CONTENTS

with

LR

© IDAF PUBLICATIONS LTD.

First published 1978.   Revised 1986.   Revised 1990.

All photographs are from the photo library of IDAF Publications and Audio-Visual Department.

The International Defence and Aid Fund for Southern Africa is a humanitarian organisation which has worked consistently for peaceful and constructive solutions to the problems created by racial oppression in Southern Africa.

It sprang from Christian and humanist opposition to the evils and injustices of apartheid in Southern Africa. It is dedicated to the achievement of free, democratic, non-racial societies throughout Southern Africa.

The objects of the Fund are:

(i)   to aid, defend and rehabilitate the victims of unjust legislation and oppressive and arbitrary procedures,

(ii) to support their families and dependants,

(iii) to keep the conscience of the world alive to the issues at stake.

In accordance with these three objects, the Fund distributes its humanitarian aid to the victims of racial injustice without any discrimination on grounds of race, colour, religious or political affiliation. The only criterion is that of genuine need.

The Fund runs a comprehensive information service on affairs in Southern Africa; this includes visual documentation. The Fund prides itself on the strict accuracy of all its information. Associated with IDAF Publications Ltd., which produces a regular news bulletin *FOCUS on Political Repression in South Africa*. It also publishes pamphlets and books and produces films and photographic exhibitions on all aspects of repression and resistance in South Africa.

British Library Cataloguing in Publications Data.

Mandela, Nelson, 1918—

> Nelson Mandela: The Struggle is my Life: his speeches and writings brought together with historical documents and accounts of Mandela in prison by fellow prisoners – 3rd ed.

1. South Africa. Black persons. Racial discrimination by society. Political aspects.

I. Title.

323.11968

ISBN 1-871863-08-2

Cover photo: Gordon Metz

Publishers' Preface to Third Edition

The first edition of Nelson Mandela's speeches and writings was published in 1978 as a tribute to him on his sixtieth birthday. He had by then spent almost 16 years as a political prisoner, and was being held on Robben Island.

The second edition was published in 1986. Mandela was then being held in Pollsmoor Prison, to which he and some other leading political prisoners had been transferred in 1982.

This third edition is being published eight weeks after Mandela's release from Victor Verster Prison where he spent the last of his 27 years of imprisonment. Its publication is intended to contribute both to the celebrations throughout the world at the release of Mandela, and to the call by the international community and the people of South Africa for the release of all political prisoners in South Africa. Mandela himself laid particular emphasis on this in a message to the international solidarity movement on 19 February:

> While I am pleased to be out of prison, my joy is not complete while some of my comrades languish in prison. I do know and trust that the same efforts will now go to securing the release of all political prisoners, particularly those on Death Row.

New material

This edition consists of all the documents in the second edition, together with two new sections in Part II. Section 14 consists of documents prepared by Mandela for his meetings last year, in July and December respectively, with P W Botha and F W De Klerk. Section 15 contains the addresses he made on his release to rallies in each of the four provinces of South Africa. Details of the additional material are given in Appendix 2. The collection of photographs has been updated and now includes pictures of Mandela after his release. The subject index has been revised to cover the new material.

One item has been removed in editing the book. The second edition contained an appendix listing honours, awards and other forms of recognition awarded to Nelson Mandela. The scale of this form of solidarity is now so great that it has become impossible to reflect it adequately in the few pages available.

London, April 1990

Publishers' Preface to Second Edition

This book was originally produced by the International Defence and Aid Fund for Southern Africa as a tribute to Nelson Mandela on the occasion of his sixtieth birthday, which he spent on Robben Island. The book has been in great damand and has sold 20,000 copies throughout the world, reflecting the extent to which the international community supports the struggle for liberation in South Africa.

The present edition is based on the original one of 1978. The opportunity has been taken to correct some minor errors, and to add a substantial amount of new material, described below.

The Fund makes this revised and up-dated version available as a further tribute to Nelson Mandela, and as a contribution to the many campaigns throughout the world calling for his release and for the release of all other political prisoners held by the apartheid regime.

The revised edition

In revising the edition of this book published in 1978, several new items have been added and one section has been omitted.

The additional material consists mainly of further documents, speeches or other writings by Mandela, included in Part II. This new material is indicated in Appendix 2, which contains a detailed index of speeches, writings and documents. In addition, document 7(h), on the stay-at-home of 1961, now includes passages on the role of the press and on opposition to the stay-at-home, which were not in the original edition *(see pp. 108ff, 111ff)*.

The section of illustrations contains new pictures from the IDAF photo library.

In Part III, 'Memoirs of the Island', there is new material entitled 'Comrade Madiba', which is extracted from the forthcoming autobiography of Michael Dingake, who was a political prisoner with Nelson Mandela.

Appendix 2, an index of the documents, speeches and writings, is more detailed than in the first edition, and the list in Appendix 3 of honours, awards and other forms of recognition accorded to Nelson Mandela, has been added. A subject index has been added.

The first edition contained a section on Nomzamo Winnie Mandela. Since 1978 she has continued to be active and, in spite of bans and harassment by the regime, has occupied a prominent and leading role in the mobilisation of resistance. To do justice to her contribution to the struggle would require a far more substantial treatment than is possible in the context of a book whose primary focus is on the writings and speeches of Nelson Mandela. Information about about Winnie Mandela can be found in a recently published book *Part of my soul* published by Penguin Books, London, 1985 and available from IDAF.

London, March 1986

I

Introduction

'The struggle is my life', wrote Nelson Mandela in a letter from underground on 26 June 1961. 'I will continue fighting for freedom until the end of my days.'

Within three years he was to be sentenced to life imprisonment on Robben Island, together with others from the Rivonia trial. 'The verdict of history', commented the London *Times*, 'will be that the ultimate guilty party is the government in power — and that already is the verdict of world opinion'. 'Most of the world', added the *New York Times*, 'regards the convicted men as heroes and freedom fighters'.[1]

Mandela would be the first to admit that he should not be singled out from the many thousands who, over decades, have struggled for freedom and justice in South Africa: dedicated, heroic and self-sacrificing men and women, some of whom have been put to death by the hangman or by Security Police interrogators. But he is perhaps the single most vital symbol not only of liberation from the tyranny of apartheid, but of a new way of life in South Africa. The occasion of his sixtieth birthday, on 18 July 1978, gave us an opportunity to celebrate the man and — through considering his actions and his writings — to reach the very heart of the struggle. The publication of this new edition allows us to include earlier material which was not previously available, as well as new material.

Nelson Rolihlahla Mandela, who was to become spokesman for his people in a period of turbulent confrontation with the state, had a traditional pastoral childhood as a member of the Tembu ruling family in the Transkei — herding sheep and helping with the ploughing and, when he listened to his cousin the Paramount Chief trying cases in the tribal court, dreaming of becoming a lawyer; dreaming too of black heroes of the past. From a Methodist school he went on to Fort Hare College to study for a BA degree but in his third year he was suspended — with other students including Oliver Tambo — for helping to organise a boycott of the Students' Representative Council after it had been deprived of its powers by the authorities. He returned home and might then have been drawn back into tribal duties and politics in the Transkei but for the fact that he wished to complete his studies, and because of the threat of an arranged marriage, both of which drove him to Johannesburg.

There he met Walter Sisulu, several years older than himself, who had worked as a miner, a servant and a factory worker, and who had educated himself and had become a fighter against injustice. It was the beginning of a remarkable friendship. Sisulu arranged for young Mandela to study law. Meanwhile, in the city and the teeming black locations of the wartime industrial boom, Mandela learned the facts of life for urban Africans under the colour bar: poverty, exclusion from skilled work, overcrowded slums and constant harassment by police, under the pass laws.

He joined the African National Congress in 1944, and, together with Sisulu, Oliver Tambo, Anton Lembede and other young men and women, helped to form its Youth League [*see document 1(a), pp. 11–20*].

Mandela was elected General Secretary; his contemporaries remember the newly graduated lawyer as tall, striking, athletic, meticulously dressed even though poor, and rather aloof. The Youth Leaguers were fired by determination to rid their people of a sense of inferiority after years of oppression; as they said in the manifesto, they would galvanise the ANC — 'a body of gentlemen with clean hands' — and they would be the 'brains trust and power station' of the spirit of African nationalism; the methods of protest — though continuing to be non-violent — should no longer be by deputations and petitions and sporadic activity: 'direct action' was the keynote.

South Africa was crucially different from the rest of the continent: a modern industrial state so organised and policed and armed that the white minority could repress the majority and maintain power, wealth and privilege. The Second World War opened up huge industrial expansion in South Africa, attracting increasing foreign investment, with consequent intensifying exploitation of cheap labour. Then in 1948 the Afrikaner Nationalist government came to power with its policy of apartheid, under which increasingly drastic laws were introduced to separate and subjugate the black population.

It was during those years and under those conditions that Mandela and his colleagues were politically educated. By 1949 they had persuaded the ANC to adopt a more militant programme of new forms of mass action by strikes, boycotts and civil disobedience against repressive legislation [*see document 1(c), pp. 28–30*]. But before such action could be organised, the police killing of 18 demonstrators on May Day 1950 precipitated a national day of protest on 26 June 1950 [*see documents 2(a) and 2(b), pp. 31–33*]. This was the first time in the history of the ANC that a national work stoppage had been called.

Exactly two years later, the Youth League's demands bore fruit: the ANC, working with the Indian Congress and other allies, organised the Defiance Campaign. This was to be directed against specific unjust laws of apartheid. Mandela was appointed national Volunteer-in-Chief; his experience of working with people of other groups had changed his political outlook, broadening his hitherto rather narrow nationalism. In a great surge of protest against selected unjust laws, all over the country men and women courted imprisonment. In disciplined groups they went through EUROPEANS ONLY entrances to railway stations and post offices; Africans broke the curfew laws, which applied only to them; a number of whites joined Indians in illegally entering African townships. In all, 8,500 went to jail until government legislation finally halted the campaign.

Mandela was one of twenty leaders who were charged and convicted at the end

2

of 1952 for organising the Defiance Campaign; he was given a nine-month suspended sentence. His contribution had been so impressive that he was elected President of the ANC (Transvaal Province) in the same year, and in response to his rising popularity the government issued him on 11 December 1952 with a banning order, prohibiting him from attending gatherings and confining him to Johannesburg. His address to the Transvaal ANC in 1953 had to be read on his behalf [*see document 3(a), pp. 34–42*].

In September 1953 the ban was renewed for two years with extra provision that he resign from the ANC. Later [*see document 10, pp. 133–60*] Mandela described what it was like: 'I found myself restricted and isolated from my fellow men, trailed by officers of the Special Branch wherever I went ... I was made, by the law, a criminal, not because of what I had done, but because of what I stood for.' When he and other organisers of the Defiance Campaign had been brought to trial under the Suppression of Communism Act, the Judge had agreed that the charge had nothing to do with communism 'as it is commonly known', and added: 'I accept the evidence that you have consistently advised your followers to follow a peaceful course of action and to avoid violence in any shape or form.' [2]

Other leaders were simultaneously banned. In the years to come, time and again the government would restrict and arrest leaders and organisers; the ANC's capacity to survive would be threatened, new methods of carrying on must continually be devised; yet the movement would never be crushed. 'To overthrow oppression', wrote Mandela, 'is the highest aspiration of every free man'. His public voice might be silenced but he worked on behind the scenes.

Meanwhile, he and Oliver Tambo had set up legal practice in Johannesburg. Even there they were harassed: ordered to move their office to the black location where they lived, they illegally remained in the city. To their office flocked victims of the system — delegations of peasants, ejected from land they had occupied for generations; husbands and wives whose life together was 'illegal' under the Urban Areas Act. Each case in court, each visit to the jails gave evidence of apartheid's brutality. 'I would say', Mandela was to tell the court at his own trial, 'that the whole life of any thinking African in this country drives him continuously to a conflict between his conscience on the one hand and the law on the other ... a law, which, in our view, is immoral, unjust and intolerable ... We must protest against it, we must oppose it, we must attempt to alter it.' [*See document 10, pp. 133–60.*]

The Congress of the People in 1955 crowned a countrywide campaign through which the ANC and its allies enabled people — workers, housewives, students, clerks, peasants, trade unionists — to express their demands; these were embraced in the Freedom Charter [*see document 4(b), pp. 61–4*]. On 26 June 1955, at Kliptown, three thousand people adopted the Freedom Charter as the policy of the Congress movement — which eventually incorporated the ANC, the SA Indian Congress, the Coloured People's Congress, the (white) Congress of Democrats and the South African Congress of Trade Unions (SACTU). For the first time the movement set out the simple objectives for a future South

Africa. The Charter begins: 'South Africa belongs to all who live in it, black and white.'

Mandela exemplified that absolute refusal to respond in kind to the racialism of the whites. Tambo has described him as passionate, fearless, impatient, sensitive — qualities which emerge in his speeches. He understood his people's needs and experiences and unremittingly articulated their basic demands. 'The people are too poor to feed their families and children', he said in his 1953 address, *No Easy Walk to Freedom* [*see document 3(a), pp. 34–42*], and this he continued to spell out until his last speech from the dock in 1964 [*see document 11(a), pp. 161–81*] in which he reiterated the demand for equal political rights, 'because without them our disabilities will be permanent'.

Over the years, Mandela attacked the steadily intensifying racial oppression in a number of articles [*see documents 5(a) to 5(f), pp. 59–86*]. He attacked such measures as Bantu Education and the segregated universities. Twenty years on, Mandela's writings are remarkable for the continuing relevance of their analysis and the accuracy of their predictions; on the Bantustan programme with its fine-sounding promises of political rights for Africans, Mandela said in 1959: 'Behind the "self-government" talk lies a grim programme of mass evictions, political persecution and police terror.'

In the mid-1950s Mandela oversaw attempts to implement the so-called 'M-Plan', named after himself, a scheme to build a mass Congress membership that would be organised into cells at the grassroots level and, through a hierarchy of leaders at intermediate levels, would be responsive to direction without the necessity of public meetings. This was a most successful method of decentralising and strengthening ANC organisation; in the words of John Gaetsewe, then General Secretary of the South African Congress of Trade Unions, 'it made the townships ours during the 'fifties and 'sixties'.[3]

The government was not slow to react against the growing unity and militancy of the people. Mandela was among the 156 people — including Chief Lutuli, President General of the ANC, Professor Z K Matthews, Oliver Tambo and Walter Sisulu — arrested at dawn on 5 December 1956 and charged with treason. Treason? Much of the evidence was farcical yet had to be seriously dealt with by the distinguished defence team and the accused, as the years passed and the trial dragged monotonously on. It was a testing time for the thirty men and women who remained after charges against the others had been dropped. Among these was Mandela: from wearying days in court, he went to his office — Tambo was keeping the practice alive — often working till late at night.

In the Treason Trial the essence of the case, as the State put it, was the belief that the liberation movement was part of an international communist-inspired effort pledged to overthrow the government by violence. Four and a half years were spent trying to prove this: the Programme of Action of 1949 and the Freedom Charter of 1955 were key documents. Mandela's evidence — partly reproduced here [*see document 6, pp. 87–94*] — and his conduct made a singular contribution. When it came to judgement, the court found that the ANC and its

4

allies were working 'to replace the present form of State with a radically and fundamentally different form of State' but 'violent means' had not been proved, nor was there proof that the ANC had been 'infiltrated' by communists. All the remaining accused were acquitted.

His first marriage (by which he had three children) having broken up, Mandela in 1958 married Nomzamo Winnie Madikizela, who had come from the Transkei to Johannesburg to qualify as a social worker and who from the start had to accept his enforced absences from their small block house in Orlando (part of what would later be called Soweto). Both husband and wife were to make an exceptional contribution to the South African liberation struggle, inspiring others with the style and spirit of their endurance.

The United Nations proclaimed 1960 Africa Year, indicating universal acceptance of the principle of African independence after years of colonial rule. In South Africa it was the year of Sharpeville, when police fired at a crowd of peacefully protesting men, women and children, killing 69 and wounding 176. As outrage spread through the world, massive demonstrations shook South Africa. The government declared a state of emergency; police and army rounded up twenty thousand people. Mandela, inevitably, was among those imprisoned. The government outlawed the ANC and the breakaway Pan Africanist Congress (which had called the Sharpeville protest). Over the following months those detained were gradually released. Among them was Mandela, whose bans had coincidentally expired — and not been renewed — early in 1961. For the first time in nine years he was free to speak and organise openly.

South Africa was about to become a republic — a white Boer republic, said the Africans. They, treated as non-citizens, had as always gone unconsulted. From all over the country African delegates — 1,400 of them — came together to confer at the specially-convened All-in African Conference at Pietermaritzburg. Unexpectedly Mandela appeared to deliver the main speech. The effect on delegates of hearing Mandela's voice once more was electric. Inspired by his strength and courage the people elected him to lead their protests and the demand for a truly representative National Convention to establish not a white republic but a new union of all South Africans. Should the government not respond to these demands, a general strike would be called by the newly-formed National Action Council, with Mandela as secretary [*see document 7(b), pp. 97–8*].

The government's immediate reaction was to instigate a fresh round of arrests. Mandela went underground. He had to assume disguises, travel about the country secretly, find places to live that were not likely to be under surveillance. There were difficulties: a well-known public figure — especially so tall and striking a man — on whom the police had a large dossier, could hardly go unrecognised, especially with the country riddled with informers. Not only he, as he contrived to go about the country organising, but all those he contacted, had to get used to wholly new methods. Not the least of his difficulties were finances:

the only car available to him at one point repeatedly broke down. At the time, he was disguised as a chauffeur.

In an open letter he explained that going underground was the only course left open to him despite the hardship it entailed: 'I have had to separate myself from my dear wife and children, from my mother and sisters, to live as an outlaw in my own land. I have had to abandon my profession and live in poverty and misery, as many of my people are doing . . . The struggle', he concluded, 'is my life' [*see document 8, pp. 119–21*].

In making the demand for a National Convention, Mandela not only wrote to the Prime Minister but also to the Leader of the Opposition in the White parliament, and called for support from all groups in the country — Coloured, Indian and White [*see documents 7(b-d), pp. 97–102*]. To Prime Minister Verwoerd, he deplored the 'savage attacks on the rights and living conditions of the African people' under a government 'notorious the world over for its obnoxious policies . . . This dangerous situation', he said, 'can be averted only by the calling of a National Convention representative of all South Africans, to draw up a non-racial and democratic constitution'. Unless that happened before Republic Day on 31 May 1961, there would be a countrywide stay-at-home from the 29th. 'We are not deterred by threats of force and violence made by you and your government.'

Government response was to arrest leaders and radicals of all races, and thousands more Africans as 'vagrants'. Police and army were called up. CAPE WHITES FORM VIGILANTE GROUPS: RAND RUSH FOR ARMS: POLICE CONFIDENT ALL IS UNDER CONTROL headlines blazoned as 29 May approached.[4] Mandela, from underground, gave an interview to a journalist who reported that 'he is not anti-White!'[5] Overseas press representatives flew in, anticipating another Sharpeville, and as Mandela continued to evade the police he became known as the 'Black Pimpernel'.

'After weeks of raids and arrests — helicopters flying low over their houses at night, flashing on powerful searchlights — the non-whites are in a harassed state. The disclosure that the police are going into the townships on Monday to hustle the residents out to work has sent a ripple of apprehension through the country', reported the London *Observer*.[6]

On Monday, 29 May, the streets of Johannesburg were almost empty of Africans. Even the police subsequently admitted that 60 per cent of African labour stayed at home in Johannesburg and Pretoria. In Port Elizabeth 75 per cent went on strike, despite threats of arrest, of being sacked by employers or evicted from homes.

The following day, two journalists from London were taken to a sparsely furnished flat in a white suburb where, in a room shaded by drawn curtains, Nelson Mandela awaited them. One of the journalists asked about the less than total response to the stay-at-home; did he concede that it had been a failure? 'In the light of the steps taken by the government to suppress it, it was a tremendous success', he replied. And he indicated what courage it took all those hundreds of

6

thousands of men and women to defy police and army and the many forms of intimidation. 'We furnish the sinews of industry and agriculture, but if the government reaction is to crush by naked force our non-violent struggle, we will have to seriously reconsider our tactics.' Later, in his report on the stay-at-home, he enlarged on this and called on 'our millions of friends outside South Africa to intensify the boycott and isolation of this government' [see document 7(f), pp. 104–5]. He concluded the interview: 'The government is spoiling for a massacre. And Africans — well, desperate people will eventually be provoked to acts of retaliation.' Soberly he reiterated: 'In my mind we are closing a chapter on this question of a non-violent policy.'[7]

Six months later, in December 1961, sabotage marked the emergence of Umkhonto we Sizwe — Spear of the Nation — in carefully planned attacks on government installations [see document 9(a), pp. 122–3].

The explosions marked a critical new stage of the struggle. Established by Mandela and other ANC and Congress leaders, Umkhonto (also abbreviated as MK) later became the armed wing of the national liberation movement; in his subsequent trial Mandela was to outline the deliberations that led to the decision to form Umkhonto and his own role in its formation. As he was to explain, quoting from the Umkhonto manifesto, the time had come when there remained only two choices, to submit or to fight. Submission was out of the question; there was no choice but to hit back.

Mandela's continued survival underground had an immensely exhilarating effect on his people as the wide-flung police net still failed to capture him. Then, early in 1962, he made a surprise appearance at a Pan-African Conference in Addis Ababa, Ethiopia. South Africa, he told delegates in a powerful speech, 'is a country torn from top to bottom by fierce racial strife and conflict and where the blood of African patriots frequently flows . . . It is a land ruled by the gun.' [See document 9(b), pp. 124–32.] He went on to visit heads of state in various parts of Africa, met political leaders in London and, in Algeria, took a course in military training. 'For the first time in my life, I was a free man', he said later.

He returned secretly to South Africa. On 5 August 1962, seventeen months from the time that he had gone underground, he was captured in Natal, apparently on a tip-off to the police by an informer. In a statement issued by the external office on 18 August 1962 calling for his release, the ANC described Mandela as a leader always 'in dynamic contact with the masses': 'his name has been a household word. Young and old composed songs about him. If it was not about his courageous leadership, it was about his success in the court of law.'

Taken to court and charged with inciting Africans to strike in 1961 and with leaving the country without valid travel documents, Mandela was sentenced in November to five years' hard labour.

In the defence, which he conducted himself, there is a passage which speaks for all political prisoners and all those who continue to be detained without charge, in solitary confinement, at the mercy of their interrogators: 'The government set out . . . not to treat with us, not to heed us, not to talk to us, but rather to present us as wild, dangerous revolutionaries, intent on disorder and riot, incapable of being dealt with in any way save by mustering an overwhelming force against us and the implementation of every possible forcible means, legal and illegal, to suppress us.' To the court he avowed: 'When my sentence has been completed . . . I will still be moved to take up again, as best I can, the struggle for the removal of injustices until they are finally abolished once and for all.' [See document 10, pp. 133–60.]

Well aware of the discriminatory nature of the white judicial system, Mandela used the dock as a place from which to confront the government and whites of South Africa, as well as the world at large, with the history and realities of the life of his people and their long struggle.

Throughout the country sabotage against Bantu Administration offices and other installations continued. Among whites an atmosphere of fear and hysteria grew. The government passed the '90 day' law — imprisonment without charge, in solitary confinement, incommunicado and under interrogation by the Security Police, for three-month periods which were renewable.

The liberation movement suffered a severe setback in July the following year when Sisulu and other underground leaders were arrested at Liliesleaf Farm in Rivonia, an outlying suburb of Johannesburg. When the 'Rivonia trial' opened in Pretoria on 9 October 1963, Nelson Mandela was brought from prison to be with them: Accused Number 1. The defence attorney, Joel Joffe, has described him during their first consultation in prison, the day before the trial opened, as: 'After a year in jail, physically a very different Mandela from the man I'd met the year before when his youthful vigour made him look much younger than forty-five. Very tall, heavily built, he'd been an amateur boxer of some ability. Now, after living on the diet prescribed for African prisoners, he looked miserably under-weight — he had withered, his face was hollow-cheeked, the skin a sickly yellowish colour. But in spirit he was undefeated, his manner was the same, friendly, easy-going, confident, and his laughter had not changed.' Joffe came to know him well in the months that followed: 'He emerged quite naturally as the leader. He had all the attributes: a strong personality, ability, stature, and calm, tact, conviction. It was part of Nelson's strength that he never dictated; he would always discuss, argue with and be guided by the opinion of his colleagues.'[8]

In the preparation of the case, the ten accused made it clear that they were not interested in a trial in law, but in a confrontation in politics. 'They were deter-mined to speak proudly of their ideals', said Joffe, 'to be defiant in face of their enemies'. Counsel warned that they were likely to be charged with trying to overthrow the state; that the penalty, if found guilty, was death. They readily admitted that most of them had taken part in a campaign designed to bring down the government and had known about or taken part in sabotage. They welcomed the opportunity to use the court as a platform from which to clarify, to the country and to the world, their position on what they considered to be the central issues of South African politics.

8

Meanwhile, reflecting worldwide anger, the United Nations, with an un-precedented vote of 106 to one, called for the immediate release of the Rivonia trialists and all South Africa's political prisoners.

Five months from the commencement of the trial, on Monday, 20 April 1964, the courtroom of the Palace of Justice was packed for the opening of the defence case. Leading counsel, Bram Fischer, QC, summarised what the defence would seek to prove, which parts of the State case it conceded, which it would deny. Then he said: 'The Defence case, my Lord, will commence with a statement from the dock by Nelson Mandela, who personally took part in the establishment of Umkhonto, and who will be able to inform the court of the beginnings of that organisation and its history up to August 1962, when he was arrested.'

Mandela rose slowly, adjusted the spectacles he wore for reading, and began: 'I am the first accused . . .' There followed his famous court statement [*see document 11(a), pp. 161–81*].

He spoke against the background of the imprisonment of the entire rank of the leadership: men — like himself — who had been preparing for the eventuality of guerilla struggle, organising the secret despatch of cadres for training abroad. Gravely, with underlying passion, he told the history of the struggle, of the founding of Umkhonto, of his own experience and political outlook. As in the Treason Trial he discussed his attitude to communism. Finally, he spelled out the wants of his people, culminating in: 'Above all, we want equal political rights . . . It is not true that the enfranchisement of all will result in racial domination . . . The ANC has spent half a century fighting against racialism. When it triumphs it will not change that policy. This then is what the ANC is fighting for . . . It is a struggle of the African people, inspired by their own suffering and their own experience. It is a struggle for the right to live.'

At this point he ceased reading. The court was still. He looked up at the Judge and quietly spoke of his dedication to this struggle; then: 'I have cherished the ideal of a democratic and free society in which all persons live together in harmony and with equal opportunities. It is an ideal which I hope to live for and to achieve. But if needs be, it is an ideal for which I am prepared to die.'

This was not rhetoric; the underlying question of the trial remained: would there be a sentence of death?

A week in mid-June 1964. The judgement was due on the Thursday. On the Monday and Tuesday Mandela, in prison in Pretoria, wrote his final papers for the London University law degree he was taking (he was to pass). On the Thursday he and all but one of the accused were found guilty. To an exchange of traditional salutes: 'Amandla!' (Power!) 'Ngawethu!' (to the People!) between the prisoners and the great crowd in the streets outside, and the singing of the anthem 'Nkosi Sikelel' iAfrika', they were driven back to jail. Their lawyers came to discuss the next day's proceedings when sentence would be passed.

'The men were calm', recalls Joffe, 'living now in the shadow of death. The only matter they wanted to discuss was how they should behave in court if the death sentence was passed. We said the Judge would first ask Nelson Mandela:

"Have you any reason to advance why the sentence of death should not be passed?" Nelson decided he would have a lot to say. If they thought by sentencing him to death they would destroy the liberation movement, they were wrong; he was prepared to die and knew his death would be an inspiration to his people in their struggle.'

Life imprisonment was the sentence on all eight convicted. Their morale was high. They were certain they would not become forgotten men, although in South Africa life imprisonment in political cases is interpreted literally, with no prospect of remission or parole or amnesty. Chief Albert Lutuli, President of the ANC, issued a statement on 12 June 1964 [*see document 11(b), pp. 181–3*] in which he recalled the contribution of Mandela and his comrades to the struggle for freedom: 'Over the long years these leaders advocated a policy of racial co-operation, of goodwill, and of peaceful struggle that made the South African liberation movement one of the most ethical and responsible of our times. In the face of bitter racial persecution, they resolutely set themselves against racialism. In the face of continued provocation, they consistently chose the path of reason . . .

'However, in the face of the uncompromising white refusal to abandon a policy which denies the African and other oppressed South Africans their rightful heritage — freedom — no one can blame brave and just men for seeking justice by the use of violent methods; nor can they be blamed if they try to create an organised force, in order ultimately to establish peace and racial harmony.

'For this, they are sentenced to be shut away for long years in the brutal and degrading prisons of South Africa . . . They represent the highest in morality and ethics in the South African political struggle . . . when they are locked away, justice and reason will have departed from the South African scene . . .'

Denis Goldberg, as a white man, was imprisoned in Pretoria; Mandela, Sisulu, Govan Mbeki, Raymond Mhlaba, Ahmed Kathrada, Elias Motsoaledi and Andrew Mlangeni were flown to South Africa's maximum security prison for black male prisoners: Robben Island.

REFERENCES

1. *The Times*, London, 12.6.64.
    New York Times, 15.6.64.
2. Mary Benson, *South Africa: Struggle for a Birthright* (IDAF, London, 1985) pp.155-6.
3. *Workers Unity*, London, May 1978.
4. *Sunday Times*, Johannesburg, May 1961.
5. *Star*, Johannesburg, May 1961.
6. *Observer*, London, 28.5.62.
7. From information supplied by Mary Benson.
8. Information from Joel Joffe.

II

Speeches, writings and documents

The following selection comprises the major speeches and writings of Nelson Mandela up to the year 1985, together with a number of other documents relating to the South African struggle for liberation. Mandela played a central role in the drafting of these, as well as in the events out of which they arose, but documents such as the ANC Youth League Manifesto, the ANC Programme of Action and the Freedom Charter were produced collectively. Such documents are indicated by the symbol ‡ after the title.

1. ANC YOUTH LEAGUE

1(a) MANIFESTO, 1944‡

Issued by the Provisional Committee of the ANC Youth League in March 1944. Mandela was a founder member of the Youth League and participated in the drafting of this manifesto.

PREAMBLE

WHEREAS Africanism must be promoted i.e. Africans must struggle for development, progress and national liberation so as to occupy their rightful and honourable place among nations of the world;

AND WHEREAS African Youth must be united, consolidated, trained and disciplined because from their ranks future leaders will be recruited;

AND WHEREAS a resolution was passed by the conference of the African National Congress held in Bloemfontein in 1943, authorising the founding and establishment of the Congress Youth League;

WE therefore assume the responsibility of laying the foundations of the said Youth League.

STATEMENT OF POLICY

South Africa has a complex problem. Stated briefly it is: The contact of the White race with the Black has resulted in the emergence of a set of conflicting living conditions and outlooks on life which seriously hamper South Africa's progress to nationhood.

The White race, possessing superior military strength and at present having superior organising skill has arrogated to itself the ownership of the land and invested itself with authority and the right to regard South Africa as a White man's country. This has meant that the African, who owned the land before the advent of the Whites, has been deprived of all security which may guarantee him an independent pursuit of destiny or ensure his leading a free and unhampered life. He has been defeated in the field of battle but refuses to accept this as meaning that he must be oppressed, just to enable the White man to further dominate him.

The African regards Civilisation as the common heritage of all Mankind and claims as full a right to make his contribution to its advancement and to live free as any White South African: further, he claims the right to all sources and agencies to enjoy rights and fulfill duties which will place him on a footing of equality with every other South African racial group.

The majority of White men regard it as the destiny of the White race to dominate the man of colour. The harshness of their domination, however, is rousing in the African feelings of hatred of everything that bars his way to full and free citizenship and these feelings can no longer be suppressed.

In South Africa, the conflict has emerged as one of race on the one side and one of ideals on the other. The White man regards the Universe as a gigantic machine hurtling through time and space to its final destruction: individuals in it are but tiny organisms with private lives that lead to private deaths: personal power, success and fame are the absolute measures of values; the things to live for. This outlook on life divides the Universe into a host of individual little entities which cannot help being in constant conflict thereby hastening the approach of the hour of their final destruction.

The African, on his side, regards the Universe as one composite whole; an organic entity, progressively driving towards greater harmony and unity whose individual parts exist merely as interdependent aspects of one whole realising their fullest life in the corporate life where communal contentment is the absolute measure of values. His philosophy of life strives towards unity and aggregation; towards greater social responsibility.

These divergences are not simplified by the fact that the two major races are on two different planes of achievement in the Civilisation of the West. This is taken advantage of to 'civilise' the African with a view to making him a perpetual minor. This obstruction of his progress is disguised as letting him 'develop along his own lines'. He is, however, suspicious of any 'lines' of development imposed on him from above and elects to develop along what the Natives' Representative Council* recently called the 'lines of his own choosing'.

*An African advisory board established in 1936 to replace the limited voting rights for Africans in the Cape Province. It had no powers and dissolved itself in 1946 after one of its members had described it as a 'toy telephone' (quoted in H J and R E Simons, *Class and Colour in South Africa* 1850–1950, IDAF, London, 1984, p.495).

In practice these divergences and conflicts work to the disadvantage of the African. South Africa's two million Whites are highly organised and are bound together by firm ties. They view South African problems through the perspective of Race destiny; that is the belief that the White race is the destined ruler and leader of the world for all time. This has made it imperative for the African to view his problems and those of his country through the perspective of Race. Viewing problems from the angle of Race destiny, the White man acts as one group in relations between Black and White. Small minorities view South African problems through the perspective of Human destiny. These number among their ranks the few Whites who value Man as Man and as above Colour. Yet these are so few that their influence on national policies is but little felt.

The advantages on the side of the Whites enable two million White men to control and dominate with ease eight million Africans and to own 87 per cent of the land while the Africans scrape a meagre existence on the remaining 13 per cent. The White man means to hold to these gains at all costs and to consolidate his position, has segregated the African in the State, the Church, in Industry, Commerce etc., in all these relegating him to an inferior position where, it is believed, the African will never menace White domination.

TRUSTEESHIP

To mislead the world and make it believe that the White man in South Africa is helping the African on the road to civilised life, the White man has arrogated to himself the title and role of Trustee for the African people.

The effects of Trusteeship alone have made the African realise that Trusteeship has meant, as it still means, the consolidation by the White man of his position at the expense of the African people, so that by the time national awakening opens the eyes of the African people to the bluff they live under, White domination should be secure and unassailable.

A hurried glance at legislation passed by the Trustees for the African during the last forty years shows what a bluff Trusteeship is. The very Act of Union* itself established as a legal right the claim of the White man to dominate the man of colour. It did not recognise the African as a citizen of the then newly formed Union; it regarded him as a beggar at the gate.

This was followed by the 1913 Land Act which deprived the African of Land and Land Security and in that way incapacitated him for that assertion of his will to be free which might otherwise have been inspired by assured security and fixed tenure. The Act drove him into urban areas where he soon made his way to skilled trades etc. But the Trustees had not brought him to urban areas to civilise him by opening to him avenues to skilled work. They had brought him so that he

---

*In 1910, following the Anglo-Boer War of 1899–1902, the whites of the four territories — Cape and Natal (formerly British) and Transvaal and Orange Free State (formerly Boer) — joined together to form the Union of South Africa under the British Crown. Only in the Cape did some blacks retain a qualified franchise: it was later withdrawn.

might be a cheap and nearby reserve of unskilled labour. This was finally established by the Colour Bar Act* which shuts Africans from skilled trades etc., thereby blocked their way to Civilisation via these channels.

In 1923 the Trustees passed the Urban Areas Act and this measure as amended warned Africans clearly that they were bidding farewell to freedom.

This Act imposed forms of control on the Africans which would have stirred into revolt any other section of the population. But because the Africans were not organised they yielded to more oppression and allowed themselves to be 'controlled' from birth to the grave. This control had the effect of forcing Africans to remain impotent under unhealthy urban conditions which were set up to add their due to the ruining of the African's resistance to disease. The legalised slums, politely called Native Locations, were one aspect of these conditions.

But the Trustees were not satisfied with the emasculation of an entire community. In the 1927 Native Administration Act,** they established the White race as the Supreme Chief of the African people. The conquest of the African was complete.

As the African accepted none of these measures to 'civilise' him without a struggle, the Trustees had always been worried by his prospects as long as the Cape Franchise remained. With little compunction, in 1936 the last door to citizenship was slammed in the face of the African by the Natives Representation Act which gave us three White men to represent eight million Africans in a house of 150 representing two million Whites. At the same time a Land Act was passed to ensure that if the 1913 Land Act had left any openings for the African, then the Natives Land and Trust Act would seal them in the name of 'humanity and Modern Civilisation'.

The 1937 Native Laws Amendment Act closed up any other loophole through which the African could have forced his way to full citizenship. Today, Trusteeship has made every African a criminal still out of prison. For all this we had to thank the philosophy of Trusteeship.

While Trustees have been very vocal in their solicitations for the African their deeds have shown clearly that talk of Trusteeship is an eyewash for the Civilised world and an empty platitude to soothe Africans into believing that after all oppression is a pleasant experience under Christian democratic rule. Trusteeship mentality is doing one thing and that very successfully, to drive the African steadily to extermination. Low wages, bad housing, inadequate health facilities, 'Native education', mass exploitation, unfixed security on land and halfhearted measures to improve the African's living conditions are all instruments and tools with which the path to African extermination is being paved.

---

*The Mines and Works Act of 1926.

**This Act made the Governor-General (representing the British Crown) 'Supreme Chief' over all African areas, which were thenceforth ruled by proclamation. When South Africa became a Republic in 1961, this power passed to the State President.

14

But Africans rejects the theory that because he is non-White and because he is a conquered race, he must be exterminated. He demands the right to be a free citizen in the South African democracy; the right to an unhampered pursuit of his national destiny and the freedom to make his legitimate contribution to human advancement.

For the last two hundred years he has striven to adapt himself to changing conditions, and has made every exertion to discover and derive the maximum benefits from the claims of the White man that they are his Trustees. Instead of meeting with encouragement commensurate with his eagerness and goodwill, he has been saddled with a load of oppression dating from the unprovoked wars of the last century and now containing such choice discriminating legislation as the 1913 Land Act, and such benefits of Trusteeship as official harshness which recently attempted to hang an African under the very roof of the very State Department established to protect him and guide him on his way to civilisation, just because he could not answer questions as quickly as the impatience of the Pass Office Trustees wanted.

In this very war* South Africa is fighting against oppression and for Freedom; a war in which she has committed herself to the principle of freedom for all. In spite of this, however, it would be the highest folly to believe that after the war South Africa will treat the Africans as citizens with the right to live free. South African blood — of Whites and Africans alike — has been shed to free the White peoples of Europe while Africans within the Union remain in bondage.

For his loyalty to the cause of human freedom and for his sacrifices in life, cash and kind, he has been promised a 'Suspense Account' — another way of telling him that, in spite of all he has done for his country in its hour of darkest need, for him there will be no freedom from fear and want.

LOSS OF FAITH IN TRUSTEESHIP

These conditions have made the African lose all faith in all talk of Trusteeship. HE NOW ELECTS TO DETERMINE HIS FUTURE BY HIS OWN EFFORTS. He has realised that to trust to the mere good grace of the White man will not free him, as no nation can free an oppressed group other than that group itself.

Self-determination is the philosophy of life which will save him from the disaster he clearly sees on his way — disaster to which Discrimination, Segregation, Pass Laws and Trusteeship are all ruthlessly and inevitably driving him.

The African is aware of the magnitude of the task before him, but has learnt that promises, no matter from what high source, are merely palliatives intended to drum him into yielding to more oppression. He has made up his mind to sweat

---

*The Second World War 1939–45, in which the Union of South Africa fought with the Allies against Nazi Germany and Fascist Italy.

for his freedom; determine his destiny himself and THROUGH HIS AFRICAN NATIONAL CONGRESS IS BUILDING A STRONG NATIONAL UNITY FRONT WHICH WILL BE HIS SUREST GUARANTEEE OF VICTORY OVER OPPRESSION.

THE AFRICAN NATIONAL CONGRESS

The African National Congress is the symbol and embodiment of the African's will to present a united national front against all forms of oppression, but this has not enabled the movement to advance the national cause in a manner demanded by prevailing conditions. And this, in turn, has drawn on it criticisms in recent times which cannot be ignored if Congress is to fulfill its mission in Africa.

The critics of Congress attribute the inability of Congress in the last twenty years to advance the national cause in a manner commensurate with the demands of the times, to weaknesses in its organisation and constitution, to its erratic policy of yielding to oppression, regarding itself as a body of gentlemen with clean hands, and to failing to see the problems of the African through the proper perspective.

Those critics further allege that in that period Congress declined and became an organisation of the privileged few — some Professionals, Small Traders, a sprinkling of Intellectuals and Conservatives of all grades. This, it is said, imparted to the Congress character taints of reactionism and conservatism which made Congress a movement out of actual touch with the needs of the rank and file of our people.

It is further contended by the critics of Congress that the privileged few who constituted the most vocal elements in Congress strongly resented any curtailment of what they considered their rights and, since the popularisation of the Congress character would have jeopardised or brought about the withdrawal of those rights by the Authorities, Congress was forced to play the dual role of being unconscious police to check the assertion of the popular will on the one hand and, on the other, of constantly warning the authorities that further curtailment of the privileges of the few would compel them, the privileged few, to yield to pressure from the avalanche of popular opinion which was tired of appeasing the Authorities while life became more intolerable.

These privileged few, so the critics of Congress maintain, are not an efficiently organised bloc. Their thinking itself lacks the national bias and this has made Congress a loose association of people who merely react negatively to given conditions, able neither to assert the national will nor to resist it openly. In this connection, Congress is accused of being partly suspicious of progressive thought and action, though it is itself unable to express correctly the views of the mass of the people.

Finally, the critics say that because the privileged few who direct Congress are poorly organised and have no marked following, Congress cannot openly defy popular wishes; hence to maintain its precarious existence, it is compelled to be very vocal against legislation that has harsh effects on the African underdog while it gives no positive lead nor has any constructive programme to enforce the repeal of all oppressive legislation.

CHALLENGE TO YOUTH

Some of these criticisms are founded on fact, it is true, but it does not advance the national cause if people concentrate on these while little or no effort is made to build Congress from within. It is admitted that in the process of our political development, our leadership made certain blunders. It was inevitable that this should have been the case, encompassed as the African people were and still are with forces inimical to their progress. But it does no good to stop at being noisy in condemning African leaders who went before us. Defects in the organisation of the people against oppression cannot be cured by mouthing criticisms and not putting our heads together to build what has been damaged and to find a way out of the present suffering.

Both the oppression and the causes that give rise to the criticisms of Congress cannot be allowed to go on indefinitely. Soon the point must be reached when African Youth, which has lived through oppression from the cradle to the present, calls a halt to it all. That point, happily, is now reached — as witness some of the clear-cut national demands by Youth at the Bloemfontein conference and the formation of Youth movements and political parties. All this is proof that Youth wants action and is in sympathy with the rank and file of our oppressed people. It is all a challenge to Youth to join in force in the national fight against oppression.

In response to the demands of the times African Youth is LAYING ITS SERVICES AT THE DISPOSAL OF THE NATIONAL LIBERATION MOVEMENT, THE AFRICAN NATIONAL CONGRESS, IN THE FIRM BELIEF, KNOWLEDGE AND CONVICTION THAT THE CAUSE OF AFRICA MUST AND WILL TRIUMPH.

CONGRESS YOUTH LEAGUE

The formation of the African National Congress Youth League is an answer and assurance to the critics of the national movement that African Youth will not allow the struggles and sacrifices of their fathers to have been in vain. Our fathers fought so that we, better equipped when our time came, should start and continue from where they stopped.

The formation of this League is an attempt on the part of Youth to impart to Congress a truly national character. It is also a protest against the lack of discipline and the absence of a clearly-defined goal in the movement as a whole.

The Congress Youth League must be the brains-trust and power-station of the spirit of African nationalism; the spirit of African self-determination; the spirit that is so discernible in the thinking of our Youth. It must be an organisation

17

where young African men and women will meet and exchange ideas in an atmosphere pervaded by a common hatred of oppression.

At this power-station the league will be a co-ordinating agency for all youthful forces employed in rousing popular political consciousness and fighting oppression and reaction. It will educate the people politically by concentrating its energies on the African homefront to make all sections of our people Congress-minded and nation-conscious.

But the Congress Youth League must not be allowed to detract Youth's attention from the organisation of Congress. In this regard, it is the first step to ensure that African Youth has direct connections with the leadership of Congress.

Circumstances call upon African Youth to make the League specialise in championing the cause of Africa; and to serve this end best, the League will sponsor a Congress political bloc, the Congress Progressive Group within the national movement. This will be the wing of the Youth League entrusted with the duty of organising Youth . . .

The Congress Progressive Group will stand for certain clear-cut national ideals within Congress; it will stand for specialisation within the national movement, to reinforce the latter's representative character and to consolidate the national unity front; it will keep a vigilant eye on all un-national tendencies on the national unity front and in Congress policies.

We must be honest enough to realise that neither Congress nor the African people can make progress as one amorphous mass. At a certain stage we must cultivate specialised political attitudes. Failure to recognise this will wreck Congress and encourage revolts from it until it ceases to be a force in national politics.

By recognising this fact, Youth does not confess sympathy with those who revolted against the national movement. These failed to realise that the formation of parties out of Congress was a serious weakening of the national unity front. They recognised the fact that Congress is a national liberation movement but were not sufficiently experienced politically to form their party within the national fold and to develop opposition from within, while strengthening the national unity front.

The result of their inexperience has been the creation of serious rifts and splits on the national unity front. For this, there can be no pardon because we cannot afford to cause any rift on the national unity front at this critical moment. By weakening the national unity front we invite more oppression for Africans after the war. By strengthening the national unity front, we are preparing a strong front against onslaughts that will be made on the real aims of the national struggle and on its significance and that will make the co-ordination of our political activities difficult, with the result that the African cannot take advantage of situations which, if intelligently exploited in time, may bring the African nearer full and free citizenship.

Congress is destined for a great purpose and mission, but shortsighted policies will cripple it and make it unable to rise to its destiny. To prevent this and therefore the setting back of the clock of African progress, African Youth must join the League in their numbers to strengthen the national movement in view of the fact that divisions just now are being sown among the people by sections of the so-called privileged few, while no convincing effort is made to narrow down and finally eliminate the gulfs that divide our people even by those who clamour loudest for national unity. Those who sow these divisions direct their activities against the national unity front in order to make the national movement incapable of expressing the wishes of the people effectively; they are the enemies of a free Africa.

The Congress is the symbol of the African people's common hatred of all oppression and of their Will to fight it relentlessly as one compact group. Youth recognises the existence of specialised attitudes and, where these lead to differences of opinion, that must be strictly a domestic matter within the national liberation movement and must in no way be allowed to interfere with the national unity front.

THE IDEAL OF NATIONAL UNITY MUST BE THE GUIDING IDEAL OF EVERY YOUNG AFRICAN'S LIFE

OUR CREED

(a) We believe in the divine destiny of nations.

(b) The goal of all our struggles is Africanism and our motto is 'AFRICA'S CAUSE MUST TRIUMPH'.

(c) We believe that the national liberation of Africans will be achieved by Africans themselves. We reject foreign leadership of Africa.

(d) We may borrow useful ideologies from foreign ideologies, but we reject the wholesale importation of foreign ideologies into Africa.

(e) We believe that leadership must be the personification and symbol of popular aspirations and ideals.

(f) We believe that practical leadership must be given to capable men, whatever their status in society.

(g) We believe in the scientific approach to all African problems.

(h) We combat moral disintegration among Africans by maintaining and upholding high ethical standards ourselves.

(i) We believe in the unity of all Africans from the Mediterranean Sea in the North to the Indian and Atlantic oceans in the South — and that Africans must speak with one voice.

OUR PROGRAMME — THE THREE-YEAR PLAN

(a) Drafting and framing of the Constitution.

(b) Improving and consolidating our financial position.

(c) Establishing the Congress Progressive Group.

(d) To win over and persuade other Youth organisations to come over to the African National Congress Youth League, i.e. to create national unity and consolidate the national unity front.

(e) To win over and persuade other African Organisations to come over to and pool their resources in the African National Congress, i.e. to create national unity and consolidate the national unity front.

(f) To work out the theories of African urbanisation and the system of Land Tenure.

(g) To make a critical study of all those forces working for or against African progress.

1(b) BASIC POLICY DOCUMENT, 1948‡

Issued by the National Executive Committee of the ANC Youth League in 1948.

The African National Congress Youth League established in April 1944 aims *inter alia*:

(a) at rallying and uniting African youth into one national Front on the basis of African Nationalism;

(b) at giving force, direction, and vigour to the struggle for African National Freedom, by assisting, supporting and reinforcing the National Movement — ANC;

(c) at studying the political, economical and social problems of Africa and the world;

(d) at striving and working for the educational, moral and cultural advancement of African youth.

In order to rally all youths under its banner, and in order to achieve the unity necessary to win the national freedom of the African people, the Congress Youth League adopts the following basic policy, which is also a basis for its political, economic, educational, cultural and social programme:

BASIC POLICY

1. African Nationalism

The African people in South Africa are oppressed as a group with a particular colour. They suffer national oppression in common with thousands and millions of oppressed Colonial peoples in other parts of the world.

African Nationalism is the dynamic National liberatory creed of the oppressed African people. Its fundamental aim is:

(i)   the creation of a united nation out of the heterogeneous tribes;
(ii) the freeing of Africa from foreign domination and foreign leadership;
(iii) the creation of conditions which can enable Africa to make her own contribution to human progress and happiness.

The African has a primary, inherent and inalienable right to Africa which is his continent and Motherland, and the Africans as a whole have a divine destiny which is to make Africa free among the peoples and nations of the earth.

In order to achieve Africa's freedom the Africans must build a powerful national liberation movement, and in order that the national movement should have inner strength and solidarity, it should adopt the national liberatory creed — African Nationalism, and it should be led by the Africans themselves.

2.   Goal of Political Action

The Congress Youth League believes that the goal of political organisation and action is the achievement of true democracy,

(i) in South Africa and
(ii) in the rest of the African continent.

In such a true democracy all the nationalities and minorities would have their fundamental human rights guaranteed in a democratic Constitution. In order to achieve this the Congress Youth League and/or the National Movement struggles for:

(a) the removal of discriminatory laws and colour bars;
(b) the admission of the Africans into the full citizenship of the country so that they have direct representation in parliament on a democratic basis.

3.   Economic Policy

The Congress Youth League holds that political democracy remains an empty form without substance unless it is properly grounded on a base of economic and, especially, industrial democracy.

The economic policy of the League can therefore be stated under the following headings:

(a) **Land:** — The League stands for far-reaching agrarian reforms in the following directions:
   (i)   the re-division of land among farmers and peasants of all nationalities in proportion to their numbers;
   (ii) the application of modern scientific methods to, and the planned development of, agriculture;
   (iii) the improvement of land, the reclamation of denuded areas and the conservation of water supplies;
   (iv) the mass education of peasants and farmers in the techniques of agricultural production.

(b) **Industry:** — The Congress Youth League aims at:
  - (i) the full industrialisation of South Africa in order to raise the level of civilisation and the standard of living of the workers;
  - (ii) the abolition of industrial colour bars and other discriminatory provisions, so that the workers of all nationalities should be able to do skilled work and so that they should get full training and education in the skill and techniques of production.
  - (iii) establishing in the Constitution the full and unhampered right of workers to organise themselves in order to increase their efficiency and protect and safeguard their interests; particularly the workers should reap and enjoy the benefits of industrial development and expansion;

(c) **Trading and Co-operation:** — In order to improve the lot of the people generally and to give strength and backbone to the National Movement, the League shall:
  - (i) encourage business, trading and commercial enterprises among Africans;
  - (ii) encourage, support and even lead workers, peasants and farmers, intellectuals and others, to engage in co-operative saving, co-operative trading, etc.

(d) **General National Economy:** — Generally the Congress Youth League aims at a National Economy which will:
  - (i) embrace all peoples and groups within the state;
  - (ii) eliminate discrimination and ensure a just and equitable distribution of wealth among the people of all nationalities;
  - (iii) as nearly as possible give all men and women an equal opportunity to improve their lot;
  - (iv) in short give no scope for the domination and exploitation of one group by another.

4. Educational Policy

(a) The ultimate goal of African Nationalism in so far as education is concerned, is a 100 per cent literacy among the people, in order to ensure the realisation of an effective democracy. Some of the means to that end are:
  - (i) free compulsory education for all children, with its concomitants of adequate accommodation, adequate training facilities and adequate remuneration for teachers;
  - (ii) mass adult education by means of night schools, adult classes, summer and winter courses and other means.

(b) All children should have access to the type of education that they are suited for. They should have access to academic, aesthetic, vocational and technical training.

(c) The aim of such education should be:
   (i) to mould the characters of the young;
   (ii) to give them a high sense of moral and ethical values;
   (iii) to prepare them for a full and responsible citizenship in a democratic society.

5. Cultural Policy

(a) Culture and civilisation have been handed down from nation to nation and from people to people, down the historic ages. One people or nation after another made its own contribution to the sum-total of human culture and civilisation. Africa has her own contribution to make. The Congress Youth League stands for a policy of assimilating the best elements in European and other civilisations and cultures, on the firm basis of what is good and durable in the African's own culture and civilisation. In this way Africa will be in a position to make her own special contribution to human progress and happiness.

(b) The Congress Youth League supports the cultural struggle of the African people and encourages works by African artists of all categories. The Congress Youth League stands for a co-ordinated development of African cultural activity.

(c) African works of art can and should reflect not only the present phase of the national liberatory struggle but also the world of beauty that lies beyond the conflict and turmoil of struggle.

6. Conclusion

The foregoing policy is largely one of ultimate objectives in general terms; although here and there it throws light on the immediate and/or near-range objectives of the National Movement.

Whilst the general policy remains fixed and unalterable, the programme of organisation and action may and shall be modified from time to time to meet new situations and conditions and to cope with the ever-changing circumstances.

By adopting this policy the Congress Youth League is forging a powerful weapon for freedom and progress.

THE POSITION OF AFRICAN NATIONALISM

In view of misunderstanding and even deliberate distortions of African nationalism, it has become necessary to re-state the position of our outlook.

1. Historical Basis of African Nationalism

More than 150 years ago, our forefathers were called upon to defend their fatherland against the foreign attacks of European settlers. In spite of bravery and unparalleled heroism, they were forced to surrender to white domination. Two main factors contributed to their defeat: firstly, the superior weapons of the white man, and secondly the fact that the Africans fought as isolated tribes, instead of pooling their resources and attacking as a united force.

2. The Birth of the African National Congress

Thus the year 1912 saw the birth of an African National Congress. The emergence of the National Congress marked the end of the old era of isolated tribal resistance, and ushered in a new era of struggle on a national rather than on a tribal plane. The ANC became the visible expression of an inner organisational plane. However imperfectly it did it, the ANC was in fact an outward expression of the African people's desire for a National Liberation Movement, capable of directing their resistance to white domination and of ultimately winning the African's national freedom.

Yet from the very outset, the ANC suffered from serious defects. The founders, great patriots no doubt, had no grasp of the concrete historical situation and its implications, and they were obsessed with imperialist forms of organisation. As a result the ANC had defects both of form and of matter and as long as these remained the ANC could not (i) create an effective organisational machinery for waging the national liberatory fight; (ii) put forward a dynamic Nationalistic programme which could inspire and cement the tribes, and be a motive power and driving force in the militant struggle for national freedom.

In spite of these serious defects, however, the event of 1912 had provided a solid basis for tribal solidarity, and for a nationally organised struggle against white domination. It was for the more politically advanced rising generations to give Congress such form and substances as would suit the organisation to its historic mission.

3. Recent Tendencies — Their Significance

Far-reaching changes have taken place in the African National Congress within recent times. During Dr A B Xuma's regime,* a policy of centralisation has been followed and an attempt made to correct, at least in form, some of the mistakes of 1912. The result has been the gaining of ground of the idea of the National Congress, with dependent provincial branches (Transvaal, Cape, Natal, OFS). Doubtless there is room for more drastic and revolutionary changes in the organisational form of Congress, if this organisation is to live up to the people's expectations. As far as the matter and substance of Congress's outlook is concerned, the year 1944 saw a historic turning point, when the Congress Youth League came into life. From the very outset, the Congress Youth League set itself, *inter alia*, the historic task of imparting dynamic substance and matter to the organisational form of the ANC. This took the form of a forthright exposition of the National Liberatory outlook — African Nationalism — which the Youth

---

*Dr Xuma was President-General of the ANC 1940–49.

League seeks to impose on the Mother Body. The first clear exponent of African nationalism was the late Anton Muziwakhe Lembede [died July 1947].

4. Basic Position of African Nationalism

The starting point of African nationalism is the historical or even pre-historical position. Africa was, has been and still is the Black man's Continent. The Europeans, who have carved up and divided Africa among themselves, dispossessed, by force of arms, the rightful owners of the land — the children of the soil. Today they occupy large tracts of Africa. They have exploited and still are exploiting the labour power of Africans and natural resources of Africa, not for the benefit of the African Peoples but for the benefit of the dominant white race and other white people across the sea. Although conquered and subjugated, the Africans have not given up, and they will never give up their claim and title to Africa. The fact that their land has been taken and their rights whittled down, does not take away or remove their right to the land of their forefathers. They will suffer white oppression, and tolerate European domination, only as long as they have not got the material force to overthrow it. There is, however, a possibility of a compromise, by which the Africans could admit the Europeans to a share of the fruits of Africa, and this is *inter alia:*

(a) that the Europeans completely abandon their domination of Africa;
(b) that they agree to an equitable and proportionate re-division of land;
(c) that they assist in establishing a free people's democracy in South Africa in particular and Africa in general.

It is known, however, that a dominant group does not voluntarily give up its privileged position. That is why the Congress Youth puts forward African Nationalism as the militant outlook of an oppressed people seeking a solid basis for waging a long, bitter, and unrelenting struggle for its national freedom.

5. Two Streams of African Nationalism

Now it must be noted that there are two streams of African Nationalism. One centres round Marcus Garvey's slogan — 'Africa for the Africans'. It is based on the 'Quit Africa' slogan and on the cry 'Hurl the White man into the sea.' This brand of African Nationalism is extreme and ultra revolutionary.

There is another stream of African Nationalism (Africanism) which is moderate, and which the Congress Youth League professes. We of the Youth League take account of the concrete situation in South Africa, and realise that the different racial groups have come to stay. But we insist that a condition for inter-racial peace and progress is the abandonment of white domination, and such a change in the basic structure of South African society that those relations which breed exploitation and human misery will disappear. Therefore our goal is the winning of national freedom for African people, and the inauguration of a people's free society where racial oppression and persecution will be outlawed.

6. Forces in the Struggle for African Freedom

(a) **Africans:** They are the greatest single group in South Africa, and they are the key to the movement for democracy in Africa, not only because Africa is their only motherland, but also because by bringing the full force of their organised numbers to bear on the national struggle, they can alter the basic position of the fight for a democratic South Africa. The only driving force that can give the black masses the self-confidence and dynamism to make a successful struggle is the creed of African Nationalism, which is professed by the Congress Youth League of South Africa. The Congress Youth League holds that the Africans are nationally oppressed, and that they can win their national freedom through a National Liberation Movement led by the Africans themselves.

(b) **Europeans:** The majority of Europeans share the spoils of white domination in this country. They have a vested interest in the exploitative caste society of South Africa. A few of them love Justice and condemn racial oppression, but their voice is negligible, and in the last analysis counts for nothing. In their struggle for freedom the Africans will be wasting their time and deflecting their forces if they look up to the Europeans either for inspiration or for help in their political struggle.

(c) **Indians:** Although, like the Africans, the Indians are oppressed as a group, yet they differ from the Africans in their historical and cultural background among other things. They have their mother-country, India, but thousands of them made South Africa and Africa their home. They, however, did not come as conquerors and exploiters, but as the exploited. As long as they do not undermine or impede out liberation struggle we should not regard them as intruders or enemies.

(d) **Coloured:** Like the Indians they differ from the Africans, they are a distinct group, suffering group oppression. But their oppression differs in degree from that of the Africans. The Coloureds have no motherland to look up to and, but for historic accidents, they might be nearer to the Africans than are the Indians, seeing they descend in part at least from the aboriginal Hottentots who with Africans and Bushmen are original children of Black Africa. Coloureds, like the Indians, will never win their national freedom unless they organise a Coloured People's National Organisation to lead in the struggle of the National Freedom of the Coloureds. The National Organisations of the Africans, Indians and Coloureds may co-operate on common issues.

7. South Africa: A Country of Nationalities

The above summary on racial groups supports our contention that South Africa is a country of four chief nationalities, three of which (the Europeans, Indians and Coloureds) are minorities, and three of which (the Africans, Coloureds and Indians) suffer national oppression . . . It is to be clearly understood that we are not against the Europeans as such — we are not against the European as a human being — but we are totally and irrevocably opposed to white domination and to oppression.

8. Fallacies and diversions that must be expected

(a) **African Nationalism and Racialism:** There is a common accusation that African Nationalism is a one-sided, racialistic outlook. The accusation is based on ignorance of African Nationalism. Ours is the sanest and at the same time the most practical and realistic view. We do not hate other racial groups. We are the overwhelming majority and, at the same time, are a downtrodden people.

(b) **Pseudo-Nationalism:** African Nationalists have to be on the lookout for people who pretend to be Nationalists when in fact they are only imperialist or capitalist agents, using Nationalistic slogans in order to cloak their reactionary position. These elements should be exposed and discredited.

(c) **Fascist Agents:** Still another group that should be closely watched and, wherever possible, ruthlessly exposed, is that section of Africans who call themselves 'Nationalists', but who are in fact agents and lackeys of Nazi and Fascist organisations. Genuine African Nationalists should be perpetually vigilant and spare no effort to denounce and eventually crush these dangerous vipers.

(d) **Vendors of Foreign Method:** There are certain groups which seek to impose on our struggle cut-and-dried formulae, which so far from clarifying the issue of our struggle, only serve to obscure the fundamental fact that we are oppressed not as a class, but as a people, as a Nation. Such wholesale importation of methods and tactics which might have succeeded in other countries, like Europe, where conditions were different, might harm the cause of our people's freedom, unless we are quick in building a militant mass liberation movement.

(e) **Tribalism:** Some people mistakenly believe that African Nationalism is a mere tribalist outlook. They fail to apprehend the fact that Nationalism is firstly a higher development of a process which was already in progress when the white man arrived, and secondly that it is a continuation of the struggle of our forefathers against foreign invasion. Tribalism itself is the mortal foe of African Nationalism, and African Nationalists everywhere should declare relentless war on centrifugal tribalism.

Conclusion drawn from above exposition

The historic task of African Nationalism (it has become apparent) is the building of a self-confident and strong African Nation in South Africa. Therefore African Nationalism transcends the narrow limits imposed by any particular sectional organisation. It is all-embracing in the sense that its field is the whole body of African people in this country. The germ of its growth was first sown within the bosom of the African National Congress, and it found its clear crystallisation in the Congress Youth League. It should now find concrete expression in the creation of a single African National Front. The strength, solidarity and permanence of such a front, will, of course, depend not on accident or chance, but on the correctness of our stand, and on the political orientation of our front. Granting that this would be anchored on African Nationalism, we should build the most powerful front in our history.

Conclusion

The position of African Nationalism has been made as clear as possible. It remains for us to stress the fact that our fundamental aim is a strong and self-confident nation. Therefore our programme is, of necessity, a many-sided one corresponding to the varied activities and aspirations of our people, and to the various avenues along which they are making an advance towards self-expression and self-realisation. Our great task is to assist and to lead our people in their Herculean efforts to emancipate themselves and to advance their cause and position economically, culturally, educationally, socially, commercially, physically and so on. But, of course, the most vital aspect of our forward struggle is the political aspect.

Therefore African Nationalists should make a scientific study and approach to the problems of Africa and the world, and place themselves in a position to give the African people a clear and fearless political leadership.

1(c) PROGRAMME OF ACTION, 1949‡

Statement of Policy adopted at ANC Annual Conference, 17 December 1949.

The fundamental principles of the programme of action of the African National Congress are inspired by the desire to achieve national freedom. By national freedom we mean freedom from White domination and the attainment of political independence. This implies the rejection of the conception of segregation, apartheid, trusteeship, or White leadership which are all in one way or another motivated by the idea of White domination or domination of the White over the Blacks. Like all other people the African people claim the right of self-determination.

With this object in view in the light of these principles we claim and will continue to fight for the political rights tabulated on page 8 of our Bill of Rights* such as:

(1) the right of direct representation in all the governing bodies of the country — national, provincial and local — and we resolve to work for the abolition of all differential institutions or bodies specially created for Africans, viz. representative councils, present form of parliamentary representation.**

(2) to achieve these objectives the following programme of action is suggested:

    (a) the creation of a national fund to finance the struggle for national liberation;

    (b) the appointment of a committee to organise an appeal for funds and to devise ways and means therefor;

---

*The Bill of Rights was adopted by the ANC in 1945, embracing claims for universal adult suffrage, equal justice in the courts and freedom of land ownership, residence and movement.

**At this period four whites known as Natives' Representatives were elected to the white parliament to represent African interests. These seats were abolished in 1959.

(c) the regular issue of propaganda material through:

    (i) the usual press, newsletter or other means of disseminating our ideas in order to raise the standard of political and national consciousness;

    (ii) establishment of a national press.

(3) appointment of a council of action whose function should be to carry into effect, vigorously and with the utmost determination, the programme of action. It should be competent for the council of action to implement our resolve to work for:

    (a) the abolition of all differential political institutions, the boycotting of which we accept, and to undertake a campaign to educate our people on this issue and, in addition, to employ the following weapons: immediate and active boycott, strike, civil disobedience, non-co-operation and such other means as may bring about the accomplishment and realisation of our aspirations;

    (b) preparations and making of plans for a national stoppage of work for one day as a mark of protest against the reactionary policy of the Government.

(4) ECONOMIC

    (a) The establishment of commercial, industrial, transport and other enterprises in both urban and rural areas;

    (b) Consolidation of the industrial organisation of the workers for the improvement of their standard of living;

    (c) Pursuant to paragraph (a) herein instructions be issued to Provincial Congresses to study the economic and social conditions in the reserves and other African settlements and to devise ways and means for their development, establishment of industries and such other enterprises as may give employment to a number of people.

(5) EDUCATION

It be an instruction to the African National Congress to devise ways and means for:

    (a) Raising the standard of Africans in the commercial, industrial and other enterprises and workers in their workers' organisations by means of providing a common educational forum wherein intellectuals, peasants and workers participate for the common good;

    (b) Establishment of national centres of education for the purpose of training and educating African youth and provision of large-scale scholarships tenable in various overseas countries.

(6) CULTURAL

    (a) To unite the cultural with the educational and national struggle;

    (b) The establishment of a national academy of arts and sciences.

(7) Congress realises that ultimately the people will be brought together by inspired leadership, under the banner of African Nationalism with courage and determination.

This ANC Programme of Action was a watershed in South African history. It laid the basis for the national campaigns of direct action and refusal to collaborate in structures provided by the government for blacks. The government's reaction was violent and intransigent: eighteen people were killed when police opened fire on May Day demonstrations in 1950, and a law was introduced (the Suppression of Communism Act, 1950, later the Internal Security Act, 1976) which made illegal all organised demands for social change and enabled the state to take administrative action against its opponents by means of banning orders.

These measures led to the National Day of Protest.

2. NATIONAL DAY OF PROTEST, 1950

2(a)   ANC STATEMENT

Issued by the National Executive Committee of the ANC at an emergency meeting on 21 May 1950.

An emergency meeting of the National Executive of the African National Congress was held at Thaba 'Nchu on Sunday, 21 May 1950, to discuss the attitude of the African National Congress to the Unlawful Organisations Bill* now before parliament, and to consider ways and means of organising and directing the opposition of the African people to the proposed legislation.

It was unanimously decided to issue the following statement:

1. Although the Unlawful Organisations Bill purports to be directed against Communism in general and the Communist Party of South Africa in particular, the ANC Executive is satisfied, from a study of the provisions of the Bill, that it is primarily directed against the Africans and other oppressed people, and is designed to frustrate all their attempts to work for the fulfilment of their legitimate demands and aspirations. The Bill is a further example of the determination of the white people of this country to keep the African in permanent subordination.

   It goes without saying that the African people are equally determined that they are not going to remain in that position forever.

   The ANC is resolved to oppose this and other measures of a similar nature by all means at its disposal.

2. As a first step it was agreed to launch a campaign for a National Day of Protest. It is suggested that, on this day, to mark their general dissatisfaction with the position in this country, the African people should refrain from going to work, and regard this day as a day of mourning for all those Africans who lost their lives in the struggle for liberation. The actual date on which the protest will be held will be announced in due course. Preparations for the day will, however, commence immediately.

2(b)   REPORT‡

Issued by the Secretary-General of the ANC, 26 July 1950, initialled by Mandela.

At the Emergency Meeting of the National Executive of the African National Congress held at Thaba 'Nchu on Sunday, 21 May 1950, the attitude of the ANC to the Suppression of Communism Act (then called the Unlawful Organisations Bill) was discussed. It was agreed to launch a campaign for a National Day of Protest. It was suggested that on that day, to mark their general dissatisfaction

---

*Enacted as the Suppression of Communism Act. After the Sharpeville massacre in 1960 a law that banned the ANC and PAC was enacted as the Unlawful Organisations Act.

with the position in this country, the African people should refrain from going to work and regard that day as a Day of Mourning for all those Africans who lost their lives in the struggle for liberation. The actual date on which the Protest would be held would be announced in due course. The Secretary-General was instructed to communicate with the leaders of the other National Organisations to establish a machinery for the implementation of this decision.

Following upon this resolution, and after consultation with leaders of other National Organisations, a National Day of Protest Co-ordinating Committee (NDPCC) was set up with headquarters in Johannesburg. The composition of the Committee was originally planned to consist of seven members from the African National Congress, and two representatives from each of the following organisations: The South African Indian Congress, the African Peoples' Organisation,* the Communist Party of South Africa and the Transvaal Council of Non-European Trade Unions. The Presidents of the ANC, the SAIC, the APO and the Chairman of the CP were to be ex-officio members of this Committee, making a total of nineteen members. Only the ANC, SAIC and the CP were actually represented on the Committee.

The African Peoples' Organisation passed the following resolution:

'That the APO supports the proposed Day of Mourning with the following proviso, namely, that proper organisation be carried out and that we then assess our organisational strength and, to expedite this matter, a United Front be established on the following basis:

1. Anti-Segregation.
2. Equal Rights for All.
3. Against the Bills.'

Furthermore, the APO felt that the precipitate manner in which the Day of Mourning was declared left the participating bodies very little time to build up their organisation and prepare their members for the Day of Protest. The Transvaal Council of Non-European Trade Unions supported the Protest morally. They sent no representatives to the Committee. The representation of the Communist Party of South Africa automatically lapsed when the Party dissolved.

On 11 June 1950, the President General, acting on the authority of the National Executive, and after consulting with the other National leaders, released a Press Statement declaring Monday, 26 June 1950 a National Day of Protest and called upon the African People in their united millions to observe it as such by refraining from going to work on that day, and appealed to all South Africans of all races to respond to the call of their leaders for the observance of this unique day in the history of South Africa. The Presidents of the SAIC and APO, and Chairman of the CP pledged the wholehearted active support of their organisations to this call and appealed to the white voters and working class of

---

*The APO was later renamed the Coloured People's Organisation (CPO) and then Coloured People's Congress (CPC).

South Africa to join the struggle for the defeat of these tyrannical measures and for the extension of democracy to all.

The headquarters of the National Day of Protest Co-ordinating Committee were at the offices of the ANC, Johannesburg. Messrs W M Sisulu and Y A Cachalia were elected Joint Secretaries. Mr N R Mandela was placed in charge of the office. Members of the National Executive and other leading members of Congress were given specific duties. Dr J S Moroka and Mr O R Tambo visited Natal to assist in the implementation of this decision. Mr Sisulu toured the Eastern Province, concentrating on Port Elizabeth and East London. Mr Gaur Rabede went to the OFS. Messrs C S Ramohanoe and E Mofutsanyana also toured the Free State. Mr D Tloome toured the Western Transvaal and Kimberley. Mr Moses Kotane was instructed to organise the Western Province.

Provincial, district, regional and local Co-ordinating Committees were established throughout the country.

Soon after the Emergency Meeting at Thaba 'Nchu, young men and women spontaneously came forward and freely placed their services at the disposal of the National Executive. Mr Diliza Mji, a fourth year medical student at the University of the Witwatersrand, gave up his studies and devoted himself full-time to the campaign. Mr Mji was sent down to Durban where he did outstanding service.

An amount of approximately £150 (one hundred and fifty pounds) was spent by the ANC before the NDPCC took over. Out of this amount £25 (twenty-five pounds) was paid to the NDPCC as a contribution by the ANC towards the funds of the Committee.

As a result of the National Day of Protest a number of people were victimised, especially in Durban, where a large number of workers lost their jobs. The Committee had to assume the responsibility of maintaining these people. To meet this situation, a fundraising campaign has been launched with the aim of raising £30,000. I might mention that a big debt was incurred by the Committee in organising the campaign for a National Day of Protest and funds have to be raised to redeem this liability. With this end in view, a team of collectors has been sent out to various parts of the country to appeal for donations. An Entertainment Committee has been set up to raise funds by staging concerts, tea-parties, bazaars and similar functions.

A further report on the results of this fundraising campaign will be submitted in due course.

Having regard to the fact that the Committee had only two weeks to prepare, and in the face of intensive and relentless police intimidation, and after studying the reports from various parts of the country, I am perfectly satisfied that, as a political strike, Monday 26 June was an outstanding success.

26 June was subsequently adopted as South African Freedom Day.

3. DEFIANCE CAMPAIGN, 1952

3(a) 'NO EASY WALK TO FREEDOM'

Presidential address by Mandela to the ANC (Transvaal) Conference, 21 September 1953. Elected ANC (Transvaal) President earlier in the year, Mandela had been served with a banning order subsequently and the address was therefore read on his behalf.

Since 1912 and year after year thereafter, in their homes and local areas, in provincial and national gatherings, on trains and buses, in the factories and on the farms, in cities, villages, shanty towns, schools and prisons, the African people have discussed the shameful misdeeds of those who rule the country. Year after year, they have raised their voices in condemnation of the grinding poverty of the people, the low wages, the acute shortage of land, the inhuman exploitation and the whole policy of white domination. But instead of more freedom, repression began to grow in volume and intensity and it seemed that all their sacrifices would end up in smoke and dust. Today the entire country knows that their labours were not in vain, for a new spirit and new ideas have gripped our people. Today the people speak the language of action: there is a mighty awakening among the men and women of our country and the year 1952 stands out as the year of this upsurge of national consciousness.

In June, 1952, the African National Congress and the South African Indian Congress, bearing in mind their responsibility as the representatives of the downtrodden and oppressed people of South Africa, took the plunge and launched the Campaign for the Defiance of the Unjust Laws. Starting off in Port Elizabeth in the early hours of 26 June and with only 33 defiers in action and then in Johannesburg in the afternoon of the same day with 106 defiers, it spread throughout the country like wildfire. Factory and office workers, doctors, lawyers, teachers, students and the clergy: Africans, Coloureds, Indians and Europeans, old and young, all rallied to the national call and defied the pass laws and the curfew and the railway apartheid regulations. By the end of the year, more than 8,500 people of all races had defied. The Campaign called for immediate and heavy sacrifices. Workers lost their jobs, chiefs and teachers were expelled from the service, doctors, lawyers and businessmen gave up their practices and businesses and elected to go to jail. Defiance was a step of great political significance. It released strong social forces which affected thousands of our countrymen. It was an effective way of getting the masses to function politically; a powerful method of voicing our indignation against the reactionary policies of the Government. It was one of the best ways of exerting pressure on the Government and extremely dangerous to the stability and security of the State. It inspired and aroused our people from a conquered and servile community of yesmen to a militant and uncompromising band of comrades-in-arms. The entire country was transformed into battle zones where the forces of liberation were locked in mortal conflict against those of reaction and evil. Our flag flew in every battlefield and thousands of our countrymen rallied around it. We held the initiative and the forces of freedom were advancing on all fronts. It was against this background and at the height of this Campaign that we held our last annual provincial Conference in Pretoria from 10th to 12th October last year. In a way, that Conference was a welcome reception for those who had returned from the battlefields and a farewell to those who were still going to action. The spirit of defiance and action dominated the entire conference.

Today we meet under totally different conditions. By the end of July last year, the Campaign had reached a stage where it had to be suppressed by the Government or it would impose its own policies on the country.

The government launched its reactionary offensive and struck at us. Between July last year and August this year 47 leading members from both Congresses in Johannesburg, Port Elizabeth and Kimberley were arrested, tried and convicted for launching the Defiance Campaign and given suspended sentences ranging from three months to two years on condition that they did not again participate in the Defiance of the Unjust Laws. In November last year, a proclamation was passed which prohibited meetings of more than ten Africans and made it an offence for any person to call upon an African to defy. Contravention of this proclamation carried a penalty of three years or a fine of three hundred pounds. In March this year the Government passed the so-called Public Safety Act which empowered it to declare a state of emergency and to create conditions which would permit of the most ruthless and pitiless methods of suppressing our movement. Almost simultaneously, the Criminal Laws Amendment Act was passed which provided heavy penalties for those convicted of Defiance offences. This Act also made provision for the whipping of defiers including women. It was under this Act that Mr Arthur Matlala, who was the local leader of the Central Branch during the Defiance Campaign, was convicted and sentenced to twelve months with hard labour plus eight strokes by the Magistrate of Villa Nora.* The Government also made extensive use of the Suppression of Communism Act. You will remember that in May last year the Government ordered Moses Kotane, Yusuf Dadoo, J B Marks, David Bopape and Johnson Ngwevela to resign from the Congresses and many other organisations and they were also prohibited from attending political gatherings. In consequence of these bans, Moses Kotane, J B Marks and David Bopape did not attend our last provincial Conference. In December last year, the Secretary-General, Mr W M Sisulu, and I were banned from attending gatherings and confined to Johannesburg for six months. Early this year, the President General, Chief Lutuli, whilst in the midst of a national tour which he was executing with remarkable energy and devotion, was prohibited for a period of twelve months from attending public gatherings and from visiting Durban, Johannesburg, Cape Town, Port Elizabeth and many other centres. A few days before the President General was banned, the President of the SAIC, Dr G M Naicker, had been served with a similar notice. Many

---

*A district in the North-Western Transvaal.

other active workers both from the African and Indian Congresses and from trade union organisations were also banned.

The Congresses realised that these measures created a new situation which did not prevail when the Campaign was launched in June 1952. The tide of defiance was bound to recede and we were forced to pause and to take stock of the new situation. We had to analyse the dangers that faced us, formulate plans to overcome them and evolve new plans of political struggle. A political movement must keep in touch with reality and the prevailing conditions. Long speeches, the shaking of fists, the banging of tables and strongly worded resolutions out of touch with the objective conditions do not bring about mass action and can do a great deal of harm to the organisation and the struggle we serve. We understood that the masses had to be prepared and made ready for new forms of political struggle. We had to recuperate our strength and muster our forces for another and more powerful offensive against the enemy. To have gone ahead blindly as if nothing had happened would have been suicidal and stupid. The conditions under which we meet today are, therefore, vastly different. The Defiance Campaign together with its thrills and adventures has receded. The old methods of bringing about mass action through public mass meetings, press statements and leaflets calling upon the people to go to action have become extremely dangerous and difficult to use effectively. The authorities will not easily permit a meeting called under the auspices of the ANC, few newspapers will publish statements openly criticising the policies of the Government and there is hardly a single printing press which will agree to print leaflets calling upon workers to embark on industrial action for fear of prosecution under the Suppression of Communism Act and similar measures. These developments require the evolution of new forms of political struggle which will make it reasonable for us to strive for action on a higher level than the Defiance Campaign. The Government, alarmed at the indomitable upsurge of national consciousness, is doing everything in its power to crush our movement by removing the genuine representatives of the people from the organisations. According to a statement made by Swart* in Parliament on 18 September 1953, there are 33 trade union officials and 89 other people who have been served with notices in terms of the Suppression of Communism Act. This does not include that formidable array of freedom fighters who have been named and blacklisted under the Suppression of Communism Act and those who have been banned under the Riotous Assemblies Act.

Meanwhile the living conditions of the people, already extremely difficult, are steadily worsening and becoming unbearable. The purchasing power of the people is progressively declining and the cost of living is rocketing. Bread is now dearer than it was two months ago. The cost of milk, meat and vegetables is beyond the pockets of the average family and many of our people cannot afford

---

*C R Swart, Minister of Justice and later first State President of the Republic of South Africa.

them. The people are too poor to have enough food to feed their families and children. They cannot afford sufficient clothing, housing and medical care. They are denied the right to security in the event of unemployment, sickness, disability, old age and where allowances are paid they are far too low for survival. Because of lack of proper medical amenities our people are ravaged by such dreaded diseases as tuberculosis, venereal disease, leprosy, pellagra, and infantile mortality is very high. The recent state budget made provision for the increase of the cost-of-living allowances for Europeans and not a word was said about the poorest and most hard-hit section of the population — the African people. The insane policies of the Government which have brought about an explosive situation in the country have definitely scared away foreign capital from South Africa and the financial crisis through which the country is now passing is forcing many industrial and business concerns to close down, to retrench their staffs and unemployment is growing every day. The farm labourers are in a particularly dire plight. You will perhaps recall the investigations and exposures of the semi-slave conditions on the Bethal farms made in 1948 by the Reverend Michael Scott and a *Guardian* Correspondent; by the *Drum* last year and the *Advance* in April this year. You will recall how human beings, wearing only sacks with holes for their heads and arms, never given enough food to eat, slept on cement floors on cold nights with only their sacks to cover their shivering bodies. You will remember how they were woken up as early as 4 am and taken to work on the fields with the indunas sjamboking* those who tried to straighten their backs, who felt weak and dropped down because of hunger and sheer exhaustion. You will also recall the story of human beings toiling pathetically from the early hours of the morning till sunset, fed only on mealie meal* served on filthy sacks spread on the ground and eating with their dirty hands. People falling ill and never once being given medical attention. You will also recall the revolting story of a farmer who was convicted for tying a labourer by his feet from a tree and having him flogged to death, pouring boiling water into his mouth whenever he cried for water. These things which have long vanished from many parts of the world still flourish in South Africa today.** None will deny that they constitute a serious challenge to Congress and we are duty bound to find an effective remedy for these obnoxious practices.

The Government has introduced in Parliament the Native Labour (Settlement of Disputes) Bill and the Bantu Education Bill. Speaking on the Labour Bill, the Minister of Labour, Ben Schoeman, openly stated that the aim of this wicked measure is to bleed African trade unions to death. By forbidding strikes and lockouts it deprives Africans of the one weapon the workers have to improve their position. The aim of the measure is to destroy the present African trade unions

---

*Induna = foreman; sjambok = whip; mealie meal = maize flour.
**These practices continue to flourish in South Africa in the 1980s. See for instance Allen Cook *Akin to Slavery*, IDAF, London, 1982.

which are controlled by the workers themselves and which fight for the improvement of their working conditions, in return for a Central Native Labour Board controlled by the Government and which will be used to frustrate the legitimate aspirations of the African worker. The Minister of Native Affairs, Verwoerd,* has also been brutally clear in explaining the objects of the Bantu Education Bill. According to him the aim of this law is to teach our children that Africans are inferior to Europeans. African education is to be taken out of the hands of people who taught equality between black and white. When this Bill becomes law, it will not be the parents but the Department of Native Affairs which will decide whether an African child should receive higher or other education. It might well be that the children of those who criticise the Government and who fight its policies will almost certainly be taught how to drill rocks in the mines and how to plough potatoes on the farms of Bethal. High education might well be the privilege of those children whose families have a tradition of collaboration with the ruling settlers.

The attitude of the Congress on these bills is very clear and unequivocal. Congress totally rejects both bills without reservation. The last provincial Conference strongly condemned the then proposed Labour Bill as a measure designed to rob the African workers of the universal right of free trade unionism and to undermine and destroy the existing African trade unions. Conference further called upon the African workers to boycott and defy the application of this sinister scheme which was calculated to further the exploitation of the African worker. To accept a measure of this nature even in a qualified manner would be a betrayal of the toiling masses. At a time when every genuine Congressite should fight unreservedly for the recognition of African trade unions and the realisation of the principle that everyone has the right to form and to join trade unions for the protection of his interests, we declare our firm belief in the principles enunciated in the Universal Declaration of Human Rights that everyone has the right to education; that education shall be directed to the full development of human personality and to the strengthening of respect for human rights and fundamental freedoms. It shall promote understanding, tolerance and friendship among the nations, racial or religious groups and shall further the activities of the United Nations for the maintenance of peace. That parents have the right to choose the kind of education that shall be given to their children.

The cumulative effect of all these measures is to prop up and perpetuate the artificial and decaying policy of the supremacy of the white men. The attitude of the Government to us is that: 'Let's beat them down with guns and batons and trample them under our feet. We must be ready to drown the whole country in blood if only there is the slightest chance of preserving white supremacy.'

But there is nothing inherently superior about the herrenvolk idea of the supremacy of the whites. In China, India, Indonesia and Korea, American,

*Dr H F Verwoerd, later Prime Minister, 1958–66.

British, Dutch and French imperialism, based on the concept of the supremacy of Europeans over Asians, has been completely and perfectly exploded. In Malaya and Indo-China British and French imperialisms are being shaken to their foundations by powerful and revolutionary national liberation movements. In Africa, there are approximately 190 million Africans as against four million Europeans. The entire continent is seething with discontent and already there are powerful revolutionary eruptions in the Gold Coast,* Nigeria, Tunisia, Kenya, the Rhodesias** and South Africa. The oppressed people and the oppressors are at loggerheads. The day of reckoning between the forces of freedom and those of reaction is not very far off. I have not the slightest doubt that when that day comes truth and justice will prevail.

The intensification of repression and the extensive use of the bans are designed to immobilise every active worker and to check the national liberation movement. But gone forever are the days when harsh and wicked laws provided the oppressors with years of peace and quiet. The racial policies of the Government have pricked the conscience of all men of good will and have aroused their deepest indignation. The feelings of the oppressed people have never been more bitter. If the ruling circles seek to maintain their position by such inhuman methods then a clash between the forces of freedom and those of reaction is certain. The grave plight of the people compels them to resist to the death the stinking policies of the gangsters that rule our country.

But in spite of all the difficulties outlined above, we have won important victories. The general political level of the people has been considerably raised and they are now more conscious of their strength. Action has become the language of the day. The ties between the working people and the Congress have been greatly strengthened. This is a development of the highest importance because in a country such as ours a political organisation that does not receive the support of the workers is in fact paralysed on the very ground on which it has chosen to wage battle. Leaders of trade union organisations are at the same time important officials of the provincial and local branches of the ANC. In the past we talked of the African, Indian and Coloured struggles. Though certain individuals raised the question of a united front of all the oppressed groups, the various non-European organisations stood miles apart from one another and the efforts of those for co-ordination and unity were like a voice crying in the wilderness and it seemed that the day would never dawn when the oppressed people would stand and fight together shoulder to shoulder against a common enemy. Today we talk of the struggle of the oppressed people which, though it is waged through their respective autonomous organisations, is gravitating towards one central command.

---

*Now Ghana.
**Southern Rhodesia, now Zimbabwe, and Northern Rhodesia, now Zambia.

Our immediate task is to consolidate these victories, to preserve our organisations and to muster our forces for the resumption of the offensive. To achieve this important task the National Executive of the ANC in consultation with the National Action Committee of the ANC and the SAIC formulated a plan of action popularly known as the 'M' Plan, and the highest importance is attached to it by the National Executive. Instructions were given to all provinces to implement the 'M' Plan without delay.*

The underlying principle of this plan is the understanding that it is no longer possible to wage our struggle mainly on the old methods of public meetings and printed circulars. The aim is:

(1) to consolidate the Congress machinery;

(2) to enable the transmission of important decisions taken on a national level to every member of the organisation without calling public meetings, issuing press statements and printing circulars;

(3) to build up in the local branches themselves local Congresses which will effectively represent the strength and will of the people;

(4) to extend and strengthen the ties between Congress and the people and to consolidate Congress leadership.

This plan is being implemented in many branches, not only in the Transvaal but also in other provinces, and is producing excellent results. The Regional Conferences held in Sophiatown, Germiston, Kliptown and Benoni on 28 June, 23 and 30 August and on 6 September 1953, which were attended by large crowds, are a striking demonstration of the effectiveness of this plan, and the National Executive must be complimented for it. I appeal to all members of the Congress to redouble their efforts and play their part truly and well in its implementation. The hard and strenuous task of recruiting members and strengthening our organisation through a house-to-house campaign in every locality must be done by you all. From now on the activity of Congressites must not be confined to speeches and resolutions. Their activities must find expression in wide-scale work among the masses, work which will enable them to make the greatest possible contact with the working people. You must protect and defend your trade unions. If you are not allowed to have your meetings publicly, then you must hold them over your machines in the factories, on the trains and buses as you travel home. You must have them in your villages and shantytowns. You must make every home, every shack and every mud structure where our people live, a branch of the trade union movement and you must *never surrender.*

You must defend the right of African parents to decide the kind of education that shall be given to their children. Teach the children that Africans are not one iota inferior to Europeans. Establish your own community schools where the

---

*In an effort to strengthen and decentralise ANC organisation, Mandela was responsible for the implementation of a plan, named after himself as 'the M Plan', to build a mass membership organised through cells at the grassroots level and through a hierarchy of leaders at intermediate level, responsive to direction without the necessity for public meetings.

right kind of education will be given to our children. If it becomes dangerous or impossible to have these alternative schools, then again you must make every home, every shack or rickety structure a centre of learning for our children. Never surrender to the inhuman and barbaric theories of Verwoerd.

The decision to defy the unjust laws enabled Congress to develop considerably wider contacts between itself and the masses and the urge to join Congress grew day by day. But due to the fact that the local branches did not exercise proper control and supervision, the admission of new members was not carried out satisfactorily. No careful examination was made of their past history and political characteristics. As a result of this, there were many shady characters ranging from political clowns, place-seekers, splitters, saboteurs, agents provocateurs to informers and even policemen, who infiltrated into the ranks of Congress. One need only refer to the Johannesburg trial of Dr Moroka and nineteen others, where a member of Congress who actually worked at the National Headquarters, turned out to be a detective-sergeant on special duty. Remember the case of Leballo of Brakpan who wormed himself into that Branch by producing faked naming letters from the Liquidator, De Villiers Louw, who had instructions to spy on us. There are many other similar instances that emerged during the Johannesburg, Port Elizabeth and Kimberley trials. Whilst some of these men were discovered there are many who have not been found out. In Congress there are still many shady characters, political clowns, place-seekers, saboteurs, provocateurs, informers and policemen who masquerade as progressives but who are in fact the bitterest enemies of our organisation. Outside appearances are highly deceptive and we cannot classify these men by looking at their faces or by listening to their sweet tongues or their vehement speeches demanding immediate action. The friends of the people are distinguishable by the ready and disciplined manner in which they rally behind their organisations and their readiness to sacrifice when the preservation of the organisation has become a matter of life and death. Similarly, enemies and shady characters are detected by the extent to which they consistently attempt to wreck the organisation by creating fratricidal strife, disseminating confusion and undermining and even opposing important plans of action to vitalise the organisation. These shady characters, by means of flattery, bribes and corruption, win the support of the weak-willed and politically backward individuals, detach them from Congress and use them in their own interests. The presence of such elements in Congress constitutes a serious threat to the struggle, for the capacity for political action of an organisation which is ravaged by such disruptive and splitting elements is considerably undermined. Here in South Africa, as in many parts of the world, a revolution is maturing; it is the profound desire, the determination and the urge of the overwhelming majority of the country to destroy for ever the shackles of oppression that condemn them to servitude and slavery. To overthrow oppression has been sanctioned by humanity and is the highest aspiration of every free man. If elements in our organisation seek to impede the realisation of this lofty purpose then these people have placed themselves outside the organisation and must be put out of action before they do more harm. To do otherwise would be a crime and a serious neglect of duty. We must rid ourselves of such elements and give our organisation the striking power of a real militant mass organisation.

Kotane, Marks, Bopape, Tloome and I have been banned from attending gatherings and we cannot join and counsel with you on the serious problems that are facing our country. We have been banned because we champion the freedom of the oppressed people of our country and because we have consistently fought against the policy of racial discrimination in favour of a policy which accords fundamental human rights to all, irrespective of race, colour, sex or language. We are exiled from our own people for we have uncompromisingly resisted the efforts of imperialist America and her satellites to drag the world into the rule of violence and brutal force, into the rule of the napalm, hydrogen and the cobalt bombs where millions of people will be wiped out to satisfy the criminal and greedy appetites of the imperial powers. We have been gagged because we have emphatically and openly condemned the criminal attacks by the imperialists against the people of Malaya, Vietnam, Indonesia, Tunisia and Tanganyika* and called upon our people to identify themselves unreservedly with the cause of world peace and to fight against the war policies of America and her satellites. We are being shadowed, hounded and trailed because we fearlessly voiced our horror and indignation at the slaughter of the people of Korea and Kenya, because we expressed our solidarity with the cause of the Kenyan people. The massacre of the Kenyan people by Britain has aroused world-wide indignation and protest. Children are being burnt alive, women are raped, tortured, whipped and boiling water poured on their breasts to force confessions from them that Jomo Kenyatta had administered the Mau Mau oath to them. Men are being castrated and shot dead. In the Kikuyu country there are some villages in which the population has been completely wiped out. We are prisoners in our own country because we dared to raise our voices against these horrible atrocities and because we expressed our solidarity with the cause of the Kenyan people.

You can see that 'there is no easy walk to freedom anywhere, and many of us will have to pass through the valley of the shadow of death again and again before we reach the mountain tops of our desires.

'Dangers and difficulties have not deterred us in the past, they will not frighten us now. But we must be prepared for them like men who mean business who do not waste energy in vain talk and idle action. The way of preparation for action lies in our rooting out all impurity and indiscipline from our organisation and making it the bright and shining instrument that will cleave its way to Africa's freedom.'**

---

*Now Tanzania.

**The quotation is taken and adapted from an article by Nehru in *The Unity of India: Collected Writings* 1937–40, Lindsay Drummond, London, 1942, p.131.

The Defiance Campaign led, amongst other developments, to the formation of anti-racialist organisations and groups among the white population. The first of these was the Congress of Democrats (COD) which later took its place in the Congress Alliance in support of the ANC. Another was the Liberal Party, formed as a non-racial party in 1952 and the subject of the article by Mandela below. The Liberal Party began with a policy of qualified franchise, which was later changed to that of universal franchise. It dissolved itself in 1967 when non-racial political parties were prohibited by law.

3(b) 'THE SHIFTING SANDS OF ILLUSION'

Article written by Mandela for the monthly journal Liberation, *June 1953.*

The Liberal Party constitution purports to uphold the 'essential dignity of every human being irrespective of race, colour, or creed, and the maintenance of his fundamental rights'. It expresses itself in favour of the 'right of every human being to develop to the fullest extent of which he is capable consistent with the rights of others'.

The new party's statement of principles thus far contents itself with the broad generalisations without any attempt to interpret them or define their practical application in the South African context. It then proceeds to announce 'that no person (should) be debarred from participation in the government or other democratic processes of the country by reason only of race, colour, or creed'. But here the neo-Liberals abandon the safe ground of generalisation and stipulate explicitly 'that political rights based on a common franchise roll be extended to all SUITABLY QUALIFIED persons'. This question-begging formulation will not for long enable our Liberals to evade the fundamental issue: which persons are 'suitably qualified'?

The democratic principle is 'one adult, one vote'. The Liberals obviously differ from this well-known conception. They are, therefore, obliged to state an alternative theory of their own. This they have, so far, failed to do. The African National Congress, the South African Indian Congress, and the Congress of Democrats stand for votes for all: the demand, a century ago, of the British Chartists for universal equal franchise rights. Does the Liberal Party support this demand? Historical reality demands a plain and unequivocal answer . . .

In South Africa, where the entire population is almost split into two hostile camps in consequence of the policy of racial discrimination, and where recent political events have made the struggle between oppressor and oppressed more acute, there can be no middle course. The fault of the Liberals — and this spells their doom — is to attempt to strike just such a course. They believe in criticising and condemning the Government for its reactionary policies but they are afraid to identify themselves with the people and to assume the task of mobilising that social force capable of lifting the struggle to higher levels.

The Liberals' credo states that to achieve their objects the party will employ 'only democratic and constitutional means and will oppose all forms of totalitarianism such as communism and fascism'. Talk of democratic and constitutional means can only have a basis in reality for those people who enjoy democratic and constitutional rights.

We must accept the fact that in our country we cannot win one single victory of political freedom without overcoming a desperate resistance on the part of the Government, and that victory will not come of itself but only as a result of a bitter struggle by the oppressed people for the overthrow of racial discrimination. This means that we are committed to struggle to mobilise from our ranks the forces capable of waging a determined and militant struggle against all forms of reaction. The theory that we can sit with folded arms and wait for a future parliament to legislate for the 'essential dignity of every human being irrespective of race, colour, or creed' is crass perversion of elementary principles of political struggle. No organisation whose interests are identical with those of the toiling masses will advocate conciliation to win its demands.

To propose in the South African context that democrats limit themselves to constitutional means of struggle is to ask the people to submit to laws enacted by a minority parliament whose composition is essentially a denial of democracy to the overwhelming majority of the population. It means that we must obey a Constitution which debars the majority from participating in the government and other democratic processes of the country by reason only of race, colour, or creed. It implies in practice that we must carry passes and permit the violation of the essential dignity of a human being. It means that we must accept the Suppression of Communism Act which legalises the gagging and persecution of leaders of the people because of their creed. It implies the acceptance of the Rehabilitation Scheme, the Bantu Authorities, the Group Areas, the Public Safety, the Criminal Law Amendment Act and all the wicked policies of the Government.

The real question is: in the general struggle for political rights can the oppressed people count on the Liberal Party as an ally? The answer is that the new party merely gives organisational expression to a tendency which has for many years existed among a section of the White ruling class and in the United Party.* This section hates and fears the idea of a revolutionary democracy in South Africa, just as much as the Malans** and the Oppenheimers*** do.

---

*White political party in opposition to Nationalist Government.
**Dr D F Malan, Prime Minister of South Africa 1948–54.
***Sir Ernest and his son and successor Harry Oppenheimer, managing directors of the Anglo-American Corporation, the most powerful mining and financial group in Southern Africa.

Rather than attempt the costly, dubious, and dangerous task of crushing the non-European mass movement by force, they would seek to divert it with fine words and promises and to divide it by giving concessions and bribes to a privileged minority (the 'suitably qualified' voters, perhaps).

It becomes clear, therefore, that the high-sounding principles enunciated by the Liberal Party, though apparently democratic and progressive in form, are essentially reactionary in content. They stand not for the freedom of the people but for the adoption of more subtle systems of oppression and exploitation. Though they talk of liberty and human dignity they are subordinate henchmen of the ruling circles. They stand for the retention of the cheap labour system and of the subordinate colonial status of the non-European masses together with the Nationalist Government whose class interests are identical with theirs. In practice they acquiesce in the slavery of the people, low wages, mass unemployment, the squalid tenements in the locations and shanty-towns.

We of the non-European liberation movement are not racialists. We are convinced that there are thousands of honest democrats among the White population who are prepared to take up a firm and courageous stand for unconditional equality, for the complete renunciation of 'White supremacy'. To them we extend the hand of sincere friendship and brotherly alliance. But no true alliance can be built on the shifting sands of evasions, illusions, and opportunism. We insist on presenting the conditions which make it reasonable to fight for freedom. The only sure road to this goal leads through the uncompromising and determined mass struggle for the overthrow of fascism and the establishment of democratic forms of government.

Two years after this article was written, the Liberal Party, although invited, did not participate in the Congress of the People, the most representative mass event up till that moment in South Africa's history.

The proposal for such a Congress was originally put forward by the veteran ANC leader Professor Z K Matthews. It was adopted by the Congress Movement consisting of the ANC, the South African Indian Congress, the Coloured People's Organisation and the (white) Congress of Democrats. These bodies each elected eight members who joined together to form a National Action Council to organise the event.

One of the Council's first tasks was to produce a leaflet calling the people of South Africa to the Congress. The leaflet was distributed in several languages to all parts of the country and to all sectors of South African society, even including the governing Nationalist Party and other exclusively white organisations, none of which responded.

The response from ordinary people, however, was 'spectacular and moving', to quote Mandela (see p.54).

4. CONGRESS OF THE PEOPLE, 1955

4(a) CALL TO THE CONGRESS‡

Leaflet issued by the National Action Council of the Congress of the People.

WE CALL THE PEOPLE OF SOUTH AFRICA BLACK AND WHITE LET US SPEAK TOGETHER OF FREEDOM! WE CALL THE FARMERS OF THE RESERVES AND TRUST LANDS.

Let us speak of the wide land, and the narrow strips on which we toil.
Let us speak of brothers without land, and of children without schooling.
Let us speak of taxes and of cattle, and of famine.
LET US SPEAK OF FREEDOM

WE CALL THE MINERS OF COAL, GOLD AND DIAMONDS.

Let us speak of the dark shafts, and the cold compounds far from our families.
Let us speak of heavy labour and long hours, and of men sent home to die.
Let us speak of rich masters and poor wages.
LET US SPEAK OF FREEDOM

WE CALL THE WORKERS OF FARMS AND FORESTS.

Let us speak of the rich foods we grow, and the laws that keep us poor.
Let us speak of harsh treatment and of children and women forced to work.
Let us speak of private prisons, and beatings and of passes.
LET US SPEAK OF FREEDOM

WE CALL THE WORKERS OF FACTORIES AND SHOPS.

Let us speak of the good things we make, and the bad conditions of our work.
Let us speak of the many passes and the few jobs.
Let us speak of foremen and of transport and of trade unions; of holidays and of houses.
LET US SPEAK OF FREEDOM

WE CALL THE TEACHERS, STUDENTS AND THE PREACHERS.

Let us speak of the light that comes with learning, and the ways we are kept in darkness.

Let us speak of great services we can render, and of the narrow ways that are open to us.

Let us speak of laws, and government, and rights.

LET US SPEAK OF FREEDOM

WE CALL THE HOUSEWIVES AND THE MOTHERS.

Let us speak of the fine children that we bear, and of their stunted lives.

Let us speak of the many illnesses and deaths, and of the few clinics and schools.

Let us speak of high prices and of shanty towns.

LET US SPEAK OF FREEDOM

ALL OF US TOGETHER — African and European, Indian and Coloured. Voter and voteless. Privileged and rightless. The happy and the homeless. All the people of South Africa; of the towns and of the countryside.

LET US SPEAK TOGETHER OF FREEDOM. And of the happiness that can come to men and women if they live in a land that is free.

LET US SPEAK TOGETHER OF FREEDOM. And of how to get it for ourselves, and for our children.

LET THE VOICE OF ALL THE PEOPLE BE HEARD. AND LET THE DEMANDS OF ALL THE PEOPLE FOR THE THINGS THAT WILL MAKE US FREE BE RECORDED. LET THE DEMANDS BE GATHERED TOGETHER IN A GREAT **CHARTER OF FREEDOM.**

WE CALL ON ALL GOOD MEN AND TRUE, to speak now of freedom, and to write their own demands into the Charter of Freedom.

WE CALL ALL WHO LOVE LIBERTY to pledge their lives from here on to win the Freedoms set out in the Charter.

WE CALL ALL THE PEOPLE OF SOUTH AFRICA TO PREPARE FOR:

THE CONGRESS OF THE PEOPLE — Where representatives of the people, everywhere in the land, will meet together in a great assembly, to discuss and adopt the Charter of Freedom.

Let us organise together for the Congress of the People.

Let us speak together of Freedom.

Let us work together for the Freedom Charter.

LET US GO FORWARD TOGETHER TO FREEDOM!

This Call to the

CONGRESS of the PEOPLE

is addressed to all South Africans, European and Non-European.

It is made by four bodies, speaking for the four sections of the people of South Africa: by the African National Congress, the South African Indian Congress, the Congress of Democrats, and the South African Coloured People's Organisation.

It calls you all to prepare to send your chosen spokesmen to:

THE CONGRESS OF THE PEOPLE

a meeting of elected representatives of all races, coming together from every town and village, every farm and factory, every mine and kraal, every street and suburb, in the whole land. Here all will speak together, freely, as equals. They will speak together of the things their people need to make them free. They will speak together of changes that must be made in our lives, our laws, our customs and our outlooks. They will speak together of freedom. And they will write their demands into:

THE FREEDOM CHARTER

This Charter will express all the demands of all the people for the good life that they seek for themselves and their children. The Freedom Charter will be our guide to those 'singing tomorrows' when all South Africans will live and work together, without racial bitterness and fear of misery, in peace and harmony.

THIS IS A CALL for an awakening of all men and women, to campaign together in the greatest movement of all our history. Our call is to you — the People of South Africa. We invite all Union-wide* Organisations to join as sponsors of the CONGRESS OF THE PEOPLE, and to take part in its direction. Those who are not afraid to hear the voice of the people will join us. We will welcome them, and work together with them as equals.

We invite all local and provincial societies, clubs, churches, trade unions, sporting bodies and other organisations to join as partners in the CONGRESS OF THE PEOPLE Committee, and to share the work. Those who are not afraid to speak of freedom will join us. We will welcome them, and work together with them as equals.

We invite all South African men and women of every race and creed to take part as organisers of the CONGRESS OF THE PEOPLE and awaken others to its message. Those who are prepared to work together for freedom and the Freedom Charter will join us. We will welcome them, and go forward together with them to freedom.

---

*South Africa was still the 'Union of South Africa'.

48

OUR CALL IS TO YOU!

- Give your time to spread the message of the CONGRESS OF THE PEOPLE.
- Become a Volunteer to organise for freedom.
- Tell your neighbours and workmates of the nation-wide elections that are coming.
- Rouse the people to discuss what they want of freedom.

LET US WORK TOGETHER FOR FREEDOM!

THE CONGRESS OF THE PEOPLE

will take place

- when all the people's demands for inclusion in the Freedom Charter have been gathered in;
- when the whole country has been awakened to speak of freedom, and the call for elections has been made;
- not later than June, 1955 — at a date and place still to be announced.

THE CONGRESS OF THE PEOPLE

will be organised

- by 50,000 Volunteers, who will give their time to carrying through the campaign as directed;
- by a network of committees in every village, town and factory, representing and uniting all sections and all races;
- by the National Action Council, composed of all national bodies that agree to act as sponsors.

DO THESE THREE THINGS — NOW!

ONE: SEND IN YOUR NAME AND ADDRESS TO A PROVINCIAL COMMITTEE OF THE CONGRESS OF THE PEOPLE, stating that you are interested and would like to assist.

Transvaal Committee, Box 11045, Johannesburg.
Natal Committee, Box 2299, Durban.
Western Cape Committee, Box 4552, Cape Town.
Eastern Cape Committee, Box 1294, Port Elizabeth.
O.F.S. Committee, 3397 Masito Street, Bloemfontein.

TWO: FORM COMMITTEES to campaign for the Congress of the People.

THREE: GATHER GROUPS to send in their demands for the Freedom Charter.

DO NOT THROW THIS LEAFLET AWAY! PASS IT ON TO A FRIEND. DISCUSS IT WITH OTHERS: SEE THAT IT IS READ BY MANY PEOPLE.

Issued by the National Action Council of the Congress of the People, Box 11045, Johannesburg.

Mary Benson describes the event itself: 'Surprisingly the authorities did not ban the Congress of the People. There were harassing tactics — withdrawal of some of the buses taking delegates from distant places, occasional road blocks, the arrest of drivers. The white Press gave it virtually no publicity . . .

On Saturday, 25 June 1955, on a battered patch of veld in Kliptown village near Johannesburg, three thousand delegates responded to this "call". Just over two thousand were Africans, with two to three hundred each of Indians, Coloured people and whites . . . It was like South Africa in miniature . . .

Meanwhile policemen slouched about, eating oranges, smoking cigarettes and swinging their rifles . . .'

Mary Benson goes on to describe how the police eventually marched on the gathering on the Sunday afternoon. The delegates maintained discipline while their papers were confiscated by the Special Branch. The provocation failed. The Congress came to its successful conclusion.*

4(b)   FREEDOM CHARTER‡

Drafted by a sub-committee of the National Action Council from contributions submitted by groups, individuals and meetings all over South Africa, approved by the ANC National Executive and adopted at the Congress of the People, Kliptown, Johannesburg, 25–26 June 1955.

Each section of the Charter was adopted by the three thousand delegates by acclamation with a show of hands and shouts of 'Afrika! Mayibuye!' **

PREAMBLE

We, the people of South Africa, declare for all our country and the world to know:

That South Africa belongs to all who live in it, black and white, and that no government can justly claim authority unless it is based on the will of the people;

That our people have been robbed of their birthright to land, liberty and peace by a form of government founded on injustice and inequality;

That our country will never be prosperous or free until all our people live in brotherhood, enjoying equal rights and opportunities;

---

*Mary Benson, *The Struggle for a Birthright*, IDAF, London, 1985, pp.174–8.
**Ibid.

50

That only a democratic state, based on the will of all the people, can secure to all their birthright without distinction of colour, race, sex or belief;

And therefore, we, the people of South Africa, black and white, together — equals, countrymen and brothers — adopt this FREEDOM CHARTER. And we pledge ourselves to strive together, sparing nothing of our strength and courage, until the democratic changes here set out have been won.

THE PEOPLE SHALL GOVERN!

Every man and woman shall have the right to vote for and stand as a candidate for all bodies which make laws.

All the people shall be entitled to take part in the administration of the country.

The rights of the people shall be the same regardless of race, colour or sex.

All bodies of minority rule, advisory boards, councils and authorities shall be replaced by democratic organs of self-government.

ALL NATIONAL GROUPS SHALL HAVE EQUAL RIGHTS!

There shall be equal status in the bodies of state, in the courts, and in the schools for all national groups and races;

All people shall have equal rights to use their own languages and to develop their own folk culture and customs;

All national groups shall be protected by law against insults to their race and national pride;

The preaching and practice of national, race or colour discrimination and contempt shall be a punishable crime;

All apartheid laws and practices shall be set aside.

THE PEOPLE SHALL SHARE IN THE COUNTRY'S WEALTH!

The national wealth of our country, the heritage of all South Africans, shall be restored to the people;

The mineral wealth beneath the soil, the banks and monopoly industry shall be transferred to the ownership of the people as a whole;

All other industries and trade shall be controlled to assist the well-being of the people;

All people shall have equal rights to trade where they choose, to manufacture and to enter all trades, crafts and professions.

THE LAND SHALL BE SHARED AMONG THOSE WHO WORK IT!

Restriction of land ownership on a racial basis shall be ended, and all the land re-divided amongst those who work it, to banish famine and land hunger;

The state shall help the peasants with implements, seed, tractors and dams to save the soil and assist the tillers;

Freedom of movement shall be guaranteed to all who work on the land;

All shall have the right to occupy land wherever they choose;

People shall not be robbed of their cattle, and forced labour and farm prisons shall be abolished.

ALL SHALL BE EQUAL BEFORE THE LAW!

No one shall be imprisoned, deported or restricted without a fair trial;

No one shall be condemned by the order of any Government official;

The courts shall be representative of all the people;

Imprisonment shall be only for serious crimes against the people, and shall aim at re-education, not vengeance;

The police force and army shall be open to all on an equal basis and shall be the helpers and protectors of the people;

All laws which discriminate on grounds of race, colour or belief shall be repealed.

ALL SHALL ENJOY EQUAL HUMAN RIGHTS!

The law shall guarantee to all their right to speak, to organise, to meet together, to publish, to preach, to worship and to educate their children;

The privacy of the house from police raids shall be protected by law;

All shall be free to travel without restriction from countryside to town, from province to province, and from South Africa abroad;

Pass laws, permits and all other laws restricting these freedoms shall be abolished.

THERE SHALL BE WORK AND SECURITY!

All who work shall be free to form trade unions, to elect their officers and to make wage agreements with their employers;

The state shall recognise the right and duty of all to work; and to draw full unemployment benefits;

Men and women of all races shall receive equal pay for equal work;

There shall be a forty-hour working week, a national minimum wage, paid annual leave, and sick leave for all workers, and maternity leave on full pay for all working mothers;

Miners, domestic workers, farm workers and civil servants shall have the same rights as all others who work;

Child labour, compound labour, the tot system* and contract labour shall be abolished.

---

*The system used on the wine farms of the Western Cape, where labourers are paid or part-paid in kind, by being supplied at various times of the day, as well as at the end of the week, with 'tots' of cheap strong wine. This and the other labour abuses mentioned still exist in the 1980s.

THE DOORS OF LEARNING AND OF CULTURE SHALL BE OPENED!

The government shall discover, develop and encourage national talent for the enhancement of our cultural life;

All the cultural treasures of mankind shall be open to all, by free exchange of books, ideas and contact with other lands;

The aim of education shall be to teach the youth to love their people and their culture, to honour human brotherhood, liberty and peace;

Education shall be free, compulsory, universal and equal for all children;

Higher education and technical training shall be opened to all by means of state allowances and scholarships awarded on the basis of merit;

Adult illiteracy shall be ended by a mass state education plan;

Teachers shall have all the rights of other citizens;

The colour bar in cultural life, in sport and in education shall be abolished.

THERE SHALL BE HOUSES, SECURITY AND COMFORT!

All people shall have the right to live where they choose, to be decently housed, and to bring up their families in comfort and security;

Unused housing space to be made available to the people;

Rent and prices shall be lowered, food plentiful and no one shall go hungry;

A preventive health scheme shall be run by the state;

Free medical care and hospitalisation shall be provided for all, with special care for mothers and young children;

Slums shall be demolished, and new suburbs built where all have transport, roads, lighting, playing fields, crèches and social centres;

The aged, the orphans, the disabled and the sick shall be cared for by the state;

Rest, leisure and recreation shall be the right of all;

Fenced locations and ghettos shall be abolished, and laws which break up families shall be repealed.

THERE SHALL BE PEACE AND FRIENDSHIP!

South Africa shall be a fully independent state, which respects the rights and sovereignty of all nations;

South Africa shall strive to maintain world peace and the settlement of all international disputes by negotiation — not war;

Peace and friendship amongst all our people shall be secured by upholding the equal rights, opportunities and status of all;

The people of the protectorates — Basutoland, Bechuanaland and Swaziland* — shall be free to decide for themselves their own future;

The right of all the peoples of Africa to independence and self-government shall be recognised, and shall be the basis of close co-operation.

---

*Now the independent States of Lesotho, Botswana and Swaziland.

Let all who love their people and their country now say, as we say here: 'THESE FREEDOMS WE WILL FIGHT FOR, SIDE BY SIDE, THROUGHOUT OUR LIVES, UNTIL WE HAVE WON OUR LIBERTY.'

4(c) 'FREEDOM IN OUR LIFETIME'

Article on the Freedom Charter by Mandela in Liberation, *June 1956.*

The adoption of the Freedom Charter by the Congress of the People was widely recognised both at home and abroad as an event of major political significance in the life of this country. In his message to the COP, Chief A J Lutuli,* the banned National President of the African National Congress, declared:

'Why will this assembly be significant and unique? Its size, I hope, will make it unique. But above all its multi-racial nature and its noble objectives will make it unique, because it will be the first time in the history of our multi-racial nation that its people from all walks of life will meet as equals, irrespective of race, colour, and creed, to formulate a freedom charter for all people in the country.'

The COP was the most spectacular and moving demonstration this country has ever seen; through it the people have given proof that they have the ability and the power to triumph over every obstacle and win the future of their dreams. Alfred Hutchinson, reporting on the COP, coined the magnificent title, 'A NEW WORLD UNFOLDS . . .', which accurately summarised the political significance of that historic gathering.

The same theme was taken up by *Liberation* of September last year when, in its editorial comment, it predicted that the textbooks of the future would treat the Kliptown meeting as one of the most important landmarks in our history. John Hatch, the Public Relations Officer of the British Labour Party, in an article published in the *New Statesman and Nation* of 28 January 1956, under the title 'The Real South African Opposition', conceded that some degree of success was achieved by the Congress Movement when it approved the Charter. Finally, in his May Day message published in *New Age,*** Moses Kotane reviewed the political achievements of 1955 and came to the conclusion that the most outstanding one was the COP, which produced the world-renowned document — the Freedom Charter — which serves as a beacon to the Congress Movement and an inspiration to the people of South Africa.

Few people will deny, therefore, that the adoption of the Charter is an event of major political significance in the life of this country. The intensive and nationwide political campaigning that preceded it, the 2,844 elected delegates of the people that attended, the attention it attracted far and wide and the favour-

---

*Ex-Chief Albert Lutuli (sometimes spelt Luthuli), President of the ANC from 1953 until its banning in 1960. Lutuli's activities in the ANC led to his dismissal by the White authorities in 1953, and after that he was often called 'Ex-Chief'.

**The newspaper of the Congress Movement.

able comment it continues to receive at home and abroad from people of diverse political opinions and beliefs long after its adoption, are evidence of this fact.

Never before has any document or conference been so widely acclaimed and discussed by the democratic movement in South Africa. Never before has any document or conference constituted such a serious and formidable challenge to the racial and anti-popular policies of the country. FOR THE FIRST TIME IN THE HISTORY OF OUR COUNTRY THE DEMOCRATIC FORCES IRRESPECTIVE OF RACE, IDEOLOGICAL CONVICTION, PARTY AFFILIATION OR RELIGIOUS BELIEF HAVE RENOUNCED AND DISCARDED RACIALISM IN ALL ITS RAMIFICATIONS, CLEARLY DEFINED THEIR AIMS AND OBJECTS AND UNITED IN A COMMON PROGRAMME OF ACTION.

The Charter is more than a mere list of demands for democratic reforms. It is a revolutionary document precisely because the changes it envisages cannot be won without breaking up the economic and political set-up of present South Africa. To win the demands calls for the organisation, launching, and development of mass struggles on the widest scale. They will be won and consolidated only as a result of a nationwide campaign of agitation; through stubborn and determined mass struggles to defeat the economic and political policies of the Nationalist Government; by repulsing onslaughts on the living standards and liberties of the people.

The most vital task facing the democratic movement in this country is to unleash such struggles and to develop them on the basis of the concrete and immediate demands of the people from area to area. Only in this way can we build a powerful mass movement, which is the only guarantee of ultimate victory in the struggle for democratic reforms. Only in this way will the democratic movement become a vital instrument for the winning of the democratic changes set out in the Charter.

Whilst the Charter proclaims democratic changes of a far-reaching nature, it is by no means a blueprint for a socialist state but a programme for the unification of various classes and groupings amongst the people on a democratic basis. Under socialism the workers hold state power. They and the peasants own the means of production, the land, the factories, and the mills. All production is for use and not for profit. The Charter does not contemplate such profound economic and political changes. Its declaration 'The People Shall Govern!' visualises the transfer of power not to any single social class but to all the people of this country, be they workers, peasants, professional men, or petty bourgeoisie.

It is true that in demanding the nationalisation of the banks, the gold mines, and the land, the Charter strikes a fatal blow at the financial and gold-mining monopolies and farming interests that have for centuries plundered the country and condemned its people to servitude. But such a step is imperative because the realisation of the Charter is inconceivable, in fact impossible, unless and until these monopolies are smashed and the national wealth of the country turned over to the people. To destroy these monopolies means the termination of the exploitation of vast sections of the populace by mining kings and land barons, and there will be a general rise in the living standards of the people. It is precisely because the Charter offers immense opportunities for an overall improvement in the material conditions of all classes and groups that it attracts such wide support.

But a mere appraisal of a document, however dynamic its provisions or content might be, is academic and valueless unless we consciously and conscientiously create the conditions necessary for its realisation. To be fruitful such appraisal must be closely linked up with the vital question of whether we have in South African society the requisite social forces that are capable of fighting for the realisation of the Charter, and whether in fact these forces are being mobilised and conditioned for this principal task.

The democratic struggle in South Africa is conducted by an alliance of various classes and political groupings amongst the non-European people supported by White democrats, African, Coloured, and Indian workers and peasants, traders and merchants, students and teachers, doctors and lawyers, and various other classes and groupings; all participate in the struggle against racial inequality and for full democratic rights. It was this alliance which launched the National Day of Protest on 26 June 1950. It was this alliance which unleashed the campaign for the Defiance of Unjust Laws on 26 June 1952. It is this same alliance that produced the Freedom Charter. In this alliance the democratic movement has the rudiments of a dynamic and militant mass movement and, provided the movement exploits the initial advantages on its side at the present moment, immense opportunities exist for the winning of the demands in the Charter within our lifetime.

The striking feature about the population of our country and its occupational distribution is the numerical preponderance of the non-Europeans over Europeans and the economic importance of the former group in the key industries. According to the 1951 population census the population of the country consists of 2,643,000 Europeans as against 10,005,000 non-Europeans, a numerical disparity which is bound to have a decisive bearing on the final outcome of the present struggle to smash the colour-bar. According to the 1953 Official Year Book of the Union of South Africa there were 46,700 Europeans employed by the gold mines and collieries at the end of 1952. The number of Africans and Coloureds employed on the mines for the same period was 452,702, a proportion of one European employee to nearly ten non-European employees. The racial composition of industrial employees in establishments with over ten employees during the period 1948-49 was as follows: Europeans 33 per cent; Africans 51.5 per cent; Asiatics 3 per cent; and Coloureds 12.5 per cent. According to the same Year Book, during 1952 there were 297,476 Europeans employed on farms occupied by Europeans and 2,188,712 Africans and 636,065 other non-Europeans.

The figures reveal the preponderant importance of the non-European people in the economic life of the country, and the key task of the movement is to stimulate and draw these forces into the struggle for democratic reforms. A significant step was taken in Johannesburg on 3 March 1955, when a new trade union centre — the South African Congress of Trade Unions★ — was formed with delegates from 34 unions with a total membership of close on 42,000, and when for the first time in the history of trade unionism in South Africa, African, Coloured, European, and Indian workers united for a fighting policy on the basis of absolute equality. With 42,000 organised workers on our side, and fighting under the flag of a trade union centre that has completely renounced racialism and committed itself to a militant and uncompromising policy, it remains for us to redouble our efforts and carry our message to every factory and mill throughout the country. The message of the new centre is bound to attract the support of the majority of the workers, for they have no interest whatsoever in the country's policy of racial discrimination.

The workers are the principal force upon which the democratic movement should rely, but to repel the savage onslaughts of the Nationalist Government and to develop the fight for democratic rights it is necessary that the other classes and groupings be joined. Support and assistance must be sought and secured from the 452,702 African and Coloured mine-workers, from the 2,834,777 non-European labourers employed on European farms and from the millions of peasants that occupy the so-called Native Reserves of the Union. The cruel and inhuman manner with which they are treated, their dreadful poverty and economic misery, make them potential allies of the democratic movement.

The non-European traders and businessmen are also potential allies, for in hardly any other country in the world has the ruling class made conditions so extremely difficult for the rise of a non-European middle class as in South Africa. The law of the country prohibits non-Europeans from owning or possessing minerals. Their right to own and occupy land is very much restricted and circum-scribed and it is virtually impossible for them to own factories and mills. There-fore they are vitally interested in the liberation of the non-European people, for it is only by destroying white supremacy and through the emancipation of the non-Europeans that they can prosper and develop as a class. To each of these classes and groups the struggle for democratic rights offers definite advantages. To every one of them the realisation of the demands embodied in the Charter would open a new career and vast opportunities for development and prosperity. These are the social forces whose alliance and unity will enable the democratic movement to vanquish the forces of reaction and win the democratic changes envisaged in the Charter.

In the present political situation in South Africa, when the Nationalist Government has gone all out to smash the people's political organisation and the trade union movement through the Suppression of Communism Act and its anti-trade union legislation, it becomes important to call upon and to stimulate every class to wage its own battles. It becomes even more important that all democratic forces be united, and the opportunities for such a united front are growing every

---

★SACTU, which later joined the Congress Alliance led by the ANC.

day. On 3 March 1955 a non-colour-bar trade union centre is formed. On 26 June the same year, in the most spectacular and moving demonstration this country has ever seen, 2,844 delegates of the people adopt the Charter, and four months thereafter more than a thousand women of all races stage a protest march to Pretoria to put their demands to the Government* — all this in the course of one year.

The rise of the Congress Movement and the powerful impact it exerts on the political scene in the country is due precisely to the fact that it has consistently followed and acted on the vital policy of democratic unity. It is precisely because of the same reason that the Congress Movement is rapidly becoming the real voice of South Africa. If this united front is strengthened and developed the Freedom Charter will be transformed into a dynamic and living instrument and we shall vanquish all opposition and win the South Africa of our dreams during our lifetime.

---

*On 27 October 1955 the ANC Women's League and the Federation of South African Women organised a protest at the Union Buildings, Pretoria, against the issuing of passes to women. This demonstration was repeated the following year on 9 August 1956, when over twenty thousand women took part.

5.   THE CONFLICT HARDENS

Articles written by Mandela for Liberation, *1955-59.*

5(a)   'PEOPLE ARE DESTROYED' (October 1955)

On the effects of apartheid, and in particular the pass laws, on people's lives.

Rachel Musi is fifty-three years of age. She and her husband had lived in Krugersdorp for thirty-two years. Throughout this period, he had worked for the Krugersdorp municipality for £7 10s. a month. They had seven children ranging from nineteen to two years of age. One was doing the final year of the Junior Certificate at the Krugersdorp Bantu High School and three were in primary schools, also in Krugersdorp. She had several convictions for brewing kaffir beer.* Because of these convictions she was arrested as an undesirable person in terms of the provisions of the Native Urban Areas Act and brought before the Additional Native Commissioner of Krugersdorp. After the arrest but before the trial her husband collapsed suddenly and died. Thereafter the Commissioner judged her an undesirable person and ordered her deportation to Lichtenburg. Bereaved and broken-hearted, and with the responsibility of maintaining seven children weighing heavily on her shoulders, an aged woman was exiled from her home and forcibly separated from her children to fend for herself among strangers in a strange environment...

In June 1952 I and about fifty other friends were arrested in Johannesburg while taking part in a defiance campaign and removed to Marshall Square. As we were being jostled into the drill yard one of our prisoners was pushed from behind by a young European constable so violently that he fell down some steps and broke his ankle. I protested, whereupon the young warrior kicked me on the leg in cowboy style. We were indignant and started a demonstration. Senior police officers entered the yard to investigate. We drew their attention to the injured man and demanded medical attention. We were curtly told that we could repeat our request the next day. And so it was that Samuel Makae spent a frightful night in the cells reeling and groaning with pain, maliciously denied medical assistance by those who had deliberately crippled him and whose duty it is to preserve and uphold the law.

In 1941 an African lad appeared before the Native Commissioner in Johannesburg charged with failing to give a good and satisfactory account of himself in terms of the above Act. The previous year he had passed the Junior Certificate with a few distinctions. He had planned to study Matric in the Cape but, because of illness, on the advice of the family doctor he decided to spend the year at home in Alexandra Township. Called upon by the police to produce proof that he had sufficient honest means of earning his livelihood, he explained that he

---

*Home-brewed alcoholic beverage, illicit brewing of which was one of the few ways African women could earn money. The word 'kaffir' is used as an insulting term for Africans but the term 'kaffir beer' was widely used in English as a name for this drink.

was still a student and was maintained by his parents. He was then arrested and ordered to work at Leeuwkop Farm Colony for six months as an idle and disorderly person. This order was subsequently set aside on review by the Supreme Court but only after the young man had languished in jail for seven weeks, with serious repercussions to his poor health . . .

The breaking up of African homes and families and the forcible separation of children from mothers, the harsh treatment meted out to African prisoners, and the forcible detention of Africans in farm colonies for spurious statutory offences are a few examples of the actual workings of the hideous and pernicious doctrines of racial inequality. To these can be added scores of thousands of foul misdeeds committed against the people by the Government; the denial to the non-European people of the elementary rights of free citizenship; the expropriation of the people from their lands and homes to assuage the insatiable appetites of European land barons and industrialists; the flogging and calculated murder of African labourers by European farmers in the countryside for being 'cheeky to the baas';* the vicious manner in which African workers are beaten up by the police and flung into jails when they down tools to win their demands; the fostering of contempt and hatred for non-Europeans; the fanning of racial prejudice between whites and non-whites, between the various non-white groups; the splitting of Africans into small hostile tribal units; the instigation of one group or tribe against another; the banning of active workers from the people's organisations, and their confinement into certain areas.

All these misdemeanours are weapons resorted to by the mining and farming cliques of this country to protect their interests and to prevent the rise of an all-powerful organised mass struggle. To them, the end justifies the means, and that end is the creation of a vast market of cheap labour for mine magnates and farmers. That is why homes are broken up and people are removed from cities to the countryside to ensure enough labour for the farms. That is why non-European political opponents of the Government are treated with such brutality. In such a set-up, African youth with distinguished scholastic careers are not a credit to the country, but a serious threat to the governing circles, for they may not like to descend to the bowels of the earth and cough their lungs out to enrich the mining magnates, nor will they elect to dig potatoes on farms for wretched rations.

Nevertheless, these methods are failing to achieve their objective. True enough they have scared and deterred certain groups and individuals, and at times even upset and temporarily dislocated our plans and schemes. But they have not halted the growing struggle of the people for liberation. Capable fighters and organisers are arising from amongst the people. The people are increasingly becoming alive to the necessity of the solidarity of all democratic forces regardless of race, party affiliation, religious belief, and ideological conviction.

---

*'Baas' is Afrikaans for 'master'.

Taking advantage of this situation, the people's organisations have embarked on a broad programme of mutual co-operation and closer relations. The Freedom Charter recently adopted by people of all races and from all walks of life now forms the ground-plan for future action.

However, the fascist regime that governs this country is not meeting this situation with arms folded. Cabinet ministers are arming themselves with inquisitorial and arbitrary powers to destroy their opponents and hostile organisations. They are building a mono-party state, the essence of which is the identification of the Nationalist Party with State power. All opposition to the Nationalists has been deemed opposition to the State. Every facet of the national life is becoming subordinated to the overriding necessity of the party's retention of power. All constitutional safeguards are being thrown overboard and individual liberties are being ruthlessly suppressed. Lynchings and pogroms are the logical weapons to be resorted to, should the onward march of the liberation movement continue to manifest itself.

The spectre of Belsen and Buchenwald is haunting South Africa. It can only be repelled by the united strength of the people of South Africa. Every situation must be used to raise the people's level of understanding. If attacks on the people's organisations, if all discriminatory measures, be they the Industrial Conciliation Amendment Act, Bantu Education, or the classification of the Coloured people, are used as a rallying point around which a united front will be built, the spectre of Belsen and Buckenwald will never descend upon us.

5(b) 'LAND HUNGER' (February 1956)

On the coercive methods used to make the 'Native Reserves' (now bantustans) into reserves of labour, and in particular on the situation in the Transkei.

The Transkeian Territories cover an area of more than four million morgen* of land, exclusive of trading sites and towns, with an African population of over three million. In comparison with the other so-called Native Reserves, this area is by far the largest single Reserve in the Union and also the greatest single reservoir of cheap labour in the country. According to official estimates, more than one-third of the total number of Africans employed on the Witwatersrand gold mines come from the Transkei.

It is thus clear that this area is the greatest single support of the most vicious system of exploitation — the gold mines. The continued growth and development of gold-mining in South Africa brought about by the discovery of gold in the Orange Free State calls for more and more of this labour at a time when the

---

*One morgen = 0.856 ha. = 2.1 acres.

Union loses about ten thousand workers a year to the Central African Federation.*

This labour problem compels South African mining circles to focus their attention more and more on the Reserves in a desperate effort to coerce every adult male African to seek employment on the mines. Recruiting agents are no longer content with discussing matters with chiefs and headmen only, as they have done in days gone by. Kraals,** drinking parties, and initiation ceremonies are given particular attention and kraal-heads and tribesmen told that fame and fortune await them if they sign up their mine contracts. Films portraying a rosy picture of conditions on the mines are shown free of charge in the villages and rural locations.

But just in case these somewhat peaceful methods of persuasion fail to induce enough recruits, the authorities have in reserve more draconian forms of coercion. The implementation of the so-called rehabilitation scheme, the enforcement of taxes, and the foisting of tribal rule upon the people are resorted to in order to ensure a regular inflow of labour.

The rehabilitation scheme, which is the trump card of both the mining and the farming industries in this sordid game of coercion, was first outlined by Dr D L Smit, then Secretary for Native Affairs, at a special session of the General Council of the Ciskei held at King William's Town in January 1945. According to the Secretary's statement the scheme had two important features, namely, the limitation of stock to the carrying capacity of the land and the replanning of the Reserves to enable the inhabitants to make the best possible use of the land.

The main object of replanning, the statement continued, would be to demarcate residential, arable, and grazing areas in order that each portion of land should be used for the purpose to which it is best suited. Rural villages would be established to provide suitable homes for the families of Africans regularly employed in industrial and other services and, therefore, unable to make efficient use of a normal allotment of land.

In point of fact, the real purpose of the scheme is to increase land hunger for the masses of the peasants in the reserves and to impoverish them. The main object is to create a huge army of migrant labourers, domiciled in rural locations in the reserves far away from the cities. Through the implementation of the scheme it is hoped that in course of time the inhabitants of the reserves will be uprooted and completely severed from their land, cattle, and sheep, to depend for their livelihood entirely on wage earnings.

By enclosing them in compounds at the centres of work and housing them in rural locations when they return home, it is hoped to prevent the emergence of a closely knit, powerful, militant, and articulate African industrial proletariat who

---

*Political federation between Northern Rhodesia (Zambia), Southern Rhodesia (Zimbabwe) and Nyasaland (Malawi), which lasted from 1953 to 1964. These years were a boom period for the mines of the Northern Rhodesian Copperbelt.

**Kraal = homestead.

62

might acquire the rudiments of political agitation and struggle. What is wanted by the ruling circles is a docile, spineless, unorganised and inarticulate army of workers.

Another method used to coerce African labour is the poll tax, also known as the general tax. When Cecil Rhodes introduced it in the old Cape Colony he openly and expressly declared that its main object would be to ensure cheap labour for industry, an object which has not changed since. In 1939, Parliament decided to make all African tax defaulters work for it, and the then Minister of Finance expressed the view that farms would benefit through this arrangement. The extent of this benefit is clearly revealed by reference to statistics. According to the 1949 official Year Book for the Union, 21,381 Africans were arrested that year for general tax. Earlier, John Burger had stated in *The Black Man's Burden* that something like sixty thousand arrests were made each year for non-payment of this tax. Since the Nationalist Party came to power these arrests have been intensified. In the Reserves, chiefs, headmen, mounted police, and court messengers comb the countryside daily for tax defaulters and, fearing arrest, thousands of Africans are forced to trek to the mines and surrounding farms in search of work. Around the jails in several parts of the country, queues of farmers are to be observed waiting for convicts.

Much has been written already on the aims and objects of the Bantu Authorities Act and on the implications of its acceptance by the Transkeian Bunga.* Here we need only reiterate that reversion to tribal rule might isolate the democratic leadership from the masses and bring about the destruction of that leadership as well as of the liberation organisations. It will also act as a delaying tactic. In course of time the wrath of the people will be directed, it is hoped, not at the oppressor but at the Bantu Authorities, who will be burdened with the dirty work of manipulating the detestable rehabilitation scheme, the collection of taxes, and the other measures which are designed to keep down the people.

It is clear, therefore, that the ruling circles attach the greatest importance to the Transkeian Territories. It is equally clear that the acceptance of tribal rule by the Bunga will henceforth be used by the Government to entice other tribal groups to accept the Act. As a matter of fact, this is precisely what the chiefs were told by Government spokesmen at the Zululand and Rustenburg Indabas.** Yet by a strange paradox the Transkei is the least politically organised area in the Union. The Transkeian Organised Bodies Association, once a powerful organisation, is for all practical purposes virtually defunct. The Cape African Teachers' Association is dominated by a group of intellectual snobs who

---

*The Bantu Authorities Act of 1951 established local 'tribal authorities' in the African reserves, which were designed to replace existing institutions such as the United Territories General Council or Bunga in the Transkei, an elected body established in 1932. Although discriminatory and largely powerless, the Bunga embodied the principle that the Transkei and its citizens were to be regarded as part of South Africa. The acceptance of the Bantu Authorities Act represented the abandonment of this principle.

**Tribal consultations.

derive their inspiration from the All-African Convention.* They are completely isolated and have no influence whatsoever with the masses of the people.

Recently, when the African National Congress declared for a boycott of Bantu Education and advocated the withdrawal of children from such schools, the AAC fought against the withdrawal and placed itself in the ridiculous position of opposing a boycott it had pretended to preach all along. This somersault completely exposed their opportunism and bankruptcy and the volume of criticism now being directed against them has temporarily silenced even the verbal theatricals for which they are famous.

Nevertheless, it is perfectly clear that the people of the Transkei are indignant. Isolated and sporadic insurrections have occurred in certain areas directed mainly against the rehabilitation scheme. Chiefs and headmen have been beaten up by their tribesmen and court actions are being fought. But in the absence of an organised peasant movement co-ordinating these isolated and sporadic outbursts, the impact of this opposition will not be sharply felt by the authorities.

Once more the problem of organisation in the countryside poses itself as one of major importance for the liberatory movement. Through the co-ordination of spontaneous and local demonstrations, and their raising to a political level, the beginnings will be found of opposition to the policy of oppressing and keeping backward the people of the Transkei. Then we can look forward to the day when the Transkei will not be a Reserve of cheap labour, but a source of strength to build a free South Africa.

5(c) 'BANTU EDUCATION GOES TO UNIVERSITY' (June 1957)

On Bantu Education and the introduction of segregated universities.

The Nationalist Government has frequently denied that it is a fascist Government inspired by the theories of the National Socialist [Nazi] Party of Hitlerite Germany. Yet the declarations it makes, the laws it passes, and the entire policy it pursues cleanly confirm this point. It is interesting to compare the colonial policy of the Hitlerite Government as outlined by the leading German theoreticians on the subject. Dr Gunther Hecht, who was regarded as an expert on colonial racial problems in the office of the German National Socialist Party, published a pamphlet in 1938 entitled *The Colonial Question and Racial Thought* in which he outlined the racial principles which were to govern the future treatment of Africans in German colonies. He declared that the German Government would not preach equality between Africans and Europeans. Africans would under no

---

*The All-African Convention came together in 1935 in the most representative black gathering ever held at that date in South Africa, since it included Indian and Coloured people. Later, as Mary Benson outlined: 'It had virtually been taken over by Coloured teachers in the Cape with pronounced Trotskyist leanings, whose organisation joined with the AAC to become ultimately the Unity Movement. In print their record was powerful: militant resolutions repeatedly called for total boycotts. In practice they achieved little.' (Mary Benson, *Struggle for a Birthright*, IDAF, London, 1985, p.122).

circumstances be allowed to leave German colonies for Europe. No African would be allowed to become a German citizen. African schools would not be permitted to preach any 'European matter' as that would foster a belief among them that Europe was the peak of cultural development and they would thus lose faith in their own culture and background. Local culture would be fostered. Higher schools and universities would be closed to them. Special theatres, cinemas, and other places of amusement and recreation would be erected for them. Hecht concluded the pamphlet by pointing out that the programme of the German Government would stand in sharp contrast to the levelling and anti-racial teachings of equality of the western colonial powers.

In this country the Government preaches the policy of baasskap,* which is based on the supremacy in all matters of the Whites over the non-Whites. They are subjected to extremely stringent regulations both in regard to their movement within the country as well as in regard to overseas travel lest they should come into contact with ideas that are in conflict with the herrenvolk policies of the Government. Through the Bantu Authorities Act and similar measures the African people are being broken up into small tribal units, isolated one from the other, in order to prevent the rise and development of national consciousness amongst them and to foster a narrow and insulated tribal outlook.

During the parliamentary debate on the second reading of the Bantu Education Bill in September 1953, the Minister of Native Affairs, Dr H F Verwoerd, who studied in German universities, outlined the educational policy of his Government. He declared that racial relations could not improve if the wrong type of education was given to Africans. They could not improve if the result of African education was the creation of a frustrated people who, as a result of the education they received, had expectations in life which circumstances in South Africa did not allow to be fulfilled; when it created people who were trained for professions not open to them; when there were people amongst them who had received a form of cultural training which strengthened their desire for white-collar occupations. Above all, good racial relations could not exist when the education was given under the control of people who believed in racial equality. It was, therefore, necessary that African education should be controlled in such a way that it should be in accord with the policy of the State.

The Bantu Education Bill has now become law and it embodies all the obnoxious doctrines enunciated by the Minister in the parliamentary debate referred to above. An inferior type of education, known as Bantu education, and designed to relegate the Africans to a position of perpetual servitude in a baasskap society, is now in force in almost all African primary schools throughout the country and will be introduced in all secondary and high schools as from next year. The Separate Universities Education Bill, now before Parliament, is a step to extend Bantu education to the field of higher education.

In terms of this Bill the Minister is empowered to establish, maintain, and

---

*baasskap = (white) supremacy.

conduct university colleges for non-Whites. The students to be admitted to the university colleges must be approved by the Minister. As from January 1958, no non-White students who were not previously registered shall be admitted to a European university without the consent of the Minister. The Bill also provides for the transfer and the control and management of the University College of Fort Hare and of the medical school for Africans at Wentworth* to the Government; all employees in these institutions will become Government employees.

The Minister can vest the control of Fort Hare in the Native Affairs Department. The Government is empowered to change the name of the college. For example, he can call it the HENDRIK FRENSCH VERWOERD University College for Bantu persons. The Minister is entitled to dismiss any member of the staff for misconduct, which includes public adverse comment upon the administration, and propagating ideas, or taking part in, or identifying himself with, any propaganda or activities calculated to impede, obstruct, or undermine the activities of any government department.

No mixed university in the country will be permitted to enrol new non-European students any more. The mixed English universities of Cape Town, Witwatersrand and Rhodes will thus be compelled to fall in line with the Afrikaans universities of Pretoria, Potchefstroom, Stellenbosch, and the Orange Free State whose doors are closed to non-Europeans.

The main purpose of the Bill is to extend the principle of Bantu education to the field of higher education. Non-Europeans who are trained at mixed universities are considered a menace to the racial policies of the Government. The friendship and inter-racial harmony that is forged through the admixture and association of various racial groups at the mixed universities constitute a direct threat to the policy of apartheid and baasskap and the Bill has been enacted to remove this threat. The type of universities the Bill envisages will be nothing more than tribal colleges, controlled by party politicians and based upon the doctrine of the perpetual supremacy of the Whites over the Blacks. Such colleges would be used by the Government to enforce its political ideology at a university level.

They will bear no resemblance whatsoever to modern universities. Not free inquiry but indoctrination is their purpose, and the education they will give will not be directed towards the unleashing of the creative potentialities of the people but towards preparing them for perpetual mental and spiritual servitude to the Whites. They will be permitted to teach only that which strictly conforms to the racial policies of the Nationalist Government. Degrees and diplomas obtained at these colleges will be held in contempt and ridicule throughout the country and abroad and will probably not be recognised outside South Africa. The decision of the Government to introduce university segregation is prompted not merely by the desire to separate non-European from European students. Its implications go

---

*Fort Hare College near Alice in the Eastern Cape was the only university for blacks in all of Southern Africa at this date. The black medical school at Wentworth in Durban was a segregated division of the University of Natal.

much further than this, for the Bill is a move to destroy the 'open' university tradition which is universally recognised throughout the civilised world and which has up to now been consistently practised by leading universities in the country for years. For centuries universities have served as centres for the dissemination of learning and knowledge to all students irrespective of their colour or creed. In multi-racial societies they serve as centres for the development of the cultural and spiritual aspects of the life of the people. Once the Bill is passed our universities can no longer serve as centres for the development of the cultural and spiritual aspects of the entire nation.

The Bill has aroused extensive and popular indignation and opposition throughout the country as well as abroad. Students and lecturers, liberals and conservatives, progressives, democrats, public men and women of all races and with varying political affiliations, have been stirred into action. A former Chief Justice of the Union, Mr Van der Sandt Centlivres, in a speech delivered at a lunch meeting of the University Club in Cape Town on 11 February this year and reported in the *Rand Daily Mail* of the 12th of the same month, said: 'I am not aware of any university of real standing in the outside world which closes its doors to students on the ground of the colour of their skins. The great universities of the world welcome students from other countries whatever the colour of their skins. They realize that the different outlook which these students bring with them advances the field of knowledge in human relations in the international sphere and contributes to their own culture.'

The attack on university freedom is a matter of vital importance and constitutes a grave challenge to all South Africans. It is perhaps because they fully appreciate this essential fact that more people are participating in the campaign against the introduction of academic segregation in the universities. Students in different parts of the country are staging mammoth demonstrations and protest meetings. Heads of universities, lecturers, men and women of all shades of opinion, have in speeches and articles violently denounced the action of the Government. All this reveals that there are many men and women in this country who are prepared to rally to the defence of traditional rights whenever they are threatened.

But we cannot for one moment forget that we are up against a fascist Government which has built up a massive coercive State apparatus to crush democracy in this country and to silence the voice of all those who cry out against the policy of apartheid and baasskap. All opposition to the Nationalist Government is being ruthlessly suppressed through the Suppression of Communism Act and similar measures. The Government, in defiance of the people's wishes, is deporting people's leaders from town and country in the most merciless and shameful manner. All rights are being systematically attacked. The right to organise, to assemble, and to agitate has been severely fettered. Trade unions and other organisations are being smashed up. Even the sacred right of freedom of religious worship, which has been observed and respected by governments down the centuries, is now being tampered with. And now the freedom of our universities is being seriously threatened. Racial persecution of the non-Whites is being intensified every day. The rule of force and violence, of terror and coercion, has become the order of the day.

Fascism has become a living reality in our country and its defeat has become the principal task of the entire people of South Africa. But the fight against the fascist policies of the Government cannot be conducted on the basis of isolated struggles. It can only be conducted on the basis of the united fight of the entire people of South Africa against all attacks of the Nationalists on traditional rights whether these attacks are launched through Parliament and other State organs or whether through extra-parliamentary forms. The more powerful the resistance of the people the less becomes the advance of the Nationalists. Hence the importance of a united front. The people must fight stubbornly and tenaciously and defend every democratic right that is being attacked or tampered with by the Nationalists.

A broad united front of all the genuine opponents of the racial policies of the Government must be developed. This is the path the people should follow to check and repel the advance of fascism in this country and to pave the way for a peaceful and democratic South Africa.

5(d) 'OUR STRUGGLE NEEDS MANY TACTICS' (February 1958)

On political tactics, in particular the boycott weapon. By 1958 there was a close working relationship between all the bodies forming the Congress Movement, headed by the ANC and consisting also of the Congresses of the Indian and Coloured peoples, and democratic whites, and the South African Congress of Trade Unions (SACTU). This came to be called the Congress Alliance. The organisation SACPO referred to by Mandela in this article is the Coloured People's Congress under its earlier name.

Political organisations in this country have frequently employed the boycott weapon in their struggle against racial discrimination and oppression. In 1947 the African National Congress decided to boycott all elections under the Native Representatives Act of 1936, as well as all elections to the United Transkeian Territories General Council, generally referred to as the Bunga, to the Advisory Boards, and all other discriminatory statutory institutions specially set up for Africans. A year earlier the South African Indian Congress had decided to boycott and had launched a resistance campaign against the Asiatic Land Tenure and Indian Representation Act which, *inter alia,* made special provision for the representation in Parliament of Indians in the Provinces of Natal and the Transvaal and for the representation in the Provincial Council of Natal of Indians in that Province. In 1957 the South African Coloured People's Organisation (SACPO) considered its attitude on the question of the election of four Europeans to represent the Coloured people in Parliament, and decided to boycott these elections as well as the election of 27 Coloured persons to the Union Council of Coloured Affairs. The same year SACPO reversed this decision and decided to participate in the parliamentary elections.

Apart from such boycotts of unrepresentative institutions, boycotts of a different kind have often been called by various organisations on matters directly affecting the people. For example, in 1949 the Western Areas Tram Fares Committee successfully boycotted the increased fares on the Johannesburg-Western Areas tram route. Similarly last year, and by means of the boycott weapon, the Alexandra People's Transport Committee achieved a brilliant victory when it rebuffed and defeated the decision of the Public Utility Transport Corporation, backed by the Government, to increase fares along the Johannesburg-Alexandra bus route. The Federation of South African Nurses and Midwives is presently campaigning for the boycott of all discriminatory provisions of the Nursing Amendment Act passed last year. By and large, boycott is recognised and accepted by the people as an effective and powerful weapon of political struggle.

Perhaps it is precisely because of its effectiveness and the wide extent to which various organisations employ it in their struggles to win their demands that some people regard the boycott as a matter of principle which must be applied invariably at all times and in all circumstances irrespective of the prevailing conditions. This is a serious mistake, for the boycott is in no way a matter of principle but a tactical weapon whose application should, like all other political weapons of the struggle, be related to the concrete conditions prevailing at the given time.

For example, the boycott by the Indian community of the representation machinery contained in the Asiatic Land Tenure and Indian Representation Act of 1946 was correct at the time not because the boycott is a correct principle but because the Indian people correctly gauged the objective situation. Firstly, the political concessions made in the Act were intended to bribe the Indian people to accept the land provisions of this Act, which deprived the Indians of their land rights — a bribe which even the Indian reactionaries were not prepared to accept. Secondly, a remarkable degree of unity and solidarity had been achieved by the Indian people in their struggle against the Act. The conservative Kajee-Pather bloc worked in collaboration with the progressive and militant Dadoo-Naicker wing of the SAIC and no less than 35,000 members had been recruited into the SAIC before the commencement of the campaign. Under these conditions the boycott proved correct and not a single Indian person registered as a voter in terms of the Act.

Similarly, the 1947 boycott resolution of the ANC was correct, in spite of the fact that no effective country-wide campaign was carried out to implement this resolution. It will be recalled that at the time, in an endeavour to destroy the people's political organisations and to divert them from these organisations, the United Party Government was fostering the illusion that the powers of the Natives Representative Council, the Bunga, the Advisory Boards, and similar institutions would be increased to such an extent that the African people would have an effective voice in the Government of the country. The agitation that followed the adoption of the boycott resolution by the ANC, inadequate as it was, helped to damage the influence of these sham institutions and to discredit those who supported them. In certain areas these institutions were completely destroyed and they have now no impact whatsoever on the outlook of the people. To put the matter crisply, the 1947 resolution completely frustrated the scheme of the United Party Government to confuse the people and to destroy their political organisation.

In some cases, therefore, it might be correct to boycott, and in others it might be unwise and dangerous. In still other cases another weapon of political struggle might be preferred. A demonstration, a protest march, a strike, or civil disobedience might be resorted to, all depending on the actual conditions at the given time.

In the opinion of some people, participation in the system of separate racial representation in any shape or form, and irrespective of any reasons advanced for doing so, is impermissible on principle and harmful in practice. According to them such participation can only serve to confuse the people and to foster the illusion that they can win their demands through a parliamentary form of struggle. In their view the people have now become so politically conscious and developed that they cannot accept any form of representation which in any way fetters their progress. They maintain that people are demanding direct representation in Parliament, in the provincial and city councils, and that nothing short of this will satisfy them. They say that leaders who talk of the practical advantages to be gained by participation in separate racial representation do not have the true interests of the people at heart. Finally, they argue that the so-called representatives have themselves expressed the view that they have achieved nothing in Parliament. Over and above this, the argument goes, the suggestion that anything could be achieved by electing such representatives to Parliament is made ridiculous by their paucity of numbers in Parliament. This view has been expressed more specifically in regard to the question of boycott of the forthcoming Coloured Parliamentary seats.

The basic error in this argument lies in the fact that it regards the boycott not as a tactical weapon to be employed if and when objective conditions permit, but as an inflexible principle which must under no circumstances be varied. Having committed this initial mistake, people who advocate this point of view are invariably compelled to interpret every effort to relate the boycott to specific conditions as impermissible deviations on questions of principle. In point of fact, total and uncompromising opposition to racial discrimination in all its ramifications, and refusal to co-operate with the Government in the implementation of its reactionary policies, are matters of principle in regard to which there can be no compromise.

In its struggle for the attainment of its demands the liberation movement avails itself of various political weapons, one of which might (but not necessarily) be the boycott. It is, therefore, a serious error to regard the boycott as a weapon that must be employed at all times and in all conditions. In this stand there is also the failure to draw the vital distinction between participation in such elections by the people who accept racial discrimination and who wish to co-operate with the Government in the oppression and exploitation of their own people on the one hand, and participation in such elections, not because of any desire to co-operate with the Government but in order to exploit them in the interest of the liberatory struggle on the other hand. The former is the course generally followed by collaborators and Government stooges and has for many years been consistently condemned and rejected by the liberation movement. The latter course, provided objective conditions permit, serves to strengthen the people's struggle against the reactionary policies of the Government.

The decision of SACPO in favour of participation in the forthcoming parliamentary elections is correct for various reasons. The principal and most urgent task facing the Congress Movement today is the defeat of the Nationalist Government and its replacement by a less reactionary one. Any step or decision which helps the movement to attain this task is politically correct. The election of four additional members to Parliament, provided they agree with the general aims of the movement and provided that they are anti-Nationalist, would contribute to the defeat of the present Government. In advocating this course it is not in any way being suggested that the salvation of the oppressed people of this country depends on the parliamentary struggle, nor is it being suggested that a United Party regime would bring about any radical changes in the political set-up in this country. It is accepted and recognised that the people of South Africa will win their freedom as a result of the pressure they put up against the reactionary policies of the Government. Under a United Party Government it will still be necessary to wage a full-scale war on racial discrimination. But the defeat of the Nationalists would at least lighten the heavy burden of harsh and restrictive legislation that is borne by the people at the present moment. There would be a breathing space during which the movement might recuperate and prepare for fresh assaults against the oppressive policies of the Government.

SACPO's struggle and influence amongst the Coloured people has grown tremendously, but it is not without opposition and there are still large numbers of Coloured people who are outside its fold. In order to succeed, a boycott would require a greater degree of unity and solidarity than has so far been achieved amongst the Coloured people. Prior to the December resolution certain Coloured organisations had indicated their willingness to participate in these elections. To boycott elections under such conditions might result in hostile and undesirable elements being returned to Parliament.

In several conferences of the ANC, both national and provincial, the view has been expressed that the 1947 boycott resolution requires to be reviewed in the light of the new conditions created as a result of the serious and dangerous attacks launched by the Nationalists on the liberation movement. The political situation has radically changed since. The political organisations of the people are functioning under conditions of semi-illegality. Legal authorities are refusing to permit meetings within their areas and it is becoming increasingly difficult to hold conferences. Some of the most experienced and active members have been deported from their homes, others have been confined to certain areas, and many have been compelled to resign from their organisations.

The present Government regards institutions such as the Advisory Boards as too advanced and dangerous, and these are being replaced by tribal institutions under the Bantu Authorities Act. Platforms for the dissemination of propaganda are gradually disappearing. Having regard to the principal task of ousting the Nationalist Government, it becomes necessary for the Congress to review its attitude towards the special provision for the representation of Africans set out in the 1936 Act. The parliamentary forum must be exploited to put forth the case for a democratic and progressive South Africa. Let the democratic movement have a voice both outside and within Parliament. Through the Advisory Boards and, if the right type of candidates are found, through Parliament, we can reach the masses of the people and rally them behind us.

5(e) 'A NEW MENACE IN AFRICA' (March 1958)

On American imperialism.

For several centuries the maritime nations of Europe exploited the peoples of Asia and Africa and interfered in numerous ways with their cherished freedoms. For several centuries the governments of Spain, Portugal, Holland, Belgium, England, France, Germany and Czarist Russia have at different historical periods created vast and mighty empires in Asia and Africa. Through armed invasion and conquest they forced the people of Asia and Africa to surrender to the expansionist policies of European capitalism. Through military plunder the people of India, Ceylon, Burma, Malaya, the East Indies and other territories lost their national independence and became colonies of foreign powers. Through force, fraud and violence, the people of North, East, West, Central and Southern Africa were relieved of their political and economic power and forced to pay allegiance to foreign monarchs. By means of unequal treaties the conquered countries were transformed into profitable fields for the investment of foreign capital. The economic wealth and resources of these colonies were exploited by and turned over to the imperialist powers not for use in the interest of the indigenous populations, but for the benefit of the metropolitan people.

In this way the spices of the East Indies, the rubber and rice of India, the gold and diamonds of South Africa, the cocoa and manganese of the Gold Coast, all found their way to the warehouses of Europe. By means of forced labour and extremely low wages the native populations were reduced to poverty and misery whilst the metropolitan populations flourished out of the raw materials seized from the colonies. To the people of Asia and Africa imperialism meant, and still means, the exploitation of the mineral and agricultural wealth of their countries by foreign powers without their consent and without compensation. It means the destruction of the economic power of the indigenous populations through the imposition of trade monopolies and excessive taxes. It means low wages and long hours of work. Above all it means the denial of political and economic rights and the perpetual subjugation of the people by a foreign power.

In exploiting the mineral and agricultural resources of a colonial country the imperialists have always tried to avoid making the issue appear one of an open clash of interests between themselves and the colonial people. Both in Asia and Africa imperialism consistently sought to divide the indigenous population by allying itself with the most reactionary elements amongst the very population it wishes to exploit. In India the feudal princes, the big landlords and industrialists became the most faithful and loyal friends of British imperialism. A similar pattern prevailed in China, the East Indies, Malaya and in other colonies. In South Africa where there were no vested interests amongst the indigenous people the position was somewhat different. British imperialism allied itself with the big farming interests, securing the support of the European section of the population by imposing a rigid colour-bar and by elevating the Europeans to a higher political and economic status. In practice imperialism is, therefore, a kind of alliance between a foreign ruling power and local reactionary elements for the exploitation by the former of the mineral and agricultural resources of a colonial country. It is precisely because of this fact that imperialism has always sought to prolong reactionary institutions in the colonial countries long after such institutions have ceased to be useful.

Concessions granted to these elements for supporting foreign rule, as well as developmental schemes designed primarily to facilitate the exploitation of the natural wealth of the exploited country, have frequently been cited to highlight the so-called benefits of imperialism to the colonial people. The building of seaports and harbours, the construction of communications, the building of hydro-electric plants, of conservation and irrigation schemes, the mapping of mineral resources, have been specifically mentioned as some of the positive steps adopted by imperialist powers to raise the living standards of dependent peoples. In point of fact these projects all serve to facilitate the exploitation of the dependent country and its people, and the export of its wealth to Europe.

THE DECLINE OF EUROPEAN IMPERIALISM

Quite naturally the colonial peoples all over the world have in various ways waged ceaseless battles against foreign domination. In many areas this battle has been decisively won whilst in others it still rages. The imperialist countries have been driven out from practically the whole of Asia and the Pacific regions. China, India, Ceylon, Burma and the United States of Indonesia have won their national independence. In Africa a large number of territories have thrown off the imperialist yoke and are now independent states. Egypt, the Sudan, Ethiopia,

Libya, Morocco, Tunisia and Ghana are no longer dependencies of foreign powers. In Algeria, Nigeria, Somalia and Uganda self-government in the near future is anticipated. All over the world the people are astir and the struggle for political progress is gathering momentum by the day. Imperialism has been weighed and found wanting. It has been fought and defeated by the united and concerted action of the common people. Its decline and fall was sealed by the Afro-Asian Conference which was held in Bandung in April, 1955, where 29 independent countries of Asia and Africa, which had recently emerged from colonial oppression, pledged themselves against colonialism and proclaimed the unity of the people of Asia and Africa in the struggle against this menace.

A NEW DANGER

Whilst the influence of the old European powers has sharply declined and whilst the anti-imperialist forces are winning striking victories all over the world, a new danger has arisen and threatens to destroy the newly-won independence of the people of Asia and Africa. It is American imperialism, which must be fought and decisively beaten down if the people of Asia and Africa are to preserve the vital gains they have won in their struggle against subjugation. The First and Second World Wars brought untold economic havoc especially in Europe, where both wars were mainly fought. Millions of people perished whilst their countries were ravaged and ruined by the war. The two conflicts resulted, on the one hand, in the decline of the old imperial powers.

On the other hand, the USA emerged from them as the richest and most powerful state in the west, firstly, because both wars were fought thousands of miles away from her mainland and she had fewer casualties. Whereas the British Empire lost 1,089,900 men, only 115,660 American soldiers died during the First World War. No damage whatsoever was suffered by her cities and industries. Secondly, she made fabulous profits from her allies out of war contracts. Due to these factors the USA grew to become the most powerful country in the west.

Paradoxically, the two world wars, which weakened the old powers and which contributed to the growth of the political and economic influence of the USA, also resulted in the growth of the anti-imperialist forces all over the world and in the intensification of the struggle for national independence. The old powers, finding themselves unable to resist the demand by their former colonies for independence and still clinging desperately to their waning empires, were compelled to lean very heavily on American aid. The USA, taking advantage of the plight of its former allies, adopted the policy of deliberately ousting them from their spheres of influence and grabbing these spheres for herself. An instance that is still fresh in our minds is that of the Middle East, where the USA assisted in the eviction of Britain from that area in order that she might gain control of the oil industry, which prior to that time was in the control of Britain.

Through the Marshall Plan the USA succeeded in gaining control of the economies of European countries and reducing them to a position analogous to that of dependencies. By establishing aggressive military blocs in Europe, the Middle East and Asia, the USA has been able to post her armies in important strategic points and is preparing for armed intervention in the domestic affairs of sovereign nations. The North Atlantic Treaty Organisation in Europe, the Baghdad Pact in the Middle East, and the South East Asian Treaty Organisation are military blocs which constitute a direct threat not only to world peace, but also to the independence of the member states.

The policy of placing reliance on American economic and military aid is extremely dangerous to the 'assisted' states themselves and has aggravated their positions. Since the Second World War, Britain, France and Holland have closely associated themselves with American plans for world conquest, and yet within that period they have lost empires in Asia, the Middle East and Africa, and they are fighting rearguard actions in their remaining colonial possessions. Their salvation and future prosperity lie not in pinning their faith on American aid and aggressive military blocs but in breaking away from her, in repudiating her foreign policy which threatens to drag them into another war, and in proclaiming a policy of peace and friendship with other nations.

US OFFENSIVE IN AFRICA

American interest in Africa has in recent years grown rapidly. This continent is rich in raw materials. It produces almost all the world's diamonds, 78 per cent of its palm oil, 68 per cent of its cocoa, half of its gold and 22 per cent of its copper. It is rich in manganese, chrome, in uranium, radium, in citrus fruits, coffee, sugar, cotton, and rubber. It is regarded by the USA as one of the most important fields of investment. According to the 'Report of the Special Study Mission to Africa, South and East of the Sahara', by the Honorable Frances P Bolton which was published in 1956 for the use of the United States Congress Committee on Foreign Affairs, by the end of World War II United States private investments in Africa amounted to scarcely £150 million. At the end of 1954 the total book value of US investments in Africa stood at £664 million.

Since then the American Government has mounted a terrific diplomatic and economic offensive in almost every part of Africa. A new organisation for the conduct of African Affairs has come into existence. The Department of State has established a new position of Deputy Assistant Secretary for African Affairs. The Bureau of African Affairs has been split into two new offices, the office of Northern African Affairs and that of Southern African Affairs. This reorganisation illustrates the increasing economic importance of Africa to the USA and the recognition by the governing circles of that state of the vital necessity for the creation and strengthening of diplomatic relations with the independent states of Africa. The USA has sent into this continent numerous 'study' and 'goodwill' missions, and scores of its leading industrialists and statesmen to survey the natural wealth of the new independent states and to establish diplomatic relations with the present regimes. Vice-President Nixon, Adlai Stevenson, the Democratic Party candidate for the American Presidency in the last elections, and scores of other leading Americans, have visited various parts of the continent to study political trends and market conditions. Today, American imperialism is a serious danger to the independent states in Africa and its people must unite before it is too late and fight it out to the bitter end.

IMPERIALISM IN DISGUISE

American imperialism is all the more dangerous because, having witnessed the resurgence of the people of Asia and Africa against imperialism and having seen the decline and fall of once powerful empires, it comes to Africa elaborately disguised. It has discarded most of the conventional weapons of the old type of imperialism. It does not openly advocate armed invasion and conquest. It purports to repudiate force and violence. It masquerades as the leader of the so-called free world in the campaign against communism. It claims that the corner-stone of its foreign policy is to assist other countries in resisting domination by others. It maintains that the huge sums of dollars invested in Africa are not for the exploitation of the people of Africa but for the purpose of developing their countries and in order to raise their living standards.

Now it is true that the new self-governing territories in Africa require capital to develop their countries. They require capital for economic development and technical training programmes, they require it to develop agriculture, fisheries, veterinary services, health, medical services, education and communications. To this extent overseas capital invested in Africa could play a useful role in the development of the self-governing territories in the continent. But the idea of making quick and high profits, which underlies all the developmental plans launched in Africa by the USA, completely effaces the value of such plans in so far as the masses of the people are concerned. The big and powerful American trade monopolies that are springing up in various parts of the continent, and which are destroying the small trader, the low wages paid the ordinary man, the resulting poverty and misery, his illiteracy and the squalid tenements in which he dwells, are the simplest and most eloquent exposition of the falsity of the argument that American investments in Africa will raise the living standards of the people of this continent.

The American brand of imperialism is imperialism all the same in spite of the modern clothing in which it is dressed and in spite of the sweet language spoken by its advocates and agents. The USA is mounting an unprecedented diplomatic offensive to win the support of the governments of the self-governing territories in the continent. It has established a network of military bases all over the continent for armed intervention in the domestic affairs of independent states should the people in these states elect to replace American satellite regimes with those who are against American imperialism. American capital has been sunk into Africa not for the purpose of raising the material standards of its people but in order to exploit them as well as the natural wealth of their continent. This is imperialism in the true sense of the word.

The Americans are forever warning the people of this continent against communism which, as they allege, seeks to enslave them and to interfere with their peaceful development. But what facts justify this warning? Unlike the USA neither the Soviet Union, the Chinese People's Republic nor any other Socialist state has aggressive military blocs in any part of the world. None of the Socialist countries has military bases anywhere in Africa, whereas the USA has built landing fields, ports and other types of strategic bases all over North Africa. In particular it has jet fields in Morocco, Libya and Liberia. Unlike the USA none of the Socialist states has invested capital in any part of Africa for the exploitation of its people. At the United Nations Organisation the Soviet Union, India and several other nations have consistently identified themselves unconditionally with the struggle of the oppressed people for freedom, whereas the USA has very often allied itself with those who stand for the enslavement of others. It was not Soviet but American planes which the French used to bomb the peaceful village of Sakiet in Tunisia. The presence of a delegation from the Chinese People's Republic at the 1955 Afro-Asian conference as well as the presence of a delegation from that country and the Soviet Union at the 1957 Cairo Afro-Asian conference show that the people of Asia and Africa have seen through the slanderous campaign conducted by the USA against the Socialist countries. They know that their independence is threatened not by any of the countries in the Socialist camp, but by the USA, who has surrounded their continent with military bases. The communist bogey is an American stunt to distract the attention of the people of Africa from the real issue facing them, namely, American imperialism.

The peoples of resurgent Africa are perfectly capable of deciding upon their own future form of government and discovering and themselves dealing with any dangers which may arise. They do not require any schooling from the USA, which — to judge from such events as the Little Rock outrage and the activities of the Un-American Witch-hunting Committee — should learn to put its own house in order before trying to teach everyone else.

The people of Africa are astir. In conjunction with the people of Asia, and with freedom-loving people all over the world, they have declared a full-scale war against all forms of imperialism. The future of this continent lies not in the hands of the discredited regimes that have allied themselves with American imperialism. It is in the hands of the common people of Africa functioning in their mass movements.

5(f) 'VERWOERD'S TRIBALISM' (May 1959)

On the bantustan policy.

'South Africa belongs to all who live in it, black and white.' *Freedom Charter.*
'All the Bantu have their permanent homes in the Reserves and their entry into other areas and into the urban areas is merely of a temporary nature and for

economic reasons. In other words, they are admitted as work-seekers, not as settlers.' Dr W W M Eiselen, Secretary of the Department of Bantu Administration and Development (article in *Optima*, March 1959).

The statements quoted above contain diametrically opposite conceptions of this country, its future, and its destiny. Obviously, they cannot be reconciled. They have nothing in common, except that both of them look forward to a future of affairs rather than that which prevails at present. At present, South Africa does not 'belong' except in a moral sense to all.

Eighty-seven per cent of the country is legally owned by members (a handful of them at that) of the dominant White minority. And at present by no means 'all' Africans have their 'permanent homes' in the Reserves. Millions of Africans were born and have their permanent homes in the towns and cities and elsewhere outside the Reserves, have never seen the Reserves, and have no desire to go there.★

It is necessary for the people of this country to choose between these two alternative paths. It is assumed that readers of *Liberation* are familiar with the detailed proposals contained in the Charter.

Let us therefore study the policies submitted by the Nationalist Party.

The newspapers have christened the Nationalists' plan as one for 'Bantustans'. The hybrid word is, in many ways, extremely misleading. It derives from the partitioning of India after the reluctant departure of the British, and as a condition thereof, into two separate states, Hindustan and Pakistan. There is no real parallel with the Nationalists' proposals, for:

(a) India and Pakistan constitute two completely separate and politically independent states.

(b) Muslims enjoy equal rights in India; Hindus enjoy equal rights in Pakistan.

(c) Partition was submitted to and approved by both parties, or at any rate fairly widespread and influential sections of each.

The Government's plans do not envisage the partitioning of this country into separate, self-governing states. They do not envisage equal rights, or any rights at all, for Africans outside the Reserves. Partition has never been approved of by Africans and never will be. For that matter it has never really been submitted to or approved of by the Whites. The term 'Bantustan' is therefore a complete misnomer, and merely tends to help the Nationalists perpetrate a fraud.

Let us examine each of these aspects in detail.

It is typical of the Nationalists' propaganda techniques that they describe their measures in misleading titles, which convey the opposite of what the measures contain. Verwoerd called his law greatly extending and intensifying the pass laws the 'Abolition of Passes' Act. Similarly, he has introduced into the current parliamentary session a measure called the 'Promotion of Bantu Self-Government Bill'. It starts off by decreeing the abolition of the tiny token representation of Africans (by Whites) in Parliament and the Cape Provincial Council.

★Under the 1913 Land Act and the 1936 Native Trust and Land Act, Africans, comprising 70 per cent of the population, were allocated 13 per cent of the land as Native Reserves.

It goes on to provide for the division of the African population into eight 'ethnic units' (the so-called Bantustans). They are: North and South Sotho, Swazi, Tsonga, Tswana, Venda, Xhosa, and Zulu. These units are to undergo a 'gradual development to self-government'.

This measure was described by the Prime Minister, Dr Verwoerd, as a 'supremely positive step' towards placing Africans 'on the road to self-government'. Mr De Wet Nel, Minister of Bantu Affairs, said the people in the Reserves 'would gradually be given more powers to rule themselves'.

The scheme is elaborated in a White Paper, tabled in the House of Assembly, to 'explain' the Bill. According to this document, the immediate objects of the Bill are:

(a) The recognition of the so-called Bantu National Units and the appointment of Commissioners-General whose task will be to give guidance and advice to the units in order to promote their general development, with special reference to the administrative field.

(b) The linking of Africans working in urban areas with territorial authorities established under the Bantu Authorities Act, by conferring powers on the Bantu authorities to nominate persons as their representatives in urban areas.

(c) The transfer to the Bantu territorial authorities, at the appropriate time, of land in their areas at present held by the Native Trust.

(d) The vesting in Bantu territorial authorities of legislative authority and the right to impose taxes, and to undertake works and give guidance to subordinate authorities.

(e) The establishment of territorial boards for the purpose of temporary liaison through Commissioners-General if during the transition period the administrative structure in any area has not yet reached the stage where a territorial authority has been established.

(f) The abolition of representation in the highest European* governing bodies.

According to the same White Paper, the Bill has the following further objects:

(a) The creation of homogeneous administrative areas for Africans by uniting the members of each so-called national group in the national unit, concentrated in one coherent homeland where possible.

(b) The education of Africans to a sound understanding of the problems of soil conversion and agriculture so that all rights over and responsibilities in respect of soil in African areas may be assigned to them.
    This includes the gradual replacement of European agricultural officers of all grades by qualified and competent Africans.

---

*Until the 1960s the word 'European' was generally used in South Africa, in the English language, to describe white South Africans. It was then replaced by the word 'white'.

(c) The systematic promotion of a diverse economy in the African areas, acceptable to Africans and to be developed by them.

(d) The education of the African to a sound understanding of the problems and aims of Bantu education so that, by the decentralisation of powers, responsibility for the different grades of education may be vested in them.

(e) The training of Africans with a view to effectively extending their own judicial system and their education to a sound understanding of the common law with a view to transferring to them responsibilities for the administration of justice in their areas.

(f) The gradual replacement of European administration officers by qualified and competent Africans.

(g) The exercise of legislative powers by Africans in respect of their areas, at first on a limited scale, but with every intention of gradually extending this power.

It will be seen that the African people are asked to pay a very high price for this so-called 'self-government' in the Reserves. Urban Africans — the workers, businessmen, and professional men and women, who are the pride of our people in the stubborn and victorious march towards modernisation and progress — are to be treated as outcasts, not even 'settlers' like Dr Verwoerd. Every vestige of rights and opportunities will be ruthlessly destroyed. Everywhere outside the Reserves an African will be tolerated only on condition that he is for the convenience of the Whites.

There will be forcible uprooting and mass removals of millions of people to 'homogeneous administrative areas'. The Reserves, already intolerably overcrowded, will be crammed with hundreds of thousands more people evicted by the Government.

In return for all these hardships, in return for Africans abandoning their birthright as citizens, pioneers, and inhabitants of South Africa, the Government promises them 'self-government' in the tiny 13 per cent that their greed and miserliness 'allocates' to us. But what sort of self-government is this that is promised?

There are two essential elements to self-government, as the term is used and understood all over the modern world. They are:

1. *Democracy.* The organs of government must be representative; that is to say, they must be freely chosen leaders and representatives of the people, whose mandate must be renewed at periodic democratic elections.

2. *Sovereignty.* The government thus chosen must be free to legislate and act as it deems fit on behalf of the people, not subject to any limitations upon its powers by any alien authority.

Neither of these two essentials is present in the Nationalist plan. The 'Bantu National Units' will be ruled in effect by the commissioners-general appointed by the Government, and administered by the Bantu Affairs Department officials under his control. When the Government says it plans gradually increasing self-government, it merely means that more powers in future will be exercised by appointed councils of chiefs and headmen. No provision is made for elections. The Nationalists say that chiefs, not elected legislatures, are 'the Bantu tradition'.

There was a time when, like all peoples on earth, Africans conducted their simple communities through chiefs, advised by tribal councils and mass meetings of the people. In those times the chiefs were indeed representative governors. Nowhere, however, have such institutions survived the complexities of modern industrial civilisation. Moreover, in South Africa we all know full well that no chief can retain his post unless he submits to Verwoerd, and many chiefs who sought the interest of their people before position and self-advancement have, like President Lutuli, been deposed.

Thus, the proposed Bantu authorities will not be, in any sense of the term, representative or democratic.

The point is made with pride by the Bantu Affairs Department itself in an official publication:

'The councillors will perform their task without fear or prejudice, because they are not elected by the majority of votes, and they will be able to lead their people onwards ... even though ... it may demand hardships and sacrifices.'

A strange paean to autocracy, from a department of a Government which claims to be democratic!

In spite of all their precautions to see that their 'territorial authorities' — appointed by themselves, subject to dismissal by themselves and under constant control by their commissioners-general and their Bantu Affairs Department — never become authentic voices of the people, the Nationalists are determined to see that even those puppet bodies never enjoy real power of sovereignty.

In his notorious (and thoroughly dishonest) article in *Optima*, Dr Eiselen draws a far-fetched comparison between the relations between the future 'Bantustans' and the Union Government, on the one hand, and those between Britain and the self-governing Dominions on the other. He foresees: 'A co-operative South African system based on the Commonwealth conception, with the Union Government gradually changing its position from guardian and trustee to become instead the senior member of a group of separate communities.'

To appreciate the full hypocrisy of this statement, it must be remembered that Dr Eiselen is an official of a Nationalist Party Government, a member of a party which has built its fortune for the past half century on its cry that it stands for full untrammelled sovereignty within the Commonwealth, that claims credit for Hertzog's achievements in winning the Statute of Westminster, which proclaims such sovereignty, and which even now wants complete independence and a republic outside the Commonwealth.*

---

*South Africa left the British Commonwealth and became a republic in 1961. General J B M Hertzog was Prime Minister 1924–39; the Statute of Westminster (1931) formally recognised the legislative independence of the dominions within the British Empire (later Commonwealth) of which South Africa was one.

It cannot be claimed, therefore, that Eiselen and Verwoerd do not understand the nature of a commonwealth, or sovereignty, or federation.

What are we to think, then, in the same article, when Dr Eiselen comes into the open, and declares: 'The utmost degree of autonomy in administrative matters which the Union Parliament is likely to be prepared to concede to these areas will stop short of actual surrender of sovereignty by the European trustee, and there is therefore no prospect of a federal system with eventual equality among members taking the place of the South African Commonwealth . . .'

There is no sovereignty then. No autonomy. No democracy. No self-government. Nothing but a crude, empty fraud, to bluff the people at home and abroad, and to serve as a pretext for heaping yet more hardships and injustices upon the African people.

Politically, the talk about self-government for the Reserves is a swindle. Economically, it is an absurdity.

The few scattered African Reserves in various parts of the Union, comprising about 13 per cent of the least desirable land area, represent the last shreds of land ownership left to the African people of their original ancestral home. After the encroachments and depredations of generations of European land-sharks, achieved by force and by cunning, and culminating in the outrageous Land Act from 1913 onwards, had turned the once free and independent Tswana, Sotho, Xhosa, Zulu, and other peasant farmers in this country into a nation of landless outcasts and roving beggars, humble 'work-seekers' on the mines and the farms where yesterday they had been masters of the land, the new White masters of the country 'generously presented' them the few remaining miserable areas as reservoirs and breeding-grounds for Black labour. These are the Reserves.

It was never claimed or remotely considered by the previous governments of the Union that these Reserves could become economically self-sufficient 'national homes' for 9,600,000 African people of this country. The final lunacy was left to Dr Verwoerd, Dr Eiselen, and the Nationalist Party.

The facts are — as every reader who remembers Govan Mbeki's brilliant series of articles on the Transkei in *Liberation** will be aware — that the Reserves are congested distressed areas, completely unable to sustain their present populations. The majority of the adult males are always away from home working in the towns, mines, or European-owned farms. The people are on the verge of starvation.

The White Paper speaks of teaching Africans soil conservation and agriculture and replacing European agricultural officers by Africans. This is merely trifling with the problem. The root problem of the Reserves is the intolerable congestion which already exists. No amount of agricultural instruction will ever enable 13 per cent of the land to sustain 66 per cent of the population.

The Government is, of course, fully aware of the fact. They have no intention of creating African areas which are genuinely self-supporting (and which could

---

*See Govan Mbeki, *South Africa: The Peasants' Revolt*, IDAF, London, 1984.

82

therefore create a genuine possibility for self-government). If such areas were indeed self-supporting, where would the Chamber of Mines and the Nationalist farmers get their supplies of cheap labour?

In the article to which I have already referred, Dr Eiselen bluntly admits: 'In fact not much more than a quarter of the community (on the Reserves) can be farmers, the others seeking their livelihood in industrial, commercial, professional, or administrative employment.'

Where are they to find such employment? In the Reserves? To anyone who knows these poverty-stricken areas, sadly lacking in modern communications, power-resources, and other needed facilities, the idea of industrial development seems far-fetched indeed. The beggarly £500,000 voted to the so-called 'Bantu Investment Corporation' by Parliament is mere eyewash: it would not suffice to build a single decent road, railway line, or power station.

The Government has already established a number of 'rural locations' — townships in the Reserves. The Eiselen article says a number more are planned: he mentions a total of no less than 96. Since the residents will not farm, how will they manage to keep alive, still less pay rents and taxes and support the traders, professional classes, and civil servants whom the optimistic Eiselen envisages will make a living there?*

Fifty-seven towns on the borders of the Reserves have been designated as centres where White capitalists can set up industries. Perhaps some will migrate, and thus 'export' their capital resources of cheap labour and land. Certainly, unlike the Reserves (which are a monument to the callous indifference of the Union Parliament to the needs of the non-voting African taxpayers), these towns have power, water, transport, railways, etc. The Nationalist Government, while it remains in office, will probably subsidise capitalists who migrate in this way. It is already doing so in various ways, thus creating unemployment in the cities. But it is unlikely that any large-scale voluntary movement will take place away from the big, established industrial centres, with their well-developed facilities, available materials, and markets.

Even if many industries were forced to move to the border areas around the Reserves it would not make one iota of difference to the economic viability of the Reserves themselves. The fundamental picture of the Union's economy could remain fundamentally the same as at present: a single integrated system based upon the exploitation of African labour by White capitalists.

Economically, the 'Bantustan' concept is just as big a swindle as it is politically.

Thus we find, if we really look into it, that this grandiose 'partition' scheme, this 'supremely positive step' of Dr Verwoerd, is like all apartheid schemes — high-sounding double talk to conceal a policy of ruthless oppression of the non-Whites and of buttressing the unwarranted privileges of the White minority, especially the farming, mining, and financial circles.

---

*History has proved Mandela's analysis accurate. These rural locations became places to which Africans were forcibly removed, and are internationally notorious for their wretched conditions.

Even if it were not so, however, even if the scheme envisaged a genuine sharing-out of the country on the basis of population figures, and a genuine transfer of power to elected representatives of the people, it would remain fundamentally unjust and dangerously unstable unless it were submitted to, accepted, and endorsed by all parties to the agreement. To think otherwise is to fly in the face of the principle of self-determination, which is upheld by all countries, and confirmed in the United Nations Charter, to which this country is pledged.

Now even Dr Eiselen recognises this difficulty to some extent. He pays lip-service to the Atlantic Charter and appeals to 'Western democracy'. He mentions the argument that apartheid would only be acceptable 'provided that the parties concerned agreed to this of their own free will'. And then he most dishonestly evades the whole issue. 'There is no reason for ruling out apartheid on the grounds that the vast majority of the population oppose it', he writes. 'The Bantu as a whole do not demand integration, in a single society. This is the idea . . . merely of a small minority.'

Even Dr Eiselen, however, has not the audacity to claim that the African people actually favour apartheid or partition.

Let us state clearly the facts of the matter, with the greatest possible clarity.

NO SERIOUS OR RESPONSIBLE LEADER, GATHERING, OR ORGANISATION OF THE AFRICAN PEOPLE HAS EVER ACCEPTED SEGREGATION, SEPARATION, OR THE PARTITION OF THIS COUNTRY IN ANY SHAPE OR FORM.

At Bloemfontein in 1956, under the auspices of the United African clergy, perhaps the most widely attended and representative gathering of African representatives of every shade of political opinion ever held, unanimously and uncompromisingly rejected the Tomlinson Report* on which the Verwoerd plan is based, and voted in favour of a single society.

Even in the rural areas, where dwell the 'good' (ie simple and ignorant) 'Bantu' of the imagination of Dr Verwoerd and Dr Eiselen, attempts to impose apartheid have met, time after time, with furious, often violent resistance. Chief after chief has been deposed or deported for resisting 'Bantu authorities' plans. Those who, out of short-sightedness, cowardice, or corruption, have accepted these plans have earned nothing but the contempt of their own people.

It is a pity that, on such a serious subject, and at such a crucial period, serious misstatements should have been made by some people who purport to speak on behalf of the Africans. For example, Mrs Margaret Ballinger, the Liberal Party MP, is reported as saying in the Assembly 'no confidence' debate:

'The Africans have given their answer to this apartheid proposition but, of course, no one ever listens to them. They have said: "If you want separation then let us have it. Give us half of South Africa. Give us the eastern half of South

---

*Report of the Commission for the Socio-Economic Development of the Bantu Areas within the Union of South Africa (UG 61/1955). This proposed that Africans be accorded political rights only in the Reserves, which were to become separate tribal 'homelands'.

Africa. Give us some of the developed resources because we have helped to develop them." ' (*SA Outlook*, March 1959.)

It is most regrettable that Mrs Ballinger should have made such a silly and irresponsible statement towards, one fears, the end of a distinguished parliamentary career. For in this instance she has put herself in the company of those who do not listen to the Africans. No Africans of any standing have ever made the proposal put forward by her.

The leading organisation of the African people is the African National Congress. Congress has repeatedly denounced apartheid. It has repeatedly endorsed the Freedom Charter, which claims South Africa 'for all its people'. It is true that occasionally individual Africans become so depressed and desperate at Nationalist misrule that they have tended to clutch at any straw to say: give us any little corner where we may be free to run our own affairs. But Congress has always firmly rejected such momentary tendencies and refused to barter our birthright, which is South Africa, for such illusory 'Bantustans'.

Commenting on a suggestion by Professor du Plessis that a federation of 'Bantustans' be established, Mr Duma Nokwe, Secretary-General of the African National Congress, totally rejected such a plan as unacceptable. The correct approach, he said, would be the extension of the franchise rights to Africans. Thereafter a National Convention of all the people of South Africa could be summoned and numerous suggestions of the democratic changes that should be brought about, including the suggestion of Professor du Plessis, could form the subject of the Convention.

Here, indeed, Mr Nokwe has put his finger on the spot. There is no need for Dr Eiselen, Mrs Ballinger, or others to argue about 'what the Africans think' about the future of this country. Let the people speak for themselves! Let us have a free vote and a free election of delegates to a national convention, irrespective of colour or nationality. Let the Nationalists submit their plan, and the Congress its Charter. If Verwoerd and Eiselen think the Africans support their schemes they need not fear such a procedure. If they are not prepared to submit to public opinion, then let them stop parading and pretending to the outside world that they are democrats, and talking revolting nonsense about 'Bantu self-government'.

Dr Verwoerd may deceive the simple-minded Nationalist voters with his talk of Bantustans, but he will not deceive anyone else, neither the African people, nor the great world beyond the borders of this country. We have heard such talk before, and we know what it means. Like everything else that has come from the Nationalist Government, it spells nothing but fresh hardships and suffering to the masses of the people.

Behind the fine talk of 'self-government' is a sinister design.

The abolition of African representation in Parliament and the Cape Provincial Council shows that the real purpose of the scheme is not to concede autonomy to Africans but to deprive them of all say in the government of the country, in exchange for a system of local government controlled by a minister who is not responsible to them but to a Parliament in which they have no voice. This is not autonomy but autocracy.

Contact between the minister and the Bantu authorities will be maintained by five commissioners-general. These officials will act as the watchdogs of the minister to ensure that the 'authorities' strictly toe the line. Their duty will be to ensure that these authorities should become the voice not of the African people but of the Nationalist Government.

In terms of the White Paper, steps will be taken to 'link' Africans working in urban areas with the territorial authorities established under the Bantu Authoritites Act, by conferring powers on these authorities to nominate persons as their representatives in urban areas. This means in effect that efforts will be made to place Africans in the cities under the control of their tribal chiefs — a retrograde step.

Nowhere in the Bill or in the various proclamations dealing with the creation of Bantu authorities is there provision for democratic elections by Africans falling within the jurisdiction of the authorities.

In the light of these facts it is sheer nonsense to talk of South Africa as being about to take a 'supremely positive step towards placing Africans on the road to self-government', or of having given them more powers to rule themselves. As Dr Eiselen clearly pointed out in his article in *Optima*, the establishment of Bantustans will not in any way affect White supremacy, since even in such areas Whites will stay supreme. The Bantustans are not intended to voice the aspirations of the African people; they are instruments for their subjection. Under the pretext of giving them self-government the African people are being split up into tribal units in order to retard their growth and development into full nationhood.

The new Bantu Bill and the policy behind it will bear heavily on the peasants in the Reserves. But it is not they who are the chief target of Verwoerd's new policy.

His new measures are aimed, in the first place, at the millions of Africans in the great cities of this country, the factory workers and intellectuals who have raised the banner of freedom and democracy and human dignity, who have spoken forth boldly the message that is shaking imperialism to its foundations throughout this great continent of Africa.

The Nationalists hate and fear that banner and that message. They will try to destroy them, by striking with all their might at the standard-bearer and vanguard of the people, the working class.

Behind the 'self-government' talks lies a grim programme of mass evictions, political persecution, and police terror. It is the last desperate gamble of a hated and doomed fascist autocracy — which, fortunately, is soon due to make its exit from the stage of history.

6. THE TREASON TRIAL, 1956-60

In response to the growing unity and strength of the Congress Movement as a united front following the adoption of the Freedom Charter, the government arrested 156 political leaders in a mass police swoop on 5 December 1956 and charged them with high treason, a grave charge carrying the death penalty. They were accused of participating in a treasonable conspiracy, inspired by international Communism, to overthrow the South African State by violent means. The trial dragged on for four years, with the last accused being acquitted in 1961.

MANDELA'S TESTIMONY, 1960

Extracts from the testimony by Mandela, responding as spokesman for the accused to questions from the bench, the prosecution and the defence lawyers on the content of ANC documents and question of violent intent on the part of those on trial.

PROSECUTION: Do you think that your People's Democracy could be achieved by a process of gradual reforms? Suppose, as a result of pressure, the ruling class were to agree next month to a qualified franchise for the Africans, an educational test perhaps — not a stringent one — and next year, as a result of further pressure, a more important concession is made — a further concession is made in 1962, and so on over a period of ten or twenty years — do you think that the People's Democracy could be achieved in that fashion?

MANDELA: Well, this is how I approach the question. I must explain at the outset that the Congress, as far as I know, has never sat down to discuss the question. . . . We demand universal adult franchise and we are prepared to exert economic pressure to attain our demands, and we will launch defiance campaigns, stay-at-homes, either singly or together, until the Government should say, 'Gentlemen, we cannot have this state of affairs, laws being defied, and this whole situation created by stay-at-homes. Let's talk.' In my own view I would say Yes, let us talk and the Government would say, 'We think that the Europeans at present are not ready for a type of government where there might be domination by non-Europeans. We think we should give you 60 seats. The African population to elect 60 Africans to represent them in Parliament. We will leave the matter over for five years and we will review it at the end of five years.' In my view, that would be a victory, my lords; we would have taken a significant step towards the attainment of universal adult suffrage for Africans, and we would then for the five years say, we will suspend civil disobedience; we won't have any stay-at-homes, and we will then devote the intervening period for the purpose of educating the country, the Europeans, to see that these changes can be brought about and that it would bring about better racial understanding, better racial harmony in the country. I'd say we should accept it, but, of course, I would not abandon the demands for the extension of the universal franchise to all Africans.

That's how I see it, my lords. Then at the end of the five-year period we will have discussions and if the Government says, 'We will give you again 40 more seats', I might say that that is quite sufficient. Let's accept it, and still demand that the franchise should be extended, but for the agreed period we should suspend civil disobedience, no stay-at-homes. In that way we would eventually be able to get everything that we want; we shall have our People's Democracy, my lords. That is the view I hold — whether that is Congress's view I don't know, but that is my view.

* * *

BENCH: Mandela, assuming you were wrong in your beliefs, do you visualise any future action on behalf of the Government, by the Government? Because I think the evidence suggests that you could not expect the Government to soften in its views. Have you any future plans in that event?

MANDELA: No, my lord. I don't think that the Congress has ever believed that its policy of pressure would ultimately fail. The Congress, of course, does not expect that one single push to coerce the Government to change its policy will succeed; the Congress expects that over a period, as a result of a repetition of these pressures, together with world opinion, that the Government notwithstanding its attitude of ruling Africans with an iron hand, that notwithstanding that, the methods which we are using will bring about a realisation of our aspirations.

PROSECUTION: Mr Mandela, whether or not there would be success ultimately, one thing is clear, is it not, and that is that the African National Congress held the view, and propagated the view, that in resisting pressure by the Congress Movement the ruling class, the Government, would not hesitate to retaliate — would not hesitate to use violence and armed force against the Congress Movement?

MANDELA: Yes, the Congress was of that view, my lords. We did expect force to be used, as far as the Government is concerned, but as far as we are concerned we took the precautions to ensure that that violence will not come from our side.

BENCH: What were those precautions?

MANDELA: Well, my lord, for example in 1952 when we launched the Defiance Campaign, and secondly, my lord, you will notice that we frequently use 'stay-at-home', not 'strike' in the ordinary sense. Now, my lord, in a strike what is usually done is to withdraw workers from a particular industry and then have pickets to prevent the people from working in those industries which are boycotted. But the Congress theory (was) that to have pickets might attract police violence. We deliberately decided to use 'stay-at-home' where people are asked to remain in their houses.

PROSECUTION: As far as you know, has the onward march of the liberatory movement continued to manifest itself?

MANDELA: Yes it has. Congress has become much more powerful and much more strong today.

PROSECUTION: And in your opinion is the possibility of this violence to which you refer therefore heightened — increased?

MANDELA: Oh, yes; we felt that the Government will not hesitate to massacre hundreds of Africans in order to intimidate them not to oppose its reactionary policy.

BENCH: Now, the difference which I want to discuss with you, what would the reaction of White supremacy be if it was made to realise that the demands of the Congress alliance would result in its supremacy being terminated once and for all?

MANDELA: Well, that has been a problem all along, my lord.

BENCH: That may be, but what do you think the reaction of White supremacy would be to that claim?

MANDELA: Well, for all I know they may be hostile to that type of thing. But already political organisations are arising in this country which themselves are striving for the extension of the franchise to the African people.

BENCH: Well, the question is now whether you can ever achieve that by the methods you are using?

MANDELA: No, but, my lord, this is what I am coming to, that already since we applied these new methods of political action, this policy of exerting pressure, we have attained — we have achieved, we have won ground. Political parties have now emerged which themselves put forward the demand of extending the franchise to the non-European people.

BENCH: Unqualified franchise? One man, one vote?

MANDELA: No, no, my lord, it is qualified.

BENCH: I would like to discuss this with you.

MANDELA: If your lordship could give me time? Now, it is true that these parties, both the Liberal Party as well as the Progressive Party* are thinking in terms of some qualified franchise. But, if your lordship bears in mind the fact that when we initiated this policy, there were no political parties — none in the Union — which thought along these lines, then your lordship will realise the revolution that has taken place in European parties in this country today. You are now having an organised body of opinion, quite apart from the Congress of Democrats, who themselves are a force, quite apart from them, you are having

---

*A small political party formed in 1960; its policies were non-racial but based on a qualified franchise. A major sponsor was Harry Oppenheimer, then the Chairman of Anglo-American Corporation. Following the break-up of the United Party in 1977, elements from it amalgamated with the Progressive Party to become the Progressive Federal Party, the main opposition party in the white parliament.

an organised body of opinion amongst Whites who put forward the view that some limited form of franchise should be extended to Africans.

BENCH: I don't think we are quite on the same — let me put it this way — wavelength. During the indictment period, did or did not — I think you said it was accepted by the Congress alliance that White supremacy would be hostile to this claim, one man one vote?

MANDELA: Yes, it is hostile, except to qualify of course that even during that period parties had already emerged which were putting forward this view, and therefore it was reasonable for us to believe that in spite of the hostility which we still encounter from the majority of the Whites, already our policy was succeeding.

★ ★ ★

BENCH: I want to know whether the Congress Alliance discussed or considered whether the — whether White supremacy in South Africa would without a show of arms surrender that which if surrendered would mean its end?

MANDELA: No, my lord. The Congress has considered the question from the point of view firstly of its experience. The Whites being eager to retain political power exclusively for themselves —

BENCH: That was considered?

MANDELA: That was considered. It was also considered that through this policy of exerting pressure we will force the Whites by using our numbers, our numerical preponderance, in forcing them to grant us what we demand, even against their will. We considered that, and we felt that that was possible.

BENCH: How would you use your numerical numbers to force White supremacy to give what you want?

MANDELA: For example by staying at home and not going to work, using our economic power for the purpose of attaining our demands. Now, my lord, we were not looking — we were not hoping that these demands were going to be realised during the period of the indictment, no. We had in mind that in the foreseeable future it will be possible for us to achieve these demands, and we worked on the basis that Europeans themselves in spite of the wall of prejudice and hostility which we encountered, that they can never remain indifferent indefinitely to our demands, because we are hitting them in the stomach with our policy of economic pressure. It is a method which is well organised. The Europeans dare not look at it with indifference. They would have to respond to it and indeed, my lord, they are responding to it.

★ ★ ★

DEFENCE *(on the basic policy document of the ANC Youth League — see above, document 1b):* What was the aim of the ANC with regard to Nationalism on the one hand and tribes on the other hand?

MANDELA: It was always the policy of the ANC to bring about out of the various African tribal groups in the country a united African community.

DEFENCE: As far as the Union of South Africa was concerned, did you regard it as a country which was subject to foreign domination?

MANDELA: We regarded it as subject to White supremacy.

DEFENCE: Apart from the question of organisation, did the Youth League feel that the methods and activity used by the ANC should be changed?

MANDELA: Up to the time that the Youth League was formed and until 1949 the only methods of political action which were adopted by the ANC were purely constitutional; deputations to see the authorities, memoranda, and the mere passing of resolutions. We felt that that policy had been tried and found wanting and we thought that the ANC, its organisers and fieldworkers, should go out into the highways and organise the masses of the African people for mass campaigns. We felt that the time had arrived for the Congress to consider the adoption of more militant forms of political action: stay-at-homes, civil disobedience, protests, demonstrations — also including the methods which had previously been employed by the ANC.

DEFENCE: Were some members of the Youth League actually in favour of expelling Communists from the ANC?

MANDELA: Yes, my lords. As a matter of fact the Youth League moved a resolution at conferences of the ANC calling on the ANC to expel Communists, but these resolutions were defeated by an overwhelming majority.

DEFENCE: On what grounds were these resolutions rejected?

MANDELA: The view of the ANC was that every person above the age of 17 years, irrespective of the political views he might have, was entitled to become a member of the ANC.

DEFENCE: What was your own view at the time?

MANDELA: At that time I strongly supported the resolution to expel the Communists from the ANC. . . .

(Mandela then went on to say that later he had worked with Communist members of the ANC.)

DEFENCE: Whatever may have been their opinions or intentions as far as you were concerned did it appear to you that they were followers of ANC policy?

MANDELA: That is correct.

DEFENCE: Did they appear loyal to it?

MANDELA: That is correct.

DEFENCE: Did you become a Communist?

MANDELA: Well, I don't know if I did become a Communist. If by Communist you mean a member of the Communist party and a person who believes in the theory of Marx, Engels, Lenin, and Stalin, and who adheres strictly to the discipline of the party, I did not become a Communist.

★ ★ ★

DEFENCE *(citing the ANC Programme of Action adopted in 1949 — see above, document 1c)*: How did you understand the new Programme of Action?

MANDELA: Up to 1949 the leaders of the ANC had always acted in the hope that by merely pleading their cause, placing it before the authorities, they, the authorities, would change their hearts and extend to them all the rights that they were demanding. But the forms of political action which are set out in the Programme of Action meant that the ANC was not going to rely on a change of heart. It was going to exert pressure to compel the authorities to grant its demands.

★ ★ ★

DEFENCE *(on the Suppression of Communism Act)*:

MANDELA: Well, in regard to the Act, the ANC took the view that the Act was an invasion of the rights of our political organisations, that it was not only aimed against the Communist Party of South Africa, but was designed to attack and destroy all the political organisations that condemned the racialist policies of the South African Government. We felt that even if it were aimed against the Communist Party of South Africa we would still oppose it, because we believe that every political organisation has a right to exist and to advocate its own point of view.

★ ★ ★

DEFENCE *(On the Defiance Campaign of 1952 — see above, document 3a)*: Do you think that, apart from the increase in your membership, it [the Defiance Campaign] had any other result?

MANDELA: Yes, most certainly. Firstly, it pricked the conscience of the European public which became aware in a much more clear manner of the sufferings and disabilities of the African people. It led directly to the formation of the Congress of Democrats. It also influenced the formation of the Liberal Party. It also led to discussions on the policies of apartheid at the United Nations and I think to that extent it was an outstanding success.

DEFENCE: Do you think it had any effect at all on the Government?

MANDELA: I think it had. After the Defiance Campaign the Government began talking about self-government for Africans, Bantustans. I do not believe, of course, that the Government was in any way sincere in saying it was part of Government policy to extend autonomy to Africans. I think they acted in order to deceive . . . but in spite of that deception one thing comes out very clearly and that is that they acknowledged the power of the Defiance Campaign, they felt that striking power of the ANC had tremendously increased. . .

BENCH: Well, as a matter of fact isn't your freedom a direct threat to the Europeans?

MANDELA: No, it is not a direct threat to the Europeans. We are not anti-white, we are against white supremacy and in struggling against white supremacy we have the support of some sections of the European population and we have made this clear from time to time. As a matter of fact, in the letter we wrote to the then Prime Minister of the country, Dr Malan, before we launched the Defiance Campaign, we said that the campaign we were about to launch was not directed against any racial group. It was a campaign which was directed against laws which we considered unjust, and time without number the ANC has explained this . . . It is quite clear that the Congress has consistently preached a policy of race harmony and we have condemned racialism no matter by whom it is professed.

* * *

BENCH *(asking about the one-party system of government)*:

MANDELA: My lord, it is not a question of form, it is a question of democracy. If democracy would be best expressed by a one-party system then I would examine the proposition very carefully. But if democracy could best be expressed by a multi-party system then I would examine that carefully. In this country, for example, we have a multi-party system at present, but so far as the non-Europeans are concerned this is the most vicious despotism you could think of.

BENCH: Are you attracted by the idea of a classless society?

MANDELA: Yes, very much so, my lord. I think that a lot of evils arise out of the existence of classes, one class exploiting others (but) . . . the ANC has no policy in any shape or form on this matter.

* * *

DEFENCE *(On the article 'The Shifting Sands of Illusion' — see above, document 3b)*: Do you adhere today to the attitude you then expressed towards the Liberal Party?

MANDELA: I still do, except that the Liberal party has now shifted a great deal from its original position. It is now working more closely with the Congress Movement and to a very large extent it has accepted a great portion of the policy of the Congress Movement. I also believe that in regard to the question of the qualified vote there has been some healthy development of outlook which brings it still closer to our policy. To that extent some of the views I expressed in that article have now been qualified.

* * *

DEFENCE *(On the issue of imperialism)*:

MANDELA: In our experience the most important thing about imperialism today is that it has gone all over the world subjugating people and exploiting them, bringing death and destruction to millions of people. That is the central thing and we want to know whether we should support and perpetuate this institution which has brought so much suffering.

The Treason Trial was in its fourth year when the shootings at Sharpeville took place on 21 March 1960. Sixty-nine Africans were killed and 176 wounded when police opened fire on an unarmed crowd. International attention was focused on South Africa. A State of Emergency was proclaimed by the government; over twenty thousand people were detained. The ANC was banned, and so was the Pan-Africanist Congress (PAC), a splinter group which had broken away from the ANC the previous year over the issue of the ANC's co-operation with non-Africans. Under pressure from the Commonwealth to change its racial policies, the South African government decided to hold a referendum among the white population to determine whether the country should become a republic outside the Commonwealth. This was viewed with grave misgivings by the Africans, who saw the proposed republic as an opportunity for the government to further institutionalise the racialist policies of the Nationalist Party, without any external check. Forty African leaders, including former members of the now-banned ANC and PAC, with Liberals and Progressives, met initially at a Consultative Conference at Orlando, Johannesburg, on 16 December 1960, to organise a united front against this threat.

Of crucial concern at the time was the situation in Pondoland, in the Transkei, where popular resistance to the imposition of the 'Bantu Authorities' system, mentioned by Mandela in document 5(f) above, had led to violent police repression and eventually to the deployment of military units against the unarmed people.

7. ALL-IN AFRICAN CONFERENCE AND 'STAY-AT-HOME'*
1960-61

7(a) CONSULTATIVE CONFERENCE OF AFRICAN LEADERS, ORLANDO, 16 DECEMBER 1960

RESOLUTIONS‡

1.   This conference agrees on the urgent need for African unity and pledges itself to work for it on the basis of the following broad principles:

(a)   The removal of the scourge of apartheid from every phase of national life.

(b)   The immediate establishment of a non-racial democracy.

(c)   The effective use of non-violent pressures against apartheid.

2.   This conference of African leaders from all walks of life, having carefully examined the grave problems of our country, places on record that:

(a)   It is convinced that the absence of fundamental rights and in particular the right to have a say in the affairs of our country is the basic cause of suffering, strife, racial tension and conflict in our country.

(b)   It is its considered view that the situation is further aggravated by the efforts of the government to muzzle the political expression of the African people by banning the African National Congress and the Pan-Africanist Congress.

(c)   There is no doubt that the imposition of a new constitution for a Nationalist Republic with contemptuous disregard for the views of the African people is a climax in this determinating process.

(d)   This conference notes with concern that the developments in South Africa are diametrically opposed to those in the rest of Africa — WHEREFORE conference warns that the situation in our country has created an atmosphere charged with the possibility of an eruption unless all sections of the people of our country halt this development. To this end the African leaders here assembled consider that the African people are the most vital and potent force to direct changes in our country and that therefore their unity is essential.

In view whereof this conference resolves that because the African people were denied participation in the Republican Referendum they do not accept its result. This conference, therefore, calls upon the African people to attend an All-in Conference representative of African people in the urban and rural areas whose purpose will be to:

(i)   demand the calling of a National Convention representing all the people of South Africa wherein the fundamental rights of the people will be considered.

---

*The concept of the 'stay-at-home' was used to describe the three-day general strike of May 1961, to protect those who took part: strike action by Africans was illegal. See Mandela's first court statement (*document 10, pp.133–60*), and the article 'General Strike' (*document 7(h), pp.107–18*).

(ii) consolidate the UNITY of the African people.

3. That to achieve the above ends a Continuation Committee be appointed which will make arrangements for an All-in African Conference which must be held by not later than the end of February 1961.

4. (a) This conference is alarmed by the use of military units in Pondoland and demands that the government withdraw them forthwith, and stop the butcherings and Pass persecutions so that an atmosphere can be created for action to be taken to redress the just grievances of the people whose existence was admitted by a Government Commission recently.

 (b) This conference hails the struggle of the Pondo people who have by their courage and determination exposed the hypocrisy which suggested that the Bantu Authorities are acceptable to the African people both in the urban and rural areas.

 (c) This conference calls upon the African people and democrats in the other racial groups to regard the Pondo people's resistance to Bantu Authorities as an integral part of the fight against apartheid.

5. That this conference suggests to the UNO to send a commission of observers to Pondoland and to use its good offices to curb the alarming military operations against unarmed people which constitute a threat to peace in South Africa.

6. This conference of African leaders welcomes the resolution of the Security Council of the UNO and in particular the visit of the Secretary-General, Mr Dag Hammarskjoeld but urges that in order to have a true view of the situation in the country he should meet African leaders.

7. This conference wishes to place on record that the raid carried out by the police on this legitimate conference of African leaders and the arbitrary arrest of some delegates demonstrates clearly the extent to which freedom of expression is being denied to Africans.

8. Conference demands the immediate lifting of the ban on the ANC and PAC, the national organisations of the people.

The Continuation Committee mentioned in the third resolution was elected and the All-in African Conference was organised at Pietermaritzburg, 25-26 March 1961. It took place against a background of a successful strike by African bus employees in Port Elizabeth, and continuing unrest in Pondoland and other rural areas.

All organisations with African membership were invited to attend, including those like the Liberal Party and Progressive Party whose membership was not exclusively or even mainly African.

Over fifteen hundred delegates of all shades of African opinion, representing all interests, and from all over the country, attended the conference.

7(b) ALL-IN AFRICAN CONFERENCE, PIETERMARITZBURG, 25-26 MARCH 1961.

By the time of this conference, Mandela had been under successive banning orders for nine years, but the current order lapsed and was not immediately renewed. He appeared at the conference and addressed it (see Introduction p.5).

RESOLUTIONS‡

A grave situation confronts the people of South Africa. The Nationalist government, after holding a fraudulent referendum among only one-fifth of the population, has decided to proclaim a white republic on 31 May, and the all-white parliament is presently discussing a constitution. It is clear that to the great disadvantage of the majority of our people such a republic will continue even more intensively the policies of racial oppression, political persecution and exploitation and the terrorisation of the non-white people which have already earned South Africa the righteous condemnation of the entire world.

In this situation it is imperative that all the African people of this country, irrespective of their political, religious or other affiliations, should unite to speak and act with a single voice.

For this purpose, we have gathered here at this solemn All-in Conference, and on behalf of the entire African nation and with a due sense of the historic responsibility which rests on us:

1. WE DECLARE that no constitution or form of government decided without the participation of the African people who form an absolute majority of the population can enjoy moral validity or merit support either within South Africa or beyond its borders.

2. WE DEMAND that a *National Convention* of elected representatives of all adult men and women on an equal basis irrespective of race, colour, creed or other limitation, be called by the Union government not later than 31 May 1961; that the convention shall have sovereign powers to determine, in any way the majority of the representatives decide, a new non-racial democratic constitution for South Africa.

3. WE RESOLVE that should the minority government ignore this demand of the representatives of the united will of the African people:
   (a) We undertake to stage countrywide demonstrations on the eve of the proclamation of the republic in protest against this undemocratic act;
   (b) We call on all Africans not to co-operate or collaborate in any way with the proposed South African republic or any other form of government which rests on force to perpetuate the tyranny of a minority, and to organise and unite in town and country to carry out constant actions to oppose oppression and win freedom;

(c) We call on the Indian and Coloured communities and all democratic Europeans to join forces with us in opposition to a regime which is bringing disaster to South Africa and to win a society in which all can enjoy freedom and security;

(d) We call on democratic people the world over to refrain from any co-operation or dealings with the South African government, to impose economic and other sanctions against this country and to isolate in every possible way the minority government whose continued disregard of all human rights and freedoms constitutes a threat to world peace.

4. WE FURTHER DECIDE that in order to implement the above decisions, conference:

(a) elects a National Action Council;

(b) instructs all delegates to return to their respective areas and form local Action Committees.

Mandela was elected secretary of the National Action Council and the only member whose identity was made public; the identities of the others were kept secret to protect them and the work they had to do. Mandela immediately went underground.

7(c) 'THE STRUGGLE FOR A NATIONAL CONVENTION'

Article written by Mandela in March 1961.

'I am attending this conference as delegate from my village. I was elected at a secret meeting held in the bushes far away from our kraals simply because in our village it is now a crime for us to hold meetings. I have listened most carefully to speeches made here and they have given me strength and courage. I now realise that we are not alone. But I am troubled by my experiences during the last weeks. In the course of our struggle against the system of Bantu Authorities, we heard many fighting speeches delivered by men we trusted most, but when the hour of decision came they did not have the courage of their convictions. They deserted us and we felt lonely and without friends. But I will go away from here refreshed and full of confidence. We must win in the end.'

These words were said at the All-in African Conference held at Pietermaritzburg on 25 and 26 March. The man who said them came from a country area where the people are waging a consistent struggle against Bantu Authorities. He wore riding breeches, a khaki shirt, an old jacket, and came to conference bare-footed. But his words held fire and dignity and his remarks, like those of other speakers, indicated that this conference was no talking shop for persons who merely wanted to let off steam, but a solemn gathering which appreciated the grave decisions it was called upon to take.

The theme of the conference was African unity and the calling, by the government, of a national convention of elected representatives of all adult men and women, on an equal basis, irrespective of race, colour or creed, with full powers to determine a new democratic constitution for South Africa.

Conference resolved that if the government failed to call this convention by 31 May, countrywide demonstrations would be held on the eve of the republic in protest against this undemocratic act.

The adoption of this part of the resolution did not mean that conference preferred a monarchy to a republican form of government. Such considerations were unimportant and irrelevant. The point at issue, and which was emphasised over and over again by delegates, was that a minority government had decided to proclaim a white republic under which the living conditions of the African people would continue to deteriorate.

Conference further resolved that, in the event of the government failing to accede to this demand, all Africans would be called upon not to co-operate with the proposed republic. All sections of our population would be asked to unite with us in opposing the Nationalists.

The resolution went further and called upon democratic people the world over to impose economic and other sanctions against the government. A National Action Council was elected to implement the above decisions.

Three other resolutions were passed in which the arrests of members of the Continuation Committee were strongly condemned; and in which conference called for the lifting of the ban imposed on the African National Congress and the Pan-Africanist Congress. The system of Bantu Authorities was attacked as a measure forcibly imposed by the government in spite of the unanimous opposition of the entire African nation.*

These resolutions were adopted unanimously by more than fifteen hundred delegates, from town and country, representing nearly one hundred and fifty political, religious, sporting, and cultural organisations.

Members of the Liberal Party, the Inter-Denominational African Ministers' Federation, the Eastwood Advisory Board, the Zenzele Club, and scores of other organisations from all over the country, spoke with one voice and jointly faced the political changes introduced by the Nationalist Government.

For thirteen hours they earnestly and calmly considered the grave political situation that has arisen in South Africa as a result of the disastrous policies of the present regime.

Now and again, discussions were interrupted by stirring tunes sung with intense feeling and tremendous enthusiasm by the entire conference. The favourite song was 'Amandla Ngawethu', composed by the freedom fighters of Port Elizabeth during the recent bus boycott in that city.

---

*The resolutions containing these points appear in document 7(a) above. Adopted by the Orlando Conference, they formed the basis for the later All-in Conference, though the final document from there only embodied the fundamental demand for a National Convention.

The gathering was a moving demonstration of comradeship and solidarity and was acclaimed by the South African press as an outstanding success.

The main resolution showed that the delegates visualised much more than a token demonstration on the chosen dates. The people contemplated a stubborn and prolonged struggle, involving masses of the people from town and country, and taking different forms in accordance with local conditions, beginning before 31 May and which would continue unabated until democratic reforms are instituted.

Delegates fully appreciated that the above decisions were not directed against any other population group in the country. They were aimed at a form of government based on brute force and condemned the world over as inhuman and dangerous. It was precisely because of this fact that conference called on the Coloured and Indian people and all European democrats to join forces with us.

It will indeed be very tragic if, in the momentous days that lie ahead, White South Africa will falter and adopt a course of action which will prevent the successful implementation of the resolutions of conference.

In the past we have been astonished by the reaction of certain political parties and 'philanthropic' associations which proclaimed themselves to be anti-apartheid but which, nevertheless, consistently opposed positive action taken by the oppressed people to defeat this same policy. Objectively, such an attitude can only serve to defend White domination and to strengthen the Nationalist Party. It also serves to weaken the impact of liberal views amongst European democrats and lays them open to the charge of being hypocritical.

All the democratic forces in this country must join in a programme of democratic changes. If they are not prepared to come along with us, they can at least be neutral and leave this government isolated and without friends.

Finally, however successful the conference was from the point of view of attendance and the fiery nature of the speeches made, these militant resolutions will remain useless and ineffective unless we translate them into practice.

If we form local action committees in our respective areas, popularise the decisions through vigorous and systematic house-to-house campaigns, we will inspire and arouse the country to implement the resolutions and to hasten the fall of the Nationalist government within our lifetime.

For the National Action Council, Mandela, who was now working underground, toured the country secretly during April and May, with Walter Sisulu, organising for the anticipated three-day stay-at-home. During this period he also addressed appeals to various sections of the population, calling for their support for the proposed National Convention; among these appeals are three letters printed here and the letter to Prime Minister Verwoerd, cited during Mandela's 1962 trial (see below pp.139–40).

APPEAL TO STUDENTS

Leaflet issued by the All-in African National Action Council, signed by Mandela [April 1961.]

AN APPEAL TO STUDENTS AND SCHOLARS

Dear Friends,

I am writing this letter on the instructions of the All-in African National Action Council which was established in terms of a resolution passed by the All-in African Conference held at Pietermaritzburg on 25 and 26 March 1961. This conference was attended by 1,500 delegates from town and country representing 145 political, religious, social, sporting and cultural organisations. Its aim was to consolidate unity amongst Africans and to consider the decision of the government to proclaim a republic on 31 May this year. It was the opinion of conference that the government was not entitled to take such a decision without first seeking the views and obtaining the express consent of the African people. Delegates felt that under the proposed republic, the racial policies of the government would be intensified resulting in a further deterioration in the living conditions of our people. In its main resolution conference called upon the government to convene a National Convention, before 31 May this year, of all South Africans, to draw up a new democratic constitution. If the government failed to call the convention before the above-mentioned date, countrywide demonstrations would be held on the eve of the republic to compel the government to do so. The resolution went further to call on the African, Coloured and Indian communities as well as European democrats not to co-operate with the proposed republic or with any government based on force. Finally, an appeal was made to democratic individuals the world over and to foreign governments not to have any dealings with the proposed republic and to apply sanctions against it.

This conference has been acclaimed throughout the country as an important landmark in the struggle of the African people to achieve unity amongst themselves. Its challenging resolution is a stirring call to an action which promises to be one of the most massive and stunning blows ever delivered by the African people against white supremacy.

In its efforts to enslave the African people the government has given particular attention to the question of education. The control of African education has been taken away from the Provincial Administrations and missionaries and is now vested in the Bantu Affairs Department so that it should conform with State policy. Instead of a free and progressive education calculated to prepare him for his responsibilities as a fully fledged citizen, the African is indoctrinated with a tribal and inferior type of education intended to keep him in a position of perpetual subservience to the whites. The matric results last year strikingly illustrated the disastrous effects of Bantu Education and show that even more tragic consequences will follow if the Nationalists are not kicked out of power. We call upon the entire South African nation to close ranks and to make a supreme effort to halt the Nationalists and to win freedom. In this situation all students have an important role to play and we appeal to you to:

1. Participate in full in the forthcoming demonstrations.
2. Refuse to participate in the forthcoming republican celebrations and in all ceremonies connected with them.
3. Popularise the Pietermaritzburg resolution amongst other students, the youth in factories, farms and in the streets, to your parents and relatives and to all people in your neighbourhood.

If you take these measures you will have made an important contribution to the historic mission of transforming our country from a white-dominated one to a free and prosperous nation.

N R MANDELA,
Secretary,
All-in African National Action Council

7(e) APPEAL TO THE PEOPLE OF NAMIBIA

Leaflet issued by the All-in African National Council, signed by Mandela [April 1961]. At this time, the country of Namibia was administered by South Africa. As 'South West Africa' the territory was represented in the Cape Town parliament by MPs voted for by a whites-only electorate, and had a South African administrator.

Some years later Mandela was to meet Andimba Herman Toivo ja Toivo and other Namibian leaders on Robben Island.

AN APPEAL TO THE PEOPLE OF SOUTH WEST AFRICA

Dear Friends,

I am writing to you in the name of the African people of the Union of South Africa, on the authority of the National Action Council set up by the All-in African Conference held in Pietermaritzburg on March 25th and 26th of this year. That conference was attended by 1,500 delegates from town and country in the Union, representing 145 political, religious, social, sporting and cultural associations. It met to consider a matter as important for your future as it is for ours — the decision of the Union government to proclaim a Republic on 31st May.

Neither your people nor ours have been consulted in this decision. The decision has been reached by a small majority vote of the white community only. It is designed to free the hands of the Verwoerd government so that it can intensify its policies of race discrimination and oppression against all of us, whether we live in the Union or in South West Africa.

The All-in Conference declared its total opposition to any form of government which relies on force alone to maintain a system of white supremacy. It called on the Union government to convene a National Convention before May 31st, composed of elected representatives of all the peoples of South Africa, with full powers to draw up and decide upon a new, democratic constitution for a multi-racial South Africa.

Conference further decided that, if the government failed to call this Convention, countrywide demonstrations would be held on the eve of the Republic, against the Republic and against the Verwoerd government. Conference called on all sections of the population, White, Coloured and Asian to refuse to co-operate in any way with the proposed Republic or with any form of white supremacist government. It called on the peoples and the governments of the world not to recognise or have any dealings with the Republic, and to apply sanctions against it.

The decisions of this conference have been acclaimed and greeted with enthusiasm by the people of South Africa. Its challenging resolution has become a stirring call to action. The people of this country are preparing for massive and stunning demonstrations against the Verwoerd government, and against the policy of white supremacy. These demonstrations will come to their full flower on May 29th, 30th and 31st.

Your future, no less than ours, is being decided by these actions on which we have embarked. Your people suffer perhaps even worse than ours under the tyranny of the Verwoerd government. Your leaders, like ours, are arrested, banished, imprisoned. Your organisations, like ours, are illegalised. Your homes, like ours, are snatched away, and your people, like ours, shifted from place to place to meet the whims of the masters of apartheid. Your movements and freedom, like ours, are everywhere chained to pass laws, imposed on your people and ours by Verwoerd's police force. The time has come to end this nightmare.

We, the African people of the Union, have always held the view that your people — like us — are ready to rule themselves, that you — like us — have the fundamental human right of deciding your own future, and claiming your own independence. We are striking out for these rights now! We ask you to join with us, to fight with us against the common enemy.

We are preparing now for a great blow against the Verwoerd government at the end of May! We call on you — the people of South West Africa. Act with us, at the same time, in whatever way your organisations decide! Let us go forward together to freedom!

In the name of the African people of the Union, I greet the people of South West Africa. The day of our liberation is dawning. Let us stand together like brothers, for liberty, for freedom and for independence.

N R MANDELA,
Secretary,
All-in African National Action Council

7(f) LETTER TO THE UNITED PARTY

Letter written by Nelson Mandela to Sir de Villiers Graaff, leader of the white opposition United Party, 23 May 1961.

23rd May, 1961

Sir De Villiers Graaff,
Leader of the Opposition,
House of Assembly,
Cape Town.

Sir,

In one week's time, the Verwoerd government intends to inaugurate its Republic. It is unnecessary to state that this intention has never been endorsed by the non-White majority of this country. The decision has been taken by little over half of the White community; it is opposed by every articulate group amongst the African, Coloured and Indian communities, who constitute the majority of this country.

The government's intentions to proceed, under these circumstances, has created conditions bordering on crisis. We have been excluded from the Commonwealth, and condemned 95 to 1 at the United Nations. Our trade is being boycotted, and foreign capital is being withdrawn. The country is becoming an armed camp, the government preparing for civil war with increasingly heavy police and military apparatus, the non-White population for a general strike and long-term non-co-operation with the Government.

None of us can draw any satisfaction from this developing crisis. We, on our part, in the name of the African people — a majority of South Africans — and on the authority given us by 1,500 elected African representatives at the Pietermaritzburg Conference of 25 and 26 March, have put forward serious proposals for a way out of the crisis. We have called on the government to convene an elected National Convention of representatives of all races without delay, and to charge that Convention with the task of drawing up a new constitution for this country which would be acceptable to all racial groups.

We can see no workable alternative to this proposal, except that the Nationalist government proceeds to enforce a minority decision on all of us, with the certain consequence of still deeper crisis, and a continuing period of strife and disaster ahead. Stated bluntly, the alternatives appear to be these: talk it out, or shoot it out. Outside of the Nationalist Party, most of the important and influential bodies of public opinion have clearly decided to talk it out. The South African Indian Congress, the only substantial Indian community organisation, has welcomed and endorsed the call for a National Convention. So, too, have the Coloured people, through the Coloured Convention movement which has the backing of the main bodies of Coloured opinion. A substantial European body of opinion, represented by both the Progressive and the Liberal Parties, has endorsed our call. Support for a National Convention has come also from the bulk of the English language press, from several national church organisations, and from many others.

But where, Sir, does the United Party stand? We have yet to hear from this most important organisation — the main organisation in fact of anti-Nationalist opinion amongst the European community. Or from you, its leader. If the country's leading statesmen fail to lead at this moment, then the worst is inevitable. It is time for you, Sir, and your Party, to speak out. Are you for a democratic and peaceable solution to our problems? Are you, therefore, *for* a National Convention? We in South Africa, and the world outside, expect an answer. Silence at this time enables Dr Verwoerd to lead us onwards towards the brink of disaster.

We realise that aspects of our proposal raise complicated problems. What shall be the basis of representation at the Convention? How shall the representatives be elected? But these are not the issues now at stake. The issue *now* is a simple one. Are all groups to be consulted before a constitutional change is made? Or only the White minority? A decision on this matter cannot be delayed. Once that decision is taken, then all other matters, of how, when and where, can be discussed, and agreement on them can be reached. On our part the door to such discussion has always been open. We have approached you and your Party before, and suggested that matters of difference be discussed. To date we have had no reply. Nevertheless we still hold the door open. But the need *now* is not for debate about differences of detail, but for clarity of principle and purpose. For a National Convention of all races? Or against?

It is still not too late to turn the tide against the Nationalist-created crisis. A call for a National Convention from you now could well be the turning point in our country's history. It would unite the overwhelming majority of our people, White, Coloured, Indian and African, for a single purpose — round-table talks for a new constitution. It would isolate the Nationalist Government, and reveal for all time that it is a minority Government, clinging tenaciously to power against the popular will, driving recklessly onward to a disaster for itself and us. Your call for a National Convention now would add such strength to the already powerful call for it that the Government would be chary of ignoring it further.

And if they nevertheless ignore the call for the Convention, the inter-racial unity thus cemented by your call would lay the basis for the replacement of this Government of national disaster by one more acceptable to the people, one prepared to follow the democratic path of consulting all the people in order to resolve the crisis.

We urge you strongly to speak out now. It is ten days to 31 May.

Yours faithfully,
(signed) Nelson Mandela.

NELSON MANDELA
All-in African National Action Council

This call for a National Convention was not answered either by the government or by the official opposition. As Republic Day approached, therefore, plans for the stay-at-home were put into action.

7(g) 'STAY-AT-HOME'

Leaflet issued by the National Action Council calling for a nationwide stay-at-home on 29, 30, 31 May 1961.

Stay at Home

PEOPLE OF SOUTH AFRICA!
THE PROTEST GOES ON
ARRESTS CANNOT STOP US

We have made our demands known to the Government. We want a National Convention to make a constitution for a democratic South Africa.

VOTES TO ALL
DECENT WAGES FOR ALL
END PASS LAWS
END MINORITY WHITE DOMINATION

VERWOERD REPLIES NO!

He mobilises the army, starts police raids, arrests our leaders and arrests thousands for passes and taxes, bans our meetings. He tries to frighten the country with wild tales of violence.

OUR ANSWER TO VERWOERD:

We are not going to be frightened by Verwoerd. WE STAND FIRM BY OUR DESICION TO STAY AT HOME ON MONDAY, TUESDAY AND WEDNESDAY.

No one who loves freedom should go to work on those three days.

LET US STAND TOGETHER, UNITED AND DISCIPLINED. DO NOT BE INTIMIDATED BY POLICE AGENTS AND PROVOCATEURS.

DOWN WITH VERWOERD'S MINORITY REPUBLIC
FORWARD TO FREEDOM IN OUR LIFETIME
A W U P A T H W A*

Issued by National Action Council

---

*Awupathwa = we shall not be dominated.

7(h) 'GENERAL STRIKE'

Statement by Mandela on behalf of the National Action Council following the stay-at-home in May 1961. Published by the underground ANC and its offices abroad, June 1961.

The statement announced the policy of non-collaboration with the government and renewed the call for an intensified international boycott and the complete isolation of South Africa.

The call of the All-in African National Action Council for a stay-at-home on 29, 30 and 31 May 1961 received solid and massive support throughout the country. This magnificent response was the result of the hard work and selfless devotion of our organisers and activists who had to overcome formidable difficulties very often involving personal risks to themselves. Defying unprecedented intimidation by the State, trailed and hounded by the Special Branch, denied the right to hold meetings, operating in areas heavily patrolled by government and municipal police and teeming with spies and informers, they stood firm as a rock and spread the stay-at-home message to millions of people throughout the country. Ever since the All-in African Conference at Pietermaritzburg, the issue that dominated South African politics and that attracted pressmen from all over the world was not the Republican celebrations organised by the government, but the stirring campaign of the African people and other non-White sections to mark our rejection of a White Republic forcibly imposed upon us by a minority.

Few political organisations could have succeeded in conducting such a stubborn and relentless campaign under conditions which, for all practical purposes, amounted to martial law. But we did so. The steps taken by the government to suppress the campaign were a measure of our strength and influence in the political life of the country and of its weakness. The government was alarmed by the tremendous impact of the demand for a national convention and the call for countrywide anti-Republican demonstrations. It realised that there would be overwhelming support for the call if the campaign was not immediately suppressed through open terror and intimidation. It also realised that the organisational machine built up to propagate the campaign was of so high a standard, and support for the idea so firm and widespread, that the situation could only be controlled by resorting to naked force. Only by mobilising the entire resources of the State could the government hope to stem the tide that was running so strongly against it.

A special law* had to be rushed through parliament to enable the government to detain without trial people connected with the organisation of the stay-at-home. The army had to be called out, European civilians armed, and the police force deployed in African townships and other areas. Meetings were banned throughout the country, and the local authorities, in collaboration with the police

---

*General Law Amendment Act, No. 39 of 1961 (5 May 1961) providing for twelve days' detention without bail or charge. This was a temporary measure, promulgated for a year at a time until it was superseded by the 90-day detention law in 1963.

force, kept vigil to ensure that no strike propaganda should be spread amongst the masses of the people. More than ten thousand innocent Africans were arrested and jailed under the pass laws and terror and intimidation became widespread. Only by adopting these strong-arm measures could the government hope to break the stay-at-home. By resorting to these drastic steps the government has in fact conceded that we are the country's most powerful and dangerous opponents to its hated policies.

On this issue, the radio, the press, and European employers played a thoroughly shameful role. At the beginning of the campaign the press gave us fairly objective coverage and, acting on information supplied by their own reporters in different parts of the country, they reported growing support for the demonstrations and correctly predicted unprecedented response to the call. Until a week or so before the stay-at-home, the South African press endeavoured to live up to the standards and ethics of honest journalism and reported news items as they were without slants and distortions. But as soon as the government showed the mailed fist and threatened action against those newspapers that gave publicity to the campaign, the Opposition press, true to tradition, beat a hurried retreat and threw all principles and ethical standards overboard.

On 18 May 1961, the Johannesburg *Rand Daily Mail* published a front-page news item alleging that the National Action Council had secret plans to bring thousands of non-whites into the central areas of cities. It also announced that the NAC had held a secret meeting the week before at which it decided to extend the duration of the stay-at-home beyond the three-day period. According to the same report, the announcement of the extension of the period would be made at the last moment to retain the element of surprise. In a front-page leading article of the same issue of this newspaper its editor stated that he and the police possessed information that some of us planned violent disturbances on the eve of the Republic.

On behalf of the NAC I immediately replied in writing and refuted all the allegations contained in the news item as sensational journalism and as the inventions of an over-enthusiastic reporter who had sucked things out of his thumbs. We reiterated that this particular campaign was planned to be disciplined and non-violent and that we had no intention whatsoever of exposing our unarmed people to situations whereby they could become targets for the trigger-happy police. In regard to the leading article, we agreed that violence was an unfortunate thing. We felt, however, that appeals for non-violence should be addressed to the government who were spoiling for a showdown and massacre and not to the African people who had repeatedly protested the peaceful and non-violent character of their campaign. We also felt it to be our duty to place on record that, if people in history had listened to appeals to drop political campaigns launched to back up the demands of an oppressed people simply because violence might occur in the course of such a campaign, the world today would still be languishing under the despotic rule of the Middle Ages. Although honour and duty obliged him to publish my reply the editor deliberately decided to suppress it. I spoke to him twice thereafter and, although he promised to attend to the matter, the reply never saw the light of day. We suspected that more was involved than met the eye.

In the evening of 29 May 1961, I made a statement to the same newspaper. I pointed out that in the light of the conditions that prevailed then, the response to the call of the NAC had been solid and substantial and that hundreds of thousands of our people had stayed away from work. I pointed out, however, that the overall response had fallen short of expectations and that we had, consequently, given instructions to our regional and local Action Committees throughout the country to swing into action and to work hard during the night to ensure greater success the following day. This statement was distorted to give the impression that we had conceded defeat and, in this distorted form, it was distributed by the *Rand Daily Mail* to other morning newspapers throughout the country — a deliberate act of sabotage.

This sudden somersault was not confined to the *Rand Daily Mail* only. With the exception of *Contact, Post, New Age, Drum,* the *World** and a few other newspapers, the Opposition press changed suddenly and simultaneously.

Undue prominence was given to statements made by government leaders, mayors of cities, managers of Non-European Affairs departments, and by employers' organisations, in which the stay-at-home was condemned and appeals made to workers to ignore the call. Statements made by the NAC were either distorted, watered down, or even suppressed deliberately. For example, on 20 May 1961 the NAC issued a press statement strongly protesting at the unwarranted arrest of more than ten thousand innocent Africans. We condemned this police action as a blatant persecution of our voteless people by a European minority which we could no longer tolerate. We placed on record that we were deeply incensed by this provocative action and demanded the immediate stopping of the arrests and the unconditional release of all those detained. Not a single Opposition newspaper published this statement, notwithstanding the extensive publicity they gave this police operation and the unwarranted compliment they paid to the same police for the courteous manner in which they were alleged to have carried out the operation. These arrests were made for the purpose of forestalling demonstrations planned by us. We had gone through numerous road blocks in various parts of the country, and it was our people who had been rounded up under a system which is rejected by the entire African nation, and which has been condemned by every government commission which considered it. Was it not important for the country to know what our views were on a matter of such importance?

The press was even more treacherous on the morning of the first day of the stay-at-home. The deliberate falsehoods spread by the police and radio were reproduced. At seven o'clock in the morning of that day, Radio South Africa broadcast news that workers throughout the country had ignored the call for a

---

*Journals reflecting anti-apartheid views or with predominantly black readerships.

stay-at-home. The country was told that this news was based on statements made at six o'clock the same morning by Colonel Spengler, head of the Witwatersrand branch of the Special Branch. Similar statements made at approximately the same time by other police officers in different parts of the country were quoted. This means that long before the factory gates were opened and, in some areas, even before the workers boarded their trains and buses to work, the police had already announced that the stay-at-home had collapsed. I cannot imagine anything more fraudulent.

The *Rand Daily Mail* issued a special edition in which it almost echoed police reports. But the truth could not be suppressed for long. The Johannesburg *Star* of the same day reported that 'Early estimates of absenteeism in Johannesburg ranged from 40 per cent to 75 per cent.' This admission was only a small portion of the truth. As the days rolled by, news came through that hundreds of thousands of workers and students throughout the country had given massive support to the call. On 3 June 1961, *Post*, a Johannesburg Sunday newspaper with a huge circulation, published reports from its team of crack reporters and photographers who had kept a continuous watch on townships in different parts of South Africa and who conducted detailed personal investigations inside and outside of these areas. Said the newspaper: 'Many thousands of workers registered their protest against the Republic and the Government's refusal to cooperate with non-Whites. THEY DID NOT GO TO WORK. They disrupted much of South African commerce and industry. Some factories worked with skeleton staffs, others closed, and many other businesses were shut down for the three days.' The leading article of the *New Age** of 8 June 1961 acclaimed the stay-at-home as the most widespread general strike on a national scale that this country had ever seen.

Contact* of 1 June 1961 wrote: 'On Tuesday 50 per cent of Indian workers in Durban were still out. Some factories showed 100 per cent success with some clothing factories 100 per cent unattended. In Durban and Pietermaritzburg most Indian businesses were closed on Monday and open again on Tuesday. Large numbers of schoolchildren kept away from school. There were attacks on buses at Cato Manor and a bus to Pietermaritzburg from a Reserve was fired on.' Sam Sly, writing in the same paper on 15 June 1961, observed: 'In defiance of that sickening and sterile rule, there were plenty of politics on plenty of campuses. Enough to bring large bands of armed police to five campuses. There was defiance, leadership, and courage amongst the students. There was political awareness, even non-racial solidarity. Before, what had one heard but minority protests lost among the sounds of the inter-varsity rugby crowd or the chatter in the students' cafeteria.'

A Port Elizabeth daily newspaper estimated that about 75 per cent of that city's non-White population stayed away on 30 May 1961.

---

*New Age was the newspaper of the Congress Movement; *Contact* that of the Liberal Party.

110

The truth had come out. From various parts of the country news came through testifying to widespread support for the call.

Students at the University College of Fort Hare, at Healdtown and Lovedale all stayed away from classes. At the University of Natal, which has about five hundred non-White students, less than fifty attended classes. Throughout the country thousands of students in primary and secondary schools stayed away from classes and boycotted republican celebrations. The Transkeian Territories have been under martial law for many months now.* The barbarous and cruel policies of the Nationalist Government find expression in extremely savage attacks on the innocent and unarmed people of these areas. Many have been murdered by the government and their stooges, thousands have been beaten up and injured, uprooted and driven away from their lands and homes. Hundreds of freedom fighters are languishing in jails for demanding freedom and justice for the people of the Transkei. Even in this area of death and hell, the flames of freedom are scorching meadows. Umtata, the capital of the area, bore witness to this fact the other day. Students of St John's College, in a militant and inspiring demonstration, showed that the days of despots and tyrants are numbered.

A detailed survey conducted by the South African Congress of Trade Unions shows that in Johannesburg, Durban, Port Elizabeth, Cape Town and other centres, the clothing, textile, laundry and dry-cleaning, food and canning, and furniture industries were severely hit.

In the light of the conditions that prevailed both before and during the three-day strike, the response from our people was magnificent indeed. The failure of the government, the employers, and the press to break us down pays tribute to the matchless courage and determination of our people and to the skilful and speedy manner in which our organisational machine was able to adapt itself to new conditions, new obstacles, new dangers.

The stay-at-home was also opposed by former members** of the Pan-Africanist Congress (PAC), the Society of Young Africa and the Sons of Zululand. The name of Peter Makhene was also mentioned. He was described as leader of the Bantu National Congress and claimed a membership of fifty thousand. The newspaper that published his statement made it clear that this gentleman is a supporter of the government and its policies. It is, therefore, part of his functions to sell apartheid to Africans. He is compelled to oppose all political organisations which fight for the defeat of the Verwoerd fascist republic. But what we want to know is where and when was this organisation established. Has it any constitution? Who are its officials? Has it had any conferences or meetings? If so, when and where? People

---

*Proclamations R400 and R413, declaring a state of emergency in the Transkei, were promulgated on 30 November and 14 December 1960. They remained in force and some of their key provisions were later incorporated into the Transkei Public Security Act of 1977.

**The term 'former members' was used to describe members of both the ANC and the PAC after the two organisations had been banned. It does not imply that the people concerned had left the organisation.

will be excused if they feel that this organisation went underground long before it was established. It simply does not exist.

The Sons of Zululand and the Society of Young Africa are not genuine organisations but cliques and sects which are completely unknown to Africans and which have never had any following whatsoever amongst our people.

The Society of Young Africa (or SOYA), like its parent body the Unity Movement from which it broke away a few years ago, is an insignificant sect of bitter and frustrated intellectuals who have completely lost confidence in themselves, who have no political ambitions whatsoever and who abhor serious political struggle. In the whole history of their existence they have never found it possible to rise above the level of saboteurs and scandalmongers. Together with the Peter Makhenes and the Sons of Zululand they invariably disappear from the political scene and suddenly come to light fighting side by side with the police to oppose the just struggles of the African people. Africans know who their friends and enemies are and these cliques are treated throughout the country with the contempt they deserve. No useful purpose will be served by wasting more ink and paper on bogus organisations which, under the pretext of ultra-revolutionary language, permit themselves to be used by the police against the struggles of their kith and kin.

The attitude of former members of the PAC on the stay-at-home has been one of shocking contradiction and amazing confusion. Nothing has been more disastrous to themselves than their pathetic attempts to sabotage the demonstrations.

First, they attended the Consultative Conference of African leaders held in Orlando in December 1960 as delegates, took part in the deliberations and fully supported the resolution adopted at that conference calling for unity amongst Africans and for a multi-racial national convention. At this conference a Continuation Committee was elected to prepare for the All-in African Conference which was subsequently held at Pietermaritzburg. Their representative served on this committee for several months with full knowledge that its main function was to unite all Africans on an anti-Republican front and for a sovereign convention of all South Africans to draw up a new democratic constitution for the country. Towards the end of February this year, and without so much as a hint to their colleagues on the Continuation Committee, they issued a press statement announcing that they would not take part in the Pietermaritzburg talks. Their failure to raise the matter in the committee before they withdrew betrays the underhand and traitorous nature of this manoeuvre and indicates that they well knew that they could find no political justification whatsoever for their action.

Secondly, there was a sharp conflict between former leaders of the PAC on the South African United Front overseas, and the local leaders. Whilst the latter opposed, the former gave support. A message from Dar-es-Salaam, signed by J J Hadebe and Gaur Radebe, former members of the ANC and PAC respectively, said:

'The South African United Front congratulates the Continuation Committee of the people's conference held at Pietermaritzburg for organising demonstrations on the eve of the South African Republic which threatens to further oppress and persecute the people.'

Even locally there were many former PAC people who bitterly disagreed with their leaders and who felt that they could not follow the stupid and disastrous blunders they were advocating.

But there was something even more disastrous and tragic than their mean and cowardly behaviour in stabbing their kith and kin at a time when maximum unity had become a matter of life and death to Africans. What shocked most people was the extent to which they completely identified themselves with the action of the police in the repression of the demonstrations. We have already indicated the unprecedented measures adopted by the government to deal with our campaign. These measures provoked strong protests from many organisations and individuals, but there was not a single word of protest from the former PAC people. Why? Precisely because their main function was to ruin African unity and to break the strike. To protest against these savage onslaughts on the African people would have been an unfriendly act to the government with whom they were now allied. They purchased collaboration with the government as the price of turning a deaf ear to the sufferings of the African people.

Authentic reports from different parts of the country revealed that the police did not interfere with the distribution of PAC leaflets and, in some areas, members of the police force even distributed leaflets purporting to have been issued by the PAC and attacking the strike.

This collaboration was not confined to negative acts of passivity. In its positive form it expressed itself in desperate attempts both by the police and the PAC people to track down the people behind the campaign. For security reasons, the identity of members of the NAC was kept a closely guarded secret. The police conducted extensive investigations to find this information in order to arrest members of this body. At the same time the PAC people called on us to publish the information and protested that we had to communicate with the press from public telephone booths. Why were they interested in this information? They knew all the members of the Continuation Committee. They withdrew from that committee and from the campaign not because they did not know its members but in spite of that knowledge. Such information was useless to them because they were out of the campaign but extremely useful to the police. On which side of the fence are these people? What sort of political organisation is this that deliberately sets traps for leaders of another political body? Who are they trying to bluff by pretending that they are still against the government and fighting for the welfare of the African people?

Differences between rival political organisations in the liberation camp on tactical questions are permissible. But for a political body which purports to be part of the liberation struggle to pursue a line which objectively supports a government that suppresses Africans is treacherous and unforgivable. We called on the African people to reject the Verwoerd republic not because we preferred a monarchical form of government, but because we felt that the introduction of a republic should only take place after seeking the views and after obtaining the express consent of the African people. We felt that the foundations of the republic, as of the State that existed prior to the proclamation of the republic, would be based on apartheid and the exploitation of the African people. The government rejected our demands, called upon the African people to ignore our call and to participate fully in the republican celebrations and to co-operate with the new government. The Africanists echoed the government by asking Africans to ignore the call but deliberately elected to remain silent on the vital question whether or not they should co-operate with the republic. An ingenious way of saying that we should participate and co-operate.

A political organisation that is forced by opportunism and petty political rivalries into allying itself with the enemies of an oppressed community is doomed. The African people demand freedom and self-rule. They refuse to co-operate with the Verwoerd republic or with any government based upon force. PAC has ruined its future by opposing this dynamic demand. That is why most Africans, including many who once supported them, are so strong in condemning their treachery.

But all this discussion has now become academic because for all practical purposes the PAC has lost considerable support even in areas where only last year it achieved spectacular success. In February this year they announced plans to stage demonstrations from 21 March 1961.* Leaflets were issued in Cape Town and were widely distributed in Langa and Nyanga African townships calling upon people to stock food and to prepare themselves for action on this date. In Johannesburg and Vereeniging stickers appeared here and there calling upon Africans to observe 21 March as the day of struggle. The whole thing fizzled out long before the much-heralded day, and when the date arrived not a single person responded either in Cape Town, Vereeniging, or Johannesburg. The episode was not regarded as sufficiently newsworthy even to be mentioned as a failure by the press either here or abroad. For the second time in two months they have suffered yet another defeat. Their efforts to sabotage the recent strike misfired badly. Hundreds of thousands of workers throughout the country, businessmen in town and country and thousands upon thousands of students in primary and secondary schools, treated the PAC with utter contempt and responded magnificently to our call. The results prove that no power on earth can stop an oppressed population determined to win its freedom. In the meantime, the PAC has been shocked and stunned by this rebuff and they sit licking their wounds, unable to look people in the face and haunted by the enormity of their outrageous crime.

One of the most significant factors about the stay-at-home was the wide support it received from students and the militant and stirring demonstrations it

---

*The first anniversary of the shootings at Sharpeville.

114

inspired amongst them. African students at Fort Hare, Natal University, Lovedale, Healdtown and in many other institutions throughout the country demonstrated their support for the call and stayed away from lectures. In primary and secondary schools throughout the country, scholars boycotted republican celebrations, refused commemoration medals, and stayed away from schools. There were militant and inspiring demonstrations at St John's College at Umtata and at the Botha Sigcau College in the Transkei. There were equally impressive ones in Kilnerton and Bloemfontein. This is an extremely significant development because students are the life-blood of a political movement and the upsurge of national consciousness amongst them spells death and destruction to those who oppose the claims and legitimate aspirations of the African people.

European students at the University of Rhodes, and at the Witwatersrand University, also played a prominent part in the demonstrations. Their support showed that even amongst the Whites the forces of challenge and opposition to White supremacy exist and are ready to join battle whenever the call is made.

On 1 June 1961, the NAC issued a press statement strongly condemning the victimisation of students who participated in the strike and demanded that the tyrannical orders for the closing of some of the colleges should be withdrawn and the colleges reopened at once. We congratulated the students for their public-spirited action in which, as befits the intellectual youth, they gave a courageous lead to the nation at a time when courage and leadership were qualities we needed most. However much the authorities may try to play down the importance and significance of this development amongst the African youth, there can be no doubt that they realise that the writing is on the wall and that the days of White supremacy in our country are numbered.

The response of the Coloured people was equally impressive. They showed immense courage and militancy. In a country where they have always been treated as an appendage of the ruling White group and in which official policy had tended to treat them differently from the rest of the non-White population, it is significant and most heartening that they decided to make common cause with us by coming out clearly against the Verwoerd republic. This development marks a landmark in the political struggles of the non-Whites in this country.

The entire Indian community threw its powerful resources behind the campaign. Indian workers stayed away from work. Businessmen closed their businesses and students stayed away from schools and refused medals.

The forces of liberation are strong and powerful and their numbers are growing. The morale is high and we look forward to the future with perfect confidence.

It would, however, be a mistake to exaggerate our success. In spite of the magnificent courage shown by our people, numerical response fell below expectations. Mistakes were committed and weaknesses and shortcomings were discovered. They must be attended to. We must make adjustments in our methods and style of work to meet contingencies which we did not anticipate.

Only in this way shall we build more strength and increase our striking power.

People expressed the view that the issue on which the people were asked to strike, namely, the demand for a national convention, lacked emotional appeal and was, in any event, too complicated an issue to arouse enthusiasm. Facts contradict this viewpoint. The success of the Pietermaritzburg conference and the deep and widespread support for the eve of the Republic demonstrations, testified to not only by our organisers and activists, but by the South African press, and the fact that hundreds of thousands of people stayed away from work notwithstanding fierce intimidation by the government and threats of dismissal by employers, indicate that this issue aroused the greatest enthusiasm. What reduced the scope and extent of what would have been an unprecedented response were the drastic measures taken by the government to suppress the strike, intimidation by employers, and the falsehoods spread by the radio and the press.

A closely related argument is that the demand for a national convention does not deal with bread-and-butter issues. Of course the African people want bread and butter. Is there anybody who does not? We demand higher wages and we want more and better food in our pantries. But we also need the vote to legislate decent laws. This is the importance of the demand for a national convention. One man, one vote, is the key to our future.

Another argument is that the strike was called by an *ad hoc* committee whose members were unknown to the public, that the voice of Chief A J Lutuli, the most powerful and popular leader of the African people, and that of the African National Congress, the sword and shield of the African people for the last fifty years, were never heard. The argument continues that the public may have doubted whether the African leaders were in fact behind the demonstration. In the first place, Chief Lutuli was a member of the Continuation Committee which organised the Pietermaritzburg conference and he sent a dynamic message to that gathering which was loudly cheered. In the second place, the names of members of the NAC were, for obvious reasons, never published and the public may never know whether or not Chief Lutuli was a member. It would have been naive for us to have stood on the mountain tops and proclaimed that he was a member directing his forces as he has always done in previous campaigns. His courage and devotion to the cause of freedom is known in every household in this country. Inside and outside committees he remains the undisputed and most respected leader of the African people and a source of tremendous inspiration to all South African freedom fighters. He is a fearless opponent of the Nationalist government and leader of all the anti-Republican forces.

Of all the observations made on the strike, none has brought forth so much heat and emotion as the stress and emphasis we put on non-violence. Our most loyal supporters, whose courage and devotion has never been doubted, unanimously and strenuously disagreed with this approach and with the assurances we gave that we would not use any form of intimidation whatsoever to induce people to stay away from work. It was argued that the soil of our beloved

116

country has been stained with the priceless blood of African patriots murdered by the Nationalist government in the course of peaceful and disciplined demonstrations to assert their claims and legitimate aspirations. It was the government that should have been told to refrain from its inhuman policy of violence and massacre, not the African people. It was further argued that it is wrong and indefensible for a political organisation to repudiate picketing, which is used the world over as a legitimate form of pressure to prevent scabbing.

Even up to the present day the question that is being asked with monotonous regularity up and down the country is this: is it politically correct to continue preaching peace and non-violence when dealing with a government whose barbaric practices have brought so much suffering and misery to Africans? With equal monotony the question is posed: have we not closed a chapter on this question? These are crucial questions that merit sane and sober reflection. It would be a serious mistake to brush them aside and leave them unanswered.

Numerous other observations were made by members of the public, by organisations and individuals, by sympathetic journals who have given us support and encouragement and by our own followers. All these have been noted. We appreciate that they were made in all humility with a view to better planning and more efficiency next time.

In rounding up this review we wish to congratulate once again all those patriotic workers, businesssmen and students, black and white, who took part in this dynamic and historic demonstration and we compliment them most heartily for their courage in the face of fierce opposition and intimidation. This patriotism, this unity and this fearless spirit are the most precious investment this country has.

The strike at the end of May was only the beginning of our campaign. We are now launching a full-scale, countrywide campaign of non-co-operation with the Verwoerd government, until we have won an elected National Convention, representing all the people of this country, with the power to draw up and enforce a new democratic constitution.

Details of the campaign will be given from time to time. But let me say now that people without votes cannot be expected to go on paying taxes to a government of White domination. People who live in poverty cannot be expected to pay rents under threats of criminal prosecution and imprisonment. Above all, those who are oppressed cannot tolerate a situation where their own people man and maintain the machinery of their own national oppression. Africans cannot serve on school boards and school committees which are part of the Nationalists' Bantu Education. This is meant to deprive Africans of true education.

Only traitors can serve on tribal councils. These are a mockery of self-government. They are meant to keep us forever in a state of slavery to Whites. We shall fight together tooth and nail, against the government plan to bring Bantu Authorities to the cities, just as our people in the rural areas have fought.

Africans cannot continue to carry passes. Thousands of our people are sent away to jail every month under the pass laws.

We ask our millions of friends outside South Africa to intensify the boycott and isolation of the government of this country, diplomatically, economically, and in every other way. The mines, industries, and farms of this country cannot carry on without the labour of Africans imported from elsewhere in Africa.

We are the people of this country. We produce the wealth of the gold mines, of the farms, and of industry. Non-collaboration is the weapon we must use to bring down the government. We have decided to use it fully and without reservation.

8. 'THE STRUGGLE IS MY LIFE': PRESS STATEMENT

Issued by Mandela on 26 June 1961 from inside South Africa, explaining his decision, in accordance with the advice of the National Action Council, to carry on his political work underground.

Published by the ANC in London.

The magnificent response to the call of the National Action Council for a three-day strike and the wonderful work done by our organisers and field workers throughout the country proves once again that no power on earth can stop an oppressed people determined to win their freedom. In the face of unprecedented intimidation by the government and employers and of blatant falsehoods and distortions by the press, immediately before and during the strike, the freedom-loving people of South Africa gave massive and solid support to the historic and challenging resolutions of the Pietermaritzburg Conference. Factory and office workers, businessmen in town and country, students in university colleges, in primary and secondary schools, inspired by genuine patriotism and threatened with loss of employment, cancellation of business licences and the ruin of school careers, rose to the occasion and recorded in emphatic tones their opposition to a White republic forcibly imposed on us by a minority. In the light of the formidable array of hostile forces that stood against us, and the difficult and dangerous conditions under which we worked, the results were most inspiring. I am confident that if we work harder and more systematically, the Nationalist government will not survive for long. No organisation in the world could have withstood and survived the full-scale and massive bombardment directed against us by the government during the last month.

In the history of our country no political campaign has ever merited the serious attention and respect which the Nationalist government gave us. When a government seeks to suppress a peaceful demonstration of an unarmed people by mobilising the entire resources of the State, military and otherwise, it concedes powerful mass support for such a demonstration. Could there be any other evidence to prove that we have become a power to be reckoned with and the strongest opposition to the government? Who can deny the plain fact that ever since the end of last month the issue that dominated South African politics was not the republican celebrations, but our plans for a general strike?

Today is 26 June, a day known throughout the length and breadth of our country as Freedom Day. On this memorable day, nine years ago, eight thousand five hundred of our dedicated freedom fighters struck a mighty blow against the repressive colour policies of the government. Their matchless courage won them the praise and affection of millions of people here and abroad. Since then we have had many stirring campaigns on this date and it has been observed by hundreds of thousands of our people as a day of dedication. It is fit and proper that on this historic day I should speak to you and announce fresh plans for the opening of the second phase in the fight against the Verwoerd republic, and for a National Convention.

You will remember that the Pietermaritzburg Resolutions warned that if the government did not call a National Convention before the end of May, 1961, Africans, Coloureds, Indians and European democrats would be asked not to collaborate with the republic or any government based on force. On several occasions since then the National Action Council explained that the last strike marked the beginning of a relentless mass struggle for the defeat of the Nationalist government, and for a sovereign multi-racial convention. We stressed that the strike would be followed by other forms of mass pressure to force the race maniacs who govern our beloved country to make way for a democratic government of the people, by the people and for the people. A full-scale and country-wide campaign of non-co-operation with the government will be launched immediately. The precise form of the contemplated action, its scope and dimensions and duration will be announced to you at the appropriate time.

At the present moment it is sufficient to say that we plan to make government impossible. Those who are voteless cannot be expected to continue paying taxes to a government which is not responsible to them. People who live in poverty and starvation cannot be expected to pay exorbitant house rents to the government and local authorities. We furnish the sinews of agriculture and industry. We produce the work of the gold mines, the diamonds and the coal, of the farms and industry, in return for miserable wages. Why should we continue enriching those who steal the products of our sweat and blood? Those who exploit us and refuse us the right to organise trade unions? Those who side with the government when we stage peaceful demonstrations to assert our claims and aspirations? How can Africans serve on School Boards and Committees which are part of Bantu Education, a sinister scheme of the Nationalist government to deprive the African people of real education in return for tribal education? Can Africans be expected to be content with serving on Advisory Boards and Bantu Authorities when the demand all over the continent of Africa is for national independence and self-government? Is it not an affront to the African people that the government should now seek to extend Bantu Authorities to the cities, when people in the rural areas have refused to accept the same system and fought against it tooth and nail? Which African does not burn with indignation when thousands of our people are sent to gaol every month under the cruel pass laws? Why should we continue carrying these badges of slavery? Non-collaboration is a dynamic weapon. We must refuse. We must use it to send this government to the grave. It must be used vigorously and without delay. The entire resources of the Black people must be mobilised to withdraw all co-operation with the Nationalist government. Various forms of industrial and economic action will be employed to undermine the already tottering economy of the country. We will call upon the international bodies to expel South Africa and upon nations of the world to sever economic and diplomatic relations with the country.

I am informed that a warrant for my arrest has been issued, and that the police are looking for me. The National Action Council has given full and serious consideration to this question, and has sought the advice of many trusted friends and

120

bodies and they have advised me not to surrender myself. I have accepted this advice, and will not give myself up to a government I do not recognise. Any serious politician will realise that under present-day conditions in this country, to seek for cheap martyrdom by handing myself to the police is naive and criminal. We have an important programme before us and it is important to carry it out very seriously and without delay.

I have chosen this latter course, which is more difficult and which entails more risk and hardship than sitting in gaol. I have had to separate myself from my dear wife and children, from my mother and sisters, to live as an outlaw in my own land. I have had to close my business, to abandon my profession, and live in poverty and misery, as many of my people are doing. I will continue to act as the spokesman of the National Action Council during the phase that is unfolding and in the tough struggles that lie ahead. I shall fight the government side by side with you, inch by inch, and mile by mile, until victory is won. What are you going to do? Will you come along with us, or are you going to co-operate with the government in its efforts to suppress the claims and aspirations of your own people? Or are you going to remain silent and neutral in a matter of life and death to my people, to our people? For my own part I have made my choice. I will not leave South Africa, nor will I surrender. Only through hardship, sacrifice and militant action can freedom be won. The struggle is my life. I will continue fighting for freedom until the end of my days.

Six months after going underground, Mandela was asked by the ANC to leave South Africa temporarily to attend the Conference of the Pan African Freedom Movement of East and Central Africa in Addis Ababa, Ethiopia. He left the country secretly and therefore, according to South African law, illegally.

9. ARMED STRUGGLE

On 16 December 1961 acts of sabotage marked the emergence of Umkhonto we Sizwe (Spear of the Nation) which was later to become the armed wing of the ANC. Mandela was a founder member and Commander-in-Chief of Umkhonto (MK).

The explosions were accompanied by the distribution of the Umkhonto we Sizwe manifesto.

9(a) UMKHONTO WE SIZWE MANIFESTO, 1961‡

Leaflet issued by Umkhonto we Sizwe (Spear of the Nation) on 16 December 1961.*

Units of Umkhonto we Sizwe today carried out planned attacks against government installations, particularly those connected with the policy of apartheid and race discrimination.

Umkhonto we Sizwe is a new, independent body, formed by Africans. It includes in its ranks South Africans of all races. It is not connected in any way with a so-called 'Committee for National Liberation' whose existence has been announced in the press. Umkhonto we Sizwe will carry on the struggle for freedom and democracy by new methods, which are necessary to complement the actions of the established national liberation organisations. Umkhonto we Sizwe fully supports the national liberation movement, and our members, jointly and individually, place themselves under the overall political guidance of that movement.

It is, however, well known that the main national liberation organisations in this country have consistently followed a policy of non-violence. They have conducted themselves peaceably at all times, regardless of government attacks and persecutions upon them, and despite all government-inspired attempts to provoke them to violence. They have done so because the people prefer peaceful methods of change to achieve their aspirations without the suffering and bitterness of civil war. But the people's patience is not endless.

The time comes in the life of any nation when there remain only two choices: submit or fight. That time has now come to South Africa. We shall not submit and we have no choice but to hit back by all means within our power in defence of our people, our future and our freedom.

---

*The date, 16 December, was made an official public holiday in South Africa commemorating the so-called 'Battle of Blood River' in Natal in 1838, where a bloody engagement was fought between the Afrikaners and the armies of Dingane, the Zulu King. For many years, it was known as 'Dingane's Day'. When the Nationalist Party came to power in 1948 they changed the name to 'Day of the Covenant', indicating their belief that the victory of the Whites had been the result of a covenant between them and God, in which they had pledged to build a church if they were victorious. For them the day is symbolic of white ascendancy over the black majority. In fact the battle was militarily inconclusive. Zulu military power was only broken later, by the British army.

The ANC observes 16 December as Heroes' Day, commemorating those who have lost their lives in the struggle against apartheid.

The government has interpreted the peacefulness of the movement as weakness; the people's non-violent policies have been taken as a green light for government violence. Refusal to resort to force has been interpreted by the government as an invitation to use armed force against the people without any fear of reprisals. The methods of Umkhonto we Sizwe mark a break with that past.

We are striking out along a new road for the liberation of the people of this country. The government policy of force, repression and violence will no longer be met with non-violent resistance only! The choice is not ours; it has been made by the Nationalist government, which has rejected every peaceable demand by the people for rights and freedom and answered every such demand with force and yet more force! Twice in the past eighteen months, virtual martial law has been imposed in order to beat down peaceful, non-violent strike action of the people in support of their rights. It is now preparing its forces — enlarging and rearming its armed forces and drawing the white civilian population into commandos and pistol clubs — for full-scale military actions against the people. The Nationalist government has chosen the course of force and massacre, now, deliberately, as it did at Sharpeville.

Umkhonto we Sizwe will be at the front line of the people's defence. It will be the fighting arm of the people against the government and its policies of race oppression. It will be the striking force of the people for liberty, for rights and for their final liberation! Let the government, its supporters who put it into power, and those whose passive toleration of reaction keeps it in power, take note of where the Nationalist government is leading the country!

We of Umkhonto we Sizwe have always sought — as the liberation movement has sought — to achieve liberation without bloodshed and civil clash. We do so still. We hope — even at this late hour — that our first actions will awaken everyone to a realisation of the disastrous situation to which the Nationalist policy is leading. We hope that we will bring the government and its supporters to their senses before it is too late, so that both the government and its policies can be changed before matters reach the desperate stage of civil war. We believe our actions to be a blow against the Nationalist preparations for civil war and military rule.

In these actions, we are working in the best interests of all the people of this country — black, brown and white — whose future happiness and well-being cannot be attained without the overthrow of the Nationalist government, the abolition of white supremacy and the winning of liberty, democracy and full national rights and equality for all the people of this country.

We appeal for the support and encouragement of all those South Africans who seek the happiness and freedom of the people of this country.

*Afrika Mayibuye!**

---

*Afrika Mayibuye = Africa Return!

9(b) ANC ADDRESS AT PAN-AFRICAN FREEDOM CONFERENCE, 1962‡

Address by Mandela on behalf of the ANC delegation to the Conference of the Pan-African Freedom Movement of East and Central Africa held in Addis Ababa in January 1962.

The delegation of the African National Congress, and I particularly, feel specially honoured by the invitation addressed to our organisation by the PAFMECA to attend this historic conference and to participate in its deliberations and decisions. The extension of the PAFMECA area to South Africa, the heart and core of imperialist reaction, should mark the beginning of a new phase in the drive for the total liberation of Africa — a phase which derives special significance from the entry into PAFMECA of the independent states of Ethiopia, Somalia, and Sudan.

It was not without reason, we believe, that the Secretariat of PAFMECA chose as the seat of this conference the great country of Ethiopia, which, with hundreds of years of colourful history behind it, can rightly claim to have paid the full price of freedom and independence. His Imperial Majesty, himself a rich and unfailing fountain of wisdom, has been foremost in promoting the cause of unity, independence, and progress in Africa, as was so amply demonstrated in the address he graciously delivered in opening this assembly. The deliberations of our conference will thus proceed in a setting most conducive to a scrupulous examination of the issues that are before us.

At the outset, our delegation wishes to place on record our sincere appreciation of the relentless efforts made by the independent African states and national movements in Africa and other parts of the world, to help the African people in South Africa in their just struggle for freedom and independence.

The movement for the boycott of South African goods and for the imposition of economic and diplomatic sanctions against South Africa has served to highlight most effectively the despotic structure of the power that rules South Africa, and has given tremendous inspiration to the liberation movement in our country. It is particularly gratifying to note that the four independent African states which are part of this conference, namely, Ethiopia, Somalia, Sudan and Tanganyika, are enforcing diplomatic and economic sanctions against South Africa. We also thank all those states that have given asylum and assistance to South African refugees of all shades of political beliefs and opinion. The warm affection with which South African freedom fighters are received by democratic countries all over the world, and the hospitality so frequently showered upon us by governments and political organisations, has made it possible for some of our people to escape persecution by the South African government, to travel freely from country to country and from continent to continent, to canvass our point of view and to rally support for our cause. We are indeed extremely grateful for this spontaneous demonstration of solidarity and support, and sincerely hope that each and every one of us will prove worthy of the trust and confidence the world has in us.

We believe that one of the main objectives of this conference is to work out concrete plans to speed up the struggle for the liberation of those territories in this region that are still under alien rule. In most of these territories the imperialist forces have been considerably weakened and are unable to resist the demand for freedom and independence — thanks to the powerful blows delivered by the freedom movements.

Although the national movements must remain alert and vigilant against all forms of imperialist intrigue and deception, there can be no doubt that imperialism is in full retreat and the attainment of independence by many of these countries has become an almost accomplished fact. Elsewhere, notably in South Africa, the liberation movement faces formidable difficulties and the struggle is likely to be long, complicated, hard, and bitter, requiring maximum unity of the national movement inside the country, and calling for level and earnest thinking on the part of its leaders, for skilful planning and intensive organisation.

South Africa is known throughout the world as a country where the most fierce forms of colour discrimination are practised, and where the peaceful struggles of the African people for freedom are violently suppressed. It is a country torn from top to bottom by fierce racial strife and conflict and where the blood of African patriots frequently flows.

Almost every African household in South Africa knows about the massacre of our people at Bulhoek, in the Queenstown district, where detachments of the army and police, armed with artillery, machine-guns, and rifles, opened fire on unarmed Africans, killing 163 persons, wounding 129, and during which 95 people were arrested simply because they refused to move from a piece of land on which they lived.*

Almost every African family remembers a similar massacre of our African brothers in South-West Africa when the South African government assembled aeroplanes, heavy machine-guns, artillery, and rifles, killing a hundred people and mutilating scores of others, merely because the Bondelswart people refused to pay dog tax.**

On 1 May 1950, 18 Africans were shot dead by the police in Johannesburg whilst striking peacefully for higher wages. The massacre at Sharpeville in March 1960 is a matter of common knowledge and is still fresh in our minds. According to a statement in parliament made by C R Swart, then Minister for Justice, between May 1948 and March 1954, 104 Africans were killed and 248 wounded by the police in the course of political demonstrations. By the middle of June 1960, these figures had risen to well over three hundred killed and five hundred wounded. Naked force and violence is the weapon openly used by the South African government to beat down the struggles of the African people and to suppress their aspirations.

The repressive policies of the South African government are reflected not only in the number of those African martyrs who perished from guns and bullets, but

---

*In 1921.
**In 1924.

in the merciless persecution of all political leaders and in the total repression of political opposition. Persecution of political leaders and suppression of political organisations became ever more violent under the Nationalist Party government. From 1952 the government used its legal powers to launch a full-scale attack on leaders of the African National Congress. Many of its prominent members were ordered by the government to resign permanently from it and never again participate in its activities. Others were prohibited from attending gatherings for specified periods ranging up to five years. Many were confined to certain districts, banished from their homes and families and even deported from the country.

In December 1956, Chief A J Lutuli, President-General of the ANC, was arrested together with 155 other freedom fighters and charged with treason. The trial which then followed is unprecedented in the history of the country, in both its magnitude and duration. It dragged on for over four years and drained our resources to the limit. In March 1960, after the murderous killing of about seventy Africans in Sharpeville, a state of emergency was declared and close on twenty thousand people were detained without trial. Even as we meet here today, martial law prevails throughout the territory of the Transkei, an area of 16,000 square miles with an African population of nearly two and a half million. The government stubbornly refuses to publish the names and number of persons detained. But it is estimated that close on two thousand Africans are presently languishing in jail in this area alone. Amongst these are to be found teachers, lawyers, doctors, clerks, workers from the towns, peasants from the country, and other freedom fighters. In this same area and during the last six months, more than thirty Africans have been sentenced to death by white judicial officers, hostile to our aspirations, for offences arising out of political demonstrations.

On 26 August 1961 the South African government even openly defied the British government when its police crossed into the neighbouring British protectorate of Basutoland* and kidnapped Anderson Ganyile, one of the country's rising freedom stars, who led the Pondo people's memorable struggles against apartheid tribal rule.

Apart from these specific instances, there are numerous other South African patriots, known and unknown, who have been sacrificed in various ways on the altar of African freedom.

This is but a brief and sketchy outline of the momentous struggle of the freedom fighters in our country, of the sacrifice they have made and of the price that is being paid at the present moment by those who keep the freedom flag flying.

For years our political organisations have been subjected to vicious attacks by the government. In 1957 there was considerable mass unrest and disturbances in the country districts of Zeerust, Sekhukhuniland, and Rustenburg. In all these

---

*Now Lesotho. Lesotho borders the Transkei area of South Africa where Ganyile was active.

126

areas there was widespread dissatisfaction with government policy and there were revolts against the pass laws, the poll tax, and government-inspired tribal authorities. Instead of meeting the legitimate political demands of the masses of the people and redressing their grievances, the government reacted by banning the ANC in all these districts. In April 1960 the government went further and completely outlawed both the African National Congress and the Pan-Africanist Congress. By resorting to these drastic methods the government had hoped to silence all opposition to its harsh policies and to remove all threats to the privileged position of the Whites in the country. It had hoped for days of perfect peace and comfort for White South Africa, free from revolt and revolution. It believe that through its strong-arm measures it could achieve what White South Africa has failed to accomplish during the last fifty years, namely, to compel Africans to accept the position that in our country freedom and happiness are the preserve of the White man.

But uneasy lies the head that wears the crown of White supremacy in South Africa. The banning and confinement of leaders, banishments and deportations, imprisonment and even death, have never deterred South African patriots. The very same day it was outlawed, the ANC issued a public statement announcing that it would definitely defy the government's ban and carry out operations from underground. The people of South Africa have adopted this declaration as their own and South Africa is today a land of turmoil and conflict.

In May last year a general strike was called. In the history of our country no strike has ever been organised under such formidable difficulties and dangers. The odds against us were tremendous. Our organisations were outlawed. Special legislation had been rushed through parliament empowering the government to round up its political opponents and to detain them without trial. One week before the strike ten thousand Africans were arrested and kept in jail until after the strike. All meetings were banned throughout the country and our field workers were trailed and hounded by members of the Security Branch. General mobilisation was ordered throughout the country and every available White man and woman put under arms. An English periodical described the situation on the eve of the strike in the following terms:

'In the country's biggest call-up since the war, scores of citizens' force and commando units were mobilised in the big towns. Camps were established at strategic points; heavy army vehicles carrying equipment and supplies moved in a steady stream along the Reef; helicopters hovered over African residential areas and trained searchlights on houses, yards, lands, and unlit areas. Hundreds of White civilians were sworn in as special constables, hundreds of white women spent weekends shooting at targets. Gun shops sold out of their stocks of revolvers and ammunition. All police leave was cancelled throughout the country. Armed guards were posted to protect power stations and other sources of essential services. Saracen armoured cars and troop carriers patrolled townships. Police vans patrolled areas and broadcast statements that Africans who struck work would be sacked and endorsed out of the town.'

This was the picture in South Africa on the eve of the general strike, but our people stood up to the test most magnificently. The response was less than we expected but we made solid and substantial achievements. Hundreds of thousands of workers stayed away from work and the country's industries and commerce were seriously damaged. Hundreds of thousands of students and schoolchildren did not go to school for the duration of the strike.

The celebrations which had been planned by the government to mark the inauguration of the republic were not only completely boycotted by the Africans, but were held in an atmosphere of tension and crisis in which the whole country looked like a military camp in a state of unrest and uncertainty. This panic-stricken show of force was a measure of the power of the liberation movement and yet it failed to stem the rising tide of popular discontent.

How strong is the freedom struggle in South Africa today? What role should PAFMECA play to strengthen the liberation movement in South Africa and speed up the liberation of our country? These are questions frequently put by those who have our welfare at heart.

The view has been expressed in some quarters outside South Africa that, in the special situation obtaining in our country, our people will never win freedom through their own efforts. Those who hold this view point to the formidable apparatus of force and coercion in the hands of the government, to the size of its armies, the fierce suppression of civil liberties, and the persecution of political opponents of the regime. Consequently, in these quarters, we are urged to look for our salvation beyond our borders.

Nothing could be further from the truth.

It is true that world opinion against the policies of the South African government has hardened considerably in recent years. The All African People's Conference held in Accra in 1958, the Positive Action Conference for Peace and Security in Africa, also held in Accra in April 1960, the Conference of Independent African States held in this famous capital in June of the same year, and the conferences at Casablanca and Monrovia last year, as well as the Lagos Conference this month, passed militant resolutions in which they sharply condemned and rejected the racial policies of the South African government. It has become clear to us that the whole of Africa is unanimously behind the move to ensure effective economic and diplomatic sanctions against the South African government.

At the international level, concrete action against South Africa found expression in the expulsion of South Africa from the Commonwealth, which was achieved with the active initiative and collaboration of the African members of the Commonwealth. These were Ghana, Nigeria, and Tanganyika (although the latter had not yet achieved its independence). Nigeria also took the initiative in moving for the expulsion of South Africa from the International Labour Organisation. But most significant was the draft resolution tabled at the fifteenth session of the United Nations which called for sanctions against South Africa. This resolution had the support of all the African members of the United Nations, with only one exception. The significance of the draft was not minimised by the fact that a milder resolution was finally adopted calling for individual or collective sanctions by member states. At the sixteenth session of the United Nations last year, the African states played a marvellous role in successfully carrying through the General Assembly a resolution against the address delivered by the South African Minister of Foreign Affairs, Mr Eric Louw, and subsequently in the moves calling for the expulsion of South Africa from the United Nations and for sanctions against her. Although the United Nations itself has neither expelled nor adopted sanctions against South Africa, many independent African states are in varying degrees enforcing economic and other sanctions against her. This increasing world pressure on South Africa has greatly weakened her international position and given a tremendous impetus to the freedom struggle inside the country. No less a danger to White minority rule and a guarantee of ultimate victory for us is the freedom struggle that is raging furiously beyond the borders of the South African territory; the rapid progress of Kenya, Uganda, and Zanzibar towards independence; the victories gained by the Nyasaland Malawi Congress; the unabated determination of Kenneth Kaunda's United National Independence Party (UNIP); the courage displayed by the freedom fighters of the Zimbabwe African People's Union (ZAPU), successor to the now banned National Democratic Party (NDP); the gallantry of the African crusaders in the Angolan war of liberation and the storm clouds forming around the excesses of Portuguese repression in Mozambique; the growing power of the independence movements in South-West Africa and the emergence of powerful political organisations in the High Commission territories* — all these are forces which cannot compromise with White domination anywhere.

But we believe it would be fatal to create the illusion that external pressures render it unnecessary for us to tackle the enemy from within. The centre and cornerstone of the struggle for freedom and democracy in South Africa lies inside South Africa itself. Apart from those required for essential work outside the country, freedom fighters are in great demand for work inside the country. We owe it as a duty to ourselves and to the freedom-loving peoples of the world to build and maintain in South Africa itself a powerful, solid movement, capable of surviving any attack by the government and sufficiently militant to fight back with a determination that comes from the knowledge and conviction that it is first and foremost by our own struggle and sacrifice inside South Africa itself that victory over White domination and apartheid can be won.

The struggle in the areas still subject to imperialist rule can be delayed and even defeated if it is unco-ordinated. Only by our combined efforts and united action can we repulse the multiple onslaughts of the imperialists and fight our way to victory. Our enemies fight collectively and combine to exploit our people.

The clear examples of collective imperialism have made themselves felt more and more in our region by the formation of an unholy alliance between the

---

*ie. the British Protectorates in Southern Africa, later Botswana, Lesotho and Swaziland.

governments of South Africa, Portugal, and the so-called Central African Federation. Hence these governments openly and shamelessly gave military assistance consisting of personnel and equipment to the traitorous Tshombe régime in Katanga.

At this very moment it has been widely reported that a secret defence agreement has been signed between Portugal, South Africa, and the Federation, following visits of Federation and South African defence ministers to Lisbon, the Federation defence minister to Luanda, and South African Defence Ministry delegations to Mozambique. Dr Salazar was quoted in the Johannesburg *Star* of 8 July 1961 as saying: 'Our relations — Mozambique's and Angola's on the one hand and the Federation and South Africa on the other — arise from the existence of our common borders and our traditional friendships that unite our Governments and our people. Our mutual interests are manifold and we are conscious of the need to cooperate to fulfil our common needs.'

Last year, Southern Rhodesian troops were training in South Africa and so were Rhodesian Air Force units. A military mission from South Africa and another from the Central African Federation visited Lourenço Marques in Mozambique, at the invitation of the Mozambique Army Command, and took part in training exercises in which several units totalling 2,600 men participated. These operations included dropping exercises for paratroopers.

A report in a South African aviation magazine, *Wings* (December 1961), states: 'The Portuguese are hastily building nine new aerodromes in Portuguese East Africa (Mozambique) following their troubles in Angola. The new 'dromes are all capable of taking jet fighters and are situated along or near the borders of Tanganyika and Nyasaland'; and gives full details.

Can anyone, therefore, doubt the role that the freedom movements should play in view of this hideous conspiracy?

As we have stated earlier, the freedom movement in South Africa believes that hard and swift blows should be delivered with the full weight of the masses of the people, who alone furnish us with one absolute guarantee that the freedom flames now burning in the country shall never be extinguished.

During the last ten years the African people in South Africa have fought many freedom battles, involving civil disobedience, strikes, protest marches, boycotts and demonstrations of all kinds. In all these campaigns we repeatedly stressed the importance of discipline, peaceful and non-violent struggle. We did so, firstly because we felt that there were still opportunities for peaceful struggle and we sincerely worked for peaceful changes. Secondly, we did not want to expose our people to situations where they might become easy targets for the trigger-happy police of South Africa. But the situation has now radically altered.

South Africa is now a land ruled by the gun. The government is increasing the size of its army, of the navy, of its air force, and the police. Pill-boxes and road blocks are being built up all over the country. Armament factories are being set up in Johannesburg and other cities. Officers of the South African army have visited Algeria and Angola where they were briefed exclusively on methods of suppressing popular struggles. All opportunities for peaceful agitation and struggle have been closed. Africans no longer have the freedom even to stay peacefully in their houses in protest against the oppressive policies of the government. During the strike in May last year the police went from house to house, beating up Africans and driving them to work.

Hence it is understandable why today many of our people are turning their faces away from the path of peace and non-violence. They feel that peace in our country must be considered already broken when a minority government maintains its authority over the majority by force and violence.

A crisis is developing in earnest in South Africa. However, no high command ever announces beforehand what its strategy and tactics will be to meet a situation. Certainly, the days of civil disobedience, of strikes, and mass demonstrations are not over and we will resort to them over and over again.

But a leadership commits a crime against its own people if it hesitates to sharpen its political weapons which have become less effective.

Regarding the actual situation pertaining today in South Africa I should mention that I have just come out of South Africa, having for the last ten months lived in my own country as an outlaw, away from family and friends. When I was compelled to lead this sort of life, I made a public statement in which I announced that I would not leave the country but would continue working underground. I meant it and I have honoured that undertaking. But when my organisation received the invitation to this conference it was decided that I should attempt to come out and attend the conference to furnish the various African leaders, leading sons of our continent, with the most up-to-date information about the situation.

During the past ten months I moved up and down my country and spoke to peasants in the countryside, to workers in the cities, to students and professional people. It dawned on me quite clearly that the situation had become explosive. It was not surprising therefore when one morning in October last year we woke up to read press reports of widespread sabotage involving the cutting of telephone wires and the blowing up of power pylons. The government remained unshaken and White South Africa tried to dismiss it as the work of criminals. Then on the night of 16 December last year the whole of South Africa vibrated under the heavy blows of Umkhonto we Sizwe (The Spear of the Nation). Government buildings were blasted with explosives in Johannesburg, the industrial heart of South Africa, in Port Elizabeth, and in Durban. It was now clear that this was a political demonstration of a formidable kind, and the press announced the beginning of planned acts of sabotage in the country. It was still a small beginning because a government as strong and as aggressive as that of South Africa can never be induced to part with political power by bomb explosions in one night and in three cities only. But in a country where freedom fighters frequently pay with their very lives and at a time when the most elaborate military preparations are being made to crush the people's struggles, planned acts of sabotage against government installations introduce a new phase in the political situation and are a demonstration of the people's unshakeable determination to win freedom whatever the cost may be. The government is preparing to strike viciously at political leaders and freedom fighters. But the people will not take these blows sitting down.

In such a grave situation it is fit and proper that this conference of PAFMECA should sound a clarion call to the struggling peoples in South Africa and other dependent areas, to close ranks, to stand firm as a rock and not allow themselves to be divided by petty political rivalries whilst their countries burn. At this critical moment in the history of struggle, unity amongst our people in South Africa and in the other territories has become as vital as the air we breathe and it should be preserved at all costs.

Finally, dear friends, I should assure you that the African people of South Africa, notwithstanding fierce persecution and untold suffering, in their ever-increasing courage will not for one single moment be diverted from the historic mission of liberating their country and winning freedom, lasting peace, and happiness.

We are confident that in the decisive struggles ahead, our liberation movement will receive the fullest support of PAFMECA and of all freedom-loving people throughout the world.

From Addis Ababa and a tour of Africa and Britain, Mandela returned to South Africa, to continue working underground. As police failed to capture him, 'he became known as the "Black Pimpernel", and fact and fantasy were joined in the stories about his daring that circulated in the African townships'. (Nelson Mandela, No Easy Walk to Freedom, *introd. Ruth First, Heinemann, London, 1964, p. 125).*

On 5 August 1962 he was arrested in Natal, and brought to trial in October.

10. 'BLACK MAN IN A WHITE COURT' FIRST COURT STATEMENT, 1962

Extracts from the court record of the trial of Mandela held in the Old Synagogue court, Pretoria, from 15 October to 7 November 1962. Mandela was accused on two counts, that of inciting persons to strike illegally (during the 1961 stay-at-home) and that of leaving the country without a valid passport. He conducted his own defence.

MANDELA: Your Worship, before I plead to the charge, there are one or two points I would like to raise.

Firstly, Your Worship will recall that this matter was postponed last Monday at my request until today, to enable Counsel to make the arrangements to be available here today.* Although Counsel is now available, after consultation with him and my attorneys, I have elected to conduct my own defence. Some time during the progress of these proceedings, I hope to be able to indicate that this case is a trial of the aspirations of the African people, and because of that I thought it proper to conduct my own defence. Nevertheless, I have decided to retain the services of Counsel, who will be here throughout these proceedings, and I also would like my attorney to be available in the course of these proceedings as well, but subject to that I will conduct my own defence.

The second point I would like to raise is an application which is addressed to Your Worship. Now at the outset, I want to make it perfectly clear that the remarks I am going to make are not addressed to Your Worship in his personal capacity, nor are they intended to reflect upon the integrity of the court. I hold Your Worship in high esteem and I do not for one single moment doubt your sense of fairness and justice. I must also mention that nothing I am going to raise in this application is intended to reflect against the Prosecutor in his personal capacity.

The point I wish to raise in my argument is based not on personal considerations, but on important questions that go beyond the scope of this present trial. I might also mention that in the course of this application I am frequently going to refer to the white man and the white people. I want at once to make it clear that I am no racialist, and I detest racialism, because I regard it as a barbaric thing, whether it comes from a black man or from a white man. The terminology that I am going to employ will be compelled on me by the nature of the application I am making.

I want to apply for Your Worship's recusal** from this case. I challenge the right of this court to hear my case on two grounds.

---

*Mandela had applied for a remand, because the trial had two and a half months previously been scheduled to take place in the Johannesburg Regional Court, where Mandela had arranged for his defence by advocate Joe Slovo. During the weekend before it opened, however, it was suddenly switched to Pretoria — and Slovo was restricted by a government banning order to the magisterial district of Johannesburg.

**Recusal = withdrawal from the case on grounds of prejudice.

Firstly, I challenge it because I fear that I will not be given a fair and proper trial. Secondly, I consider myself neither legally nor morally bound to obey laws made by a parliament in which I have no representation.

In a political trial such as this one, which involves a clash of the aspirations of the African people and those of whites, the country's courts, as presently constituted, cannot be impartial and fair.

In such cases, whites are interested parties. To have a white judicial officer presiding, however high his esteem, and however strong his sense of fairness and justice, is to make whites judges in their own case.

It is improper and against the elementary principles of justice to entrust whites with cases involving the denial by them of basic human rights to the African people.

What sort of justice is this that enables the aggrieved to sit in judgement over those against whom they have laid a charge?

A judiciary controlled entirely by whites and enforcing laws enacted by a white parliament in which Africans have no representation — laws which in most cases are passed in the face of unanimous opposition from Africans —

MAGISTRATE: I am wondering whether I shouldn't interfere with you at this stage, Mr Mandela. Aren't we going beyond the scope of the proceedings? After all is said and done, there is only one court today and that is the White Man's court. There is no other court. What purpose does it serve you to make an application when there is only one court, as you know yourself. What court do you wish to be tried by?

MANDELA: Well, Your Worship, firstly I would like Your Worship to bear in mind that in a series of cases our courts have laid it down that the right of a litigant to ask for a recusal of a judicial officer is an extremely important right, which must be given full protection by the court, as long as that right is exercised honestly. Now I honestly have apprehensions, as I am going to demonstrate just now, that this unfair discrimination throughout my life has been responsible for very grave injustices, and I am going to contend that that race discrimination which outside this court has been responsible for all my troubles, I fear in this court is going to do me the same injustice. Now Your Worship may disagree with that, but Your Worship is perfectly entitled, in fact, obliged to listen to me and because of that I feel that Your Worship —

MAGISTRATE: I would like to listen, but I would like you to give me the grounds for your application for me to recuse myself.

MANDELA: Well, these are the grounds, I am developing them, sir. If Your Worship will give me time —

MAGISTRATE: I don't wish to go out of the scope of the proceedings.

MANDELA: — Of the scope of the application. I am within the scope of the application, because I am putting forward grounds which in my opinion are likely not to give me a fair and proper trial.

MAGISTRATE: Anyway proceed.

MANDELA: As your Worship pleases. I was developing the point that a judiciary controlled entirely by whites and enforcing laws enacted by a white parliament in which we have no representation, laws which in most cases are passed in the face of unanimous opposition from Africans, cannot be regarded as an impartial tribunal in a political trial where an African stands as an accused.

The Universal Declaration of Human Rights provides that all men are equal before the law, and are entitled without any discrimination to equal protection of the law. In May 1951, Dr D F Malan, then Prime Minister, told the Union parliament that this provision of the Declaration applies in this country. Similar statements have been made on numerous occasions in the past by prominent whites in this country, including judges and magistrates. But the real truth is that there is in fact no equality before the law whatsoever as far as our people are concerned, and statements to the contrary are definitely incorrect and misleading.

It is true that an African who is charged in a court of law enjoys, on the surface, the same rights and privileges as an accused who is white in so far as the conduct of this trial is concerned. He is governed by the same rules of procedure and evidence as apply to a white accused. But it would be grossly inaccurate to conclude from this fact that an African consequently enjoys equality before the law.

In its proper meaning equality before the law means the right to participate in the making of the laws by which one is governed, a constitution which guarantees democratic rights to all sections of the population, the right to approach the court for protection or relief in the case of the violation of rights guaranteed in the constitution, and the right to take part in the administration of justice as judges, magistrates, attorneys-general, law advisers and similar positions.

In the absence of these safeguards the phrase 'equality before the law', in so far as it is intended to apply to us, is meaningless and misleading. All the rights and privileges to which I have referred are monopolised by whites, and we enjoy none of them.

The white man makes all the laws, he drags us before his courts and accuses us, and he sits in judgement over us.

It is fit and proper to raise the question sharply, what is this rigid colour-bar in the administration of justice? Why is it that in this courtroom I face a white magistrate, am confronted by a white prosecutor, and escorted into the dock by a white orderly? Can anyone honestly and seriously suggest that in this type of atmosphere the scales of justice are evenly balanced?

Why is it that no African in the history of this country has ever had the honour of being tried by his own kith and kin, by his own flesh and blood?

I will tell Your Worship why: the real purpose of this rigid colour-bar is to ensure that the justice dispensed by the courts should conform to the policy of the country, however much that policy might be in conflict with the norms of justice accepted in judiciaries throughout the civilised world.

I feel oppressed by the atmosphere of white domination that lurks all around in this courtroom. Somehow this atmosphere calls to mind the inhuman injustices caused to my people outside this courtroom by this same white domination.

It reminds me that I am voteless because there is a parliament in this country that is white-controlled. I am without land because the white minority has taken a lion's share of my country and forced me to occupy poverty-stricken Reserves, over-populated and over-stocked. We are ravaged by starvation and disease . . .

MAGISTRATE: What has that got to do with the case, Mr Mandela?

MANDELA: With the last point, Sir, it hangs together, if Your Worship will give me the chance to develop it.

MAGISTRATE: You have been developing it for quite a while now, and I feel you are going beyond the scope of your application.

MANDELA: Your Worship, this to me is an extremely important ground which the court must consider.

MAGISTRATE: I fully realise your position, Mr Mandela, but you must confine yourself to the application and not go beyond it. I don't want to know about starvation. That in my view has got nothing to do with the case at the present moment.

MANDELA: Well, Your Worship has already raised the point that here in this country there is only a white court. What is the point of all this? Now if I can demonstrate to Your Worship that outside this courtroom race discrimination has been used in such a way as to deprive me of my rights, not to treat me fairly, certainly this is a relevant fact from which to infer that wherever race discrimination is practised, this will be the same result, and this is the only reason why I am using this point.

MAGISTRATE: I am afraid that I will have to interrupt you, and you will have to confine yourself to the reasons, the real reasons for asking me to recuse myself.

MANDELA: Your Worship, the next point which I want to make is this: I raise the question, how can I be expected to believe that this same racial discrimination which has been the cause of so much injustice and suffering right through the years should now operate here to give me a fair and open trial? Is there no danger that an African accused may regard the courts not as impartial tribunals, dispensing justice without fear or favour, but as instruments used by the white man to punish those amongst us who clamour for deliverance from the fiery furnace of white rule. I have grave fears that this system of justice may enable the guilty to drag the innocent before the courts. It enables the unjust to prosecute and demand vengeance against the just. It may tend to lower the standards of fairness and justice applied in the country's courts by white judicial officers to black litigants. This is the first ground for this application: that I will not receive a fair and proper trial.

136

The second ground of my objection is that I consider myself neither morally nor legally obliged to obey laws made by a parliament in which I am not represented.

That the will of the people is the basis of the authority of government is a principle universally acknowledged as sacred throughout the civilised world, and constitutes the basic foundations of freedom and justice. It is understandable why citizens, who have the vote as well as the right to direct representation in the country's governing bodies, should be morally and legally bound by the laws governing the country.

It should be equally understandable why we, as Africans, should adopt the attitude that we are neither morally nor legally bound to obey laws which we have not made, nor can we be expected to have confidence in courts which enforce such laws.

I am aware that in many cases of this nature in the past, South African courts have upheld the right of the African people to work for democratic changes. Some of our judicial officers have even openly criticised the policy which refuses to acknowledge that all men are born free and equal, and fearlessly condemned the denial of opportunities to our people.

But such exceptions exist in spite of, not because of, the grotesque system of justice that has been built up in this country. These exceptions furnish yet another proof that even among the country's whites there are honest men whose sense of fairness and justice revolts against the cruelty perpetrated by their own white brothers to our people.

The existence of genuine democratic values among some of the country's whites in the judiciary, however slender they may be, is welcomed by me. But I have no illusions about the significance of this fact, healthy a sign as it might be. Such honest and upright whites are few and they have certainly not succeeded in convincing the vast majority of the rest of the white population that white supremacy leads to dangers and disaster.

However, it would be a hopeless commandant who relied for his victories on the few soldiers in the enemy camp who sympathise with his cause. A competent general pins his faith on the superior striking power he commands and on the justness of his cause which he must pursue uncompromisingly to the bitter end.

I hate race discrimination most intensely and in all its manifestations. I have fought it all during my life; I fight it now, and will do so until the end of my days. Even although I now happen to be tried by one whose opinion I hold in high esteem, I detest most violently the set-up that surrounds me here. It makes me feel that I am a black man in a white man's court. This should not be. I should feel perfectly at ease and at home with the assurance that I am being tried by a fellow South African who does not regard me as an inferior, entitled to a special type of justice.

This is not the type of atmosphere most conducive to feelings of security and confidence in the impartiality of a court.

The court might reply to this part of my argument by assuring me that it will try my case fairly and without fear or favour, that in deciding whether or not I am guilty of the offence charged by the State, the court will not be influenced by the colour of my skin or by any other improper motive.

That might well be so. But such a reply would completely miss the point of my argument.

As already indicated, my objection is not directed to Your Worship in his personal capacity, nor is it intended to reflect upon the integrity of the court. My objection is based upon the fact that our courts, as presently constituted, create grave doubts in the minds of an African accused, whether he will receive a fair and proper trial.

This doubt springs from objective facts relating to the practice of unfair discrimination against the black man in the constitution of the country's courts. Such doubts cannot be allayed by mere verbal assurances from a presiding officer, however sincere such assurances might be. There is only one way, and one way only, of allaying such doubts, namely, by removing unfair discrimination in judicial appointments. This is my first difficulty.

I have yet another difficulty about similar assurances Your Worship might give. Broadly speaking, Africans and whites in this country have no common standard of fairness, morality, and ethics, and it would be very difficult to determine on my part what standard of fairness and justice Your Worship has in mind.

In their relationship with us, South African whites regard it as fair and just to pursue policies which have outraged the conscience of mankind and of honest and upright men throughout the civilised world. They suppress our aspirations, bar our way to freedom, and deny us opportunities to promote our moral and material progress, to secure ourselves from fear and want. All the good things of life are reserved for the white folk and we blacks are expected to be content to nourish our bodies with such pieces of food as drop from the tables of men with white skins. This is the white man's standard of justice and fairness. Herein lies his conceptions of ethics. Whatever he himself may say in his defence, the white man's moral standards in this country must be judged by the extent to which he has condemned the vast majority of its inhabitants to serfdom and inferiority.

We, on the other hand, regard the struggle against colour discrimination and for the pursuit of freedom and happiness as the highest aspiration of all men. Through bitter experience, we have learnt to regard the white man as a harsh and merciless type of human being whose contempt for our rights, and whose utter indifference to the promotion of our welfare, makes his assurances to us absolutely meaningless and hypocritical.

I have the hope and confidence that Your Worship will not hear this objection lightly nor regard it as frivolous. I have decided to speak frankly and honestly because the injustice I have referred to contains the seeds of an extremely dangerous situation for our country and people. I make no threat when I say that unless these wrongs are remedied without delay, we might well find that even

138

plain talk before the country's courts is too timid a method to draw the attention of the country to our political demands.

Finally, I need only to say that the courts have said that the possibility of bias and not actual bias is all that needs be proved to ground an application of this nature. In this application I have merely referred to certain objective facts, from which I submit that the possibility be inferred that I will not receive a fair and proper trial.

MAGISTRATE: Mr Prosecutor, have you anything to say?

PROSECUTOR: Very briefly, Your Worship, I just wish to point out that there are certain legal grounds upon which an accused person is entitled to apply for the recusal of a judicial officer from the case in which he is to be tried. I submit that the Accused's application is not based on one of those principles, and I ask the Court to reject it.

MAGISTRATE: [*to Mandela*] Your application is dismissed. Will you now plead to your charges?

MANDELA: I plead NOT GUILTY to both charges, to all the charges.

Among the witnesses was Mr Barnard, the private secretary to the then Prime Minister, Dr H F Verwoerd, whom Mandela cross-examined on the subject of a letter sent by Mandela to the Prime Minister demanding a National Convention in May 1961. In cross-examining the witness, Mandela first read the contents of the letter:

'I am directed by the All-in African National Action Council to address your government in the following terms:

'The All-in African National Action Council was established in terms of a resolution adopted at a conference held at Pietermaritzburg on 25 and 26 March 1961. This conference was attended by 1,500 delegates from town and country, representing 145 religious, social, cultural, sporting, and political bodies.

'Conference noted that your government, after receiving a mandate from a section of the European population, decided to proclaim a republic on 31 May.

'It was the firm view of delegates that your government, which represents only a minority of the population in this country, is not entitled to take such a decision without first seeking the views and obtaining the express consent of the African people. Conference feared that under this proposed republic your government, which is already notorious the world over for its obnoxious policies, would continue to make even more savage attacks on the rights and living conditions of the African people.

'Conference carefully considered the grave political situation facing the African people today. Delegate after delegate drew attention to the vicious manner in which your government forced the people of Zeerust, Sekhukhuniland, Pondoland, Nongoma, Tembuland and other areas to accept the unpopular system of Bantu Authorities, and pointed to numerous facts and incidents which indicate the rapid manner in which race relations are deteriorating in this country.

'It was the earnest opinion of Conference that this dangerous situation could be averted only by the calling of a sovereign national convention representative of all South Africans, to draw up a new non-racial and democratic Constitution. Such a convention would discuss our national problems in a sane and sober manner, and would work out solutions which sought to preserve and safeguard the interests of all sections of the population.

'Conference unanimously decided to call upon your government to summon such a convention before 31 May.

'Conference further decided that unless your government calls the convention before the above-mentioned date, countrywide demonstrations would be held on the eve of the republic in protest. Conference also resolved that in addition to the demonstrations, the African people would be called upon to refuse to co-operate with the proposed republic.

'We attach the Resolutions of the Conference for your attention and necessary action.

'We now demand that your government call the convention before 31 May, failing which we propose to adopt the steps indicated in paragraphs 8 and 9 of this letter.

'These demonstrations will be conducted in a disciplined and peaceful manner.

'We are fully aware of the implications of this decision, and the action we propose taking. We have no illusions about the counter-measures your government might take in this matter. After all, South Africa and the world know that during the last thirteen years your government has subjected us to merciless and arbitrary rule. Hundreds of our people have been banned and confined to certain areas. Scores have been banished to remote parts of the country, and many arrested and jailed for a multitude of offences. It has become extremely difficult to hold meetings, and freedom of speech has been drastically curtailed. During the last twelve months we have gone through a period of grim dictatorship, during which seventy-five people were killed and hundreds injured while peacefully demonstrating against passes.

'Political organisations were declared unlawful, and thousands flung into jail without trial. Your government can only take these measures to suppress the forthcoming demonstrations, and these measures have failed to stop opposition to the policies of your government. We are not deterred by threats of force and violence made by you and your government, and will carry out our duty without flinching.'

MANDELA: You remember the contents of this letter?

WITNESS: I do.

MANDELA: Did you place this letter before your Prime Minister?

WITNESS: Yes.

MANDELA: On what date? Can you remember?

WITNESS: It is difficult to remember, but I gather from the date specified on the date stamp, the Prime Minister's Office date stamp.

MANDELA: That is 24 April. Now was any reply given to this letter by the Prime Minister? Did he reply to this letter?

WITNESS: He did not reply to the writer.

MANDELA: He did not reply to the letter. Now, will you agree that this letter raises matters of vital concern to the vast majority of the citizens of this country?

WITNESS: I do not agree.

MANDELA: You don't agree? You don't agree that the question of human rights, of civil liberties, is a matter of vital importance to the African people?

WITNESS: Yes, that is so, indeed.

MANDELA: Are these things mentioned here?

WITNESS: Yes, I think so.

MANDELA: They are mentioned. You agree that this letter deals with matters of vital importance to the African people in this country? You have already agreed that this letter raises questions like the rights of freedom, civil liberties, and so on?

WITNESS: Yes, the letter raises it.

MANDELA: Important questions to any citizen?

WITNESS: Yes.

MANDELA: Now, you know of course that Africans don't enjoy the rights demanded in this letter. They are denied the rights of government?

WITNESS: Some rights.

MANDELA: No African is a member of parliament?

WITNESS: That is right.

MANDELA: No African can be a member of the Provincial Council, of the Municipal Councils?

WITNESS: Yes.

MANDELA: Africans have no vote in this country?

WITNESS: They have got no vote as far as parliament is concerned.

MANDELA: Yes, that is what I am talking about, I am talking about parliament, and other government bodies of the country, the Provincial Councils, the Municipal Councils. They have no vote?

WITNESS: That is right.

MANDELA: Would you agree with me that in any civilised country in the world it would be at least most scandalous for a Prime Minister to fail to reply to a letter raising vital issues affecting the majority of the citizens of that country. Would you agree with that?

WITNESS: I don't agree with that.

MANDELA: You don't agree that it would be irregular for a Prime Minister to ignore a letter raising vital issues affecting the vast majority of the citizens of that country?

WITNESS: This letter has not been ignored by the Prime Minister.

MANDELA: Just answer the question. Do you regard it proper for a Prime Minister not to respond to pleas made in regard to vital issues by the vast majority of the citizens of the country? You say that is not wrong?

WITNESS: The Prime Minister did respond to the letter.

MANDELA: Mr Barnard, I don't want to be rude to you. Will you confine yourself to answering my questions? The question I am putting to you is, do you agree that it is most improper on the part of a Prime Minister not to reply to a communication raising vital issues affecting the vast majority of the country?

WITNESS: I do not agree in this special case, because . . .

MANDELA: As a general proposition? Would you regard it as improper, speaking generally, for a Prime Minister not to respond to a letter of this nature, that is, a letter raising vital issues affecting the majority of the citizens?

PROSECUTOR: (*Intervened with objections to the line of questioning*)

MANDELA: You say that the Prime Minister did not ignore this letter?

WITNESS: He did not acknowledge the letter to the writer.

MANDELA: This letter was not ignored by the Prime Minister?

WITNESS: No, it was not ignored.

MANDELA: It was attended to?

WITNESS: It was indeed.

MANDELA: In what way?

WITNESS: According to the usual procedure, and that is that the Prime Minister refers correspondence to the respective Minister, the Minister most responsible for that particular letter.

MANDELA: Was this letter referred to another Department?

WITNESS: That is right.

MANDELA: Which Department?

WITNESS: The Department of Justice.

MANDELA: Can you explain why I was not favoured with the courtesy of an acknowledgement of this letter, and also the explanation that it had been referred to the appropriate Department for attention?

WITNESS: When a letter is replied to and whether it should be replied to, depends on the contents of the letter in many instances.

MANDELA: My question is, can you explain to me why I was not favoured with the courtesy of an acknowledgement of the letter, irrespective of what the Prime Minister is going to do about it? Why was I not favoured with this courtesy?

WITNESS: Because of the contents of this letter.

MANDELA: Because it raises vital issues?

WITNESS: Because of the contents of the letter.

MANDELA: I see. This is not the type of thing the Prime Minister would ever consider responding to?

WITNESS: The Prime Minister did respond.

MANDELA: You say that the issues raised in this letter are not the type of thing your Prime Minister could ever respond to?

WITNESS: The whole tone of the letter was taken into consideration.

MANDELA: The tone of the letter demanding a National Convention? Of all South Africans? That is the tone of the letter? That is not the type of thing your Prime Minister could ever respond to?

WITNESS: The tone of the letter indicates whether, and to what extent, the Prime Minister responds to correspondence.

MANDELA: I want to put it to you that in failing to respond to this letter, your Prime Minister fell below the standards which one expects from one in such a position.

Now this letter, Exhibit 18, is dated 26 June 1961, and it is also addressed to the Prime Minister, and it reads as follows:

'I refer you to my letter of 20 April 1961, to which you do not have the courtesy to reply or acknowledge receipt. In the letter referred to above I informed you of the resolutions passed by the All-in African National Conference in Pietermaritzburg on 26 March 1961, demanding the calling by your government before 31 May 1961 of a multi-racial and sovereign National Convention to draw up a new non-racial and democratic Constitution for South Africa. The Conference Resolution which was attached to my letter indicated that if your government did not call this convention by the specific date, country-wide demonstrations would be staged to mark our protest against the White republic forcibly imposed on us by a minority. The Resolution further indicated that in addition to the demonstrations, the African people would be called upon not to co-operate with the republican government, or with any government based on force. As your government did not respond to our demands, the All-in African National Council, which was entrusted by the Conference with the task of implementing its resolutions, called for a General Strike on the 29, 30 and 31 of last month. As predicted in my letter of 30 April 1961, your government sought to suppress the strike by force. You rushed a special law in parliament authorising the detention without trial of people connected with the organisation of the strike. The army was mobilised and European civilians armed. More than ten thousand innocent Africans were arrested under the pass laws and meetings banned throughout the country. Long before the factory gates were opened on Monday, 29 May 1961, senior police officers and Nationalist South Africans spread a deliberate falsehood and announced that the strike had failed. All these measures failed to break the strike and our people stood up magnificently and gave us solid and substantial support. Factory and office workers, businessmen in town and country, students in university colleges, in the primary and secondary schools, rose to the occasion and recorded in clear terms their opposition to the republic. The government is guilty of self-deception if they say that non-Europeans did not respond to the call. Considerations of honesty demand of your government to realise that the African people who constitute four-fifths of the country's population are against your republic. As indicated above, the Pietermaritzburg resolution provided that in addition to the countrywide demonstrations, the African people would refuse to co-operate with the republic or any form of government based on force. Failure by your government to call the convention makes it imperative for us to launch a full-scale and countrywide campaign for non-co-operation with your government. There are two alternatives before you. Either you accede to our demands and call a National Convention of all South Africans to draw up a democratic Constitution, which will end the frightful policies of racial oppression pursued by your government. By pursuing this course and abandoning the repressive and dangerous policies of your government, you may still save our country from economic dislocation and ruin and from civil strife and bitterness. Alternatively, you may choose to persist with the present policies which are cruel and dishonest and which are opposed by millions of people here and abroad. For our own part, we wish to make it perfectly clear that we shall never cease to fight against repression and injustice, and we are resuming active opposition against your régime. In taking this decision we must again stress that we have no illusions of the serious implications of our decision. We know that your government will once again unleash all its fury and barbarity to persecute the African people. But as the result of the last strike has clearly proved, no power on earth can stop an oppressed people determined to win their freedom. History punishes those who resort to force and fraud to suppress the claims and legitimate aspirations of the majority of the country's citizens.'

MANDELA: This is the letter which you received on 28 June 1961? Again there was no acknowledgement or reply by the Prime Minister to this letter?

WITNESS: I don't think it is — I think it shouldn't be called a letter in the first instance, but an accumulation of threats.

MANDELA: Whatever it is, there was no reply to it?

WITNESS: No.

Another witness to be called was Warrant Officer Baardman, member of the police Special Branch in Bloemfontein. He was cross-examined by Mandela:

MANDELA: Is it true to say that the present constitution of South Africa was passed at a National Convention representing whites only?

WITNESS: I don't know, I was not there.

MANDELA: But from your knowledge?

WITNESS: I don't know, I was not there.

MANDELA: You don't know at all?

WITNESS: No, I don't know.

MANDELA: You want this court to believe that, that you don't know?

WITNESS: I don't know, I was not there.

MANDELA: Just let me put the question. You don't know that the National Convention in 1909 was a convention of whites only?

WITNESS: I don't know, I was not there.

MANDELA: Do you know that the Union Parliament is an all-White parliament?

WITNESS: Yes, with representation for non-Whites.

MANDELA: Now, I just want to ask you one or two personal questions. What standard of education have you passed?

WITNESS: Matriculation.

MANDELA: When was that?

WITNESS: In 1932.

MANDELA: In what medium did you write it?

WITNESS: In my mother tongue. (*Here the witness meant Afrikaans.*)

MANDELA: I notice you are very proud of this?

WITNESS: I am.

MANDELA: You know of course that in this country we have no language rights as Africans?

WITNESS: I don't agree with you.

MANDELA: None of our languages is an official language, for example. Would you agree with that?

WITNESS: They are perhaps not in the Statute Book as official languages, but no one forbids you from using your own language.

MANDELA: Will you answer the question? Is it true that in this country there are only two official languages, and they are English and Afrikaans?

WITNESS: I agree entirely. By name they are the two official languages, but no one has ever forbidden you to use your own language.

MANDELA: Is it true that there are only two official languages in this country, that is English and Afrikaans?

WITNESS: To please you, that is so.

MANDELA: Is it true that the Afrikaner people in this country have fought for equality of English and Afrikaans? There was a time, for example, when Afrikaans was not the official language in the history of the various colonies, like the Cape?

WITNESS: Yes, I agree with you entirely. Constitutionally, the Afrikaner did fight for his language but not through agitators.

On the third day of the trial Mandela again applied for the recusal of the magistrate.

MANDELA: I want to make application for the recusal of Your Worship from this case. As I indicated last Monday, I hold Your Worship in high esteem, and I do not for one single moment doubt Your Worship's sense of fairness and justice. I still do, as I assured Your Worship last Monday. I make this application with the greatest of respect. I have been placed in possession of information to the effect that after the adjournment yesterday, Your Worship was seen leaving the courtroom in the company of Warrant Officer Dirker of the Special Branch, and another member of the Special Branch. As Your Worship will remember, Warrant Officer Dirker gave evidence in this case on the first day of the trial. The State Prosecutor then indicated that he would be called later, on another aspect of this case. I was then given permission by the court to defer my cross-examination of this witness until then. The second member of the Special Branch who was in the company of Your Worship, has been seen throughout this trial assisting the State Prosecutor in presenting the case against me. Your Worship was seen entering a small blue Volkswagen car; it is believed that Your Worship sat in front, as Warrant Officer Dirker drove the car. And this other member of the Special Branch sat behind. At about ten to two Your Worship was seen returning with Warrant Officer Dirker and this other member of the Special Branch.

Now, it is not known what communication passed between Your Worship and Warrant Officer Dirker and this other member of the Special Branch. I, as an accused, was not there, and was not represented. Now, these facts have created an impression in my mind that the court has associated itself with the State case. I am left with the substantial fear that justice is being administered in a secret manner. It is an elementary rule of justice that a judicial officer should not communicate or associate in any manner whatsoever with a party to those proceedings. I submit that Your Worship should not have acted in this fashion, and I must therefore ask Your Worship to recuse yourself from this case.

MAGISTRATE: I can only say this, that it is not for me here to give you any reasons. I can assure you, as I here now do, that I did not communicate with these two gentlemen, and your application is refused.

Another police witness was Mr A Moolla, an Indian member of the Special Branch, who was also cross-examined by Mandela:

146

MANDELA: You know about the Group Areas Act?

WITNESS: I do.

MANDELA: You know that it is intended to set certain areas for occupation by the various population groups in the country?

WITNESS: Yes, I do know.

MANDELA: And you know that it has aroused a great deal of feeling and opposition from the Indian community in this country?

WITNESS: Well, not that I know of. I think that most of the Indians are satisfied with it.

MANDELA: Is this a sincere opinion?

WITNESS: That is my sincere opinion, from people that I have met.

MANDELA: And are you aware of the attitude of the South African Indian Congress, about the Group Areas?

WITNESS: Yes.

MANDELA: What is the attitude of the South African Indian Congress?

WITNESS: The South African Indian Congress is against it.

MANDELA: And the attitude of the Transvaal Indian Congress?

WITNESS: Also.

MANDELA: They are against it?

WITNESS: Yes.

MANDELA: And the Transvaal Indian Youth Congress?

WITNESS: Also.

MANDELA: The Cape Indian Assembly, also against it?

WITNESS: Yes. Well, the Cape Indian Assembly I do not know about.

MANDELA: Well, you can take it from me that it is against it. Now, of course, if the Group Areas Act is carried out in its present form, it means that a large number of Indian merchants would lose their trading rights in areas which have been declared White Areas?

WITNESS: That is right.

MANDELA: And a large number of members of the Indian community who are living at the present moment in areas which might or have been declared as White Areas, would have to leave those homes, and have to go where they are to be stationed?

WITNESS: I think they will be better off than where . . .

MANDELA: Answer the question. You know that?

WITNESS: Yes, I know that.

MANDELA: You say that the Indian merchant class in this country, who are going to lose their business rights, are happy about it?

WITNESS: Well, not all.

MANDELA: Not all. And you are saying that those members of the Indian community who are going to be driven away from the areas where they are living at present would be happy to do so?

WITNESS: Yes, they would be.

MANDELA: Well, Mr Moolla, I want to leave it at that, but just to say that you have lost your soul.

Following the closure of the prosecution case against him, Mandela addressed the court:

I am charged with inciting people to commit an offence by way of protest against the law, a law which neither I nor any of my people had any say in preparing. The law against which the protest was directed is the law which established a republic in the Union of South Africa. I am also charged with leaving the country without a passport. This court has found that I am guilty of incitement to commit an offence in opposition to this law as well as of leaving the country. But in weighing up the decision as to the sentence which is to be imposed for such an offence, the court must take into account the question of responsibility, whether it is I who is responsible or whether, in fact, a large measure of the responsibility does not lie on the shoulders of the government which promulgated that law, knowing that my people, who constitute the majority of the population of this country, were opposed to that law, and knowing further that every legal means of demonstrating that opposition had been closed to them by prior legislation, and by government administrative action.

The starting point in the case against me is the holding of the conference in Pietermaritzburg on 25 and 26 March last year [1961], known as the All-in African Conference, which was called by a committee which had been established by leading people and spokesmen of the whole African population, to consider the situation which was being created by the promulgation of the republic in the country, without consultation with us, and without our consent. That conference unanimously rejected the decision of the government, acting only in the name of and with the agreement of the white minority of this country, to establish a republic.

It is common knowledge that the conference decided that, in place of the unilateral proclamation of a republic by the white minority of South Africans only, it would demand in the name of the African people the calling of a truly national convention representative of all South Africans, irrespective of their colour, black and white, to sit amicably round a table, to debate a new constitution for South Africa, which was in essence what the government was doing by the proclamation of a republic, and furthermore, to press on behalf of the

African people, that such new constitution should differ from the constitution of the proposed South African Republic by guaranteeing democratic rights on a basis of full equality to all South Africans of adult age. The conference had assembled, knowing full well that for a long period the present National Party Government of the Union of South Africa had refused to deal with, to discuss with, or to take into consideration the views of, the overwhelming majority of the South African population on this question. And, therefore, it was not enough for this conference just to proclaim its aim, but it was also necessary for the conference to find a means of stating that aim strongly and powerfully, despite the government's unwillingness to listen.

Accordingly, it was decided that should the government fail to summon such a National Convention before 31 May 1961, all sections of the population would be called on to stage a general strike for a period of three days, both to mark our protest against the establishment of a republic, based completely on white domination over a non-white majority, and also, in a last attempt to persuade the government to heed our legitimate claims, and thus to avoid a period of increasing bitterness and hostility and discord in South Africa.

At that conference, an Action Council was elected, and I became its secretary. It was my duty, as secretary of the committee, to establish the machinery necessary for publicising the decision of this conference and for directing the campaign of propaganda, publicity, and organisation which would flow from it.

The court is aware of the fact that I am an attorney by profession and no doubt the question will be asked why I, as an attorney who is bound, as part of my code of behaviour, to observe the laws of the country and to respect its customs and traditions, should willingly lend myself to a campaign whose ultimate aim was to bring about a strike against the proclaimed policy of the government of this country.

In order that the court shall understand the frame of mind which leads me to action such as this, it is necessary for me to explain the background to my own political development and to try to make this court aware of the factors which influenced me in deciding to act as I did.

Many years ago, when I was a boy brought up in my village in the Transkei, I listened to the elders of the tribe telling stories about the good old days, before the arrival of the white man. Then our people lived peacefully, under the democratic rule of their kings and their amapakati,* and moved freely and confidently up and down the country without let or hindrance. Then the country was ours, in our own name and right. We occupied the land, the forests, the rivers; we extracted the mineral wealth beneath the soil and all the riches of this beautiful country. We set up and operated our own government, we controlled our own armies and we organised our own trade and commerce. The elders would tell tales of the wars fought by our ancestors in defence of the fatherland, as well as the acts of valour performed by generals and soldiers during those epic days. The names of Dingane and Bambata, among the Zulus,

---

*Amapakati = 'insiders', those of highest rank next to the king.

of Hintsa, Makana, Ndlambe of the Amaxhosa, of Sekhukhuni and others in the north, were mentioned as the pride and glory of the entire African nation.

I hoped and vowed then that, among the treasures that life might offer me, would be the opportunity to serve my people and make my own humble contribution to their freedom struggles.

The structure and organisation of early African societies in this country fascinated me very much and greatly influenced the evolution of my political outlook. The land, then the main means of production, belonged to the whole tribe, and there was no individual ownership whatsoever. There were no classes, no rich or poor and no exploitation of man by man. All men were free and equal and this was the foundation of government. Recognition of this general principle found expression in the constitution of the council, variously called Imbizo, or Pitso, or Kgotla, which governs the affairs of the tribe. The council was so completely democratic that all members of the tribe could participate in its deliberations. Chief and subject, warrior and medicine man, all took part and endeavoured to influence its decisions. It was so weighty and influential a body that no step of any importance could ever be taken by the tribe without reference to it.

There was much in such a society that was primitive and insecure and it certainly could never measure up to the demands of the present epoch. But in such a society are contained the seeds of revolutionary democracy in which none will be held in slavery or servitude, and in which poverty, want, and insecurity shall be no more. This is the inspiration which, even today, inspires me and my colleagues in our political struggle.

When I reached adult stature, I became a member of the African National Congress. That was in 1944 and I have followed its policy, supported it, and believed in its aims and outlook for eighteen years. Its policy was one which appealed to my deepest inner convictions. It sought for the unity of all Africans, overriding tribal differences among them. It sought the acquisition of political power for Africans in the land of their birth. The African National Congress further believed that all people, irrespective of the national groups to which they may belong, and irrespective of the colour of their skins, all people whose home is South Africa and who believe in the principles of democracy and of equality of men, should be treated as Africans; that all South Africans are entitled to live a free life on the basis of fullest equality of the rights and opportunities in every field, of full democratic rights, with a direct say in the affairs of the government.

These principles have been embodied in the Freedom Charter, which none in this country will dare challenge for its place as the most democratic programme of political principles ever enunciated by any political party or organisation in this country. It was for me a matter of joy and pride to be a member of an organisation which has proclaimed so democratic a policy and which campaigned for it militantly and fearlessly. The principles enumerated in the Charter have not been those of African people alone, for whom the African National Congress has always been the spokesman. Those principles have been adopted as well by the

Indian people and the South African Indian Congress; by a section of the Coloured people, through the South African Coloured People's Congress, and also by a farsighted, forward-looking section of the European population, whose organisation in days gone by was the South African Congress of Democrats. All these organisations, like the African National Congress, supported completely the demand for one man, one vote.

Right at the beginning of my career as an attorney I encountered difficulties imposed on me because of the colour of my skin, and further difficulty surrounding me because of my membership and support of the African National Congress. I discovered, for example, that, unlike a white attorney, I could not occupy business premises in the city unless I first obtained ministerial consent in terms of the Urban Areas Act. I applied for that consent, but it was never granted. Although I subsequently obtained a permit, for a limited period, in terms of the Group Areas Act, that soon expired, and the authorities refused to renew it. They insisted that my partner, Oliver Tambo, and I should leave the city and practise in an African location at the back of beyond, miles away from where clients could reach us during working hours. This was tantamount to asking us to abandon our legal practice, to give up the legal service of our people, for which we had spent many years training. No attorney worth his salt will agree easily to do so. For some years, therefore, we continued to occupy premises in the city, illegally. The threat of prosecution and ejection hung menacingly over us throughout that period. It was an act of defiance of the law. We were aware that it was, but, nevertheless, that act had been forced on us against our wishes, and we could do no other than to choose between compliance with the law and compliance with our consciences.

In the courts where we practised we were treated courteously by many officials but we were very often discriminated against by some and treated with resentment and hostility by others. We were constantly aware that no matter how well, how correctly, how adequately we pursued our career of law, we could not become a prosecutor, or a magistrate, or a judge. We became aware of the fact that as attorneys we often dealt with officials whose competence and attainments were no higher than ours, but whose superior position was maintained and protected by a white skin.

I regarded it as a duty which I owed, not just to my people, but also to my profession, to the practice of law, and to justice for all mankind, to cry out against this discrimination, which is essentially unjust and opposed to the whole basis of the attitude towards justice which is part of the tradition of legal training in this country. I believed that in taking up a stand against this injustice I was upholding the dignity of what should be an honourable profession.

Nine years ago the Transvaal Law Society applied to the Supreme Court to have my name struck off the roll because of the part I had played in a campaign initiated by the African National Congress, a campaign for the Defiance of Unjust Laws. During the campaign more than eight thousand of the most advanced and farseeing of my people deliberately courted arrest and imprisonment by breaking specified laws, which we regarded then, as we still do now, as unjust and repressive. In the opinion of the Law Society, my activity in connection with that campaign did not conform to the standards of conduct expected from members of our honourable profession, but on this occasion the Supreme Court held that I had been within my rights as an attorney, that there was nothing dishonourable in an attorney identifying himself with his people in their struggle for political rights, even if his activities should infringe upon the laws of the country; the Supreme Court rejected the application of the Law Society.

It would not be expected that with such a verdict in my favour I should discontinue my political activities. But Your Worship may well wonder why it is that I should find it necessary to persist with such conduct, which has not only brought me the difficulties I have referred to, but which has resulted in my spending some four years on a charge before the courts of high treason, of which I was subsequently acquitted, and of many months in jail on no charge at all, merely on the basis of the government's dislike of my views and of my activities during the whole period of the Emergency of 1960.

Your Worship, I would say that the whole life of any thinking African in this country drives him continuously to a conflict between his conscience on the one hand and the law on the other. This is not a conflict peculiar to this country. The conflict arises for men of conscience, for men who think and who feel deeply in every country. Recently in Britain, a peer of the realm, Earl Russell, probably the most respected philosopher of the Western world, was sentenced, convicted for precisely the type of activities for which I stand before you today, for following his conscience in defiance of the law, as a protest against a nuclear weapons policy being followed by his own government. For him, his duty to the public, his belief in the morality of the essential rightness of the cause for which he stood, rose superior to this high respect for the law. He could not do other than to oppose the law and to suffer the consequences for it. Nor can I. Nor can many Africans in this country. The law as it is applied, the law as it has been developed over a long period of history, and especially the law as it is written and designed by the Nationalist government, is a law which, in our view, is immoral, unjust, and intolerable. Our consciences dictate that we must protest against it, that we must oppose it, and that we must attempt to alter it.

Always we have been conscious of our obligations as citizens to avoid breaches of the law, where such breaches can be avoided, to prevent a clash between the authorities and our people, where such clash can be prevented, but nevertheless, we have been driven to speak up for what we believe is right, and to work for it and to try and bring about changes which will satisfy our human conscience.

Throughout its fifty years of existence the African National Congress, for instance, has done everything possible to bring its demands to the attention of successive South African governments. It has sought at all times peaceful solutions for all the country's ills and problems. The history of the ANC is filled with instances where deputations were sent to South African governments either

152

on specific issues or on the general political demands of our people. I do not wish to burden Your Worship by enunciating the occasions when such deputations were sent; all that I wish to indicate at this stage is that, in addition to the efforts made by former presidents of the ANC, when Mr Strijdom became Prime Minister of this country, my leader, Chief A J Lutuli, then President of our organisation, made yet another effort to persuade this government to consider and to heed our point of view. In his letter to the Prime Minister at the time, Chief Lutuli exhaustively reviewed the country's relations and its dangers, and expressed the view that a meeting between the government and African leaders had become necessary and urgent.

This statesmanlike and correct behaviour on the part of the leader of the majority of the South African population did not find an appropriate answer from the leader of the South African government. The standard of behaviour of the South African government towards my people and its aspirations has not always been what it should have been, and is not always the standard which is to be expected in serious high-level dealings between civilised peoples. Chief Lutuli's letter was not even favoured with the courtesy of an acknowledgement from the Prime Minister's office.

This experience was repeated after the Pietermaritzburg conference, when I, as Secretary of the Action Council, elected at that conference, addressed a letter to the Prime Minister, Dr Verwoerd, informing him of the resolution which had been taken, and calling on him to initiate steps for the convening of such a national convention as we suggested, before the date specified in the resolution. In a civilised country one would be outraged by the failure of the head of government even to acknowledge receipt of a letter, or to consider such a reasonable request put to him by a broadly representative collection of important personalities and leaders of the most important community of the country. Once again, government standards in dealing with my people fell below what the civilised world would expect. No reply, no response whatsoever, was received to our letter, no indication was even given that it had received any consideration whatsoever. Here we, the African people, and especially we of the National Action Council, who had been entrusted with the tremendous responsibility of safeguarding the interests of the African people, were faced with this conflict between the law and our conscience. In the face of the complete failure of the government to heed, to consider, or even to respond to our seriously proposed objections and our solutions to the forthcoming republic, what were we to do? Were we to allow the law which states that you shall not commit an offence by way of protest, to take its course and thus betray our conscience and our belief? Were we to uphold our conscience and our beliefs to strive for what we believe is right, not just for us, but for all the people who live in this country, both the present generation and for generations to come, and thus transgress against the law? This is the dilemma which faced us, and in such a dilemma, men of honesty, men of purpose, and men of public morality and of conscience can only have one answer. They must follow the dictates of their conscience irrespective of the consequences which might overtake them for it. We of the Action Council, and I particularly as Secretary, followed my conscience.

If I had my time over I would do the same again, so would any man who dares call himself a man. We went ahead with our campaign as instructed by the conference and in accordance with its decisions.

The issue that sharply divided white South Africans during the referendum for a republic did not interest us. It formed no part in our campaign. Continued association with the British monarchy on the one hand, or the establishment of a Boer republic on the other — this was the crucial issue in so far as the White population was concerned and as it was put to them in the referendum. We are neither monarchists nor admirers of a Voortrekker type of republic. We believe that we were inspired by aspirations more worthy than either of the groups who took part in the campaign on these. We were inspired by the idea of bringing into being a democratic republic where all South Africans will enjoy human rights without the slightest discrimination; where African and non-African would be able to live together in peace, sharing a common nationality and a common loyalty to this country, which is our homeland. For these reasons we were opposed to the type of republic proposed by the Nationalist Party government, just as we have been opposed previously to the constitutional basis of the Union of South Africa as a part of the British Empire. We were not prepared to accept, at a time when constitutional changes were being made, that these constitutional changes should not affect the real basis of a South African constitution, white supremacy and white domination, the very basis which has brought South Africa and its constitution into contempt and disrepute throughout the world.

I wish now to deal with the campaign itself, with the character of the campaign, and with the course of events which followed our decision. From the beginning our campaign was a campaign designed to call on people as a last extreme, if all else failed, if all discussions failed to materialise, if the government showed no sign of taking any steps to attempt either to treat with us or to meet our demands peacefully, to strike, that is to stay away from work, and so to bring economic pressure to bear. There was never any intention that our demonstrations, at that stage, go further than that. In all our statements, both those which are before the court, and those which are not before the court, we made it clear that that strike would be a peaceful protest, in which people were asked to remain in their homes. It was our intention that the demonstration should go through peacefully and peaceably, without clash and conflict, as such demonstrations do in every civilised country.

Nevertheless, around that campaign and our preparations for that campaign was created the atmosphere for civil war and revolution. I would say deliberately created. Deliberately created not by us, Your Worship, but by the government, which set out from the beginning of this campaign not to treat with us, not to heed us, not to talk to us, but rather to present us as wild, dangerous revolutionaries, intent on disorder and riot, incapable of being dealt with in any way save by mustering an overwhelming force against us and the implementation of every

154

possible forcible means, legal and illegal, to suppress us. The government behaved in a way no civilised government should dare behave when faced with a peaceful, disciplined, sensible, and democratic expression of the views of its own population. It ordered the mobilisation of its armed forces to attempt to cow and terrorise our peaceful protest. It arrested people known to be active in African politics and in support of African demands for democratic rights, passed special laws enabling it to hold them without trial for twelve days instead of the forty-eight hours which had been customary before, and hold them, the majority of them, never to be charged before the courts, but to be released after the date for the strike had passed. If there was a danger during this period that violence would result from the situation in the country, then the possibility was of the government's making. They set the scene for violence by relying exclusively on violence with which to answer our people and their demands. The counter-measures which they took clearly reflected growing uneasiness on their part, which grew out of the knowledge that their policy did not enjoy the support of the majority of the people, while ours did. It was clear that the government was attempting to combat the intensity of our campaign by a reign of terror. At the time the newspapers suggested the strike was a failure and it was said that we did not enjoy the support of the people. I deny that. I deny it and I will continue to deny it as long as this government is not prepared to put to the test the question of the opinion of the African people by consulting them in a democratic way. In any event, the evidence in this case has shown that it was a substantial success. Our campaign was an intensive campaign and met with tremendous and over-whelming response from the population. In the end, if a strike did not materialise on the scale on which it had been hoped it would, it was not because the people were not willing, but because the overwhelming strength, violence, and force of the government's attack against our campaign had for the time being achieved its aim of forcing us into submission against our wishes and against our conscience.

I wish again to return to the question of why people like me, knowing all this, knowing in advance that this government is incapable of progressive democratic moves so far as our people are concerned, knowing that this government is incapable of reacting towards us in any way other than by the use of over-whelming brute force, why I and people like me nevertheless decide to go ahead to do what we must do. We have been conditioned to our attitudes by the history which is not of our making. We have been conditioned by the history of White governments in this country to accept the fact that Africans, when they make their demands strongly and powerfully enough to have some chance of success, will be met by force and terror on the part of the government. This is not some-thing we have taught the African people, this is something the African people have learned from their own bitter experience. We learned it from each succes-sive government. We learned it from the government of General Smuts at the time of two massacres of our people: the 1921 massacre in Bulhoek when more than a hundred men, women, and children were killed, and from the 1924 massacre — the Bondelswart massacre in South-West Africa, in which some two hundred Africans were killed. We have continued to learn it from every successive government.

Government violence can do only one thing, and that is to breed counter-violence. We have warned repeatedly that the government, by resorting continually to violence, will breed in this country counter-violence amongst the people, till ultimately, if there is no dawning of sanity on the part of the government — ultimately, the dispute between the government and my people will finish up by being settled in violence and by force. Already there are indications in this country that people, my people, Africans, are turning to deliberate acts of violence and of force against the government, in order to persuade the government, in the only language which this government shows by its own behaviour that it understands.

Elsewhere in the world, a court would say to me, 'You should have made representations to the government.' This court, I am confident, will not say so. Representations have been made, by people who have gone before me, time and time again. Representations were made in this case by me; I do not want again to repeat the experience of those representations. The court cannot expect a respect for the processes of representation and negotiation to grow amongst the African people, when the government shows every day, by its conduct, that it despises such processes and frowns upon them and will not indulge in them. Nor will the court, I believe, say that, under the circumstances, my people are condemned forever to say nothing and to do nothing. If this court says that, or believes it, I think it is mistaken and deceiving itself. Men are not capable of doing nothing, of saying nothing, of not reacting to injustice, of not protesting against oppression, of not striving for the good of society and the good life in the ways they see it. Nor will they do so in this country.

Perhaps the court will say that despite our human rights to protest, to object, to make ourselves heard, we should stay within the letter of the law. I would say, Sir, that it is the government, its administration of the law, which brings the law into such contempt and disrepute that one is no longer concerned in this country to stay within the letter of the law. I will illustrate this from my own experience. The government has used the process of law to handicap me, in my personal life, in my career, and in my political work, in a way which is calculated, in my opinion, to bring about a contempt for the law. In December 1952 I was issued with an order by the government, not as a result of a trial before a court and a conviction, but as a result of prejudice, or perhaps Star Chamber procedure behind closed doors in the halls of government. In terms of that order I was confined to the magisterial district of Johannesburg for six months and, at the same time, I was prohibited from attending gatherings for a similar period. That order expired in June 1953 and three months thereafter, again without any hearing, without any attempt to hear my side of the case, without facing me with charges, or explanations, both bans were renewed for a further period of two years. To these bans a third was added: I was ordered by the Minister of Justice to resign altogether from the African National Congress, and never again to become a member or to participate in its activities. Towards the end of 1955, I found myself free and able to move around once again, but not for long. In February 1956 the bans were again renewed, administratively, again without hearing, this time for five years. Again, by order of the government, in the name of the law, I found myself restricted and isolated from my fellow men, from people who think like me and believe like me. I found myself trailed by officers of the Security Branch of the Police Force wherever I went. In short, I found myself treated as a criminal — an unconvicted criminal. I was not allowed to pick my company, to frequent the company of men, to participate in their political activities, to join their organisations. I was not free from constant police surveillance. I was made, by the law, a criminal, not because of what I had done, but because of what I stood for, because of what I thought, because of my conscience. Can it be any wonder to anybody that such conditions make a man an outlaw of society? Can it be wondered that such a man, having been outlawed by the government, should be prepared to lead the life of an outlaw, as I have led for some months, according to the evidence before this court?

It has not been easy for me during the past period to separate myself from my wife and children, to say goodbye to the good old days when, at the end of a strenuous day at an office, I could look forward to joining my family at the dinner-table, and instead to take up the life of a man hunted continuously by the police, living separated from those who are closest to me, in my own country, facing continually the hazards of detection and of arrest. This has been a life infinitely more difficult than serving a prison sentence. No man in his right senses would voluntarily choose such a life in preference to the one of normal family social life which exists in every civilised community.

But there comes a time, as it came in my life, when a man is denied the right to live a normal life, when he can only live the life of an outlaw because the government has so decreed to use the law to impose a state of outlawry upon him. I was driven to this situation, and I do not regret having taken the decisions that I did take. Other people will be driven in the same way in this country, by this very same force of police persecution and of administrative action by the government, to follow my course, of that I am certain. The decision that I should continue to carry out the decisions of the Pietermaritzburg conference, despite police persecution all the time, was not my decision alone. It was a decision reached by me, in consultation with those who were entrusted with the leadership of the campaign and its fulfilment. It was clear to us then, in the early periods of the campaign, when the government was busy whipping up an atmosphere of hysteria as the prelude to violence, that the views of the African people would not be heard, would not find expression, unless attempts were made deliberately by those of us entrusted with the task of carrying through the strike call to keep away from the illegal, unlawful attacks of the Special Branch, the unlawful detention of people for twelve days without trial, and unlawful and illegal intervention by the police and the government forces in legitimate political activity of the population. I was, at the time of the Pietermaritzburg conference, free from bans for a short time, and a time which I had no reason to expect would prolong itself for very long. Had I remained in my normal surroundings, carrying on my normal life, I would have again been forced by government action to a position of an outlaw. That I was not prepared to do while the commands of the Pietermaritzburg conference to me remained unfulfilled. New situations require new tactics. The situation, which was not of our making, which followed the Pietermaritzburg conference required the tactics which I adopted, I believe, correctly.

A lot has been written since the Pietermaritzburg conference, and even more since my arrest, much of which is flattering to my pride and dear to my heart, but much of which is mistaken and incorrect. It has been suggested that the advances, the articulateness of our people, the successes which they are achieving here, and the recognition which they are winning both here and abroad are in some way the result of my work. I must place on record my belief that I have been only one in a large army of people, to all of whom the credit for any success of achievement is due. Advance and progress is not the result of my work alone, but of the collective work of my colleagues and I, both here and abroad. I have been fortunate throughout my political life to work together with colleagues whose abilities and contributions to the cause of my people's freedom have been greater and better than my own, people who have been loved and respected by the African population generally as a result of the dedicated way in which they have fought for freedom and for peace and justice in this country. It distresses me to read reports that my arrest has been instigated by some of my colleagues for some sinister purposes of their own. Nothing could be further from the truth. I dismiss these suggestions as the sensational inventions of unscrupulous journalists. People who stoop to such unscrupulous manoeuvres as the betrayal of their own comrades have no place in the good fight which I have fought for the freedom of the African people, which my colleagues continue to fight without me today. Not just I alone, but all of us are willing to pay the penalties which we may have to pay, which I may have to pay for having followed my conscience in pursuit of what I believe is right. So are we all. Many people in this country have paid the price before me, and many will pay the price after me.

I do not believe, Your Worship, that this court, in inflicting penalties on me for the crimes for which I am convicted, should be moved by the belief that penalties deter men from the course that they believe is right. History shows that penalties do not deter men when their conscience is aroused, nor will they deter my people or the colleagues with whom I have worked before.

I am prepared to pay the penalty even though I know how bitter and desperate is the situation of an African in the prisons of this country. I have been in these prisons and I know how gross is the discrimination, even behind the prison walls, against Africans, how much worse is the treatment meted out to African prisoners than that accorded to whites. Nevertheless, these considerations do not sway me from the path that I have taken, nor will they sway others like me. For to men, freedom in their own land is the pinnacle of their ambitions, from which nothing can turn men of conviction aside. More powerful than my fear of the dreadful conditions to which I might be subjected is my hatred for the dreadful conditions to which my people are subjected outside prison throughout this country.

I hate the practice of race discrimination, and in my hatred I am sustained by the fact that the overwhelming majority of mankind hate it equally. I hate the systematic inculcation of children with colour prejudice and I am sustained in that hatred by the fact that the overwhelming majority of mankind, here and abroad, are with me in that. I hate the racial arrogance which decrees that the good things of life shall be retained as the exclusive right of a minority of the population, and which reduces the majority of the population to a position of subservience and inferiority, and maintains them as voteless chattels to work where they are told and behave as they are told by the ruling minority. I am sustained in that hatred by the fact that the overwhelming majority of mankind both in this country and abroad are with me.

Nothing that this court can do to me will change in any way that hatred in me, which can only be removed by the removal of the injustice and the inhumanity which I have sought to remove from the political and social life of this country.

Whatever sentence Your Worship sees fit to impose upon me for the crime for which I have been convicted before this court, may it rest assured that when my sentence has been completed I will still be moved, as men are always moved, by their consciences; I will still be moved by my dislike of the race discrimination against my people when I come out from serving my sentence, to take up again, as best I can, the struggle for the removal of those injustices until they are finally abolished once and for all.

I now wish to deal with the Second Count.

When my colleagues and I received the invitation to attend the Conference of the Pan-African Freedom Movement for East and Central Africa, it was decided that I should leave the country and join our delegation to Addis Ababa, the capital of Ethiopia, where the conference would be held. It was part of my mandate to tour Africa and make direct contact with African leaders on the continent.

I did not apply for a passport because I knew very well that it would not be granted to me. After all, the Nationalist Party government, throughout the fourteen years of its oppressive rule, had refused permission to leave the country to many African scholars, educationalists, artists, sportsmen, and clerics, and I wished to waste none of my time by applying for a passport.

The tour of the continent made a forceful impression on me. For the first time in my life I was a free man; free from white oppression, from the idiocy of apartheid and racial arrogance, from police molestation, from humiliation and indignity. Wherever I went I was treated like a human being. I met Rashidi Kawawa, Prime Minister of Tanganyika, and Julius Nyerere. I was received by Emperor Haile Selassie, by General Abboud, President of Sudan, by Habib Bourguiba, President of Tunisia, and by Modibo Keita of the Republic of Mali. I

159

met Léopold Senghor, President of Senegal, Presidents Sékou Touré and Tubman, of Guinea and Liberia, respectively.

I met Ben Bella, the President of Algeria, and Colonel Boumedienne, the Commander-in-Chief of the Algerian Army of National Liberation. I saw the cream and flower of the Algerian youth who had fought French imperialism and whose valour had brought freedom and happiness to their country.

In London I was received by Hugh Gaitskell, Leader of the Labour Party, and by Jo Grimond, Leader of the Liberal Party, and other prominent Englishmen.

I met Prime Minister Obote of Uganda, distinguished African nationalists like Kenneth Kaunda, Oginga Odinga, Joshua Nkomo, and many others. In all these countries we were showered with hospitality, and assured of solid support for our cause.

In its efforts to keep the African people in a position of perpetual subordination, South Africa must and will fail. South Africa is out of step with the rest of the civilised world, as is shown by the resolution adopted last night by the General Assembly of the United Nations Organisation which decided to impose diplomatic and economic sanctions. In the African states, I saw black and white mingling peacefully and happily in hotels, cinemas, trading in the same areas, using the same public transport, and living in the same residential areas.

I had to return home to report to my colleagues and to share my impressions and experiences with them.

I have done my duty to my people and to South Africa. I have no doubt that posterity will pronounce that I was innocent and that the criminals that should have been brought before this court are the members of the Verwoerd government.

At the end of this trial, on 7 November 1962, Mandela was convicted and sentenced to three years' imprisonment on the charge of incitement and two years for leaving the country without valid travel documents.

At the close of the trial the crowd ignored a special prohibition on all demonstrations relating to trials and marched through the streets singing a freedom song, 'Tshotsholoza Mandela', a call to Mandela to continue the struggle.

11. THE RIVONIA TRIAL, 1963-64

On 11 July police raided a farm at Rivonia, near Johannesburg, and arrested several senior members of the Congress Alliance. On 9 October 1963 ten men appeared in court on charges of sabotage, among them Mandela, who was brought from prison to stand trial as the first accused.

The State alleged that the accused had embarked on a campaign to overthrow the government by violent revolution. There were four charges under security legislation: the Sabotage Act, the Suppression of Communism Act and the Criminal Law Amendment Act. The charge sheet listed 193 acts of sabotage committed between 27 June 1962 and the date of the Rivonia raid, allegedly carried out by persons recruited by the accused in their capacity as members of the High Command of Umkhonto.

Charges against one of the accused were later withdrawn, and another was acquitted at the conclusion of the trial.

Mandela chose not to give evidence in his own defence or be cross-examined, but only to make a statement.

11(a) SECOND COURT STATEMENT, 1964*

Mandela's statement from the dock in Pretoria Supreme Court, 20 April 1964, at the opening of the defence case.

I am the first accused.

I hold a Bachelor's Degree in Arts and practised as an attorney in Johannesburg for a number of years in partnership with Oliver Tambo. I am a convicted prisoner serving five years for leaving the country without a permit and for inciting people to go on strike at the end of May 1961.

At the outset, I want to say that the suggestion made by the State in its opening that the struggle in South Africa is under the influence of foreigners or communists is wholly incorrect. I have done whatever I did, both as an individual and as a leader of my people, because of my experience in South Africa and my own proudly felt African background, and not because of what any outsider might have said.

In my youth in the Transkei I listened to the elders of my tribe telling stories of the old days. Amongst the tales they related to me were those of wars fought by our ancestors in defence of the fatherland. The names of Dingane and Bambata, Hintsa and Makana, Squngthi and Dalasile, Moshoeshoe and Sekhukhuni, were praised as the glory of the entire African nation. I hoped then that life might offer me the opportunity to serve my people and make my own humble contribution to their freedom struggle. This is what has motivated me in all that I have done in relation to the charges made against me in this case.

---

*It is customary to omit sections of this statement which deal in detail with points of evidence made by some witnesses. These were clearly important at the time in the trial, but have little meaning for readers today, and only serve to lessen the impact of the statement as a whole. As in the previous edition of this book, this custom is followed here.

Having said this, I must deal immediately and at some length with the question of violence. Some of the things so far told to the court are true and some are untrue. I do not, however, deny that I planned sabotage. I did not plan it in a spirit of recklessness, nor because I have any love of violence. I planned it as a result of a calm and sober assessment of the political situation that had arisen after many years of tyranny, exploitation, and oppression of my people by the Whites.

I admit immediately that I was one of the persons who helped to form Umkhonto we Sizwe, and that I played a prominent role in its affairs until I was arrested in August 1962.

In the statement which I am about to make I shall correct certain false impressions which have been created by State witnesses. Amongst other things, I will demonstrate that certain of the acts referred to in the evidence were not and could not have been committed by Umkhonto. I will also deal with the relationship between the African National Congress and Umkhonto, and with the part which I personally have played in the affairs of both organisations. I shall deal also with the part played by the Communist Party. In order to explain these matters properly, I will have to explain what Umkhonto set out to achieve; what methods it prescribed for the achievement of these objects, and why these methods were chosen. I will also have to explain how I became involved in the activities of these organisations.

I deny that Umkhonto was responsible for a number of acts which clearly fell outside the policy of the organisation, and which have been charged in the indictment against us. I do not know what justification there was for these acts, but to demonstrate that they could not have been authorised by Umkhonto, I want to refer briefly to the roots and policy of the organisation.

I have already mentioned that I was one of the persons who helped to form Umkhonto. I, and the others who started the organisation, did so for two reasons. Firstly, we believed that as a result of government policy, violence by the African people had become inevitable, and that unless responsible leadership was given to canalise and control the feelings of our people, there would be outbreaks of terrorism which would produce an intensity of bitterness and hostility between the various races of this country which is not produced even by war. Secondly, we felt that without violence there would be no way open to the African people to succeed in their struggle against the principle of white supremacy. All lawful modes of expressing opposition to this principle had been closed by legislation, and we were placed in a position in which we had either to accept a permanent state of inferiority, or to defy the government. We chose to defy the law. We first broke the law in a way which avoided any recourse to violence; when this form was legislated against, and then the government resorted to a show of force to crush opposition to its policies, only then did we decide to answer violence with violence.

But the violence which we chose to adopt was not terrorism. We who formed Umkhonto were all members of the African National Congress, and had behind us the ANC tradition of non-violence and negotiation as a means of solving political disputes. We believe that South Africa belongs to all the people who live in it, and not to one group, be it black or white. We did not want an inter-racial war, and tried to avoid it to the last minute. If the court is in doubt about this, it will be seen that the whole history of our organisation bears out what I have said, and what I will subsequently say, when I describe the tactics which Umkhonto decided to adopt. I want, therefore, to say something about the African National Congress.

The African National Congress was formed in 1912 to defend the rights of the African people which had been seriously curtailed by the South Africa Act, and which were then being threatened by the Native Land Act. For thirty-seven years — that is, until 1949 — it adhered strictly to a constitutional struggle. It put forward demands and resolutions; it sent delegations to the government in the belief that African grievances could be settled through peaceful discussion and that Africans could advance gradually to full political rights. But White governments remained unmoved, and the rights of Africans became less instead of becoming greater. In the words of my leader, Chief Lutuli, who became President of the ANC in 1952, and who was later awarded the Nobel Peace Prize: 'Who will deny that thirty years of my life have been spent knocking in vain, patiently, moderately, and modestly at a closed and barred door? What have been the fruits of moderation? The past thirty years have seen the greatest number of laws restricting our rights and progress, until today we have reached a stage where we have almost no rights at all.'

Even after 1949, the ANC remained determined to avoid violence. At this time, however, there was a change from the strictly constitutional means of protest which had been employed in the past. The change was embodied in a decision which was taken to protest against apartheid legislation by peaceful, but unlawful, demonstrations against certain laws. Pursuant to this policy the ANC launched the Defiance Campaign, in which I was placed in charge of volunteers. This campaign was based on the principles of passive resistance. More than 8,500 people defied apartheid laws and went to jail. Yet there was not a single instance of violence in the course of this campaign on the part of any defier. I and 19 colleagues were convicted for the role which we played in organising the campaign, but our sentences were suspended mainly because the Judge found that discipline and non-violence had been stressed throughout. This was the time when the volunteer section of the ANC was established, and when the word 'Amadelakufa'* was first used: this was the time when the volunteers were asked to take a pledge to uphold certain principles. Evidence dealing with volunteers and their pledges has been introduced into this case, but completely out of context. The volunteers were not, and are not, the soldiers of a black army pledged to fight a civil war against the whites. They were, and are, dedicated workers who are prepared to lead campaigns initiated by the ANC to distribute leaflets, to organise strikes, or do whatever the particular campaign required.

---

*Amadelakufa = those who are prepared to make sacrifices.

They are called volunteers because they volunteer to face the penalties of imprisonment and whipping which are now prescribed by the legislature for such acts.

During the Defiance Campaign, the Public Safety Act and the Criminal Law Amendment Act were passed. These statutes provided harsher penalties for offences committed by way of protests against laws. Despite this, the protests continued and the ANC adhered to its policy of non-violence. In 1956, 156 leading members of the Congress Alliance, including myself, were arrested on a charge of high treason and charges under the Suppression of Communism Act. The non-violent policy of the ANC was put in issue by the State, but when the court gave judgement some five years later, it found that the ANC did not have a policy of violence. We were acquitted on all counts, which included a count that the ANC sought to set up a communist state in place of the existing regime. The government has always sought to label all its opponents as communists. This allegation has been repeated in the present case but, as I will show, the ANC is not and never has been a communist organisation.

In 1960 there was the shooting at Sharpeville, which resulted in the proclamation of a state of emergency and the declaration of the ANC as an unlawful organisation. My colleagues and I, after careful consideration, decided that we would not obey this decree. The African people were not part of the government and did not make the laws by which they were governed. We believed in the words of the Universal Declaration of Human Rights, that 'the will of the people shall be the basis of authority of the Government', and for us to accept the banning was equivalent to accepting the silencing of the Africans for all time. The ANC refused to dissolve, but instead went underground. We believed it was our duty to preserve this organisation, which had been built up with almost fifty years of unremitting toil. I have no doubt that no self-respecting White political organisation would disband itself if declared illegal by a government in which it had no say.

In 1960 the government held a referendum which led to the establishment of the republic. Africans, who constituted approximately 70 per cent of the population of South Africa, were not entitled to vote, and were not even consulted about the proposed constitutional change. All of us were apprehensive of our future under the proposed White republic, and a resolution was taken to hold an All-in African Conference to call for a National Convention, and to organise mass demonstrations on the eve of the unwanted republic, if the government failed to call the convention. The conference was attended by Africans of various political persuasions. I was the Secretary of the conference and undertook to be responsible for organising the national stay-at-home which was subsequently called to coincide with the declaration of the republic. As all strikes by Africans are illegal, the person organising such a strike must avoid arrest. I was chosen to be this person, and consequently I had to leave my home and family and my practice and go into hiding to avoid arrest.

The stay-at-home, in accordance with ANC policy, was to be a peaceful demonstration. Careful instructions were given to organisers and members to avoid any recourse to violence. The government's answer was to introduce new and harsher laws, to mobilise its armed forces, and to send Saracens,* armed vehicles, and soldiers into the townships in a massive show of force designed to intimidate the people. This was an indication that the government had decided to rule by force alone, and this decision was a milestone on the road to Umkhonto.

Some of this may appear irrelevant to this trial. In fact, I believe none of it is irrelevant because it will, I hope, enable the court to appreciate the attitude eventually adopted by the various persons and bodies concerned in the national liberation movement. When I went to jail in 1962, the dominant idea was that loss of life should be avoided. I now know that this was still so in 1963.

I must return to June 1961. What were we, the leaders of our people, to do? Were we to give in to the show of force and the implied threat against future action, or were we to fight it and, if so, how?

We had no doubt that we had to continue the fight. Anything else would have been abject surrender. Our problem was not whether to fight, but was how to continue the fight. We of the ANC had always stood for a non-racial democracy, and we shrank from any action which might drive the races further apart than they already were. But the hard facts were that fifty years of non-violence had brought the African people nothing but more and more repressive legislation, and fewer and fewer rights. It may not be easy for this court to understand, but it is a fact that for a long time the people had been talking of violence — of the day when they would fight the White man and win back their country — and we, the leaders of the ANC, had nevertheless always prevailed upon them to avoid violence and to pursue peaceful methods. When some of us discussed this in May and June of 1961, it could not be denied that our policy to achieve a non-racial State by non-violence had achieved nothing, and that our followers were beginning to lose confidence in this policy and were developing disturbing ideas of terrorism.

It must not be forgotten that by this time violence had, in fact, become a feature of the South African political scene. There had been violence in 1957 when the women of Zeerust were ordered to carry passes; there was violence in 1958 with the enforcement of cattle culling in Sekhukhuniland; there was violence in 1959 when the people of Cato Manor protested against pass raids; there was violence in 1960 when the government attempted to impose Bantu Authorities in Pondoland. Thirty-nine Africans died in these disturbances. In 1961 there had been riots in Warmbaths, and all this time the Transkei had been a seething mass of unrest. Each disturbance pointed clearly to the inevitable growth among Africans of the belief that violence was the only way out — it showed that a government which uses force to maintain its rule teaches the oppressed to use force to oppose it. Already small groups had arisen in the urban areas and were spontaneously making plans for violent forms of political struggle. There now arose a danger that these groups would adopt terrorism against

---

*Saracen armoured vehicles: British-made military troop carriers.

Africans, as well as Whites, if not properly directed. Particularly disturbing was the type of violence engendered in places such as Zeerust, Sekhukhuniland, and Pondoland amongst Africans. It was increasingly taking the form, not of struggle against the government — though this is what prompted it — but of civil strife amongst themselves, conducted in such a way that it could not hope to achieve anything other than a loss of life and bitterness.

At the beginning of June 1961, after a long and anxious assessment of the South African situation, I and some colleagues came to the conclusion that, as violence in this country was inevitable, it would be unrealistic and wrong for African leaders to continue preaching peace and non-violence at a time when the government met our peaceful demands with force.

This conclusion was not easily arrived at. It was only when all else had failed, when all channels of peaceful protest had been barred to us, that the decision was made to embark on violent forms of political struggle, and to form Umkhonto we Sizwe. We did so not because we desired such a course, but solely because the government had left us with no other choice. In the manifesto of Umkhonto, published on 16 December 1961, which is Exhibit AD, we said: 'The time comes in the life of any nation when there remain only two choices — submit or fight. That time has now come to South Africa. We shall not submit and we have no choice but to hit back by all means in our power in defence of our people, our future, and our freedom.'

This was our feeling in June of 1961 when we decided to press for a change in the policy of the national liberation movement. I can only say that I felt morally obliged to do what I did.

We who had taken this decision started to consult leaders of various organisations, including the ANC. I will not say whom we spoke to, or what they said, but I wish to deal with the role of the African National Congress in this phase of the struggle, and with the policy and objectives of Umkhonto we Sizwe.

As far as the ANC was concerned, it formed a clear view which can be summarised as follows:

(a) It was a mass political organisation with a political function to fulfil. Its members had joined on the express policy of non-violence.

(b) Because of all this, it could not and would not undertake violence. This must be stressed. One cannot turn such a body into the small, closely knit organisation required for sabotage. Nor would this be politically correct, because it would result in members ceasing to carry out this essential activity: political propaganda and organisation. Nor was it permissible to change the whole nature of the organisation.

(c) On the other hand, in view of this situation I have described, the ANC was prepared to depart from its fifty-year-old policy of non-violence to this extent that it would no longer disapprove of properly controlled violence. Hence members who undertook such activity would not be subject to disciplinary action by the ANC.

166

I say 'properly controlled violence' because I made it clear that if I formed the organisation I would at all times subject it to the political guidance of the ANC and would not undertake any different form of activity from that contemplated without the consent of the ANC. And I shall now tell the court how that form of violence came to be determined.

As a result of this decision, Umkhonto was formed in November 1961. When we took this decision, and subsequently formulated our plans, the ANC heritage of non-violence and racial harmony was very much with us. We felt that the country was drifting towards a civil war in which blacks and whites would fight each other. We viewed the situation with alarm. Civil war could mean the destruction of what the ANC stood for; with civil war, racial peace would be more difficult than ever to achieve. We already have examples in South African history of the results of war. It has taken more than fifty years for the scars of the South African War* to disappear. How much longer would it take to eradicate the scars of inter-racial civil war, which could not be fought without a great loss of life on both sides?

The avoidance of civil war had dominated our thinking for many years, but when we decided to adopt violence as part of our policy, we realised that we might one day have to face the prospect of such a war. This had to be taken into account in formulating our plans. We required a plan which was flexible and which permitted us to act in accordance with the needs of the times; above all, the plan had to be one which recognised civil war as the last resort, and left the decision on this question to the future. We did not want to be committed to civil war, but we wanted to be ready if it became inevitable.

Four forms of violence were possible. There is sabotage, there is guerrilla warfare, there is terrorism, and there is open revolution. We chose to adopt the first method and to exhaust it before taking any other decision.

In the light of our political background the choice was a logical one. Sabotage did not involve loss of life, and it offered the best hope for future race relations. Bitterness would be kept to a minimum and, if the policy bore fruit, democratic government could become a reality. This is what we felt at the time, and this is what we said in our manifesto (Exhibit AD):

'We of Umkhonto we Sizwe have always sought to achieve liberation without bloodshed and civil clash. We hope, even at this late hour, that our first actions will awaken everyone to a realisation of the disastrous situation to which the Nationalist policy is leading. We hope that we will bring the government and its supporters to their senses before it is too late, so that both the government and its policies can be changed before matters reach the desperate stage of civil war.'

The initial plan was based on a careful analysis of the political and economic situation of our country. We believed that South Africa depended to a large extent on foreign capital and foreign trade. We felt that planned destruction of power plants, and interference with rail and telephone communications, would tend to scare away capital from the country, make it more difficult for goods from

---

*The Anglo-Boer War of 1899-1902.

the industrial areas to reach the seaports on schedule, and would in the long run be a heavy drain on the economic life of the country, thus compelling the voters of the country to reconsider their position.

Attacks on the economic lifelines of the country were to be linked with sabotage on government buildings and other symbols of apartheid. These attacks would serve as a source of inspiration to our people. In addition, they would provide an outlet for those people who were urging the adoption of violent methods and would enable us to give concrete proof to our followers that we had adopted a stronger line and were fighting back against government violence.

In addition, if mass action were successfully organised and mass reprisals taken, we felt that sympathy for our cause would be roused in other countries, and that greater pressure would be brought to bear on the South African government.

This then was the plan. Umkhonto was to perform sabotage, and strict instructions were given to its members right from the start, that on no account were they to injure or kill people in planning or carrying out operations. These instructions have been referred to in the evidence of 'Mr X' and 'Mr Z'.*

The affairs of the Umkhonto were controlled and directed by a National High Command, which had powers of co-option and which could, and did, appoint Regional Commands. The High Command was the body which determined tactics and targets and was in charge of training and finance. Under the High Command there were Regional Commands which were responsible for the direction of the local sabotage groups. Within the framework of the policy laid down by the National High Command, the Regional Commands had authority to select the targets to be attacked. They had no authority to go beyond the prescribed framework and thus had no authority to embark upon acts which endangered life, or which did not fit into the overall plan of sabotage. For instance, Umkhonto members were forbidden ever to go armed into operation. Incidentally, the terms High Command and Regional Command were an importation from the Jewish national underground organisation Irgun Zvai Leumi, which operated in Israel between 1944 and 1948.

Umkhonto had its first operation on 16 December 1961, when government buildings in Johannesburg, Port Elizabeth and Durban were attacked. The selection of targets is proof of the policy to which I have referred. Had we intended to attack life we would have selected targets where people congregated, and not empty buildings and power stations. The sabotage which was committed before 16 December 1961 was the work of isolated groups and had no connection whatever with Umkhonto. In fact, some of these and a number of later acts were claimed by other organisations.

The manifesto of Umkhonto was issued on the day that operations commenced. The response to our actions and manifesto among the white population was characteristically violent. The government threatened to take strong action, and called upon its supporters to stand firm and to ignore the

---

*State witnesses in the trial whose names were withheld.

demands of the Africans. The whites failed to respond by suggesting change; they responded to our call by suggesting the laager.*

In contrast, the response of the Africans was one of encouragement. Suddenly there was hope again. Things were happening. People in the townships became eager for political news. A great deal of enthusiasm was generated by the initial successes, and people began to speculate on how soon freedom would be obtained.

But we in Umkhonto weighed up the white response with anxiety. The lines were being drawn. The whites and blacks were moving into separate camps, and the prospects of avoiding a civil war were made less. The white newspapers carried reports that sabotage would be punished by death. If this was so, how could we continue to keep Africans away from terrorism?

Already scores of Africans had died as a result of racial friction. In 1920 when the famous leader, Masabala, was held in Port Elizabeth jail, 24 of a group of Africans who had gathered to demand his release were killed by the police and white civilians. In 1921, more than one hundred Africans died in the Bulhoek affair. In 1924 over two hundred Africans were killed when the Administrator of South-West Africa led a force against a group which had rebelled against the imposition of dog tax. On 1 May 1950, 18 Africans died as a result of police shootings during the strike. On 21 March 1960, 69 unarmed Africans died at Sharpeville.

How many more Sharpevilles would there be in the history of our country? And how many more Sharpevilles could the country stand without violence and terror becoming the order of the day? And what would happen to our people when that stage was reached? In the long run we felt certain we must succeed, but at what cost to ourselves and the rest of the country? And if this happened, how could black and white ever live together again in peace and harmony? These were the problems that faced us, and these were our decisions.

Experience convinced us that rebellion would offer the government limitless opportunities for the indiscriminate slaughter of our people. But it was precisely because the soil of South Africa is already drenched with the blood of innocent Africans that we felt it our duty to make preparations as a long-term undertaking to use force in order to defend ourselves against force. If war were inevitable, we wanted the fight to be conducted on terms most favourable to our people. The fight which held out prospects best for us and the least risk of life to both sides was guerrilla warfare. We decided, therefore, in our preparations for the future, to make provision for the possibility of guerrilla warfare.

All whites undergo compulsory military training, but no such training was given to Africans. It was in our view essential to build up a nucleus of trained men who would be able to provide the leadership which would be required if guerrilla warfare started. We had to prepare for such a situation before it became too late to make proper preparations. It was also necessary to build up a nucleus

---

*Laager = closed defensive position. This refers to the defensive camps of wagons used by white settlers during their intrusion into Southern Africa.

169

of men trained in civil administration and other professions, so that Africans would be equipped to participate in the government of this country as soon as they were allowed to do so.

At this stage it was decided that I should attend the Conference of the Pan-African Freedom Movement for Central, East and Southern Africa, which was to be held early in 1962 in Addis Ababa, and, because of our need for preparation, it was also decided that, after the conference, I would undertake a tour of the African states with a view to obtaining facilities for the training of soldiers, and that I would also solicit scholarships for the higher education of matriculated Africans. Training in both fields would be necessary, even if changes came about by peaceful means. Administrators would be necessary who would be willing and able to administer a non-racial state and so would men be necessary to control the army and police force of such a state.

It was on this note that I left South Africa to proceed to Addis Ababa as a delegate of the ANC. My tour was a success. Wherever I went I met sympathy for our cause and promises of help. All Africa was united against the stand of White South Africa, and even in London I was received with great sympathy by political leaders such as Mr Gaitskell and Mr Grimond. In Africa I was promised support by such men as Julius Nyerere, now President of Tanganyika; Mr Kawawa, then Prime Minister of Tanganyika; Emperor Haile Selassie of Ethiopia; General Abboud, President of the Sudan; Habib Bourguiba, President of Tunisia; Ben Bella, now President of Algeria; Modibo Keita, President of Mali; Leopold Senghor, President of Senegal; Sékou Touré, President of Guinea; President Tubman of Liberia; and Milton Obote, Prime Minister of Uganda. It was Ben Bella who invited me to visit Oujda, the headquarters of the Algerian Army of National Liberation, the visit which is described in my diary, one of the exhibits.

I started to make a study of the art of war and revolution and, whilst abroad, underwent a course in military training. If there was to be guerrilla warfare, I wanted to be able to stand and fight with my people and to share the hazards of war with them. Notes of lectures which I received in Algeria are contained in Exhibit 16, produced in evidence. Summaries of books on guerrilla warfare and military strategy have also been produced. I have already admitted that these documents are in my writing, and I acknowledge that I made these studies to equip myself for the role which I might have to play if the struggle drifted into guerrilla warfare. I approached this question as every African nationalist should do. I was completely objective. The court will see that I attempted to examine all types of authority on the subject — from the East and from the West, going back to the classic work of Clausewitz, and covering such a variety as Mao Tse Tung and Che Guevara on the one hand, and the writings on the Anglo-Boer War on the other. Of course, these notes are merely summaries of the books I read and do not contain my personal views.

I also made arrangements for our recruits to undergo military training. But here it was impossible to organise any scheme without the co-operation of the ANC offices in Africa. I consequently obtained the permission of the ANC in

170

South Africa to do this. To this extent then there was a departure from the original decision of the ANC, but it applied outside South Africa only. The first batch of recruits actually arrived in Tanganyika when I was passing through that country on my way back to South Africa.

I returned to South Africa and reported to my colleagues on the results of my trip. On my return I found that there had been little alteration in the political scene save that the threat of a death penalty for sabotage had now become a fact. The attitude of my colleagues in Umkhonto was much the same as it had been before I left. They were feeling their way cautiously and felt that it would be a long time before the possibilities of sabotage were exhausted. In fact, the view was expressed by some that the training of recruits was premature. This is recorded by me in the document which is Exhibit R.14. After a full discussion, however, it was decided to go ahead with the plans for military training because of the fact that it would take many years to build up a sufficient nucleus of trained soldiers to start a guerilla campaign, and whatever happened the training would be of value.

I wish to turn now to certain general allegations made in this case by the State. But before doing so, I wish to revert to certain occurrences said by witnesses to have happened in Port Elizabeth and East London. I am referring to the bombing of private houses of pro-government persons during September, October and November 1962. I do not know what justification there was for these acts, nor what provocation had been given. But if what I have said already is accepted, then it is clear that these acts had nothing to do with the carrying out of the policy of Umkhonto.

One of the chief allegations in the indictment is that the ANC was a party to a general conspiracy to commit sabotage. I have already explained why this is incorrect but how, externally, there was a departure from the original principle laid down by the ANC. There has, of course, been overlapping of functions internally as well, because there is a difference between a resolution adopted in the atmosphere of a committee room and the concrete difficulties that arise in the field of practical activity. At a later stage the position was further affected by bannings and house arrests, and by persons leaving the country to take up political work abroad. This led to individuals having to do work in different capacities. But though this may have blurred the distinction between Umkhonto and the ANC, it by no means abolished that distinction. Great care was taken to keep the activities of the two organisations in South Africa distinct. The ANC remained a mass political body of Africans only carrying on the type of political work they had conducted prior to 1961. Umkhonto remained a small organisation recruiting its members from different races and organisations and trying to achieve its own particular object. The fact that members of Umkhonto were recruited from the ANC, and the fact that persons served both organisations, like Solomon Mbanjwa, did not, in our view, change the nature of the ANC or give it a policy of violence. This overlapping of officers, however, was more the exception than the rule. This is why persons such as 'Mr X' and 'Mr Z', who were on the Regional Command of their respective areas, did not participate in any of the ANC committees or activities, and why people such as Mr Bennett Mashiyana and Mr Reginald Ndubi did not hear of sabotage at their ANC meetings.

Another of the allegations in the indictment is that Rivonia was the headquarters of Umkhonto. This is not true of the time when I was there. I was told, of course, and knew that certain of the activities of the Communist Party were carried on there. But this is no reason (as I shall presently explain) why I should not use the place.

I came there in the following manner:

(a) As already indicated, early in April 1961 I went underground to organise the May general strike. My work entailed travelling throughout the country, living now in African townships, then in country villages and again in cities.

During the second half of the year I started visiting the Parktown home of Arthur Goldreich, where I used to meet my family privately. Although I had no direct political association with him, I had known Arthur Goldreich socially since 1958.*

(b) In October, Arthur Goldreich informed me that he was moving out of town and offered me a hiding place there. A few days thereafter, he arranged for Michael Harmel to take me to Rivonia. I naturally found Rivonia an ideal place for the man who lived the life of an outlaw. Up to that time I had been compelled to live indoors during the daytime and could only venture out under cover of darkness. But at Liliesleaf** I could live differently and work far more efficiently.

(c) For obvious reasons, I had to disguise myself and I assumed the fictitious name of David. In December, Arthur Goldreich and his family moved in. I stayed there until I went abroad on 11 January 1962. As already indicated, I returned in July 1962 and was arrested in Natal on 5 August.

(d) Up to the time of my arrest, Liliesleaf farm was the headquarters of neither the African National Congress nor Umkhonto. With the exception of myself, none of the officials or members of these bodies lived there, no meetings of the governing bodies were ever held there, and no activities connected with them were either organised or directed from there. On numerous occasions during my stay at Liliesleaf farm I met both the Executive Committee of the ANC, as well as the NHC, but such meetings were held elsewhere and not on the farm.

(e) Whilst staying at Liliesleaf farm, I frequently visited Arthur Goldreich in the main house and he also paid me visits in my room. We had numerous

---

*Arthur Goldreich was among those arrested in connection with the Rivonia case. Later he and three others in custody escaped from jail by bribing a guard, and fled the country.

**Liliesleaf was the name of the farm in the district of Rivonia, on the northern outskirts of Johannesburg, where the arrests took place. At the time it was let to Arthur Goldreich.

political discussions covering a variety of subjects. We discussed ideological and practical questions, the Congress Alliance, Umkhonto and its activities generally, and his experiences as a soldier in the Palmach, the military wing of the Haganah. Haganah was the political authority of the Jewish National Movement in Palestine.

(f) Because of what I had got to know of Goldreich, I recommended on my return to South Africa that he should be recruited to Umkhonto. I do not know of my personal knowledge whether this was done.

Another of the allegations made by the State is that the aims and objects of the ANC and the Communist Party are the same. I wish to deal with this and with my own political position, because I must assume that the State may try to argue from certain exhibits that I tried to introduce Marxism into the ANC. The allegation as to the ANC is false. This is an old allegation which was disproved at the Treason Trial and which has again reared its head. But since the allegation has been made again, I shall deal with it as well as with the relationship between the ANC and the Communist Party and Umkhonto and that party.

The ideological creed of the ANC is, and always has been, the creed of African Nationalism. It is not the concept of African Nationalism expressed in the cry, 'Drive the White man into the sea.' The African Nationalism for which the ANC stands is the concept of freedom and fulfilment for the African people in their own land. The most important political document ever adopted by the ANC is the Freedom Charter. It is by no means a blueprint for a socialist state. It calls for redistribution, but not nationalisation, of land; it provides for nationalisation of mines, banks, and monopoly industry, because big monopolies are owned by one race only, and without such nationalisation racial domination would be perpetuated despite the spread of political power. It would be a hollow gesture to repeal the Gold Law prohibitions against Africans when all gold mines are owned by European companies. In this respect the ANC's policy corresponds with the old policy of the present Nationalist Party which, for many years, had as part of its programme the nationalisation of the gold mines which, at that time, were controlled by foreign capital. Under the Freedom Charter, nationalisation would take place in an economy based on private enterprise. The realisation of the Freedom Charter would open up fresh fields for a prosperous African population of all classes, including the middle class. The ANC has never at any period of its history advocated a revolutionary change in the economic structure of the country, nor has it, to the best of my recollection, ever condemned capitalist society.

As far as the Communist Party is concerned, and if I understand its policy correctly, it stands for the establishment of a State based on the principles of Marxism. Although it is prepared to work for the Freedom Charter, as a short-term solution to the problems created by white supremacy, it regards the Freedom Charter as the beginning, and not the end, of its programme.

The ANC, unlike the Communist Party, admitted Africans only as members.

Its chief goal was, and is, for the African people to win unity and full political rights. The Communist Party's main aim, on the other hand, was to remove the capitalists and to replace them with a working-class government. The Communist Party sought to emphasise class distinctions whilst the ANC seeks to harmonise them. This is a vital distinction.

It is true that there has often been close co-operation between the ANC and the Communist Party. But co-operation is merely proof of a common goal — in this case the removal of white supremacy — and is not proof of a complete community of interests.

The history of the world is full of similar examples. Perhaps the most striking illustration is to be found in the co-operation between Great Britain, the United States of America, and the Soviet Union in the fight against Hitler. Nobody but Hitler would have dared to suggest that such co-operation turned Churchill or Roosevelt into communists or communist tools, or that Britain and America were working to bring about a communist world.

Another instance of such co-operation is to be found precisely in Umkhonto. Shortly after Umkhonto was constituted, I was informed by some of its members that the Communist Party would support Umkhonto, and this then occurred. At a later stage the support was made openly.

I believe that communists have always played an active role in the fight by colonial countries for their freedom, because the short-term objects of communism would always correspond with the long-term objects of freedom movements. Thus communists have played an important role in the freedom struggles fought in countries such as Malaya, Algeria, and Indonesia, yet none of these states today are communist countries. Similarly in the underground resistance movements which sprung up in Europe during the last world war, communists played an important role. Even General Chiang Kai-Shek, today one of the bitterest enemies of communism, fought together with the communists against the ruling class in the struggle which led to his assumption of power in China in the 1930s.

This pattern of co-operation between communists and non-communists has been repeated in the national liberation movement of South Africa. Prior to the banning of the Communist Party, joint campaigns involving the Communist Party and the Congress movements were accepted practice. African communists could, and did, become members of the ANC, and some served on the national, provincial, and local committees. Amongst those who served on the National Executive are Albert Nzula, a former Secretary of the Communist Party, Moses Kotane, another former Secretary, and J B Marks, a former member of the Central Committee.

I joined the ANC in 1944, and in my younger days I held the view that the policy of admitting communists to the ANC, and the close co-operation which existed at times on specific issues between the ANC and the Communist Party, would lead to a watering down of the concept of African Nationalism. At that stage I was a member of the African National Congress Youth League, and was one of a group which moved for the expulsion of communists from the ANC.

This proposal was heavily defeated. Amongst those who voted against the proposal were some of the most conservative sections of African political opinion. They defended the policy on the ground that from its inception the ANC was formed and built up, not as a political party with one school of political thought, but as a Parliament of the African people, accommodating people of various political convictions, all united by the common goal of national liberation. I was eventually won over to this point of view and I have upheld it ever since.

It is perhaps difficult for white South Africans, with an ingrained prejudice against communism, to understand why experienced African politicians so readily accept communists as their friends. But to us the reason is obvious. Theoretical differences amongst those fighting against oppression is a luxury we cannot afford at this stage. What is more, for many decades communists were the only political group in South Africa who were prepared to treat Africans as human beings and their equals; who were prepared to eat with us; talk with us, live with us, and work with us. They were the only political group which was prepared to work with the Africans for the attainment of political rights and a stake in society. Because of this, there are many Africans who today tend to equate freedom with communism. They are supported in this belief by a legislature which brands all exponents of democratic government and African freedom as communists and bans many of them (who are not communists) under the Suppression of Communism Act. Although I have never been a member of the Communist Party, I myself have been named under that pernicious Act because of the role I played in the Defiance Campaign. I have also been banned and imprisoned under that Act.

It is not only in internal politics that we count communists as amongst those who support our cause. In the international field, communist countries have always come to our aid. In the United Nations and other Councils of the world the communist bloc has supported the Afro-Asian struggle against colonialism and often seems to be more sympathetic to our plight than some of the Western powers. Although there is a universal condemnation of apartheid, the communist bloc speaks out against it with a louder voice than most of the white world. In these circumstances, it would take a brash young politician, such as I was in 1949, to proclaim that the communists are our enemies.

I turn now to my own position. I have denied that I am a communist, and I think that in the circumstances I am obliged to state exactly what my political beliefs are.

I have always regarded myself, in the first place, as an African patriot. After all, I was born in Umtata, 46 years ago. My guardian was my cousin, who was the acting paramount chief of Tembuland, and I am related both to the present paramount chief of Tembuland, Sabata Dalindyebo, and to Kaizer Matanzima, the Chief Minister of the Transkei.

Today I am attracted by the idea of a classless society, an attraction which springs in part from Marxist reading and, in part, from my admiration of the structure and organisation of early African societies in this country. The land, then the main means of production, belonged to the tribe. There were no rich or poor and there was no exploitation.

It is true, as I have already stated, that I have been influenced by Marxist thought. But this is also true of many of the leaders of the new independent states. Such widely different persons as Gandhi, Nehru, Nkrumah, and Nasser all acknowledge this fact. We all accept the need for some form of socialism to enable our people to catch up with the advanced countries of this world and to overcome their legacy of extreme poverty. But this does not mean we are Marxists.

Indeed, for my own part, I believe that it is open to debate whether the Communist Party has any specific role to play at this particular stage of our political struggle. The basic task at the present moment is the removal of race discrimination and the attainment of democratic rights on the basis of the Freedom Charter. In so far as that Party furthers this task, I welcome its assistance. I realise that it is one of the means by which people of all races can be drawn into our struggle.

From my reading of Marxist literature and from conversations with Marxists, I have gained the impression that communists regard the parliamentary system of the West as undemocratic and reactionary. But, on the contrary, I am an admirer of such a system.

The Magna Carta, the Petition of Rights, and the Bill of Rights are documents which are held in veneration by democrats throughout the world.

I have great respect for British political institutions, and for the country's system of justice. I regard the British parliament as the most democratic institution in the world, and the independence and impartiality of its judiciary never fail to arouse my admiration.

The American Congress, that country's doctrine of separation of powers, as well as the independence of its judiciary, arouses in me similar sentiments.

I have been influenced in my thinking by both West and East. All this has led me to feel that in my search for a political formula, I should be absolutely impartial and objective. I should tie myself to no particular system of society other than of socialism. I must leave myself free to borrow the best from the West and from the East . . .

There are certain exhibits which suggest that we received financial support from abroad, and I wish to deal with this question.

Our political struggle has always been financed from internal sources — from funds raised by our own people and by our own supporters. Whenever we had a special campaign or an important political case — for example, the Treason Trial — we received financial assistance from sympathetic individuals and organisations in the Western countries. We had never felt it necessary to go beyond these sources.

But when in 1961 the Umkhonto was formed, and a new phase of struggle introduced, we realised that these events would make a heavy call on our slender resources, and that the scale of our activities would be hampered by the lack of funds. One of my instructions, as I went abroad in January 1962, was to raise funds from the African states.

I must add that, whilst abroad, I had discussions with leaders of political movements in Africa and discovered that almost every single one of them, in areas which had still not attained independence, had received all forms of assistance from the socialist countries, as well as from the West, including that of financial support. I also discovered that some well-known African states, all of them non-communists, and even anti-communists, had received similar assistance.

On my return to the Republic, I made a strong recommendation to the ANC that we should not confine ourselves to Africa and the Western countries, but that we should also send a mission to the socialist countries to raise the funds which we so urgently needed.

I have been told that after I was convicted such a mission was sent, but I am not prepared to name any countries to which it went, nor am I at liberty to disclose the names of the organisations and countries which gave us support or promised to do so.

As I understand the State case, and in particular the evidence of 'Mr X', the suggestion is that Umkhonto was the inspiration of the Communist Party, which sought by playing upon imaginary grievances to enrol the African people into an army which ostensibly was to fight for African freedom, but in reality was fighting for a communist state. Nothing could be further from the truth. In fact the suggestion is preposterous. Umkhonto was formed by Africans to further their strugggle for freedom in their own land. Communists and others supported the movement, and we only wish that more sections of the community would join us.

Our fight is against real, and not imaginary, hardships or, to use the language of the State Prosecutor, 'so-called hardships'. Basically, we fight against two features which are the hallmarks of African life in South Africa and which are entrenched by legislation which we seek to have repealed. These features are poverty and lack of human dignity, and we do not need communists or so-called 'agitators' to teach us about these things.

South Africa is the richest country in Africa, and could be one of the richest countries in the world. But it is a land of extremes and remarkable contrasts. The whites enjoy what may well be the highest standard of living in the world, whilst Africans live in poverty and misery. Forty per cent of the Africans live in hopelessly overcrowded and, in some cases, drought-stricken Reserves, where soil erosion and the overworking of the soil make it impossible for them to live properly off the land. Thirty per cent are labourers, labour tenants, and squatters on white farms and work and live under conditions similar to those of the serfs of the Middle Ages. The other 30 per cent live in towns where they have developed economic and social habits which bring them closer in many respects to white standards. Yet most Africans, even in this group, are impoverished by low incomes and high cost of living.

The highest paid and the most prosperous section of urban African life is in Johannesburg. Yet their actual position is desperate. The latest figures were given on 25 March 1964 by Mr Carr, Manager of the Johannesburg Non-European Affairs Department. The poverty datum line for the average African family in Johannesburg (according to Mr Carr's department) is R42.84 per month. He showed that the average monthly wage is R32.24 and that 46 per cent of all African families in Johannesburg do not earn enough to keep them going.

Poverty goes hand in hand with malnutrition and disease. The incidence of malnutrition and deficiency diseases is very high amongst Africans. Tuberculosis, pellagra, kwashiorkor, gastro-enteritis and scurvy bring death and destruction of health. The incidence of infant mortality is one of the highest in the world. According to the Medical Officer of Health for Pretoria, tuberculosis kills forty people a day (almost all Africans), and in 1961 there were 58,491 new cases reported. These diseases not only destroy the vital organs of the body, but they result in retarded mental conditions and lack of initiative, and reduce powers of concentration. The secondary results of such conditions affect the whole community and the standard of work performed by African labourers.

The complaint of Africans, however, is not only that they are poor and the whites are rich, but that the laws which are made by the whites are designed to preserve this situation. There are two ways to break out of poverty. The first is by formal education, and the second is by the worker acquiring a greater skill at his work and thus higher wages. As far as Africans are concerned, both these avenues of advancement are deliberately curtailed by legislation.

The present government has always sought to hamper Africans in their search for education. One of their early acts after coming into power was to stop subsidies for African school feeding. Many African children who attended schools depended on this supplement to their diet. This was a cruel act.

There is compulsory education for all white children at virtually no cost to their parents, be they rich or poor. Similar facilities are not provided for the African children, though there are some who receive such assistance. African children, however, generally have to pay more for their schooling than whites. According to figures quoted by the South African Institute of Race Relations in its 1963 journal, approximately 40 per cent of African children in the age group between seven and fourteen do not attend school. For those who do attend school, the standards are vastly different from those afforded to white children. In 1960-61 the *per capita* government spending on African students at State-aided schools was estimated at R12.46. In the same years, the *per capita* spending on white children in the Cape Province (which are the only figures available to me) was R144.57. Although there are no figures available to me, it can be stated, without doubt, that the white children on whom R144.57 per head was being spent all came from wealthier homes than African children on whom R12.46 per head was being spent.

The quality of education is also different. According to the Bantu Educational Journal, only 5,660 African children in the whole of South Africa passed their

Junior Certificate in 1962, and in that year only 362 passed matric.* This is presumably consistent with the policy of Bantu education about which the present Prime Minister said, during the debate on the Bantu Education Bill in 1953: 'When I have control of Native education I will reform it so that Natives will be taught from childhood to realise that equality with Europeans is not for them . . . People who believe in equality are not desirable teachers for Natives. When my Department controls Native education it will know for what class of higher education a Native is fitted, and whether he will have a chance in life to use his knowledge.'

The other main obstacle to the economic advancement of the African is the industrial colour-bar under which all the better jobs of industry are reserved for whites only. Moreover, Africans who do obtain employment in the unskilled and semi-skilled occupations which are open to them are not allowed to form trade unions which have recognition under the Industrial Conciliation Act. This means that strikes of African workers are illegal, and that they are denied the right of collective bargaining which is permitted to the better-paid white workers. The discrimination in the policy of successive South African governments towards African workers is demonstrated by the so-called 'civilised labour policy' under which sheltered, unskilled government jobs are found for those white workers who cannot make the grade in industry, at wages which far exceed the earnings of the average African employee in industry.

The government often answers its critics by saying that Africans in South Africa are economically better off than the inhabitants of the other countries in Africa. I do not know whether this statement is true and doubt whether any comparison can be made without having regard to the cost-of-living index in such countries. But even if it is true, as far as the African people are concerned it is irrelevant. Our complaint is not that we are poor by comparison with people in other countries, but that we are poor by comparison with the white people in our own country, and that we are prevented by legislation from altering this imbalance.

The lack of human dignity experienced by Africans is the direct result of the policy of white supremacy. White supremacy implies black inferiority. Legislation designed to preserve white supremacy entrenches this notion. Menial tasks in South Africa are invariably performed by Africans. When anything has to be carried or cleaned the white man will look around for an African to do it for him, whether the African is employed by him or not. Because of this sort of attitude, whites tend to regard Africans as a separate breed. They do not look upon them as people with families of their own; they do not realise that they have emotions — that they fall in love like white people do; that they want to be with their

---

*The Junior Certificate examination is generally taken by white children at the age of 15, and they do not normally leave school before this. Matriculation is taken two years later and qualifies students for higher education. The educational system, however, ensures that very few Africans reach Junior Certificate level, so that what represents a basic standard for whites is one of achievement for Africans. Even fewer attain matriculation level.

wives and children like white people want to be with theirs; that they want to earn enough money to support their families properly, to feed and clothe them and send them to school. And what 'house-boy' or 'garden-boy' or labourer can ever hope to do this?

Pass laws, which to the Africans are among the most hated bits of legislation in South Africa, render any African liable to police surveillance at any time. I doubt whether there is a single African male* in South Africa who has not at some stage had a brush with the police over his pass. Hundreds and thousands of Africans are thrown into jail each year under pass laws. Even worse than this is the fact that pass laws keep husband and wife apart and lead to the breakdown of family life.

Poverty and the breakdown of family life have secondary effects. Children wander about the streets of the townships because they have no schools to go to, or no money to enable them to go to school, or no parents at home to see that they go to school, because both parents (if there be two) have to work to keep the family alive. This leads to a breakdown in moral standards, to an alarming rise in illegitimacy, and to growing violence which erupts not only politically, but everywhere. Life in the townships is dangerous. There is not a day that goes by without somebody being stabbed or assaulted. And violence is carried out of the townships in the white living areas. People are afraid to walk alone in the streets after dark. Housebreakings and robberies are increasing, despite the fact that the death sentence can now be imposed for such offences. Death sentences cannot cure the festering sore.

Africans want to be paid a living wage. Africans want to perform work which they are capable of doing, and not work which the government declares them to be capable of. Africans want to be allowed to live where they obtain work, and not be endorsed out of an area because they were not born there. Africans want to be allowed to own land in places where they work, and not to be obliged to live in rented houses which they can never call their own. Africans want to be part of the general population, and not confined to living in their own ghettoes. African men want to have their wives and children to live with them where they work, and not be forced into an unnatural existence in men's hostels. African women want to be with their menfolk and not be left permanently widowed in the Reserves. Africans want to be allowed out after eleven o'clock at night and not to be confined to their rooms like little children. Africans want to be allowed to travel in their own country and to seek work where they want to and not where the Labour Bureau tells them to. Africans want a just share in the whole of South Africa; they want security and a stake in society.

Above all, we want equal political rights, because without them our disabilities will be permanent. I know this sounds revolutionary to the whites in this country,

---

*Until the 1950s only African men (over the age of 16) had to carry passes. Then, under the terms of the Abolition of Passes and Co-ordination of Documents Act of 1952, women were made to carry them too. Passes were abolished only in the sense that the official designation of the documents (made more comprehensive by the new law) was changed from 'Pass' to 'Reference Book'.

because the majority of voters will be Africans. This makes the white man fear democracy.

But this fear cannot be allowed to stand in the way of the only solution which will guarantee racial harmony and freedom for all. It is not true that the enfranchisement of all will result in racial domination. Political division, based on colour, is entirely artificial and, when it disappears, so will the domination of one colour group by another. The ANC has spent half a century fighting against racialism. When it triumphs it will not change that policy.

This then is what the ANC is fighting. Their struggle is a truly national one. It is a struggle of the African people, inspired by their own suffering and their own experience. It is a struggle for the right to live.

During my lifetime I have dedicated myself to this struggle of the African people. I have fought against white domination, and I have fought against black domination. I have cherished the ideal of a democratic and free society in which all persons live together in harmony and with equal opportunities. It is an ideal which I hope to live for and to achieve. But if needs be, it is an ideal for which I am prepared to die.

On 11 June 1964, at the conclusion of the trial, Mandela and seven others —
Walter Sisulu, Govan Mbeki, Raymond Mhlaba, Elias Motsoaledi, Andrew
Mlangeni, Ahmed Kathrada and Denis Goldberg — were convicted. Mandela
was found guilty on four charges of sabotage and like the others was sentenced to life
imprisonment.

11(b) STATEMENT BY CHIEF LUTULI

Press statement by Chief Albert Lutuli issued by the ANC, 12 June 1964,
following the Rivonia verdict and released by the ANC office in London.

Sentences of life imprisonment have been pronounced on Nelson Mandela, Walter Sisulu, Ahmed Kathrada, Govan Mbeki, Denis Goldberg, Raymond Mhlaba, Elias Motsoaledi and Andrew Mlangeni in the 'Rivonia trial' in Pretoria.

Over the long years these leaders advocated a policy of racial co-operation, of goodwill, and of peaceful struggle that made the South African liberation movement one of the most ethical and responsible of our time. In the face of the most bitter racial persecution, they resolutely set themselves against racialism; in the face of continued provocation, they consistently chose the path of reason.

The African National Congress, with allied organisations representing all racial sections, sought every possible means of redress for intolerable conditions, and held consistently to a policy of using militant, non-violent means of struggle. Their common aim was to create a South Africa in which all South Africans would live and work together as fellow-citizens, enjoying equal rights without discrimination on grounds of race, colour or creed.

To this end, they used every accepted method: propaganda, public meetings and rallies, petitions, stay-at-home strikes, appeals, boycotts. So carefully did they educate the people that in the four-year-long Treason Trial, one police witness after another voluntarily testified to this emphasis on non-violent methods of struggle in all aspects of their activities.

But finally all avenues of resistance were closed; the African National Congress and other organisations were made illegal; their leaders jailed, exiled or forced underground. The government sharpened its oppression of the peoples of South Africa, using its all-white parliament as the vehicle for making repression legal, and utilising every weapon of this highly industrialised and modern state to enforce that 'legality'. The stage was even reached where a white spokesman for the disenfranchised Africans was regarded by the government as a traitor. In addition, sporadic acts of uncontrolled violence were increasing throughout the country. At first in one place, then in another, there were spontaneous eruptions against intolerable conditions; many of these acts increasingly assumed a racial character.

The African National Congress never abandoned its method of a militant, non-violent struggle, and of creating in the process a spirit of militancy in the people. However, in the face of the uncompromising white refusal to abandon a policy which denies the African and other oppressed South Africans their rightful heritage — freedom — no one can blame brave and just men for seeking justice by the use of violent methods; nor could they be blamed if they tried to create an organised force in order to ultimately establish peace and racial harmony.

For this, they are sentenced to be shut away for long years in the brutal and degrading prisons of South Africa. With them will be interred this country's hopes for racial co-operation. They will leave a vacuum in leadership that may only be filled by bitter hate and racial strife.

They represent the highest in morality and ethics in the South African political struggle; this morality and ethics has been sentenced to an imprisonment it may never survive. Their policies are in accordance with the deepest international principles of brotherhood and humanity; without their leadership, brotherhood and humanity may be blasted out of existence in South Africa for long decades to come. They believe profoundly in justice and reason; when they are locked away, justice and reason will have departed from the South African scene.

This is an appeal to save these men, not merely as individuals, but for what they stand for. In the name of justice, of hope, of truth and of peace, I appeal to South Africa's strongest allies, Britain and America. In the name of what we have come to believe Britain and America stand for, I appeal to those two powerful countries to take decisive action for full-scale action for sanctions that would precipitate the end of the hateful system of apartheid.*

I appeal to all governments throughout the world, to people everywhere, to organisations and institutions in every land and at every level, to act now to impose such sanctions on South Africa that will bring about the vital necessary change and avert what can become the greatest African tragedy of our times.

---

*In fact Britain and the US, together with France, have consistently vetoed mandatory United Nations resolutions in the Security Council calling for sanctions against South Africa under Chapter VII of the UN Charter. Eventually in 1977 the Western nations agreed to a mandatory arms embargo, while continuing to oppose all forms of economic sanctions. At the same time the Security Council unanimously adopted another resolution calling on South Africa to release all those imprisoned under its security laws. In the 1980s the governments of both Britain and the US moved towards closer relations with the South African government. The British Prime Minister invited the South African Prime Minister to visit Britain in 1984. In the United States the Reagan administration pursued a policy of 'constructive engagement' with the regime. Later, in 1985, following international outrage resulting from extended international television coverage of police repression in South Africa, both governments adopted limited sanctions policies, though they stopped well short of the boycott and isolation of the South African government called for by Mandela on behalf of the National Action Council in 1961 (*see document 7(h), pp.107–18*).

12. ROBBEN ISLAND

On 13 June 1964, Nelson Mandela was sent back to Robben Island maximum security prison.

Due to close censorship and monitoring of writing materials, correspondence and study activities, no substantial memoirs or prison letters on political topics have come out of South African prisons. However, the letter below by Mandela did come out of Robben Island, and political messages were also sent out, both from the Island and, later, from Pollsmoor Prison.

Descriptions of the conditions which Mandela and other political prisoners experienced on Robben Island, and of the part he played in the struggles there, will be found in Chapter 14 in the form of accounts by fellow prisoners who were released after completing their sentences.

12(a) 'RELEASE US OR TREAT US AS POLITICAL PRISONERS'

Letter addressed to the Minister of Justice, Cape Town, from Nelson Mandela, Robben Island Prison, dated 22 April 1969. Published by the ANC in 1978.

Dear Sir,

My colleagues have requested me to write and ask you to release us from prison and, pending your decision on the matter, to accord us the treatment due to political prisoners. At the outset we wish to point out that in making this application we are not pleading for mercy but are exercising the inherent right of all people incarcerated for their political beliefs.

The persons whose names appear in schedule A attached to this letter live in the single cell section* of Robben Island Prison and are completely isolated from the rest of the prisoners on the island. For this reason we are unable to furnish you with a full list of all the persons on this island and in other prisons on behalf of whom this application is made.

Prior to our conviction and imprisonment we were members of well-known political organisations which fought against political and racial persecution, and which demanded full political rights for the African, Coloured and Indian people of this country. We completely rejected, as we still do, all forms of white domination, and more particularly the policy of separate development, and demanded a democratic South Africa free from the evils of colour oppression, and where all South Africans, regardless of race or belief, would live together in peace and harmony on a basis of equality.

All of us, without exception, were convicted and sentenced for political activities which we embarked upon as part and parcel of our struggle to win for our people the right of self-determination, acknowledged throughout the civilised

---

*The leading figures amongst the political prisoners were held in the single cell section in isolation from the rest: in the section each prisoner was in a separate or single cell, in contrast to the majority, who shared communal cells.

world as the inalienable birthright of all human beings. These activities were inspired by the desire to resist racial policies and unjust laws which violate the principle of human rights and fundamental freedoms that forms the foundation of democratic government.

In the past the governments of South Africa have treated persons found guilty of offences of this nature as political offenders who were released from prison, in some cases, long before their sentences expired. In this connection we refer you to the cases of Generals Christiaan de Wet, J C C Kemp and others who were charged with high treason arising out of the 1914 Rebellion. Their case was in every respect more serious than ours. Twelve thousand rebels took to arms and there were no less than 322 casualties. Towns were occupied and considerable damage caused to government installations, while claims for damage to private property amounted to R500,000. These acts of violence were committed by white men who enjoyed full political rights, who belonged to political parties that were legal, who had newspapers that could publicise their views. They were able to move freely up and down the country espousing their cause and rallying support for their ideas. They had no justification whatsoever for resorting to violence. The leader of the Orange Free State rebels, de Wet, was sentenced to six years' imprisonment plus a fine of R4,000. Kemp received a sentence of seven years and a fine of R2,000. The rest were given comparatively lighter sentences.

In spite of the gravity of their offences, de Wet was released within six months of his conviction and sentence, and the rest within a year. This event occurred a little more than half a century ago, yet the government of the day showed much less intransigence in its treatment of this category of prisoner than the present government seems prepared to do 54 years later with black politicians who have even more justification to resort to violence than the 1914 rebels. This government has persistently spurned our aspirations, suppressed our political organisations and imposed severe restrictions on known activists and field workers.

It has caused hardship and disruption of family life by throwing into prison hundreds of otherwise innocent people. Finally it has instituted a reign of terror unprecedented in the history of the country and closed all channels of constitutional struggle. In such a situation resort to violence was the inevitable alternative of freedom fighters who had the courage of their convictions. No men of principle and integrity could have done otherwise. To have folded arms would have been an act of surrender to a government of minority rule and a betrayal of our cause. World history in general, and that of South Africa in particular, teaches that resort to violence may in certain cases be perfectly legitimate.

In releasing the rebels soon after their convictions the Botha-Smuts government acknowledged this vital fact. We firmly believe that our case is no less different, and we accordingly ask you to make this privilege available to us. As indicated above, there were 322 casualties in the Rebellion. By way of contrast, we draw attention to the fact that in committing acts of sabotage we took special precautions to avoid loss of life, a fact which was expressly acknowledged by both the trial judge and the prosecution in the Rivonia case.

An examination of the attached schedule shows that if we use de Wet's case as the standard, then every one of us ought to have been released by now. Of the 23 persons whose names are listed therein, eight are doing life imprisonment, ten are serving sentences ranging from ten to twenty years, and five between two and ten years.

Of those doing imprisonment for life, seven have completed four years ten months, and one has done four years and four months. The man with the longest sentence amongst those serving terms between ten and twenty years is Billy Nair, who has already completed a quarter of his sentence. Joe Gqabi, Samson Fadana and Andrew Masondo, the first to be convicted in this group, have each completed six years of their respective sentences of twelve, eight and thirteen years. The last men to be sentenced in the same group were Jackson Fuzile and Johannes Dangala, who received twelve and seven years respectively. Fuzile has completed a quarter of his sentence whereas Dangala will have done exactly half of his on 19 May 1969. Every one of those serving terms between two and ten years has at least completed a quarter of his sentence.

Our claim for release becomes even stronger when examined in relation to the cases of Robey Leibbrandt, Holm, Pienaar Strauss and others. Leibbrandt, a national of the Union of South Africa, arrived in the Union from Germany at a time when that country was at war with the Union. He then proceeded to set up a paramilitary underground organisation with the purpose of overthrowing the government and establishing in its place one modelled on that of Nazi Germany. He was found guilty of high treason and sentenced to death, later commuted to imprisonment for life. Holm, Pienaar and Strauss were also imprisoned for high treason, it being alleged that they collaborated with the enemy in prosecuting the war against the Union and its allies. On coming to power, however, the present government released these and other prisoners sentenced for treason and sabotage, notwithstanding the fact that they had been arrested in circumstances which made them appear to many South Africans as traitors to their own country. Again by way of contrast, we draw attention to the fact that our activities were at all times actuated by the noblest ideals that men can cherish, namely, the desire to serve our people in their just struggle to free themselves from a government founded on injustice and inequality.

We further wish to remind you that in 1966 your predecessors released Spike de Keller, Stephanie Kemp, Alan Brooks and Tony Trew, all of whom originally appeared jointly with Edward Joseph Daniels (whose names appear in the schedule) on a charge of sabotage. Kemp, Brooks and Trew pleaded guilty to an alternative charge, and a separation of trial was ordered. The case against Daniels and de Keller proceeded on the main charge and on 17 November 1964 they were found guilty and sentenced to fifteen and ten years respectively. Kemp, Brooks and Trew were found guilty on the alternative and sentenced five, four and four years respectively, each of which was partly suspended. We are informed that de Keller was released after he had served approximately two years, or less, of his sentence of ten years, whilst Kemp, Brooks and Trew were also released before they had completed their sentences.

186

Photo: Eli Weinberg

At the age of nineteen in Umtata, Transkei   Photo: P. K. A. Gaeshwe

Photo: Eli Weinberg

The house at 'The Great Place' where Mandela lived from the late 1920s to 1939   *Photo: Peter Davis*

In the legal office shared with O. R. Tambo (see sign on window)   *Photo: Jurgen Schadeberg*

Photo: Eli Weinberg

Photo: Eli Weinberg

Yusuf Dadoo, President Transvaal Indian Congress, addressing a meeting outside Johannesburg City Hall during the Defiance Campaign. Mandela stands to the left of Dadoo   *Photographer unknown*

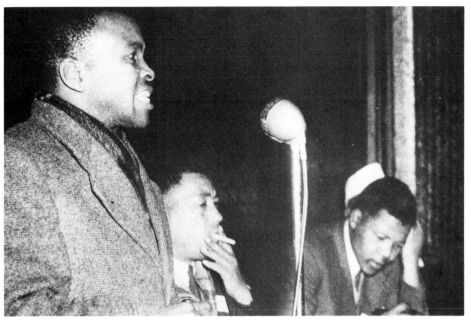

David Bopape, Secretary ANC Transvaal, Walter Sisulu, Secretary General ANC, Mandela, Volunteer-in-Chief, Defiance Campaign, 1952   *Photographer unknown*

Yusuf Dadoo and Mandela after their arrest during the Defiance Campaign, 1952   *Photo: Eli Weinberg*

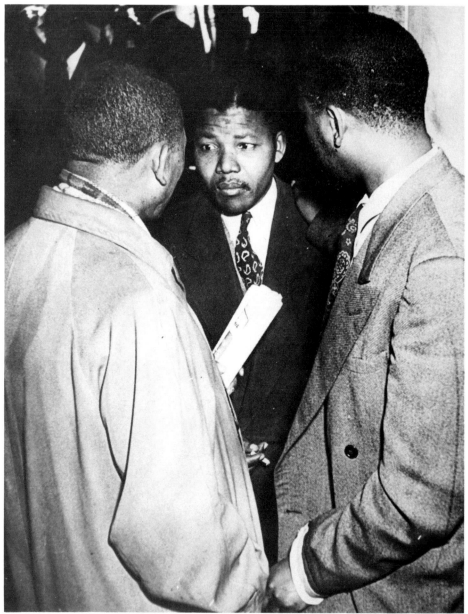

Mandela at the Transvaal Supreme Court, 1952, after receiving a 9-month suspended sentence under the Suppression of Communism Act

Photographer unknown

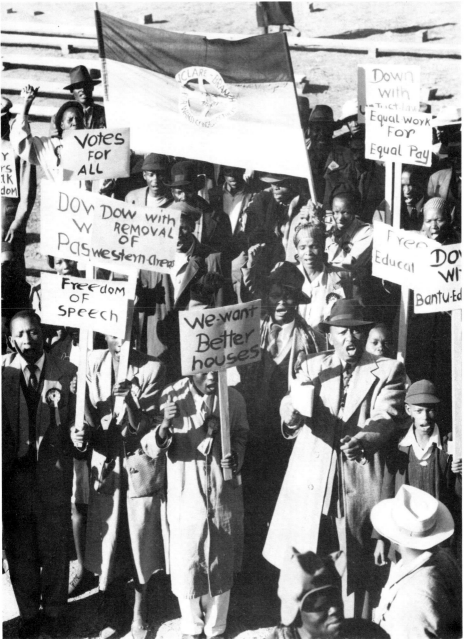

Congress of the People, Kliptown, 1955   *Photo: Eli Weinberg*

The accused — Mandela is in the centre of the 3rd row from the bottom

Montage: Eli Weinberg

Photographer unknown

Washing cups during a recess of the Treason Trial
Photographer unknown

Treason trialists arriving at court, Drill Hall, Johannesburg, December 1956. With Mandela (seen on the right) are Patrick Molaoa and Robert Resha   *Photographer unknown*

Demonstration outside Treason Trial Court, December 1956   *Photo: Eli Weinberg*

During Treason Trial   *Photographer unknown*

Accused and supporters celebrate the end of the Treason Trial, April 1961, when the court acquitted and discharged all the accused. Mandela appears facing the camera on the right and Winnie Mandela is behind him on the right   *Photographer unknown*

Winnie and Nelson on their wedding day, 14 June 1958   Photo: Eli Weinberg

At the funeral of Ida Mntwana, who died during the Treason Trial. Winnie and other leaders of the ANC Women's League carry the coffin

Photo: Eli Weinberg

Winnie and Nelson celebrate the end of the State of Emergency, December 1960   *Photographer unknown*

IF GOVERNMENT REFUSES NATIONAL CONVENTION...

ALL-IN CONFERENCE CALLS FOR ACTION

Vol. 7, No. 24. Registered at the G.P.O. as a Newspaper — 6d.

SOUTHERN EDITION — Thursday, March 30, 1961 — 5c.

Mass Demonstrations On Eve of Republic

Photos by Joe Gqabi and Bala Govender
and story from M. P. Naicker

MARITZBURG

THE ALL AFRICAN PEOPLE'S CONFERENCE HELD AT PIETERMARITZBURG LAST SATURDAY WAS AN UNQUALIFIED SUCCESS.

Over 1,400 delegates attended and unanimously demanded . . .
● "That a National Convention of elected representatives of all adult men and women on an equal basis irrespective of race, colour, creed or other limitations be called not later than May 31, 1961."

The conference also resolved:
● That should the minority Government ignore this demand of the representatives of the united will of the African people:
1. To call on the people to organise mass demonstrations throughout the country on the eve of the declaration of the Republic on May 31.
2. To call on all Africans not to co-operate or collaborate with the proposed S.A. Republic or any other

form of Government which rests on force to perpetuate the tyranny of a minority; and, to organise and unite in town and country to carry out constant actions to oppose oppression and win freedom.

3. To call on the Indian and Coloured communities and all democratic Europeans to join forces with us in opposition to a regime which is bringing South Africa to disaster . . .

The highlights of this magnificent Conference were . . . .
● The patience and seriousness with which the delegates from all over South Africa met and discussed the problems that faced them. They conferred throughout Saturday night, even though many of them were tired after travelling the previous night in order to get to Conference . . .
● The inspiring opening address by Mr. Nelson Mandela, former President of the banned African National Congress (Transvaal), whose every sentence was either cheered or greeted with cries of "shame" when he referred to atrocities perpetrated against the people by the Nationalist Government.

● The representative character of the delegates, old and young, who had travelled many miles to be at Conference. There were delegates from Thogazi in Zululand; St. Faith's, near Port Shepstone; Ixopo, New Hanover, Tembuland, Pondoland, Zeerust and Sekhukhuneland. They came from New Brighton and Moroka, Alexandra and Langa.

(Continued on page 3)

Mr. Nelson Mandela delivering his inspiring opening address to the Maritzburg conference.

AFRICA DAY SPECIAL

In commemoration of Africa Day (April 15), New Age will distribute FREE with each copy of the paper — published on Thursday, April 13, a portrait of Chief A. J. Lutuli. Order your copy now.

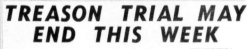

TREASON TRIAL MAY END THIS WEEK

JOHANNESBURG

THERE WAS AN ELECTRIC ATMOSPHERE IN THE TREASON TRIAL COURT WHEN THE JUDGES ADJOURNED THE CASE LAST FRIDAY UNTIL WEDNESDAY OF THIS WEEK. IT LOOKED AS THOUGH AFTER FOUR AND A HALF YEARS OF PAINFUL NEVER-ENDING EVIDENCE AND ARGUMENT THE BIG CASE MIGHT SUDDENLY COLLAPSE.

The judges broke into the Defence argument when Advocate A. Fischer was on his feet arguing on the meetings the 28 accused had addressed. The presiding judge, Mr. Justice Rumpff, said the Bench thought it might shorten the proceedings if it interrupted the Defence argument and adjourned for six days for the judges to consider the legal points so far argued.

The Crown argument has lasted almost four months. The Defence has been arguing for three weeks. This is the second interruption of the Defence argument by the Bench. The first was to call on the Crown to answer the weighty legal arguments advanced by the Defence before its case was fully argued. This second adjournment was called for by the Bench after Mr. Trengove had already completed the Crown's reply to the Defence legal argument.

(Continued on page 6)

Abandoning the first hall, which had been wired by the Special Branch, the people marched two miles in the rain to another hall in Plessislaer where the conference eventually took place.

Front page of New Age, the weekly newspaper of the Congress Alliance, 31 March 1961

With Oliver Tambo in Addis Ababa, 1962   *Photographer unknown*

At the Algerian Military Headquarters, 1962　　　　　　　　　　　　*Photographer unknown*

Outside Westminster Abbey, London 1962　　　　　　　　　　　　*Photo: Mary Benson*

In hiding, after his return from abroad, 1962   *Photo: Eli Weinberg*

Winnie Mandela leaving court during Mandela's trial in 1962

Winnie with Zinzi and Zenani, 1961

Mandela and Sisulu, prison yard, Robben Island, 1966   *Photographer unknown*

The prison yard, Robben Island. The political prisoners, on the right, are sewing mailbags   *Photographer unknown*

Winnie Mandela at Hector Petersen's funeral (he was the first child to die in the Soweto Massacre), June 1976
Photo: Peter Magubane

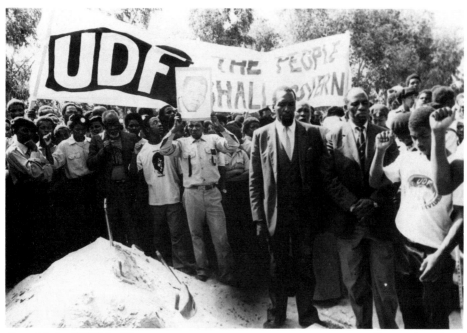

Funeral during 1985 State of Emergency   *Photographer unknown*

Jesse Jackson, US black leader, with O. R. Tambo to his right (front) addresses the 'March Against Apartheid', Trafalgar Square, London, November 1985   *Photo: Gerzy Dabrowski*

Banner at Memorial Meeting, Middleburg, Cape, March 1986   *Photo: Gillian Edelstein*

Zinzi Mandela at Jabulani Stadium, Soweto, 10 February 1985, reading her father's statement rejecting the government's offer of his conditional release
Photo: Morris Zwi

Police prevented this message of the people to Nelson Mandela being delivered to him
Photographer unknown

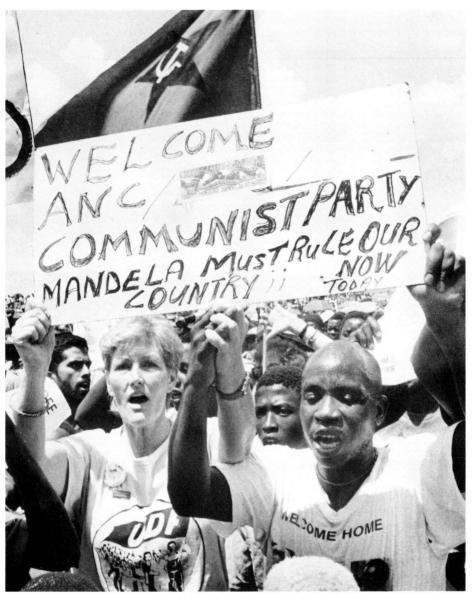

Supporters celebrate the unbanning of the African National Congress and the South African Communist Party at a rally before a march to the Alexandra Civic Centre where they called on members of the government-created town council to resign and join the ANC. 3 February 1990.

Photo: Anna Zieminski

Part of a rally in Soweto to welcome home from prison seven ANC leaders who were released on 15 October. The seven were Walter Sisulu, Raymond Mhlaba, Ahmed Kathrada, Elias Motsoaledi, Andrew Mlangeni, Wilton Mkwayi and Oscar Mpetha. 29 October 1989.

Photo: Anna Zieminski

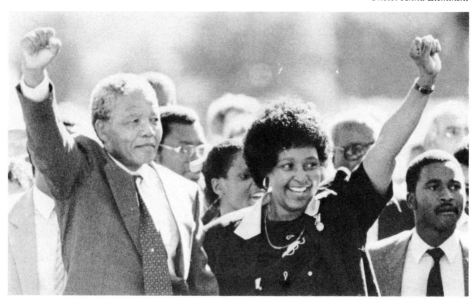

Nelson Mandela walks through the gates of Victor Verster prison with Winnie Mandela on his release from 27 years imprisonment. 11 February 1990.

Photo: Paul Weinberg

Two of the thousands of supporters who gathered in Cape Town's Grand Parade for the first glimpse of Nelson Mandela on the day of his release. 11 February 1990.

Photo: Paul Grendon

Nelson Mandela.   *Photo: Paul Weinberg*

Part of a rally in Soweto to celebrate the release of Mandela. 11 February 1990.

Photo: Anna Zieminski

Soweto residents gather outside Nelson Mandela's home to celebrate his release. 11 February 1990.

Photo: Cedric Nunn

Nelson Mandela addresses a 'Welcome Home Rally' in Soweto. 13 February 1990.

Photo: Gill de Vlieg.

Part of the mass rally in Durban to greet Mandela. 25 February 1990.   Photo: Guy Tillim

Nelson Mandela met by Zambian President Kenneth Kaunda (right) on his arrival at Lusaka airport. 27 February 1990.

           Photo: Cedric Nunn

Nelson Mandela with (left to right): Ingvar Carlsson, Prime Minister of Sweden; Alfred Nzo, Secretary General of the ANC; and Thabo Mbeki, Secretary for International Affairs of the ANC, at a press conference in Stockholm during Mandela's visit to Sweden. 13 March 1990.

Photo: Tim Sambrooke

Nelson Mandela and Oliver Tambo, re-united in Stockholm after 28 years. 12 March 1990.

Photo: Anders Holmstrom

We do not in any way begrudge those who were fortunate enough to be released and who escape the hardship of prison life and are happy to know that they now lead a normal life. But we refer to their case for the limited purpose of showing that our request is reasonable, and also to stress that a government is expected to be consistent in its policy and to accord the same treatment to its citizens.

There is one important difference between our case and that of de Wet and Leibbrandt. They were released only after the rebellion had been crushed and after Germany had been conquered and they were thus no threat to the safety of the State when they were freed.

In our case, however, it may be argued that our revolution is planned for the future and that security considerations require that we be treated differently. Add to this the fact that our convictions have not changed and our dreams are still the same as they were before we were jailed; all of which would seem to confirm the opinion that our case is distinguishable from all the previous ones. We feel sure, however, that you will not be tempted to think along these lines, as such an argument would carry sinister implications. It would mean that if security considerations today require that we should be kept in prison, we would not be released when we complete our respective sentences, if the present situation remains unaltered, or if the position worsens. The plain truth is that the racial strife and conflict that seriously threatens the country today is due solely to the shortsighted policies and crimes committed by the government.

The only way to avert disaster is not to keep innocent men in jail but to abandon your provocative actions and to pursue sane and enlightened policies. Whether or not evil strife and bloodshed are to occur in this country rests entirely on the government. The continued suppression of our aspirations and reliance on rule through coercion drives our people more and more to violence. Neither you nor I can predict the price the country will have to pay at the end of that strife. The obvious solution is to release us and to hold a round table conference to consider an amicable solution.

Our main request is that you release us and, pending your decision, you treat us as political prisoners. This means that we should be provided with good diet, proper clothing outfit, bed and mattress, newspapers, radios, bioscope,* better contact with our families here and abroad.

Treatment as political prisoners implies the freedom to obtain all reading material that is not banned and to write books for publication. We would expect to be given the option to work as one desires and to decide the trades one would like to learn. In this connection we wish to point out that some of these privileges were enjoyed both by the 1914 rebels as well as by Leibbrandt and colleagues, all of whom were treated as political prisoners.

The prison authorities attempt to answer our demand for treatment as political prisoners by pointing out that we were convicted by the courts for contravening

---

*ie. cinema.

the laws of the country, that we are like any other criminals and, therefore, cannot be treated as political offenders.

This is a spurious argument which flies in the face of the facts. On this view de Wet, Kemp, Maritz, Leibbrandt and others were ordinary criminals. Treason, sabotage, membership of an illegal organisation were all criminal offences then as now. Why then were they treated differently? It seems to us that the only difference between the two cases is one of colour.

Serious differences of opinion on a specific issue had emerged amongst the Whites, and those who lost in the contest that flowed from these differences eventually found themselves behind bars. On all other issues, especially on the major question of colour both victor and vanquished were in agreement. The conflict having been solved, it was possible for the government to adopt a conciliatory attitude and to extend to the prisoners all sorts of indulgences. But today the position is altogether different. This time the challenge comes, not from the white man, but mainly from black politicians who disagree with the government on almost everything under the sun. The victory of our cause means the end of white rule.

In this situation the government regards the prison not as an institution of rehabilitation but as an instrument of retribution, not to prepare us to lead a respectable and industrious life when released, and to play our role as worthy members of society, but to punish and cripple us, so that we should never again have the strength and courage to pursue our ideals. This is our punishment for raising our voices against the tyranny of colour. This is the true explanation for the bad treatment we receive in prison — pick and shovel work continuously for the last five years, a wretched diet, denial of essential cultural material and isolation from the world outside the jail. This is the reason why privileges normally available to other prisoners, including those convicted of murder, rape and crimes involving dishonesty, are withheld from political offenders.

We get no remission of sentence. Whilst the ordinary prisoner is classified in C group on admission, political offenders are put in D, which carries the least privileges. Those of us who managed to reach A group are denied privileges normally enjoyed by criminals in the same group. We are compelled to do pick and shovel work, are not allowed newspapers, radios, bioscope; contact visits* and even groceries are given grudgingly.

---

*Visits where a prisoner may embrace visitors. Mandela's first contact visit with his wife was in May 1984, fifteen years after this letter was written. His wife describes it: 'Can you imagine! We last touched his hand in 1962. When I arrived at Pollsmoor Prison — Zeni and her youngest were with me — Sergeant Gregory called me to the office. I got a terrible shock, I thought Nelson was sick, because that's very unusual. He said: "As from now on you will be able to have different visits. I thought I should bring the news gently to you." We kissed Nelson and held him a long time. It is an experience one just can't put into words. It was fantastic and hurting at the same time. He clung to the child right through the visit. Gregory, his warder, was so moved he looked the other way. That the system could have been so cruel as to deny us that right for the last twenty-two years! Why deny that right to a man who is jailed for life?' (Winnie Mandela, *Part of My Soul*, Penguin, London 1985, p 144). In fact Mandela had been allowed contact visits on previous occasions with his daughter Zeni, apparently for diplomatic reasons, because she is married to a member of the royal family of Swaziland. The first was in 1978.

188

As already indicated in the second paragraph above, I make this application on behalf of all my colleagues on the island and in other jails and I trust that any concessions that may be granted will be made available to all without exception.

The Prisons Act of 1959 gives you the necessary powers to grant the relief we seek. Under its provisions you are entitled to release us on parole or probation. de Wet and others were released under the former method. In conclusion, we place on record that the years we have spent on this island have been difficult years. Almost every one of us has had a full share in one way or another of the hardships that face non-white prisoners. These hardships have at times been the result of official indifference to our problems, other times they were due to plain persecution. But things have somewhat eased and we hope even better days will come. All that we wish to add is that we trust that when you consider this application you will bear in mind that the ideas that inspire us, and the convictions that give form and direction to our activities constitute the only solution to the problems of our country and are in accordance with the enlightened conceptions of the human family.

Yours faithfully,

Signed N Mandela

12(b) 'UNITE! MOBILISE! FIGHT ON! BETWEEN THE ANVIL OF UNITED MASS ACTION AND THE HAMMER OF THE ARMED STRUGGLE WE SHALL CRUSH APARTHEID!'

This message was Mandela's call after the Soweto uprising of 1976.* It was published by the ANC on 10 June 1980, with an introduction by O R Tambo, now President of the ANC.

The African National Congress brings you this URGENT CALL TO UNITY AND MASS ACTION by political prisoners on Robben Island to all patriots of our motherland. Nelson Mandela and hundreds of our comrades have been in the racist regime's prisons for more than 17 years. This message by Nelson Mandela addressed to the struggling masses of our country was written to deal with the present crisis gripping our enemy and in the aftermath of the Soweto uprisings. It was smuggled out of Robben Island prison under very difficult conditions and has taken over two years to reach us. None the less we believe the message remains fresh and valid and should be presented to our people. His call to unity and mass

---

*On 16 June 1976, police opened fire on schoolchildren marching in protest against the education imposed on them by the apartheid system. This sparked a national uprising against the whole system of apartheid. By the end of the uprising, at least 618 black people had been killed and 1,500 injured, according to the South African Institute of Race Relations. Most of the casualties were school pupils shot by the police. Some press reports put the figure substantially higher.

action is of particular importance in this Year of the Charter — 25th anniversary of the Freedom Charter. The ANC urges you to respond to this call and make 1980 a year of united mass struggle.

Oliver Tambo: President, ANC

*   *   *

MANDELA'S CALL

RACISTS RULE BY THE GUN!

The gun has played an important part in our history. The resistance of the black man to white colonial intrusion was crushed by the gun. Our struggle to liberate ourselves from white domination is held in check by force of arms. From conquest to the present the story is the same. Successive white regimes have repeatedly massacred unarmed defenceless blacks. And wherever and whenever they have pulled out their guns the ferocity of their fire has been trained on the African people.

Apartheid is the embodiment of the racialism, repression and inhumanity of all previous white supremacist regimes. To see the real face of apartheid we must look beneath the veil of constitutional formulas, deceptive phrases and playing with words.

The rattle of gunfire and the rumbling of Hippo armoured vehicles since June 1976 have once again torn aside that veil. Spread across the face of our country, in black townships, the racist army and police have been pouring a hail of bullets killing and maiming hundreds of black men, women and children. The toll of the dead and injured already surpasses that of all past massacres carried out by this regime.

Apartheid is the rule of the gun and the hangman. The Hippo, the FN rifle* and the gallows are its true symbols. These remain the easiest resort, the ever-ready solution of the race-mad rulers of South Africa.

VAGUE PROMISES, GREATER REPRESSION . . .

In the midst of the present crisis, while our people count the dead and nurse the injured, they ask themselves: what lies ahead?

From our rulers we can expect nothing. They are the ones who give orders to the soldier crouching over his rifle: theirs is the spirit that moves the finger that caresses the trigger.

Vague promises, tinkerings with the machinery of apartheid, constitution juggling, massive arrests and detentions side by side with renewed overtures aimed at weakening and forestalling the unity of us blacks and dividing the forces of change — these are the fixed paths along which they will move. For they are neither capable nor willing to heed the verdict of the masses of our people.

---

*Standard NATO weapon.

THE VERDICT OF JUNE 16!

That verdict is loud and clear: apartheid has failed. Our people remain unequivocal in its rejection. The young and the old, parent and child, all reject it. At the forefront of this 1976/77 wave of unrest were our students and youth. They come from the universities, high schools and even primary schools. They are a generation whose whole education has been under the diabolical design of the racists to poison the minds and brainwash our children into docile subjects of apartheid rule. But after more than twenty years of Bantu Education the circle is closed and nothing demonstrates the utter bankruptcy of apartheid as the revolt of our youth.

The evils, the cruelty and the inhumanity of apartheid have been there from its inception. And all blacks — Africans, Coloureds and Indians — have opposed it all along the line. What is now unmistakeable, what the current wave of unrest has sharply highlighted, is this: that despite all the window-dressing and smooth talk, apartheid has become intolerable.

This awareness reaches over and beyond the particulars of our enslavement. The measure of this truth is the recognition by our people that under apartheid our lives, individually and collectively, count for nothing.

UNITE!

We face an enemy that is deeprooted, an enemy entrenched and determined not to yield. Our march to freedom is long and difficult. But both within and beyond our borders the prospects of victory grow bright.

The first condition for victory is black unity. Every effort to divide the blacks, to woo and pit one black group against another, must be vigorously repulsed. Our people — African, Coloured, Indian and democratic whites — must be united into a single massive and solid wall of resistance, of united mass action.

Our struggle is growing sharper. This is not the time for the luxury of division and disunity. At all levels and in every walk of life we must close ranks. Within the ranks of the people differences must be submerged to the achievement of a single goal — the complete overthrow of apartheid and racist domination.

VICTORY IS CERTAIN!

The revulsion of the world against apartheid is growing and the frontiers of white supremacy are shrinking. Mozambique and Angola are free and the war of liberation gathers force in Namibia and Zimbabwe. The soil of our country is destined to be the scene of the fiercest fight and the sharpest battles to rid our continent of the last vestiges of white minority rule.

The world is on our side. The OAU, the UN and the anti-apartheid movement continue to put pressure on the racist rulers of our country. Every effort to isolate South Africa adds strength to our struggle.

At all levels of our struggle, within and outside the country, much has been achieved and much remains to be done. But victory is certain!

WE SALUTE ALL OF YOU!

We who are confined within the grey walls of the Pretoria regime's prisons reach out to our people. With you we count those who have perished by means of the gun and the hangman's rope. We salute all of you — the living, the injured and the dead. For you have dared to rise up against the tyrant's might.

Even as we bow at their graves we remember this: the dead live on as martyrs in our hearts and minds, a reproach to our disunity and the host of shortcomings that accompany divisions among the oppressed, a spur to our efforts to close ranks, and a reminder that the freedom of our people is yet to be won.

We face the future with confidence. For the guns that serve apartheid cannot render it unconquerable. Those who live by the gun shall perish by the gun.

UNITE! MOBILISE! FIGHT ON!

Between the anvil of united mass action and the hammer of the armed struggle we shall crush apartheid and white minority racist rule.

AMANDLA NGAWETHU!*
MATLA KE A RONA!

---

*'Power to the People!' in Zulu and Sotho.

13. POLLSMOOR — 1985

In April 1982 Nelson Mandela was transferred to Pollsmoor maximum security prison near Cape Town on the mainland, together with Walter Sisulu, Ahmed Kathrada, Raymond Mhlaba and Andrew Mlangeni. The reasons for the transfer were not clear.*

Their conditions were suddenly worse. On the island, each man had a cell; now, they all had to share one large cell with a sixth prisoner. On the island, they had moved freely about the communal section; now, they were isolated from all other prisoners. On the island, they could walk to work outdoors; now, they had an exercise yard attached to the cell from which they could only see a little patch of sky. Improvements they had fought for, over twenty years, were left behind.

In spite of the conditions, Mandela and the other imprisoned leaders still participated in the struggle for freedom. Mandela's status as a leader continued to grow, as it had throughout his imprisonment.

The period between the uprising of 1976 (see previous chapter) and the events of 1985 which provided the context for the statements in this chapter, was marked by an intensification of every aspect of the struggle for liberation.

The ANC's armed struggle was set back by ruthless repression in the 1960s. It was renewed in the mid-1970s after the ANC had rebuilt its underground structures and it received added impetus after the uprising of 1976. There was a dramatic increase in the number of people leaving the country for military training and in the following years Umkhonto we Sizwe carried out attacks with increasing frequency on strategic targets, buildings involved in the administration of apartheid, police stations and installations of the South African Defence Force.

During 1984 and 1985 the armed struggle entered a new phase as part of the liberation movement's shift to a more generalised offensive aimed at making South Africa ungovernable and at making the apartheid system unworkable. The distinction between actions carried out by trained guerillas and attacks of a more spontaneous character arising out of mass resistance became less sharp. The ANC's National Consultative Conference held in Zambia in June 1985 (and to which Mandela and other imprisoned leaders sent the message in document 13(b)) issued a call for a 'people's war', for the forging of closer links between guerillas and political activists and for an active engagement of the armed forces of apartheid.

---

*Winnie Mandela discussed the reason for the transfer with her husband on a visit: 'He had no idea. The most logical reason seems to have been that it was for administrative reasons. He told me that the very day he was transferred, he had been consulting a lawyer from Cape Town about the education of young prisoners on the island.' Nelson Mandela had just been awarded the Jahawarlal Nehru Peace Prize and was planning to use the prize money to help young prisoners with their education, as he had done on previous occasions. 'The Prisons Department', Winnie Mandela wrote, 'must have got worried about the extent to which he was doing this sort of programme. The island became known as Mandela University. Youths who had left school having Standard 6 emerged from the island with degrees. In his absence that programme came to an end.' (Winnie Mandela, *Part of My Soul*, Penguin, London, 1985, pp 141-2.)

These developments were accompanied by processes of both underground and legal mobilisation for the liberation struggle. After the banning in 1977 of almost all the legal organisations of resistance, the following years saw a broad and deeply rooted growth of new legal structures of open resistance. The initial stage consisted of the formation of a large number of local, community-based organisations. They mobilised support around specific aspects of the apartheid system affecting the lives of the majority of the population — high rents, transport costs, low wages, and inferior education. National organisations of pupils and students were also formed and there was a tremendous growth of independent black and non-racial trade unions.

Over the next few years, particularly in the course of mass political campaigns such as the boycott of elections to apartheid institutions, the links between the new organisations developed. Their specific struggles were integrated into the overall struggle against the apartheid system. This took place at first on a regional and ad hoc basis, and then in 1983 assumed a national and more permanent form with the emergence of the United Democratic Front (UDF) (of which Mandela was made a patron). The UDF was formed specifically around opposition to the new apartheid constitution, in order to campaign for boycotts of the elections to the new Black Local Authorities in November 1983 and the first elections to the Indian and Coloured chambers of the segregated tricameral parliament in August 1984.

By the end of 1984 plans to preserve the apartheid system by adapting it to the new conditions in South Africa faced a major challenge. Boycotts of elections to apartheid political structures, protests against apartheid education, resistance to increased rents, all contributed to a mobilisation of resistance to the system as a whole and to the general offensive against the regime.

In July 1985, after months of steadily more violent repressive action, the government declared a State of Emergency.

One aspect of the political mobilisation described above was increasingly open and organised expression of support for the ANC and for Nelson Mandela, with calls for his release and the release of all other political prisoners. Surveys of black opinion during the first half of the 1980s consistently showed that despite 25 years of being banned and operating underground, the ANC was still the most popular political organisation in South Africa and Nelson Mandela the most popular leader. In January 1985 faced with mounting resistance to which it was responding with increasing violence the government offered to release Nelson Mandela on condition that he renounced his commitment to the ANC's armed struggle. His rejection of that offer is contained in the following document.

13(a) 'I AM NOT PREPARED TO SELL THE BIRTHRIGHT OF THE PEOPLE TO BE FREE.'

On 31 January 1985 the State President of South Africa, P W Botha, speaking in parliament, offered Mandela his freedom on condition that he 'unconditionally rejected violence as a political weapon'.

194

This was the sixth offer of release reported to have been made to Mandela. Previous offers were conditional on his going to live in the Transkei bantustan. He rejected them all on the grounds that he rejected the bantustans and all who collaborated in their establishment and maintenance.

Mandela's response to the latest offer was read on his behalf by his daughter Zinzi to a mass meeting in Jabulani Stadium, Soweto, on 10 February, 1985. This text was published by the ANC in London.

On Friday my mother and our attorney saw my father at Pollsmoor Prison to obtain his answer to Botha's offer of conditional release. The prison authorities attempted to stop this statement being made but he would have none of this and made it clear that he would make the statement to you, the people.

Strangers like Bethell from England and Professor Dash from the United States have in recent weeks been authorised by Pretoria to see my father without restriction, yet Pretoria cannot allow you, the people, to hear what he has to say directly. He should be here himself to tell you what he thinks of this statement by Botha. He is not allowed to do so. My mother, who also heard his words, is also not allowed to speak to you today.

My father and his comrades at Pollsmoor Prison send their greetings to you, the freedom-loving people of this our tragic land, in the full confidence that you will carry on the struggle for freedom. He and his comrades at Pollsmoor Prison send their very warmest greetings to Bishop Desmond Tutu. Bishop Tutu has made it clear to the world that the Nobel Peace Prize belongs to you who are the people. We salute him.

My father and his comrades at Pollsmoor Prison are grateful to the United Democratic Front who without hesitation made this venue available to them so that they could speak to you today. My father and his comrades wish to make this statement to you, the people, first. They are clear that they are accountable to you and to you alone. And that you should hear their views directly and not through others. My father speaks not only for himself and for his comrades at Pollsmoor Prison, but he hopes he also speaks for all those in jail for their opposition to apartheid, for all those who are banished, for all those who are in exile, for all those who suffer under apartheid, for all those who are opponents of apartheid and for all those who are oppressed and exploited.

Throughout our struggle there have been puppets who have claimed to speak for you. They have made this claim, both here and abroad. They are of no consequence. My father and his colleagues will not be like them. My father says:

I am a member of the African National Congress. I have always been a member of the African National Congress and I will remain a member of the African National Congress until the day I die. Oliver Tambo is much more than a brother to me. He is my greatest friend and comrade for nearly fifty years. If there is any one amongst you who cherishes my freedom, Oliver Tambo cherishes it more, and I know that he would give his life to see me free. There is no difference between his views and mine.

I am surprised at the conditions that the government wants to impose on me. I am not a violent man. My colleagues and I wrote in 1952 to Malan asking for a round table conference to find a solution to the problems of our country, but that was ignored. When Strijdom was in power, we made the same offer. Again it was ignored. When Verwoerd was in power we asked for a national convention for all the people in South Africa to decide on their future. This, too, was in vain.

It was only then, when all other forms of resistance were no longer open to us, that we turned to armed struggle. Let Botha show that he is different to Malan, Strijdom and Verwoerd. Let him renounce violence. Let him say that he will dismantle apartheid. Let him unban the people's organisation, the African National Congress. Let him free all who have been imprisoned, banished or exiled for their opposition to apartheid. Let him guarantee free political activity so that people may decide who will govern them.

I cherish my own freedom dearly, but I care even more for your freedom. Too many have died since I went to prison. Too many have suffered for the love of freedom. I owe it to their widows, to their orphans, to their mothers and to their fathers who have grieved and wept for them. Not only I have suffered during these long, lonely, wasted years. I am not less life-loving than you are. But I cannot sell my birthright, nor am I prepared to sell the birthright of the people to be free. I am in prison as the representative of the people and of your organisation, the African National Congress, which was banned.

What freedom am I being offered while the organisaton of the people remains banned? What freedom am I being offered when I may be arrested on a pass offence? What freedom am I being offered to live my life as a family with my dear wife who remains in banishment in Brandfort? What freedom am I being offered when I must ask for permission to live in an urban area? What freedom am I being offered when I need a stamp in my pass to seek work? What freedom am I being offered when my very South African citizenship is not respected?

Only free men can negotiate. Prisoners cannot enter into contracts. Herman Toivo ja Toivo, when freed, never gave any undertaking, nor was he called upon to do so.

I cannot and will not give any undertaking at a time when I and you, the people, are not free.

Your freedom and mine cannot be separated. I will return.

13(b) MESSAGE TO THE SECOND NATIONAL CONSULTATIVE CONFERENCE OF THE ANC, ZAMBIA, JUNE 1985

This message, from the leaders in Pollsmoor and Robben Island prisons, and signed on their behalf by Nelson Mandela, was read to the Conference and later presented to a press conference in Lusaka on 25 June 1985 by the President of the ANC.

We were most delighted to hear that the ANC will soon have another Conference. We sincerely hope that such an occasion will constitute yet another milestone in our history. It is most satisfying, especially in our present position, to belong to a tested organisation which exercises so formidable an impact on the situation in our country, which has established itself firmly as the standard bearer of such a rich tradition, and which has brought us such coveted laurels.

As you know, we always try to harmonise our own views and responses with those of the movement at large. For this reason, we find it rewarding indeed to know that, despite the immense distance and the years which separate us, as well as the lack of effective communication channels, we still remain a closely knit organisation, ever conscious of the crucial importance of unity, and of resisting every attempt to divide and confuse.

We feel sure that all those delegates who will attend will go there with one central issue uppermost in their minds: that out of the Conference the ANC will emerge far stronger than ever before. Unity is the rock on which the African National Congress was founded; it is the principle which has guided us down the years as we feel our way forward.

In the course of its history, the ANC has survived countless storms and risen to eminence partly because of the sterling qualities of its membership, and partly because each member has regarded himself or herself as the principal guardian of that unity. All discussions, contributions and criticism have generally been balanced and constructive and, above all, they have been invariably subjected to the over-riding principle of maximum unity. To lose sight of this basic principle is to sell our birthright, to betray those who paid the highest price so that the ANC should flourish and triumph.

In this connection, the positions taken by Oliver Tambo on various issues and also stressed by Joe Slovo inspired us tremendously. Both drew attention to vital issues which, in our opinion, are very timely. They must be highlighted and kept consciously in mind as we try to sort out the complicated problems which face the movement, and as we try to hammer out the guidelines for future progress.

These remarks are the clearest expression of that enduring identity of approach of members of the movement wherever they may be, and a summary of achievements of which we are justly proud. In particular, we fully share the view that the ANC has raised mass political consciousness to a scale unknown in our experience. It is in this spirit that we send you our greetings and best wishes. We hold your hands firmly across the miles.

14. VICTOR VERSTER

In July 1985, six months after P W Botha had said that Nelson Mandela could go free if he renounced the ANC's armed struggle, and after months of steadily more violent repressive action including the occupation of townships by troops, the government announced a partial State of Emergency affecting much of the country. In the rest of the country the apartheid regime relied on repressive laws such as the Internal Security Act and others in force in bantustan areas. During the year 11,000 people were detained without trial.

The emergency was lifted in March 1986 when South Africa was visited by the Commonwealth Eminent Persons Group (EPG). The mission of the EPG, some of whose members visited Mandela in Pollsmoor Prison, was to meet all the relevant parties in order to encourage the process of dialogue as a way forward. However in May, just as it was putting its 'negotiating concept' to the government, South African forces carried out raids on the capital cities of Botswana, Zambia and Zimbabwe, thereby bringing the initiative to an end. In June 1986 a national State of Emergency was declared.

Three and a half years later, when Mandela was released from prison, the State of Emergency was still in force, having been renewed in June of each year since 1986. Throughout these years the regime's forces used the emergency powers in an attempt to suppress protest and to destroy the structures of organised resistance. The authorities detained tens of thousands without trial, imposed even harsher censorship of information than that which already existed as well as restrictions on meetings, controls on movement, prohibitions on the activities of organisations and restrictions on organisers and activists. Over four thousand people were killed in the period after July 1985 and many more injured, in most cases as a result of armed violence by the regime's regular forces and by 'vigilantes', unofficial armed groups linked to the official forces. In spite of these conditions of extreme repression the forces of resistance proved resilient and by 1989 were able to engage in a campaign of mass defiance of apartheid laws and the emergency regulations. Central to this campaign was an affirmation of support for the ANC and by the end of the year the organisation, although still legally proscribed, had effectively unbanned itself.

When the national State of Emergency was declared Mandela was still in Pollsmoor Prison, but in August 1988 he was diagnosed as having tuberculosis and was moved to Tygerberg Hospital. On his recovery he was moved, in December 1988, to Victor Verster Prison where he was held on his own in a house in the prison complex.

Speculation concerning Mandela's release, almost continuous since P W Botha's conditional offer in January 1985, became intense from the time he was taken to Tygerberg Hospital. Although Botha was still insisting on renunciation of armed struggle as a condition of Mandela's release, the government had since August 1987 begun to develop a more flexible policy on the release of political prisoners. In November of that year Govan Mbeki, one of the ANC's leaders, was released after spending nearly 24 years of a life sentence in prison. He was however quickly placed under restriction orders as the regime reacted repressively to the mass political activity which followed his release. A shift in policy came in April 1989 when Botha, choosing words that were widely interpreted as avoiding the demand that Mandela should renounce armed struggle, said that he could be released on the basis of a commitment 'to a peaceful settlement of South Africa's future'. In July he had a meeting with Mandela. Then in October eight leading political prisoners were unconditionally released. Seven of them were ANC members: Walter Sisulu, Ahmed Kathrada, Raymond Mhlaba, Andrew Mlangeni and Elias Motsoaledi (all sentenced to life imprisonment in the Rivonia Trial, with Mandela), Wilton Mkwayi, and Oscar Mpetha. The eighth prisoner released was Jafta Masemola of the PAC, imprisoned in 1963.

From 1986 Mandela received many visits by government ministers. In an international press conference the day after his release, he spoke of these meetings:

I have been having discussions with the government over the last three years on two separate but related questions. The first one in which I had been negotiating with the government was the release of my comrades, Mr Sisulu and others. As far as that is concerned, I have been negotiating. But the second issue has been one of a meeting between the ANC and the government. There I have been acting purely as a facilitator to bring these two major political organisations to the negotiating table. In the course of my attempt to secure results . . . I met a number of cabinet ministers. The first, of course, was Mr Kobie Coetsee. I had countless meetings with him. The second has been Dr Gerrit Viljoen, whom I have met about four times since he took over his new portfolio. As you know, I had met the former State President Mr P W Botha. That meeting has been misunderstood. There is a submission that this was a propaganda ploy on the part of the President at the time. It is not so. This meeting was requested by me and the former State President merely responded to my request for him to see me. Secondly, it has been suggested that this was an attempt on the part of the former State President to do something that would embarrass Mr De Klerk, and that is not so. Minister De Klerk was involved right at the outset in the arrangements for the meeting. He was kept informed and he himself was in line with the fact that this discussion should take place.

Asked to comment on suggestions by the government that he was willing to act as mediator, Mandela replied:

In a sense I have been acting as a mediator, because I believe that the first step towards a solution of our problems is a meeting between the ANC and the government. So I have been playing that role, but now that I am released, it is for the ANC to determine what role I should play.

Document 14(a) which follows was prepared by Mandela for the meeting with P W Botha on 5 July 1989. The same document was discussed when on 13 December 1989 he met F W De Klerk who had succeeded Botha as State President.

A second document, 14(b), was also discussed at the meeting with De Klerk. It modified what the first had to say about the process of negotiations. The first had suggested two stages of negotiations. Stage one would involve a meeting between the government and the ANC in order to discuss preconditions for negotiations, and the second stage would be the actual negotiations. The second document, which was forwarded to De Klerk on 12 December, the day before the two met, presents the process as it is conceived in guidelines formulated by the ANC for a genuinely negotiated end to apartheid. These principles were incorporated in the Organisation of African Unity's Harare Declaration of August 1989 which laid the basis for an international consensus arrived at by the United Nations General Assembly in December 1989. Mandela, in the second document, said that the 'two-stage' approach had been his own thoughts at the time, but that he now favoured working on the formula since adopted by the ANC. This placed the onus on the government to create a climate conducive to negotiations by eliminating the obstacles to negotiations which it has created by its repressive measures. The necessary steps were: the release of all political prisoners, without restrictions being imposed on them; the lifting of all bans and restrictions on all proscribed and restricted organisations and persons; the removal of all troops from the townships; an end to the State of Emergency and the repeal of all legislation designed to circumscribe political activity, such as, and including, the Internal Security Act; and an end to all political trials and executions.

14(a) DOCUMENT PREPARED BEFORE MEETING WITH P W BOTHA ON 5 JULY 1989

The deepening political crisis in our country has been a matter of grave concern to me for quite some time and I now consider it necessary in the national interest for the African National Congress and the government to meet urgently to negotiate an effective political settlement.

At the outset I must point out that I make this move without consultation with the ANC. I am a loyal and disciplined member of the ANC, my political loyalty is owed primarily, if not exclusively to this organisation and particularly to our Lusaka headquarters where the official leadership is stationed and from where our affairs are directed. In the normal course of events, I would put my views to the organisation first, and if these views were accepted, the organisation would then decide on who were the best qualified members to handle the matter on its behalf and on exactly when to make the move. But in my current circumstances I cannot follow this course, and this is the only reason why I am acting on my own initiative, in the hope that the organisation will, in due course, endorse my action.

I must stress that no prisoner, irrespective of his status or influence, can conduct negotiations of this nature from prison. In our special situation, negotiation on political matters is literally a matter of life and death which requires to be handled by the organisation itself through its appointed representatives.

The step I am taking should, therefore, not be seen as the beginning of actual negotiations between the government and the ANC. My task is a very limited one, and that is to bring the country's two major political bodies to the negotiating table. I must further point out that the question of my release from prison is not an issue, at least at this stage of discussions, and I am certainly not asking to be freed. But I do hope that the government will, as soon as possible, give me the opportunity from my present quarters to sound the views of my colleagues inside and outside the country on this move.

Only if this initiative is formally endorsed by the ANC will it have any significance.

I will touch presently on some of the problems which seem to constitute an obstacle to a meeting between the ANC and the government. But I must emphasise right at this stage that this step is not a response to the call by the government on ANC leaders to declare whether or not they are nationalists and to renounce the South African Communist Party before there can be negotiations: no self-respecting freedom fighter will take orders from the government on how to wage the freedom struggle against that same government and on who his allies in the freedom struggle should be. To obey such instructions would be a violation of the long-standing and fruitful solidarity which distinguishes our liberation movement, and a betrayal of those who have worked so closely and suffered so much with us for almost 70 years.

Far from responding to that call, my intervention is influenced by purely domestic issues, by the civil strife and ruin into which the country is now sliding. I am disturbed, as many other South Africans no doubt are, by the spectre of a South Africa split into two hostile camps – blacks on one side (the term 'blacks' is used in a broad sense to indicate all those who are not whites) and whites on the other, slaughtering one another; by acute tensions which are building up dangerously in practically every sphere of our lives, a situation which, in turn, foreshadows more violent clashes in the days ahead. This is the crisis that has forced me to act.

I must add that the purpose of this discussion is not only to urge the government to talk to the ANC, but it is also to acquaint you with the views current among blacks, especially those in the Mass Democratic Movement. If I am unable to express those views frankly and freely, you will never know how the majority of South Africans think on the policy and actions of the government; you will never know how to deal with their grievances and demands.

It is perhaps proper to remind you that the media here and abroad has given certain public figures in this country a rather negative image not only in regard to human rights questions, but also in respect of their prescriptive stance when dealing with black leaders generally. The impression is shared not only by the vast majority of blacks but also by a substantial section of the whites. If I had allowed myself to be influenced by this impression, I would not even have thought of making this move.

Nevertheless, I come here with an open mind and the impression I will carry away from this meeting will be determined almost exclusively by the manner in which you respond to my proposal. It is in this spirit that I have undertaken this mission, and I sincerely hope that nothing will be done or said here which will force me to revise my views on this aspect.

I have already indicated that I propose to deal with some of the obstacles to a meeting between the government and the ANC. The government gives several reasons why it will not negotiate with us. However, for purposes of this discussion, I will confine myself to only three main demands set by the government as a precondition for negotiation, namely that the ANC must first renounce violence, break with the SACP and abandon its demand for majority rule.

The position of the ANC on the question of violence is very simple. The organisation has no vested interest in violence. It abhors any action which may cause loss of life, destruction of property and misery to the people. It has worked long and patiently for a South Africa of common values and for an undivided and peaceful non-racial state. But we consider the armed struggle a legitimate form of self-defence against a morally repugnant system of government which will not allow even peaceful forms of protest.

It is more than ironical that it should be the government which demands that we should renounce violence. The government knows only too well that there is not a single political organisation in this country, inside and outside parliament, which can ever compare with the ANC in its total commitment to peaceful change. Right from the early days of its history, the organisation diligently sought peaceful solutions and, to that extent, it talked patiently to successive South African governments, a policy we tried to follow in dealing with the present government. Not only did the government ignore our demands for a meeting, instead it took advantage of our commitment to a non-violent struggle and unleashed the most violent form of racial oppression this country has ever seen. It stripped us of all basic human rights, outlawed our organisations and barred all channels of peaceful resistance. It met our just demands with force and, despite the grave problems facing the country, it continues to refuse to talk to us. There can only be one answer to this challenge: violent forms of struggle.

Down the years oppressed people have fought for their birthright by peaceful means, where that was possible, and through force where peaceful channels were closed. The history of this country also confirms this vital lesson. Africans as well as Afrikaners were, at one time or other, compelled to take up arms in defence of their freedom against British imperialism. The fact that both were finally defeated by superior arms, and by the vast resources of that empire, does not negate this lesson. But from what has happened in South Africa during the last 40 years, we must conclude that now that the roles are reversed, and the Afrikaner is no longer a freedom fighter, but is in power, the entire lesson of history must be brushed aside. Not even a disciplined non-violent protest will now be tolerated. To the government a black man has neither a just cause to espouse nor freedom rights to defend. The whites must have the monopoly of political power, and of committing violence against innocent and defenceless people.

That situation was totally unacceptable to us and the formation of Umkhonto we Sizwe was introduced to end that monopoly, and to forcibly bring home to the government that the oppressed people of this country were prepared to stand up and defend themselves.

It is significant to note that throughout the past four decades, and more especially over the last 26 years, the government has met our demands with force only, and has done hardly anything to create a suitable climate for dialogue. On the contrary, the government continues to govern with a heavy hand, and to incite whites against negotiation with the ANC. The publication of the booklet 'Talking with the ANC . . .' which completely distorts the history and policy of the ANC, the extremely offensive language used by government spokesmen against freedom fighters, and the intimidation of whites who want to hear the views of the ANC at first hand, are all part of the government's strategy to wreck meaningful dialogue.

It is perfectly clear on the facts that the refusal of the ANC to renounce violence is not the real problem facing the government. The truth is that the government is not yet ready for negotiation and for the sharing of political power with blacks. It is still committed to white domination and, for that reason, it will only tolerate those blacks who are willing to serve on its apartheid structures. Its policy is to remove from the political scene blacks who refuse to conform, who reject white supremacy and its apartheid structures, and who will insist on equal rights with whites. This is the reason for the government's refusal to talk to us, and for its demand that we disarm ourselves, while it continues to use violence against our people. This is the reason for its massive propaganda campaign to discredit the ANC, and present it to the public as a communist-dominated organisation bent on murder and destruction. In this situation the reaction of the oppressed people is clearly predictable.

White South Africa must accept the plain fact that the ANC will not suspend, to say nothing of abandoning, the armed struggle until the government shows its willingness to surrender the monopoly of political power, and to negotiate directly and in good faith with the acknowledged black leaders. The renunciation of violence by either the government or the ANC should not be a pre-condition to but the result of negotiation. Moreover, by ignoring credible black leaders, and imposing a succession of still-born negotiation structures, the government is not only squandering the country's precious resources, but it is in fact discrediting the negotiation process itself, and prolonging the civil strife. The position of the ANC on the question of violence is, therefore, very clear. A government which used violence against blacks many years before we took up arms, has no right whatsoever to call on us to lay down arms.

I have already pointed out that no self-respecting freedom fighter will allow the government to prescribe who his allies in the freedom struggle should be, and that to obey such instructions would be a betrayal of those who have suffered repression with us for so long. We equally reject the charge that the ANC is dominated by the SACP and we regard the accusation as part of the smearing campaign the government is waging against us. The accusation has, in effect, also been refuted by two totally independent sources. In January 1987 the American State Department published a report on the activities of the SACP in this country which contrasts very sharply with the subjective picture the government has tried to paint against us over the years. The essence of that report is that, although the influence of the SACP on the ANC is strong, it is unlikely that the Party will ever dominate the ANC. The same point is made somewhat differently by Mr Ismail Omar, member of the President's Council, in his book *Reform in Crisis* published in 1988, in which he gives concrete examples of important issues of the day over which the ANC and the SACP have differed. He also points out that the ANC enjoys greater popular support than the SACP. He adds that, despite the many years of combined struggle, the two remain distinct organisations with ideological and policy differences which preclude a merger of identity. These observations go some way towards disproving the accusation. But since the allegation has become the focal point of government propaganda against the ANC, I propose to use this opportunity to give you that correct information, in the hope that this will help you to see the matter in its proper perspective, and to evaluate your strategy afresh.

Cooperation between the ANC and SACP goes back to the early twenties and has always been, and still is, strictly limited to the struggle against racial oppression and for a just society. At no time has the organisation ever adopted or cooperated with communism itself. Apart from the question of cooperation between the two organisations, members of the SACP have always been free to join the ANC. But once they do so, they become fully bound by the policy of the organisation set out in the Freedom Charter. As members of the ANC engaged in the anti-apartheid struggle, their Marxist ideology is not directly relevant. The SACP has throughout the years accepted the leading role of the ANC, a position which is respected by the SACP members who join the ANC.

There is, of course, a firmly established tradition in the ANC in terms of which any attempt is resisted, from whatever quarter, which is intended to undermine cooperation between the two organisations. Even within the ranks of the ANC there have been, at one time or other, people - and some of them were highly respected and influential individuals - who were against this cooperation and who wanted SACP members expelled from the organisation. Those who persisted in these activities were themselves ultimately expelled, or they broke away in despair. In either case their departure ended their political careers, or they formed other political organisations which, in due course, crumbled into splinter groups. No dedicated ANC member will ever heed the call to break with the SACP. We regard such a demand as a purely divisive government strategy. It is in fact a call on us to commit suicide. Which man of honour will ever desert a life-long friend at the instance of a common opponent and still retain a measure of credibility among his people? Which opponent will ever trust such a treacherous freedom fighter? Yet this is what the government is, in effect, asking us to do: to desert our faithful allies. We will not fall into that trap.

The government also accuses us of being agents of the Soviet Union. The truth is that the ANC is non-aligned, and we welcome support from the East and the West, from the socialist and capitalist countries. The only difference, as we have explained on countless occasions before, is that the socialist countries supply us with weapons, which the West refuses to give us. We have no intention whatsoever of changing our stand on this question.

The government's exaggerated hostility to the SACP, and its refusal to have any dealings with that party have a hollow ring. Such an attitude is not only out of step with the growing cooperation between the capitalist and socialist countries in different parts of the world, but it is also inconsistent with the policy of the government itself, when dealing with our neighbouring states. Not only has South Africa concluded treaties with the Marxist states of Angola and Mozambique - quite rightly in our opinion - but she also wants to strengthen ties with Marxist Zimbabwe. The government will certainly find it difficult, if not altogether impossible, to reconcile its readiness to work with foreign Marxists for the peaceful resolution of mutual problems, with its uncompromising refusal to talk to South African Marxists.

The reason for this inconsistency is obvious. As I have already said, the government is still too deeply committed to the principle of white domination and, despite lip-service to reform, it is deadly opposed to the sharing of political power with blacks, and the SACP is merely being used as a smokescreen to retain the monopoly of political power. The smearing campaign against the ANC also helps the government to evade the real issue at stake, namely, the exclusion from political power of the black majority by a white minority, which is the source of all our troubles.

Concerning my own personal position, I have already informed you that I will not respond to the government's demand that ANC members should state whether they are members of the SACP or not. But because much has been said by the media, as well as by government leaders regarding my political beliefs, I propose to use this opportunity to put the record straight. My political beliefs have been explained in the course of several political trials in which I was charged, in the policy documents of the ANC, and in my autobiography *The Struggle is My Life* which I wrote in prison in 1975. I stated in these trials and publications that I did not belong to any organisation apart from the ANC. In my address to the court which sentenced me to life imprisonment in June 1964, I said:

'Today I am attracted by the idea of a classless society, an attraction which springs in part from Marxist reading, and, in part, from my admiration of the structure and organisation of early African societies in this country . . . It is true, as I have already stated, that I have been influenced by Marxist thought. But this is also true of many of the leaders of the new independent states. Such widely different persons as Gandhi, Nehru, Nkrumah and Nasser all acknowledge this fact. We all accept the need for some form of socialism to enable our people to catch up with the advanced countries of the world, and to overcome their legacy of extreme poverty.'

My views are still the same. Equally important is the fact that many ANC leaders who are labelled communists by the government, embrace nothing different from these beliefs.

The term 'communist' when used by the government has a totally different meaning from the conventional one. Practically every freedom fighter who receives his military training or education in the socialist countries is to the government a communist. It would appear to be established government policy that, as long as the National Party is in power in this country, there can be no black freedom struggle, and no black freedom fighter. Any black political organisation which, like us, fights for the liberation of its people through armed struggle, must invariably be dominated by the SACP.

This attitude is not only the result of government propaganda, it is a logical consequence of white supremacy. After more than 300 years of racial indoctrination, the country's whites have developed such deep-seated contempt for blacks as to believe that we cannot think for ourselves, that we are incapable of fighting for political rights without incitement by some white agitation. In accusing the ANC of domination by the SACP, and in calling on ANC members to renounce the party, the government is deliberately exploiting that contempt.

The government is equally vehement in condemning the principle of majority rule. The principle is rejected despite the fact that it is a pillar of democratic rule in many countries of the world. It is a principle which is fully accepted in the white politics of this country. Only now that the stark reality has dawned that apartheid has failed, and that blacks will one day have an effective voice in government, are we told by whites here, and by their Western friends, that majority rule is a disaster to be avoided at all costs. Majority rule is acceptable to whites as long as it is considered within the context of white politics. If black political aspirations are to be accommodated, then some other formula must be found, provided that that formula does not raise blacks to a position of equality with whites.

Yet majority rule and internal peace are like the two sides of a single coin, and white South Africa simply has to accept that there will never be peace and stability in this country until the principle is fully applied. It is precisely because of its denial that the government has become the enemy of practically every black man. It is that denial that has sparked off the current civil strife.

By insisting on compliance with the above mentioned conditions before there can be talks, the government clearly confirms that it wants no peace in this

206

country but turmoil, no strong and independent ANC, but a weak and servile organisation playing a supportive role to white minority rule, not a non-aligned ANC, but one which is a satellite of the West, and which is ready to serve the interests of capitalism.

No worthy leaders of a freedom movement will ever submit to conditions which are essentially terms of surrender dictated by a victorious commander to a beaten enemy, and which are really intended to weaken the organisation to humiliate its leadership.

The key to the whole situation is a negotiated settlement, and a meeting between the government and the ANC will be the first major step towards lasting peace in the country, better relations with our neighbour states, admission to the Organisation of African Unity, re-admission to the United Nations and other world bodies, to international markets and improved international relations generally. An accord with the ANC, and the introduction of a non-racial society is the only way in which our rich and beautiful country will be saved from the stigma which repels the world.

Two political issues will have to be addressed at such a meeting; firstly, the demand for majority rule in a unitary state, secondly, the concern of white South Africa over this demand, as well as the insistence of whites on structural guarantees that majority rule will not mean domination of the white minority by blacks. The most crucial task which will face the government and the ANC will be to reconcile these two positions. Such reconciliation will be achieved only if both parties are willing to compromise. The organisation will determine precisely how negotiations should be conducted.

It may well be that this should be done at least in two stages. The first, where the organisation and the government will work out together the pre-conditions for a proper climate for negotiations. Up to now both parties have simply been broadcasting their conditions for negotiations without putting them directly to each other. The second stage would be the actual negotiations themselves when the climate is ripe for doing so. Any other approach would entail the danger of an irresolvable stalemate.

Lastly, I must point out that the move I have taken provides you with the opportunity to overcome the current deadlock, and to normalise the country's political situation. I hope you will seize it without delay. I believe that the overwhelming majority of South Africans, black and white, hope to see the ANC and the government working closely together to lay the foundations for a new era in our country, in which racial discrimination and prejudice, coercion and confrontation, death and destruction will be forgotten.

14(b) 'A DOCUMENT TO CREATE A CLIMATE OF UNDERSTANDING'.

Document forwarded by Nelson Mandela to F W De Klerk on 12 December 1989.

Mr President,

I hope that Ministers Kobie Coetsee and Gerrit Viljoen have informed you that I deeply appreciate your decision in terms of which eight fellow-prisoners were freed on 15 October 1989, and for advising me of the fact in advance. The release was clearly a major development which rightly evoked praise here and abroad.

In my view it has now become urgent to take other measures to end the present deadlock, and this will certainly be achieved if the government first creates a proper climate for negotiation, followed by a meeting with the ANC. The conflict which is presently draining South Africa's life blood, either in the form of peaceful demonstrations, acts of violence or external preasure, will never be settled until there is an agreement with the ANC. To this end I have spent more than three years urging the Government to negotiate with the ANC. I hope I will not leave this place with empty hands.

The Government insists on the ANC making an honest commitment to peace before it will talk to the organisation. This is the pre-condition we are required to meet before the Government will negotiate with us. It must be made clear at the outset that the ANC will never make such a commitment at the instance of the Government, or any other source for that matter. We would have thought that the history of this country's liberation movement, especially during the last 41 years, would have made that point perfectly clear.

The whole approach of the Government to the question of negotiation with the ANC is totally unacceptable, and requires to be drastically changed. No serious political organisation will ever talk peace when an aggressive war is being waged against it. No proud people will ever obey orders from those who have humiliated and dishonoured them for so long.

Besides, the pre-condition that we should commit ourselves to peace is inconsistent with the statement you made in Nigel shortly before the last general election, in which you appealed to black leaders to come forward to negotiate with the Government, and to refrain from setting pre-conditions for such negotiations. It was generally assumed that the appeal was addressed to blacks as a whole and not, as now appears, only to those who work in apartheid structures.

In the light of subsequent Government policy statements, the perception has deepened that the Nigel statement was no more than mere rhetoric. Although the Government called on blacks to set no pre-conditions, it considers itself free to do exactly that. That is the reason why it prescribes to us to make a commitment to peace before we can talk.

The Government ought to be aware that readiness to negotiate is in itself an honest commitment to peace. In this regard, the ANC is far ahead of the Government. It has repeatedly declared its willingness to negotiate, provided a proper climate for such negotiations exists. The organisation has recently published a clear and detailed plan to this effect, which has already been approved by the Frontline States, the Organisation of African Unity, the Non-Aligned Movement and by almost all the members of the Commonwealth of Nations.

Equally relevant is the fact that on many occasions in the past, the ANC has explicitly acknowledged its commitment to peaceful solutions, if channels for doing so are available. As recently as 24 October 1989, the *Star* reported as follows:

'The ANC says it is committed to a peaceful solution in South Africa but accuses the Government of rhetoric . . . At present there is really no serious indication from the Government itself about a peaceful solution to the political crisis . . . Five years ago, President P W Botha spoke virtually the same words but nothing happened. It is history now that the ANC has made impassioned overtures to every single Government of South Africa in vain. Every manoeuvre was met with a negative response, and at times violence.'

This and similar other previous statements clearly show that the ANC has an established record of commitment to peace, and that its armed struggle is a purely defensive measure against the violence of the Government. This point was stressed by Mr Oliver Tambo. President of the ANC, during an interview with *Cape Times* editor, Anthony Heard, on 4 November 1985, when he said:

'The unfortunate thing is that people tend to be worried about the violence that comes from the oppressed . . . Really, there would be no violence at all if we did not have the violence of the apartheid system.'

There is neither logic nor common sense in asking the ANC to do now what it has consistently done on countless occasions before. It is the Government, not the ANC, that started civil war in this country, and that does not want reconciliation and peace. How does one work for reconciliation and peace under a State of Emergency, with black areas under military occupation, when people's organisations are banned, leaders are either in exile, prison or restricted, when the policy of apartheid with its violence is still being enforced, and when no conditions for free political expression exist?

Serious doubts have also been expressed as to whether the Government would be prepared to meet the ANC even when it fully complied with your demand. Political commentators point out that, during the series of discussions you and other Government members held recently with the 'homeland' leaders and their urban counterparts, you avoided meeting the very organisations which, together with the ANC, hold the key to peace in the country. The United Democratic

Front and its main affiliates, the Congress of South African Trade Unions, Natal Indian Congress and Transvaal Indian Congress, are all non-violent and peaceful organisations. Why then did the Government ignore them if commitment to peace is the only qualification for participation in negotiations?

In your inaugural address on 20 September 1989, you made an important statement which must have had a formidable impact inside and outside the country. You said:

'There is but one way to peace, to justice for all, that is the way of reconciliation, of together seeking mutually acceptable solutions, of together discussing what the new South Africa should look like, of constitutional negotiation with a view to a permanent understanding.'

The cornerstone of that address was the idea of reconciliaton, in which you pleaded for a new spirit and approach. By reconciliation, in this context, was understood the situation where opponents, and even enemies for that matter, would sink their differences and lay down their arms for the purpose of working out a peaceful solution, where the injustices and grievances of the past would be buried and forgotten, and a fresh start made. That is the spirit in which the people of South Africa would like to work together for peace; those are the principles which should guide those who love their country and its people, who want to turn South Africa into a land of hope. In highlighting this theme in your address, you sparked off a groundswell of expectations from far and wide. Many people felt that, at last, the South Africa of their dreams was about to be born.

We also understood your appeal for reconciliation and justice for all not to be directed to those blacks who operate apartheid structures. Apart from a few notable exceptions, these blacks are the creation of the National Party and, throughout the years, they have served as its loyal agents in its various strategies to cling to minority rule. Their principal role has been, and still is, to make the struggle for majority rule in a unitary state far more difficult to achieve. For the last three decades, they have been used to defend the NP's policy of group domination – now referred to as group rights – and they have no tradition of militant resistance against racial discrimination. There is thus no conflict to be reconciled between the NP and these people.

The appeal could not have been directed to any of the opposition parties in Parliament either. Although the NP has made positive initiatives here and there, its public image is still tarnished by a cloud of distrust and suspicion, and by an inherent vagueness and indecision as far as the really basic issues are concerned. Many people see no fundamental difference between its policies and those of the Conservative Party. Both are regarded as apartheid parties, the only difference being that one is more blunt than the other in its defence of white privilege.

Although the Democratic Party is the most progressive parliamentary party, and despite the existence of important policy differences between that party and the NP, the relations between the two parties are not so bitter as to justify a call for reconciliation and peace by a head of state. The fairly even relations between the two parties is clearly illustrated by the fact that the DP is not banned, none of its leaders are restricted, imprisoned, driven into exile or executed for purely political offences, as is happening to our people.

The conflict which we believed you wanted to settle was that between the Government, on the one hand, and the ANC and other extra-parliamentary organisations, on the other. It is the activities of these organisations which have turned South Africa into a land of acute tensions and fear. It is on this level that the country desperately yearns for reconciliation and justice for all. As pointed out on another occasion, dialogue with the ANC and the mass democratic movement is the only way of stopping violence and bringing peace to the country. It is, therefore, ironical that it is precisely these organisations with whom the Government is not at all prepared to talk.

It is common knowledge that the Government has been sharply criticised, and even condemned, in the past, for squandering precious resources, and for wasting much energy and time discussing with people who can play no significant role in the resolution of the current conflict in the country. Past experience shows that the Government would prefer to make peace with those who accept its policies, rather than those who reject them, with its friends rather than its opponents. It is to be hoped that this time, the Government will not repeat that costly mistake. To continue to ignore this criticism, and to confine consultations on the political crisis almost entirely to those individuals and organisations which help the Government to maintain the *status quo*, will certainly deepen the distrust and suspicion which impede real progress on negotiations.

In my lengthy discussions with the team of Government officials, I repeatedly urged that negotiation between the ANC and the Government should preferably be in two stages; the first being where the Government and the ANC would together work out the pre-conditions for negotiations. The second stage would consist of the actual negotiations themselves when the climate for doing so was ripe. These were my personal views and not those of the ANC, which sees the problem quite differently. It seems to me that now that I am aware of the attitude of the ANC on the matter, an attitude which is perfectly sound, we should work on the formula indicated by the organisation for the resolution of the present obstacles to negotiation.

The principal source of almost all our problems in this country is undoubtedly the policy of apartheid, which the Government now admits is an unjust system, and from which it claims to be moving away. This means that organisations and people who were banned, restricted, driven into exile, imprisoned or executed for their anti-apartheid activities were unjustly condemned. The very first step on the way to reconciliation is obviously the dismantling of apartheid, and all measures used to enforce it. To talk of reconciliation before this major step is taken is totally unrealistic.

The five-year plan of the NP, with its outdated concept of group rights, has aggravated the position almost beyond repair. It is yet another example of the Government's attempt 'to modernise apartheid without abandoning it'. What the plan means, in effect, is that after resisting racial oppression for so many years, and after making such heavy sacrifices during which countless lives were lost, we should at the height of that heroic struggle, yield to a disguised form of minority rule. In a nutshell, the plan means that blacks will taste real freedom in the world to come. In this one, whites will go on preaching reconciliation and peace, but continue to hold firmly and defiantly to power and to enforce racial separation, the very issues which have caused so much agony and bitterness in the country. Insistence on such a plan will render meaningless all talk of 'reconciliation and justice for all; of together seeking mutually acceptable solutions, of together discussing what the new South Africa should look like, of constitutional negotiation with a view to a permanent understanding'.

We equally reject, out of hand, the Government's plan to hold racially based elections to determine those who should take part in negotiations. Commentators of different political views consider it absurd for the Government to advocate essentially racist procedures, where the overwhelming majority of the population is striving for a non-racial system of government.

The Government argues that our situation is a complex one, and that a lasting solution will only be found after years of consultation and planning. We totally reject that view. There is nothing complicated in replacing minority rule with majority rule, group domination with a non-racial social order. The position is complicated simply because the Government itself is not yet ready to accept the most obvious solution which the majority demands, and believes that a racial solution can still be imposed on the country.

The Government claims that the ANC is not the sole representative of black aspirations in this country; therefore, it (the Government) cannot be expected to have separate discussions with the organisation. It can only do so in the presence of other organisations. We reject this argument as yet another example of the Government's intransigence. All those who resort to such an argument make themselves wide open to the charge of using double standards.

It is now public knowledge that the Government has on numerous occasions held separate discussions with each of the 'homeland' leaders and with their urban counterparts. For the Government now to refuse us this privilege would not only be inconsistent with its own actions, but would seriously undermine the confidence-building exercises on which we have embarked, compelling all those involved to seek mutually acceptable solutions under very grave difficulties. Equally important is the fact that there is a war between the ANC and the Government, and a cease-fire to end hostilities will have to be negotiated first, before talks to normalise the situation can begin. Only the Government and the ANC and its allies can take part in such talks, and no third party would be needed.

I must now refer to a different but related matter, which I hope will receive your urgent attention, that is the release of four fellow-prisoners who were sentenced to life imprisonment by a Natal court in 1978, and who are presently held in Robben Island. They are:

Mr Matthew Meyiwa (66 years)

Mr Elphas Mdlalose (66 years)

Mr Anthony Xaba (56 years)

Mr John Nene (±56 years)

They were first sentenced in 1964, Mr Mdlalose to 10 years' imprisonment and the rest to eight years. In 1978 they were again convicted and sentenced, this time to life imprisonment. For reasons which were carefully explained to Ministers Gerrit Viljoen and Kobie Coetsee on 10 October 1989, and to the Government team on 16 November 1989, I had expected Messrs Mdlalose and Meyiwa to be freed together with the eight fellow-prisoners mentioned above. I was indeed extremely distressed when the two were not included. Bearing in mind all the surrounding circumstances to the case, the fact that these four persons are not first offenders should be regarded as a mitigating, and not as an aggravating factor.

I would like to believe that my exploratory efforts during the last three years have not been in vain, that I have an important role still to play in helping to bring about a peaceful settlement, that the initiatives you have already taken will soon be followed by other developments on the really fundamental issues that are agitating our people, and that in our life-time our country will rid itself of the pestilence of racialism in all its forms.

In conclusion, Mr President, I should add that, in helping to promote dialogue between the ANC and the Government, I hope to be able to avoid any act which may be interpreted as an attempt on my part to drive a wedge between you and the NP, or to portray you in a manner not consistent with your public image. I trust that you and other members of the Government will fully reciprocate.

15. RELEASE

The apartheid regime took its first concrete steps towards a negotiated end to apartheid in February 1990, but without irrevocably committing itself to that path. In a speech at the opening of parliament on 2 February, F W De Klerk initiated the process by announcing a number of measures including the unbanning of political organisations; the lifting of restrictions on some (but not all) restricted individuals; the release of some (but not all) political prisoners; a suspension of executions; and the repeal of some of the emergency regulations. He also announced that Nelson Mandela would soon be released.

For its part the ANC welcomed the developments as positive and important, but called on the government to take the remaining steps needed to clear the way for negotiations.

On 11 February 1990, Nelson Mandela walked out through the gates of Victor Verster Prison. Thousands of people were waiting outside the gates and along the route to Cape Town to welcome him. Across the world millions of people watched the event on television.

Asked the next day to describe his own emotions as he came out of prison, Mandela replied:

I must confess that I am unable to describe my emotions. I was completely overwhelmed by the enthusiasm. It is something I did not expect. I would be merely rationalising if I told you that I am able to describe my own feelings. It was breathtaking. That's all I can say.

That evening in Cape Town he addressed the first of four huge rallies, one in each of South Africa's provinces. Estimates of attendances at the rallies indicate that altogether around half a million people heard him speak in the Cape, Transvaal, Natal and Orange Free State. What he said at each rally differed, combining varying themes of national concern with issues specific to the province in which he was speaking.

The texts of the four addresses are reproduced below.

15(a) ADDRESS TO RALLY IN CAPE TOWN, 11 FEBRUARY 1990

Friends, comrades and fellow South Africans. I greet you all in the name of peace, democracy and freedom for all.

I stand here before you not as a prophet but as a humble servant of you, the people. Your tireless and heroic sacrifices have made it possible for me to be here today. I therefore place the remaining years of my life in your hands.

On this day of my release, I extend my sincere and warmest gratitude to the millions of my compatriots and those in every corner of the globe who have campaigned tirelessly for my release.

I send special greetings to the people of Cape Town, this city which has been

214

my home for three decades. Your mass marches and other forms of struggle have served as a constant source of strength to all political prisoners.

I salute the African National Congress. It has fulfilled our every expectation in its role as leader of the great march to freedom.

I salute our President, Comrade Oliver Tambo, for leading the ANC even under the most difficult circumstances.

I salute the rank and file members of the ANC. You have sacrificed life and limb in the pursuit of the noble cause of our struggle.

I salute combatants of Umkhonto we Sizwe, like Solomon Mahlangu* and Ashley Kriel† who have paid the ultimate price for the freedom of all South Africans.

I salute the South African Communist Party for its sterling contribution to the struggle for democracy. You have survived 40 years of unrelenting persecution. The memory of great communists like Moses Kotane, Yusuf Dadoo, Bram Fischer and Moses Mabhida will be cherished for generations to come.

I salute General Secretary Joe Slovo, one of our finest patriots. We are heartened by the fact that the alliance between ourselves and the Party remains as strong as it always was.

I salute the United Democratic Front, the National Education Crisis Committee, the South African Youth Congress, the Transvaal and Natal Indian Congresses and COSATU and the many other formations of the Mass Democratic Movement.

I also salute the Black Sash and the National Union of South African Students. We note with pride that you have acted as the conscience of white South Africa. Even during the darkest days in the history of our struggle you held the flag of liberty high. The large-scale mass mobilisation of the past few years is one of the key factors which led to the opening of the final chapter of our struggle.

I extend my greetings to the working class of our country. Your organised strength is the pride of our movement. You remain the most dependable force in the struggle to end exploitation and oppression.

I pay tribute to the many religious communities who carried the campaign for justice forward when the organisations for our people were silenced.

I greet the traditional leaders of our country - many of you continue to walk in the footsteps of great heroes like Hintsa and Sekhukune‡.

I pay tribute to the endless heroism of youth, you, the young lions. You, the young lions, have energised our entire struggle.

I pay tribute to the mothers and wives and sisters of our nation. You are the

---

* Executed on 6 April 1979.

† Shot dead by police in July 1987.

‡ Chiefs who led resistance to the advance of white settlers in the 19th century, in the Eastern Cape and Northern Transvaal respectively.

rock-hard foundation of our struggle. Apartheid has inflicted more pain on you than on anyone else.

On this occasion, we thank the world community for their great contribution to the anti-apartheid struggle. Without your support our struggle would not have reached this advanced stage. The sacrifice of the frontline states will be remembered by South Africans forever.

My salutations would be incomplete without expressing my deep appreciation for the strength given to me during my long and lonely years in prison by my beloved wife and family. I am convinced that your pain and suffering was far greater than my own.

Before I go any further I wish to make the point that I intend making only a few preliminary comments at this stage. I will make a more complete statement only after I have had the opportunity to consult with my comrades.

Today the majority of South Africans, black and white, recognise that apartheid has no future. It has to be ended by our own decisive mass action in order to build peace and security. The mass campaign of defiance and other actions of our organisation and people can only culminate in the establishment of democracy. The destruction caused by apartheid on our sub-continent is incalculable. The fabric of family life of millions of my people has been shattered. Millions are homeless and unemployed. Our economy lies in ruins and our people are embroiled in political strife. Our resort to the armed struggle in 1960 with the formation of the military wing of the ANC, Umkhonto we Sizwe, was a purely defensive action against the violence of apartheid. The factors which necessitated the armed struggle still exist today. We have no option but to continue. We express the hope that a climate conducive to a negotiated settlement will be created soon so that there may no longer be the need for the armed struggle.

I am a loyal and disciplined member of the African National Congress. I am therefore in full agreement with all of its objectives, strategies and tactics.

The need to unite the people of our country is as important a task now as it always has been. No individual leader is able to take on this enormous task on his own. It is our task as leaders to place our views before our organisation and to allow the democratic structures to decide. On the question of democratic practice, I feel duty bound to make the point that a leader of the movement is a person who has been democratically elected at a national conference. This is a principle which must be upheld without any exceptions.

Today, I wish to report to you that my talks with the government have been aimed at normalising the political situation in the country. We have not as yet begun discussing the basic demands of the struggle. I wish to stress that I myself have at no time entered into negotiations about the future of our country except to insist on a meeting between the ANC and the government.

Mr De Klerk has gone further than any other Nationalist president in taking real steps to normalise the situation. However, there are further steps as outlined in the Harare Declaration that have to be met before negotiations on the basic demands of our people can begin. I reiterate our call for, *inter alia*, the immediate ending of the State of Emergency and the freeing of all, and not only some, political prisoners. Only such a normalised situation, which allows for free political activity, can allow us to consult our people in order to obtain a mandate.

The people need to be consulted on who will negotiate and on the content of such negotiations. Negotiations cannot take place above the heads or behind the backs of our people. It is our belief that the future of our country can only be determined by a body which is democratically elected on a non-racial basis. Negotiations on the dismantling of apartheid will have to address the over-whelming demand of our people for a democratic, non-racial and unitary South Africa. There must be an end to white monopoly on political power and a fundamental restructuring of our political and economic systems to ensure that the inequalities of apartheid are addressed and our society thoroughly democ-ratised.

It must be added that Mr De Klerk himself is a man of integrity who is acutely aware of the dangers of a public figure not honouring his undertakings. But as an organisation we base our policy and strategy on the harsh reality we are faced with. And this reality is that we are still suffering under the policy of the Nationalist government.

Our struggle has reached a decisive moment. We call on our people to seize this moment so that the process towards democracy is rapid and uninterrupted. We have waited too long for our freedom. We can no longer wait. Now is the time to intensify the struggle on all fronts. To relax our efforts now would be a mistake which generations to come will not be able to forgive. The sight of freedom looming on the horizon should encourage us to redouble our efforts.

It is only through disciplined mass action that our victory can be assured. We call on our white compatriots to join us in the shaping of a new South Africa. The freedom movement is a political home for you too. We call on the international community to continue the campaign to isolate the apartheid regime. To lift sanctions now would be to run the risk of aborting the process towards the complete eradication of apartheid.

Our march to freedom is irreversible. We must not allow fear to stand in our way. Universal suffrage on a common voters' role in a united democratic and non-racial South Africa is the only way to peace and racial harmony.

In conclusion I wish to quote my own words during my trial in 1964. They are true today as they were then:

'I have fought against white domination and I have fought against black domination. I have cherished the ideal of a democratic and free society in which all persons live together in harmony and with equal opportunities. It is an ideal which I hope to live for and to achieve. But if needs be, it is an ideal for which I am prepared to die.'

15(b) ADDRESS TO RALLY IN SOWETO, 13 FEBRUARY 1990

Comrades, friends and the people of Soweto at large, I greet you in the name of the heroic struggle of our people to establish justice and freedom for all in our country.

I salute our President, Comrade Oliver Tambo, for his leadership of the ANC that has put our organisation and the hopes of the people it represents on the political centre stage in South Africa.

I salute our rank and file members and combatants of the ANC who have sacrificed all for the love of their country and their people.

I salute the South African Communist Party for its consistent and determined contribution to the struggle for a democratic government in South Africa. Our alliance is built on the unshakable foundation of our united struggle for a non-racial democracy.

I salute the United Democratic Front, the Congress of South African Trade Unions, the National Education Crisis Committee and many other formations of the MDM. The work of the UDF has ensured that none of the reformist strategies of the government have succeeded.

I salute the working class of our country. Our movement would not be where it is without your organised strength. You are an indispensable force in the struggle to end exploitation and oppression in South Africa.

We salute the victory of SWAPO, with whom we shared trenches of battle against colonialism and apartheid. You have established your right to self-determination and your victory is our victory.

I pay tribute to the many religious leaders who carried the struggle for justice forward, and held our banner high during the most brutal periods of repression against our people.

I salute the courage and the heroism of the youth of South Africa, organised under the South African Youth Congress. At this point I wish to pay tribute to comrade Hector Petersen* who together with hundreds of young activists was mowed down by apartheid bullets in 1976. We gained inspiration by your courage and conviction during our lonely years on the Island.

Today, my return to Soweto fills my heart with joy. At the same time I also return with a deep sense of sadness. Sadness to learn that you are still suffering under an inhuman system. The housing shortage, the schools crisis, unemployment and the crime rate still remain.

I am even more proud to be a member of this community because of the pioneering role it has played in the struggle for the democratisation of local government. You have built democratic structures of local government in Soweto such as street committees and civic organisations that give practical

---

* A 13-year-old schoolboy who was the first to be killed by the police who fired on school children in Soweto on 16 June 1976.

import to our desire to let the people govern. I fully support the call made by our people for democratic systems of local government that will have a single tax base. In this regard I believe that the campaigns for open cities must receive our active support.

As proud as I am to be part of the Soweto community, I have been greatly disturbed by the statistics of crime that I have read in the newspapers. Although I understand the deprivations our people suffer I must make it clear that the level of crime in our township is unhealthy and must be eliminated as a matter of urgency. It is through the creation of democratic and accountable structures that we can achieve this. I salute the Anti-crime Campaigns conducted by our organisations.

The crisis in education that exists in South Africa demands special attention. The education crisis in black schools is a political crisis. It arises out of the fact that our people have no vote and therefore cannot make the government of the day responsive to their needs. Apartheid education is inferior and a crime against humanity. Education is an area that needs the attention of all our people, students, parents, teachers, workers and all other organised sectors of our community. Let us build disciplined structures, Student Representative Councils, a united national teachers organisation, parent structures and parent-teacher-student associations and the National Education Crisis Committee.

It has been the policy of the ANC that though the school and the entire education system is a site of struggle, the actual process of learning must take place in the schools. I want to add my voice, therefore, to the call made at the beginning of the year that all students must return to school and learn. We must continue our struggle for People's Education within the school system and utilise its resources to achieve our goals. I call on the government to build more schools, to train and employ more teachers and to abandon its policy of forcing our children out of the school system by use of various measures such as the age restrictions and their refusal to admit those who fail their classes. We have consistently called for a unitary non-racial education system that develops the potential of all our youth.

As I said when I stood in the dock at the Rivonia Trial 27 years ago and as I said on the day of my release in Cape Town, the ANC will pursue the armed struggle against the government as long as the violence of apartheid continues. Our armed combatants act under the political leadership of the ANC. Cadres of our People's Army are skilled, not only in military affairs, but act as the political commissars of our movement. We are therefore disturbed that there are certain elements amongst those who claim to support the liberation struggle who use violence against our people. The hijacking and setting alight of vehicles, and the harassment of innocent people are criminal acts that have no place in our struggle. We condemn that. Our major weapon of struggle against apartheid oppression and exploitation is our people organised into mass formations of the Democratic Movement. This is achieved by politically organising our people - not through the use of violence against our people.

I call in the strongest possible way for us to act with the dignity and discipline that our just struggle for freedom deserves. Our victories must be celebrated in peace and joy. In particular I call on our people in Natal to unite against the perpetrators of violence. I call on the leadership of the UDF, COSATU and Inkatha to take decisive steps to revive the peace initiative and end the scourge on our proud history. Let us act with political foresight and develop bold steps to end the mindless violence. Joint initiatives at local, regional and national levels between the parties concerned must call for restraint. The security forces must be compelled to act with absolute impartiality and to arrest those offenders who continue with violence.

We are disturbed that attempts are being made to disrupt the unity of the oppressed by stirring tensions between African and Indian communities of Natal. Let us build on the proud tradition of unity in action as embodied in the Xuma-Naicker-Dadoo Pact* which was fully endorsed by our great hero Chief Luthuli.

I am also concerned by the ongoing violence perpetrated by certain sections of the security forces against our peaceful marches and demonstrations. We condemn this. I understand that implementing apartheid laws has made it extremely difficult for many honest policemen to fulfill their role as servants of the public. You are seen in the eyes of many of our people as an instrument of repression and injustice. We call on the police to abandon apartheid and to serve the interests of the people. Join our march to a new South Africa where you also have a place. We note with appreciation that there are certain areas where policemen are acting with restraint and fulfilling the real role of protecting all our people irrespective of their race.

Much debate has been sparked off by the ANC policies on the economy relating to nationalisation and the redistribution of wealth. We believe that apartheid has created a heinous system of exploitation in which a racist minority monopolises economic wealth while the vast majority of oppressed black people are condemned to poverty. South Africa is a wealthy country. It is the labour of black workers that has built the cities, roads and factories we see. They cannot be excluded from sharing this wealth. The ANC is just as committed to economic growth and productivity as the present employers claim to be. Yet we are also committed to ensure that a democratic government has the resources to address the inequalities caused by apartheid.

Our people need proper housing, not ghettos like Soweto. Workers need a living wage - and the right to join unions of their own choice and to participate in determining policies that affect their lives.

Our history has shown that apartheid has stifled growth, created mass unemployment and led to spiralling inflation that has undermined the standards

---

* A pact between the leaders of the ANC and the Transvaal and Natal Indian Congresses which laid the foundations of unity between Africans and Indians in the struggle.

of living of the majority of our people, both black and white. Only a participatory democracy involving our people in the structures of decision making at all levels of society can ensure that this is corrected. We will certainly introduce policies that address the economic problems that we face.

We call on employers to recognise the fundamental rights of workers in our country. We are marching to a new future based on strong foundations of respect for each other achieved through bona fide negotiations. In particular we call for genuine negotiations to achieve a fair Labour Relations Act and mechanisms to resolve conflict. Employers can play their role in shaping the new South Africa by acknowledging these rights. We call on workers, black and white, to join industrial trade unions organised under the banner of our non-racial progressive federation, the Congress of South African Trade Unions, which has played an indispensable role in our struggle against apartheid.

A number of obstacles to the creation of a non-racial democratic South Africa remain and need to be tackled. The fears of whites about their rights and place in a South Africa they do not control exclusively are an obstacle we must understand and address. I stated in 1964 that I and the ANC are as opposed to black domination as we are to white domination. We must accept however that our statements and declarations alone will not be sufficient to allay the fears of white South Africans. We must clearly demonstrate our goodwill to our white compatriots and convince them by our conduct and arguments that a South Africa without apartheid will be a better home for all. A new South Africa has to eliminate the racial hatred and suspicion caused by apartheid and offer guarantees to all its citizens of peace, security and prosperity. We call on those, who out of ignorance, have collaborated with apartheid in the past, to join our liberation struggle. No man or woman who has abandoned apartheid will be excluded from our movement towards a non-racial united and democratic South Africa, based on one person one vote on a common voters' roll.

Our primary task remains to unite our people across the length and breadth of our country. Our democratic organisations must be consolidated in all our sectors. Democratic political practice and accountable leadership must be strengthened on all fronts. Our struggle against apartheid, though seemingly uncertain must be intensified on all fronts. Let each one of you and all of our people give the enemies of peace and liberty no space to take us back to the dark hell of apartheid. It is only disciplined mass action that assures us of the victory we seek.

Go back to your schools, factories, mines and communities. Build on the massive energies that recent events in our country have unleashed by strengthening disciplined mass organisations.

We are going forward. The march towards freedom and justice is irreversible. I have spoken about freedom in my lifetime. Your struggles, your commitment and your discipline have released me to stand here before you today. These basic principles will propel us to a free, non-racial, democratic, united South Africa that we have struggled and died for.

15(c) ADDRESS TO RALLY IN DURBAN, 25 FEBRUARY 1990

The symbol '*' indicates the start of a passage delivered in Zulu and translated into English and '+' marks where the text reverts into original English.

Friends, comrades, and the people of Natal, I greet you all. I do so in the name of peace, the peace that is so desperately and urgently needed in this region.

In Natal, apartheid is a deadly cancer in our midst, setting house against house, and eating away at the precious ties that bound us together. This strife among ourselves wastes our energy and destroys our unity. My message to those of you involved in this battle of brother against brother is this: take your guns, your knives, and your pangas‡, and throw them into the sea. Close down the death factories. End this war now!

We also come together today to renew the ties that make us one people, and to reaffirm a single united stand against the oppression of apartheid. *We have gathered here to find a way of building even greater unity than we already have. Unity is the pillar and foundation of our struggle to end the misery which is caused by the oppression which is our greatest enemy. This repression and the violence it creates cannot be ended if we fight and attack each other.

+The people of Natal have fought a long struggle against oppression. The victory of the army of King Cetshwayo kaMpande at the Battle of Isandlwana in 1879 has been an inspiration for those of us engaged in the struggle for justice and freedom in South Africa. At Isandlwana, disciplined Zulu regiments, armed only with shields and spears, but filled with courage and determination, thrust back the guns and cannon of the British imperialists. When the British finally managed to defeat the Zulu kingdom, they divided it into 13 new chiefdoms. Later, they annexed the area and gave the land to white farmers. In 1906, in the reign of Dinizulu kaCetshwayo, the colonialists introduced the Poll Tax (Head Tax) and other regulations designed to force Africans to work for wages on white farms. The Zulu people, led by Chief Bambatha, refused to bow their proud heads and a powerful spirit of resistance developed, which, like the battle of Isandlwana, inspired generations of South Africans.

The ANC pays tribute to these heroic struggles of the Zulu people to combat oppression. And we are very proud that from the ranks of the Zulu people have emerged outstanding cadres of the ANC and national leaders like Dube§, Seme¶, Luthuli. We remember another son of Natal, the young and talented Communist Party organiser, Johannes Nkosi, who, with three others, was brutally murdered in 1930, when he led a march into Durban to protest against the hated pass laws.

Another strand in the struggle against oppression began with the formation,

---

‡ Machetes, widely used in Natal's sugar growing areas for cutting cane.

§ Rev. John Langalibelele Dube, first President of the ANC.

¶ Pixley ka Isaka Seme, ANC founder member and its President between 1930-7.

right here in Natal, of the first black political organisation in Africa. The Natal Indian Congress, founded in 1894, began a tradition of extra-parliamentary protest that continues into the present. The next decade saw the increasing radicalisation of Indian politics under the leadership of Mahatma Gandhi.

*In 1906, at the time when Bambatha led sections of Africans in a war to destroy the Poll Tax, our brothers who originated from India, led by Mahatma Gandhi, fought against the oppression of the British Government. In 1913, we see Indian workers striking in the sugar-cane plantations and in the coal mines. These actions show the oppressed of South Africa waging a struggle to end exploitation and oppression, mounting an important challenge to the repressive British rule.

+In the passive resistance campaign of 1946, over 2,000 Indians went to jail, many for occupying land reserved for whites. The campaign made clear the common nature of Indian and African oppression and the necessity of united resistance. In 1947, this led to the Xuma-Naicker-Dadoo Pact, and to the joint action of Africans and Indians in the Defiance Campaign of 1952. We remind the people of Natal of this long and proud tradition of cooperation between Africans and Indians against racial discrimination and other forms of injustice and oppression. We are extremely disturbed by recent acts of violence against our Indian compatriots. The perpetrators of these acts are enemies of the liberation movement.

Another great struggle in Natal has been that of the workers. In 1926, the Durban branch of the ICU powerfully voiced the grievances of migrant workers on the docks, railways and local industries. In the 1970s Durban workers led the country in a movement to organise and fought for workers' rights. In January 1973, 2,000 workers at the Coronation Brick and Tile factory in Durban came out on strike. They were followed by workers all over Durban. Out of these strikes grew a host of new union federations and, eventually COSATU, the biggest and most powerful labour organisation in our history. We recognise that battles won in industrial disputes can never be permanently secure without the necessary political changes. Our Defiance Campaign has succeeded in forcing the government to scrap discriminatory laws and has brought us to the point where we are to glimpse the outlines of a new South Africa. The Mass Democratic Movement stands as testimony to the powerful alliance of workers and progressive political organisations.

Whites, too, have made a contribution to the struggle in Natal. It began with the lonely voices of Bishop Colenso and his daughters who denounced imperialist injustices against the Zulu people and who campaigned vigorously for the freedom of their leaders. The Natal Liberal Party waged steadfast campaigns against removals, and its work has been continued into the present by people like Peter Brown. Whites also contributed significantly to the resurgence of labour struggles in the 1970s through the Wages Commission and the Trade Unions Advisory and Coordinating Council.

Our struggle has won the participation of every language and colour, every stripe and hue in this country. These four strands of resistance and organisation have inspired all South Africans, and provide the foundations of our struggle today. We salute your proud and courageous history. *No people can boast more proudly of having ploughed a significant field in the struggle than the people of Natal.

+The past is a rich resource on which we can draw in order to make decisions for the future, but it does not dictate our choices. We should look back at the past and select what is good, and leave behind what is bad. The issue of chiefship is one such question. Not only in Natal, but all through the country, there have been chiefs who have been good and honest leaders who have piloted their people through the dark days of oppression with skill. These are the chiefs who have looked after the interests of their people and who enjoy the support of their people. We salute these traditional leaders. But there have been many bad chiefs who have profited from apartheid and who have increased the burden on their people. We denounce this misuse of office in the strongest terms. There are also chiefs who have collaborated with the system, but who have since seen the error of their ways. We commend their change of heart. Chiefly office is not something that history has given to certain individuals to use or abuse as they see fit. Like all forms of leadership, it places specific responsibilities on its holders. As Luthuli, himself a chief, put it: 'A chief is primarily a servant of the people. He is the voice of his people.'

The Zulu royal house continues today to enjoy the respect of its subjects. It has a glorious history. We are confident that its members will act in ways that will promote the well-being of all South Africans.

The ANC offers a home to all who subscribe to the principles of a free, democratic, non-racial and united South Africa. We are committed to building a single nation in our country. Our new nation will include blacks and whites, Zulus and Afrikaners, and speakers of every other language. ANC President-General Chief Luthuli said: 'I personally believe that here in South Africa, with all of our diversities of colour and race, we will show the world a new pattern for democracy. I think that there is a challenge to us in South Africa, to set a new example for the world.' This is the challenge we face today.

To do this we must eliminate all forms of factionalism and regionalism. We praise organisations which have fought to retain the dignity of our people. Although there are fundamental differences between us, we commend Inkatha for their demand over the years for the unbanning of the ANC and the release of political prisoners, as well as for their stand of refusing to participate in a negotiated settlement without the creation of the necessary climate. This stand of Inkatha has contributed in no small measure to making it difficult for the regime to implement successive schemes designed to perpetuate minority rule.

The 1986 Indaba‡ solution proposed for Natal broke new ground in so far as

---

‡ A proposal for a change in the structure of regional government in Natal.

it addressed the question of the exclusion from political power of the African population of Natal and sought to make regional change pioneer national change. But we are now on the threshold of a very different scenario for national change. We are on the edge of a much greater step forward, for all our people throughout South Africa. There can be no separate solution for Natal under these conditions, nor can it be argued any longer that there is a need. We believe Inkatha and all the people of Natal would genuinely welcome a unitary, non-racial democratic South Africa, the goal of millions throughout the country. Our call is, 'One nation, one country.' *We must be one people across the whole of South Africa!

+Yet even now as we stand together on the threshold of a new South Africa, Natal is in flames. Brother is fighting brother in wars of vengeance and retaliation. Every family has lost dear ones in this strife. In the last few years of my imprisonment my greatest burden, my deepest suffering, was caused by reports which reached me of the terrrible things which were happening here. *All of us are bereft of loved ones. All of us are aggrieved. Your tears are mine. What has happened has happened and must be accepted by you [the people of this region *(here Mandela evoked the terms of traditional praise songs in addressing the people)*]. +I extend my condolences to all of you who have lost your loved ones in this conflict.

It is my duty to remind you, in the middle of our great sufferings, of the responsibility which we bear today. If we do not bring a halt to this conflict, we will be in a grave danger of corrupting the proud legacy of our struggle. We endanger the peace process in the whole of the country.

Apartheid is not yet dead. Equality and democracy continue to elude us. We do not have access to political power. We need to intensify our struggle to achieve our goals. But we cannot do this as long as the conflict amongst ourselves continues. Vigilantes, thugs and gangs like the notorious Sinyoras, have taken advantage of the hardships experienced by our people to profit and gain for themselves. We can stop them, and the descent into lawlessness and violence only by ceasing our feuds. We recognise that in order to bring war to an end, the two sides must talk. We are pleased to inform you that we are presently preparing for a meeting in the near future, between ourselves and the present Zulu monarch, King Zwelithini Goodwill kaBhekuzulu. It is my earnest wish that the meeting will establish a basis on which we can build a real peace.

Repeating the call made by Comrade Walter Sisulu at the Conference for a Democratic Future, we extend the hand of peace to Inkatha and hope that it might one day be possible for us to share a platform with its leader, Chief Mangosuthu Gatsha Buthelezi. We recognise the right of all organisations which are not racist to participate in political life. We commend the actions of those who have involved themselves actively in the search for peace in Natal. We commend the joint UDF-COSATU team. We also commend Dr Dhlomo, Dr Mdlalose, and Messrs Nkheli, Ndlovu and Zondi from Inkatha, as well as the churches in Natal, and certain business sectors, notably the Pietermaritzburg

Chamber of Commerce. Our search for peace is a search for strength.

As a result of our historic struggles we, in the Mass Democratic Movement and in the ANC, are the premier political force in the country. This pre-eminence confers on us responsibilities over and above the concerns of power politics. We have a duty to look beyond our own ranks and our immediate concerns. We must strive more earnestly to unite all the people of our country and to nurture that unity into a common nationhood. Wherever divisions occur, such as in the strife here in Natal, it is a reflection against us and our greater societal goals. We need to look critically and candidly at aspects of our own practices which may not be acceptable or wise. We need to be rigorous in identifying our own contribution to the escalation of violence where it may occur. We have a greater purpose than the defeat of rival oppressed groups. It is the creation of a healthy and vibrant society.

We condemn, in the strongest possible terms, the use of violence as a way of settling differences amongst our people. *Great anger and violence can never build a nation. The apartheid regime uses this strife as a pretext for further oppression.

+We would like to see in members of all seasoned political organisations the total absence of intolerance towards those who differ from us on questions of strategy and tactics. Those who approach problems with intolerant attitudes are no credit to the struggle: they actively endanger our future.

The youth have been the shock troops of our struggle. We salute them for the ground which they have gained. Only through commitment have these victories been won; only through discipline can they be consolidated and made to last. *The youth must be like the warriors who fought under Shaka, the son of Senzangakhona, fighting with great bravery and skill. These heroes obeyed the commands of their commanders and their leaders. Today the community says, the world says, and I say: end this violence. Let us not be ruled by anger. +Our youth must be ready to demonstrate the same perfect discipline as the armies of King Shaka. If they do not, we will lose the ground which we have gained at such great cost.

The parties to the conflict in Natal have disagreed about a great deal. We have reached a stage where none of the parties can be regarded as right or wrong. Each carries a painful legacy of the past few years. But both sides share a common enemy: the enemy is that of inadequate housing, forced removals, lack of resources as basic as that of water, and rising unemployment. The Freedom Charter asserts that there should be houses, security and comfort for all. We demand that the government provides these basic necessities of life. *The shortage of housing, water and work opportunities, the forced removal of people and the destruction of their houses: these are our problems. They must not make us enemies. We must take lessons from what happened in Lamontville when they said: *Asinamali* – We have no money!‡ – they were expressing collectively the

‡ A slogan of the 1983 campaign against rent increases in Durban townships.

226

problems of the whole community.

+It is thus vital that we end the conflict in Natal, and end it now. Everyone must commit themselves to peace. Women of Natal, in the past and at crucial moments, you have shown greater wisdom than your menfolk. It was you who, in 1929 and again in 1959, identified and struck out at one of the roots of our oppression. You launched powerful campaigns against beer halls. *Women such as Dorothy Nyembe, Gladys Manzi and Ruth Shabane showed sharpness of mind by closing down the beer halls when the men were rendered useless by alcohol and families were being broken up. I hope that the women will again stand up and put their shoulders to the wheel together with the community to end the strife and violence. +More recently, the women of Chesterville arranged all-night vigils to protect their children. Mothers, sisters and daughters of Natal, it falls to you once again to intervene decisively.

I call on the women of Natal. *Each and every one of you must play your part! +I charge you with a special responsibility here today. It is you, in your wisdom now, who must begin the work of bringing peace to Natal. Tell your sons, your brothers, and your husbands, that you want peace and security. It is you who must show them the real enemy. *All women know of mass poverty and homelessness, of children dying from diseases caused by hunger, poverty and repression. We must therefore end the strife and the fighting and the misunderstanding in the community so that we defeat our common enemy, the apartheid regime. +Open the cooking pots and ask the men why there is so little food inside. When the rains come into your homes, place the hands of your men in the pools on the floor, and ask them, why? When your child ails, and you have no money to take it to a doctor, ask them, why? There is only one answer, and that answer is our common deprivation. Go out and meet the women on the other side. Their story is the same. Then take your men with you. I want to hear from you. From each and every community, I want a report. I want to hear the story of how you made the peace. We place our trust in you.

Viva our mothers!
Viva our sisters!
Viva the women of our land!

I call on the people of Inanda. Join hands. All of you from Clermont, join hands; Hambanathi, Hammarsdale, Chesterville and Mpophomeni, join hands. People of Ashdown, Esikhaweni, Mbali, and Trustfeed, join hands. Those of you who are from Maphumulo's area, you too. Residents of Durban and Pietermaritzburg, it is your turn. Those from strife-torn Umlazi and tragic KwaMashu, join hands also. I know each one of these names from my time in prison. I know each as an explosion of conflict. And those of you whose homes I have not named, you too should join hands. We are many thousands gathered here in this stadium today. Let us now pledge ourselves to peace and to unity. Join hands all of you and raise them up for all to see.

A great deal of energy has been wasted by our people in violent actions across the towns and villages of this province. If we could channel this energy towards the real enemy of the people, apartheid, we could be free within days. We have already waited for our freedom for far too long. We can wait no longer. Join forces, Indians, Coloureds, Africans and freedom-loving Whites, to give apartheid its final blow. In the process, let us develop active democracy. Democratic structures which serve the people must be established in every school, township, village, factory and farm.

Since my release, I have become more convinced than ever that the real makers of history are the ordinary men and women of our country; their participation in every decision about the future is the only guarantee of true democracy and freedom. Undue reliance should not be placed on a white-minority regime concerned to protect white-minority rights as far as it can. Nor should our reliance be placed on the abilities of the statesmen amongst us and our political leaders to negotiate an acceptable settlement. It is only the united action of you, the people, that will ensure that freedom is finally achieved. I call, therefore, for an all-round intensification of our struggle. *Together we shall conquer!

MAYIBUYE iAFRIKA
AMANDLA!

15(d) ADDRESS TO RALLY IN BLOEMFONTEIN, 25 FEBRUARY 1990

The symbol '' marks the begining of a passage delivered in Sotho and translated into English, and '+' marks where the text reverts to original English.*

My dear compatriots, I greet you in the name of our glorious movement, the African National Congress. I greet you in the name of our president, Oliver Tambo.

Let me express my pleasure and appreciation at the warm welcome you have given us. Your great numbers here are a clear indication that the ANC is alive and well here in the Free State.

The importance of today's rally is enhanced by the fact that Bloemfontein is the birthplace of the ANC. *The ANC is a child of Bloemfontein. +The umbilical cord of the ANC is buried here. Today, we are like children returning to their mother. The African National Congress was formed in Bloemfontein in 1912. In his opening address to the delegates, Pixley Seme, the first Secretary of the ANC, commented that the vast majority of our people were treated as 'hewers of wood and drawers of water'. He pointed out that most of our people had no voice in the making of the laws of the country. He emphasised that the ANC was formed to create national unity and to defend the rights and privileges of African peoples.

228

We salute the founding fathers and mothers of our glorious organisation. We proudly affirm that almost 80 years after its formation, the ANC remains firmly committed to the central vision of its founders; indeed we have extended the boundaries of their vision, embracing within our ranks Africans, Indians, Coloureds and Whites to become an organisation that is truly national. In this respect, we stand apart from every other political organisation in this country.

In these many decades of unremitting struggle, the ANC has established itself as the chief architect of national liberation, the embodiment of the aspirations of our people and the resounding voice of the oppressed which cannot be silenced. We have been unrivalled in our commitment to peace, justice and equality for all. We have guided our struggle to the point where our freedom from the chains of apartheid is not wishful thinking. It is the future which we demand for ourselves and make for our children.

Today, the Nationalist government envies the international acclaim which we have won. Our ambassadors and diplomats are received in the numerous capitals of the world, while those of the regime remain outcast in the community of nations. We praise the Organisation of African Unity for the steadfast support which they have given us in making known to the world the illegitimacy of the apartheid government. Their help will never be forgotten.

Today, our organisation stands as the most powerful symbol of the global rejection of racism. From very humble beginnings, from a meeting of only 100 delegates 78 years ago, we have become an organisation of hundreds of thousands, embodying the aspirations of millions, and an inspiration to yet more.

What have we done to win the respect of kings, presidents, prime ministers and millions of ordinary persons everywhere?

We have stood fearless before the guns of apartheid. The blood of our martyrs has stained the floors and walls of apartheid jails. Yet we have never faltered in our quest to create a South Africa where freedom, peace, justice and equality prevail. This is the noble mission of the ANC and one which we will never forsake.

The march to freedom has not been easy. Along the way we have had to develop organisational capacity, tactical flexibility, and a breadth of vision to keep our ship afloat on the stormy seas on which we have sailed. We began as a racially restricted organisation, articulating the demands of only Africans. The 1940s represented a crucial turning point in the history of the ANC. In that decade the ANC recognised that freedom was only possible when the masses were involved in the struggle for their own liberation.

Mass action became, and remains, a cornerstone of the ANC's commitment to transforming the political landscape of this country. Some of the leaders who effected that policy shift are still with us. I salute our President Oliver Tambo, and our veteran leaders Walter Sisulu and Govan Mbeki for their participation in the Youth League which spearheaded this important policy shift.

The formation of the people's army, Umkhonto we Sizwe, in 1961 is another major landmark in the history of our struggle. Umkhonto we Sizwe was formed to defend our people against the violence of apartheid. I salute our brave warriors. Your contribution to the struggle for peace is immeasurable. I salute all those who have fallen in battle. You have not died in vain. Martyrs to our cause, your courage enables us to remain unflinchingly committed to our goal of creating a non-racial democracy in a unitary South Africa. Let us observe a minute's silence for all those who have died.

I salute each and every one of you here today. It is due to your courage and steadfastness that I stand before you here, representing the ANC, an ANC which unites not only Africans as envisaged by the founding fathers – but all South Africans. Since the historic Morogoro conference in Tanzania in 1968 we are proud to be able to count within our ranks Africans, Coloureds, Indians and Whites. We are 'one nation in one country'.

Here, in one of the heartlands of conservative Afrikanerdom, I want to pay tribute to Comrade Bram Fischer, a heroic Afrikaner and a born son of the Free State. We call on all other peace-loving Afrikaners to join our ranks. Let the proud spirit that moved you to name this area the Free State in 1854 now guide you in the pursuit of a still greater freedom.

We in the ANC are committed not only to freedom within our country. We seek freedom from tyranny in the entire region. The evil hand of apartheid forces has been active in Mozambique. The government of South Africa has repeatedly allowed sections of its forces to violate the sovereignty of Mozambique. In spite of the Nkomati Accord, the security establishment has continued to support Renamo. Recently it has been claimed that the continued aid which Renamo receives comes from private sources in South Africa, and right-wing elements in the United States. I call on Mr De Klerk to demonstrate the same integrity which I observed around the circumstances of my release by passing legislation which makes the rendition of assistance to Renamo a punishable offence. The government of the United States should do the same.

More refugees have died attempting to cross the fence of death separating South Africa and Mozambique than died crossing the Berlin Wall. That fence must go. The people of Mozambique are our brothers and sisters. We must accept refugees from Mozambique in line with the terms of the Geneva Conventions and we must recognise that we have a special responsibility in this regard because of the regime's role in creating devastation in Mozambique. The South African government must cease to be the terror and scourge of our people and their neighbours.

The ANC is committed to using every method that may further the goals of peace on the sub-continent and national liberation. Negotiations with the regime are one of these methods. Through negotiations we hope to demonstrate to all parties concerned the moral superiority of our cause and the justness of our demands. At the same time, we hope to show more clearly our understanding of the genuine anxieties and fears of the other parties in this conflict. The end goal is to arrive at a democratic non-racial South Africa which guarantees equal rights, privileges and protection to all South Africans. Where there is true peace, everyone is a winner.

The ANC is committed to the process of achieving peace as set out in the Harare Declaration and which is supported by the international community. We note that the government has failed to meet all the pre-conditions set out in the Declaration. We hope, however, that in the preliminary talks soon to be held with the government, the regime will realise the necessity of meeting those demands.

We must be flexible in tactics but stand firm on principles. There may be some in our ranks who are sceptical of talks about talks. We say, however, that the ANC has nothing to fear about enjoying open debate with anyone who is genuinely prepared to listen. We must seize this opportunity to demonstrate the correctness of our views and to win more people over to our side. In this struggle we hold the moral high ground. We must maintain it. The long years of our struggle provide us with the experience and the skills necessary to steer a steady course at this time. Our hard-fought campaigns have steeled us.

Today I pay tribute to the valiant struggles of the women of the Orange Free State. In 1913 the centre of Bloemfontein was invaded by hundreds of women. Their cause: the much-hated passes for women. After numerous representations and petitions to the authorities, the women declared: 'We have done with pleading, we now demand!' Like wildfire, their protest spread to other towns in the Free State, from Winburg in the north and to Jagersfontein in the south. These early struggles paid off when, ten years later, women were exempted from carrying passes under legislation enacted in parliament. It was not until 1963, fifty years after their protest, that the government finally succeeded in forcing women to carry passes. Our women are still looking for freedom. In the forthcoming talks with the government we will echo their call, 'We have done with pleading, we now demand.'

In prison we were deeply moved by the plight of the 500,000 people, discarded, displaced, and dumped on open ground without shelter at Onver-wacht, later called Botshabelo. In the ten years since then Botshabelo has become, after Soweto, the largest township in the country. We reiterate our commitment to providing a shelter for every head in this country.

In 1987, in further defiance of the laws of economic gravity, Pretoria attempted to incorporate Botshabelo into Qwa-Qwa‡. I salute the brave fight of the people of Botshabelo to remain part of South Africa. I salute your efforts to try to force the authorities to provide better social services and basic amenities like electricity, piped water, sewerage disposal, clinics and tarred roads. But the people of Botshabelo still seek an end to their poverty and distress. It is clear that

---

‡ One of South Africa's ten bantustans.

there is nothing free about the Free State today.

The Orange Free State has abundant resources — gold, diamonds and a fertile soil. The food produced here fills the tables of people right across South Africa. Its gold and diamonds enrich many. Yet many of you, the people of the Orange Free State, live in poverty. The ANC remains committed to a more equal distribution of the wealth of this country. The people who work must enjoy the fruits of their labour.

Today I wish to pay tribute to the trade unions which, against all odds, have organised the workers into a force to be reckoned with. In particular, the National Union of Mineworkers has been a vanguard in the articulation and protection of workers' rights.

We condemn the absence of legal protection for farm workers and the opportunities for gross exploitation which exist on farms. The country recoils in horror at the repeated reports of farmworkers being beaten to death by racist farmers. It is painful for me to see that magistrates — officials charged with the execution of justice — consider a human life to be worth a fine of R100 or a suspended sentence.

Bloemfontein is the judicial capital of the country. I wish to reiterate here the ANC's total commitment to the rule of law. Sadly, but not surprisingly, this government has systematically undermined this time-honoured judicial principle of all civilised societies. Under the State of Emergency the police headquarters have taken over as the judicial capital. Not all judges and magistrates have defended and spoken out against those laws which constitute a travesty of justice. Their failure is a national shame. But, we praise those judges and magistrates who have defended the integrity and independence of the courts and whose enlightened judgements are beacons of hope for the future.

I understand that implementing apartheid laws has made it extremely difficult for many honest policemen to fulfill their role as servants of the public. You are seen in the eyes of many of our people as an instrument of repression and injustice. We call on the police to abandon apartheid and to serve the interests of the people. Join our march to a new South Africa where you also have a place. We note with appreciation that there are certain areas where policemen are acting with restraint and fulfilling the real role of protecting all our people, irrespective of their race. But we view with horror the moral decay within certain sections of the security establishment. The collapse of good conscience and the absence of accountability and public scrutiny have led to crimes against humanity and violations of international law. We call on Mr De Klerk to show good faith in this matter by suspending Mr Adriaan Vlok‡ and dismissing General Magnus Malan§.

The Free State is seen by our people as a bastion of white conservatism. We

‡ Minister of Law and Order.
§ Minister of Defence.

serve notice that this state of affairs must be remedied. Whilst we cannot yet say that we are satisfied, at least municipal authorities like those of Johannesburg, Pretoria and Cape Town have opened their amenities to all South Africans. It is in the interest of the municipal authorities of the Orange Free State to contribute towards the creation of a conflict-free South Africa. Opening up amenities to all would be a step in the right direction. We urge you to do so without delay.

Comrades and friends gathered here today, you have urgent tasks ahead of you. Build democratic organisations through the length and breadth of the Orange Free State. Every youth, every woman, every worker, every township dweller must join organisations where they exist and, where they do not exist, they must be formed.

Finally, I look forward to the day when this city will welcome back Comrade Tambo, Comrade Slovo, and all our brothers and sisters from exile, as well as those who still languish in jail. The child conceived here in 1912 returns to its mother, older, stronger and wiser. The full-grown ANC leads our country to freedom.

AMANDLA!

III

Memoirs of the Island

1 ROBBEN ISLAND, BY S R 'MAC' MAHARAJ

S R 'Mac' Maharaj was sentenced to 12 years' imprisonment for sabotage in December 1964, and spent all but three months of his sentence on Robben Island, in the same section as Mandela and other ANC leaders.

1(a) 'Esiqithini'

This piece was written as a tribute, on the occasion of Nelson Mandela's sixtieth birthday on 18 July 1978.

On 7 November 1978 Nelson Mandela will be commencing his seventeenth year in prison. He and hundreds of his fellow freedom fighters from South Africa and Namibia are incarcerated in the fortified island-prison known as Robben Island, which guards the entrance to Cape Town harbour.

Robben Island, better known simply as *esiqithini* ('at the island') among the African people, is intimately woven into the history of black resistance to colonialism and the struggle for national liberation. To it was banished Autshumayo, known in the books of the racist historians as Harry the Strandloper [Beachcomber], at the end of the 1658 war between the Khoi Khoi people and the Dutch. He is the only prisoner known to have successfully escaped from the island. He was followed by a long line of patriots and freedom fighters — heroes like Makana, commander of the Xhosa army in the fourth Xhosa war of resistance, Maqoma, commander in the fifth Xhosa war of resistance in 1834, Langalibalele, the Hlubi Chief sentenced for 'high treason' by a special court in Natal in 1873. Among others who lived and died on the island was Sheik Abdul Rahman Mantura, a political exile from Java.

Robben Island — notorious political prison, one time leper colony, Second World War naval fortress — a tiny outcrop of limestone, bleak, windswept and caught in the wash of the icy Benguella current from the Antarctic. It is an island crisscrossed with subterranean tunnels which were constructed as part of its fortifications and it has camouflaged heavy artillery facing outward towards the Atlantic Ocean. It is an island whose history counts the years of bondage of the black man in South Africa and it has been the home of Nelson Mandela for more than a decade and a half. In the early 1960s, when Verwoerd served as the White premier and Vorster was his Minister of Justice, the island was once more re-established as a political prison. By incarcerating Nelson Mandela and other freedom fighters there they hoped to wipe their names from the lips of the people of South Africa, to bury them living into oblivion.

But the name of Nelson Mandela lives on in the hearts and minds of his people and of all democrats throughout the world.

When Albert J Lutuli, President of the vanguard revolutionary organisation of the peoples of South Africa — the African National Congress — died in 1967 a young South African poet, Jennifer Davis, in a tribute to him wrote these lines:

> Bounded
> You gave me knowledge
> Of freedom.
>
> Silenced
> You taught me how
> To speak.

So it is with Nelson Mandela and his colleagues. Within his lifetime Nelson has become a living legend and the people, through their actions, give the lie to the designs of the race-mad rulers of South Africa.

Since early 1976 South Africa has once more been in the throes of a rising tide of revolt. In the wave of uprisings that swept across the country thousands of militants, especially young militants, have been gunned down by the police and army, whisked away by the Security Police into detention without trial to be tortured, interrogated and in many cases murdered, while others have been brought before the racist courts charged for daring to rise in revolt.

In the midst of this massive inflow into the prisons one prisoner was on his way out of prison. Towards the end of 1976 I was completing my twelve-year sentence on Robben Island. In November 1976 I was removed from Robben Island to be placed under five-year house arrest in Durban on release. En route I passed through five different prisons in all four provinces of South Africa. In each of these prisons I was held in solitary confinement in order, among other things, to be kept apart from the young militants who were being crowded into the prisons.

In all five prisons, despite the conditions of solitary confinement, I managed to establish contact with some of the men. Some were being held incommunicado in detention, others had already been sentenced. Whenever the prison authorities became aware that I had established some form of contact they hastily removed me from the prison. As soon as the detainees and other prisoners learnt of my presence in the prison and knew where I came from the first questions they asked me were: 'Do you know Nelson Mandela? What kind of man is he?'

Most of the youth who are now in the forefront of the struggle inside South Africa have neither met Mandela nor heard him speak. Indeed, when he was first imprisoned in 1962 they were mere infants. But the militant youth know of Mandela, who continues to grow in stature even from within the fastness of Robben Island prison. In June 1976 the Vice-President of the University of Zululand branch of the South African Students' Organisation (SASO), Wiseman Khuzwayo, spoke to a meeting using the text of Nelson Mandela's address to the court in the Rivonia trial as the basis of his speech. He and other students were immediately detained and eventually tried and acquitted of sabotage in connection with, amongst other things, the burning down of the administration block on the campus. The security police spared no torture while interrogating Wiseman to get him to surrender the book of Mandela's speeches they believed him to possess.

Is it true to speak of the identification of the masses in South Africa with Nelson Mandela? In order to grasp the relation between Nelson and the people we need to understand the forces that have moulded him into what he is.

Nelson Mandela entered prison as the first commander-in-chief of Umkhonto we Sizwe, the military wing of the African National Congress. On 16 December 1961 Umkhonto announced its existence with a series of explosions that rocked the major centres of South Africa. In a manifesto put out that day it stated: 'The people's patience is not endless. The time comes in the life of any nation when there remain only two choices: submit or fight. That time has now come in South Africa.' The birth of Umkhonto marked a turning-point in the struggle in South Africa: the time had come for the people, led by the African National Congress, to meet the violence of the racist State, its police and its army with armed struggle.

It has been a long, hard road to give effective shape and form to that recognition. The essential point is that side by side with the slow and painful advances registered so far, we have reached the point where at the mass level the armed struggle has come to be accepted as the crucial weapon in the armoury of the liberation movement if victory is to be achieved. The fact of young militants coming forward on a mass scale to face the tanks and rifles of the enemy with sticks and stones and bare hands underlines this lesson. In their search for the way forward the identification of the masses with Nelson Mandela is an identification that goes beyond the person of Mandela and sees him as the first commander-in-chief of Umkhonto. It is an identification that leads the masses forward and into the ranks of Umkhonto we Sizwe and the African National Congress.

Nelson Mandela the individual cannot be separated from Umkhonto and the ANC. He is above all a product of the ANC and the whole course of his political development has been within the ranks of the ANC. This development has encompassed not simply a growing sharpness and depth in his political consciousness but, equally significantly, finding his way to working as part of an organisation, a team, a collective. Both inside and outside prison, the struggle continues.

236

1(b) Interview with 'Mac' Maharaj

'Mac' Maharaj was interviewed in London in 1978 by a member of the Research, Information and Publications Department of IDAF.

CONDITIONS

Q. *What kind of cell does Mandela have?*

A. He has been living in a concrete cell, outside walls of grey stone 7 ft by 7 ft and about 9 ft high. It was lit with one 40 watt globe. It had originally no furnishings except for a bed roll and mat, no bench, no table, nothing. Then as a result of demands made by us some were provided with small tables 2 ft by 2 ft 6 in and later on it was extended to all the prisoners in that section and they built post office type counters against the wall without benches, you had to stand and work. They then provided benches and one wooden shelf, just a plank to keep your books on but we ourselves got cardboard paper and plastic and made cupboards for ourselves. Somewhere around 1973-74 when Nelson was ill he was granted a bed for the first time, so in his cell there is a bed. Then I think, oh yes, as a result of his back trouble he received a chair instead of a bench.

Q. *Does he have hot water to wash in?*

A. From the beginning of our imprisonment up to 1973 we only had access to cold water. There were periods when they changed the water for bathing to sea water instead of brack water. They reverted to brack water for washing and provided fresh water brought from the mainland in drums for us to drink from. They introduced hot water into the isolation section in 1973 — a little earlier in the main sections of the prison. There are communal showers. Now again, typically of the administration, you will find that these facilities which you begin to enjoy are then used as forms of punishment. It is difficult to talk of hot water for showering without remembering that in mid-winter we will find that when we are engaged in some struggle against the authorities, suddenly there is no hot water and that will go on for weeks and weeks. The same thing will happen with the taped music they were playing for us. Once you've got used to it the next thing it is used as a form of punishment — it is taken away. Of course they do not say it is a form of punishment but you will find that it's out of order for six months or a year.

Q. *What toilet facilities are available?*

A. In the single cell section we have communal toilets to which we have no access except when the cells are opened. In your cells when you are confined — and you spend an average of 15 hours on weekdays, and during weekends up to 17 hours or more in your cell — you are provided with a sanitary pail, and you are given a plastic bottle which takes about 1½ pints of water for drinking purposes or any other use while you are locked up.

Q. *What diet does Mandela have? How does it compare with that of other prisoners?*

A. Right at the beginning of his imprisonment and when Nelson got to Robben Island as part of the Rivonia group he was offered by the head of prison security a special diet. Nelson refused because he realised that it was a subterfuge based not on his actual medical condition but merely a roundabout way of giving him a diet different from his colleagues. So his diet has been the normal prisoners' diet which of course discriminates on the basis of whether you are African, Coloured, or Indian. Just to illustrate how it works: there is porridge for breakfast (maize-meal porridge) for all — but African comrades are allowed half a tablespoon of sugar — Indians and Coloureds one tablespoon. At lunchtime Africans may be given plain boiled mealies and perhaps boiled samp the next day, both being different forms of maize. Now Indians and Coloureds in the same section might also get samp but not on the day when the African comrades get it, and then the next day might get mealie rice which is just more crushed maize. So that although you have to eat food which is classified differently according to race, in fact it is mostly different forms of the same thing — maize. Now Nelson is treated in the same way with the difference that in recent years his meal has been salt-free.

In 1973-74 when he was not well — the result of high blood pressure — he was given treatment, a bed and he was put on a supplementary medical diet. He also has to have a salt-free diet so that his food comes separately. It's the same food but it's prepared without salt and in addition he has been given milk.

Q. *How are prisoners separated from each other and how many groups are there?*

A. When I was on the island there were three groups of prisoners — those in the 'single cells', which included the prisoners from the Rivonia trial and others and Toivo of SWAPO. Then there are the main sections which are communal cells divided into two sections with a wall separating them. One houses primarily the South African political prisoners but includes some short-term Namibian prisoners. Then there is the other communal section, a smaller section housing primarily the Namibian comrades, but it includes some South Africans sentenced under the Terrorism Act including quite a few ANC men.

Since March 1977 another communal section has been built where they now hold the people sentenced in the last two years, particularly the younger ones, in an attempt to keep them isolated from the bulk of the prisoners.

We don't know how they categorised us — I don't know why they put me in the single cells, for instance.

Q. *The thirty or so of you in the special section — were you all in single cells?*

A. All of us. This is the particular characteristic of the section that it is single cells, a cell for each person and you all have the same conditions.

Q. *Mandela is now an 'A' Group prisoner. What does this mean in terms of letters and visits?*

A. Well, he is allowed three outgoing and three incoming letters a month. He is allowed two visits of two people at a time for half an hour per visit per month.

238

According to regulations 'A' group prisoners should be allowed 'contact' visits, but political prisoners are not allowed these. Also, 'A' group prisoners should be allowed access to newspapers and radio broadcasts, which again they are not allowed.

Q. *What work has Mandela done on the island? What is he doing now?*

A. When Nelson was sentenced in 1962 he was kept in Pretoria Central jail in solitary confinement. He was then shifted to Robben Island in 1963 — he stayed two weeks on Robben Island without work, confined to his cell. Suddenly he was taken back to Pretoria into solitary and then brought to trial in the Rivonia case. He was sentenced in June 1964, taken with his comrades to Robben Island, kept in a zinc section (a temporary section) in total isolation and solitary confinement and then brought to the present single cells which were specially built for the Rivonia men. There they were first kept in total isolation.

They were then put to breaking stones in the yard with a four-pound hammer, crushing them to little pieces. This is where I joined them and we did that job until February 1965 when we were taken to the lime quarry, which meant digging limestone with a pick and shovel, cutting it and loading it on to trucks. This work was our main form of activity right until 1973-74. It was interspersed with very short bouts of other work — at one time building a road to the airport of Robben Island and at other times repairing the surface of the hardground road. In 1973-74 we were taken for the first time to the sea where we collected sea-weed with our bare hands. This was alternate work, we sometimes did seaweed work, sometimes the lime work. The lime work was one the authorities had promised the Red Cross they would stop and despite their promises they only stopped it somewhere around 1975.

The latest report I have is that since I left the island at the beginning of November 1976 the comrades in the single cells have not been out to work at all and have therefore spent virtually a year and a half in total inactivity. This is at a time when their studies have been curtailed, which means that most of those in the single cells are not studying. They are therefore confined once more, as we were when we were breaking stones, to the little quadrangle which is slightly larger than a tennis court and they therefore have no chance of even seeing a blade of grass except when they go out to receive visits.

Q. *Tell us about this quadrangle?*

A. It's supposed to be an exercise yard and in about 1975 they allowed us to construct a volleyball court in it. We constructed it ourselves and adjusted it into a sort of tennis court — but with 30 prisoners you must appreciate you can't all play tennis and not all of them are fit enough to play tennis. In fact, I have one comrade who says that at present they are not working and it is completely monotonous, he says weekends have lost their meaning; every day is just the same. And of course, we have repeatedly demanded creative work: pottery, carpentry, basket-making, where you work at your own speed and you do something creative and can see what you are producing. But the authorities have been adamant in refusing this kind of work.

Q. *What is a routine day for Mandela on the island? Could you give a brief summary of a day for the single cell prisoners?*

A. I'll give a typical day of the last two years of my prison life, that is between 1974 and 1976.

You are woken up at different times in winter or summer, earlier in summer, later in winter. Summer at five, winter about six. When you are woken up you go out through the corridor into a section where there are communal baths and toilets. You are allowed about half an hour for everyone to wash and to clean their sanitary pails. There are about four sinks where all 30 may wash and shave. It is mandatory that you shave, as well as clean your sanitary pail. If you want to have a bath you must have it within that half an hour.

Then you collect your food. The food is brought in drums into the section, left at the gate where it is collected and we then dish it out ourselves, organising ourselves into teams voluntarily to do this work. You have your breakfast and within an hour from opening the doors you are supposed to fall in, unless of course the warders are late. You then go out to work. There were times in the early years when we were allowed the luxury of walking to our workplace, which enabled us to see something of the island, but then they began to move us by truck to prevent us from coming across any other prisoners. You get to work and you go down to work, say clearing seaweed, and you go on doing this until lunch-break, which is an hour's break. The food is brought in drums, we dish it out and we sit down on the ground — open air, no tables — for eating utensils we are provided with a spoon and a steel plate. You knock off work at any time between half past three and four, the timing being determined by the fact that you must be back in the prison and given about half an hour for all the prisoners to have a bath and the food to be dished out and cleared by the prisoners. Then you are locked up by half past four or quarter to five so that the warders can sign off by five and the next shift of warders can come on. And from five if you are not allowed study privilege you are allowed to be up and about in your cell until eight o'clock when you are supposed to be in bed. Those who are allowed to study at the level of matriculation (which is roughly the equivalent of ordinary level GCE) are allowed until ten o'clock at night to study; those who are allowed university status could go on until eleven. When you are supposed to go to sleep the lights remain on and you are meant to be in bed, not even reading. If a warder finds you reading after those hours he can have you charged and punished for it. In the early 1970s they introduced a canned music service. This music was played from lock-up or from about six to eight pm. Neither at Christmas, New Year or any other occasion are you allowed to sing or whistle, either individually or communally. That is the typical day.

Q. *Are you allowed to talk to each other when you are in your cells, in the evening or at any other time?*

A.   When we got there we were told that this was solitary confinement, which meant that we were not allowed to talk to each other at all, even when we were in our cells. In the cells there are windows overlooking the corridor and cells on either side of the corridor, and it is possible to whisper to your neighbour. But that was illegal and we were punished. Of course they justified this on the grounds that we were in solitary confinement. One of our lines of attack was that they had no right to put us in solitary confinement. The first sign of caving in from the authorities was to say that we were no longer in solitary confinement but in 'isolation'. And then we challenged that and said isolation conditions don't permit them to stop us from talking, and secondly that these conditions did not conform to isolation, and thirdly we were not supposed to be under isolation. Eventually as a result of defying these orders we reached a tacit understanding where a prisoner may talk to his fellow prisoners from his cell up to eight pm. Then of course when the music came it became impossible to talk. In any case those studying don't want to hear the others shouting and talking across to each other.

We are therefore now allowed to talk at work. The name 'isolation' for the section has been dropped by the authorities and they now refer to it as the 'single cells'.

Q.   *When are the prisoners in the single cells allowed into the courtyard?*

A.   Now that they are not working their life will be the way it was on some days (when I was in prison) when, for lack of warders or some other reason, you didn't go out to work even though it wasn't a public holiday. You'd be let out later, say by eight o'clock in the morning, you'd be left in the confines of that quadrangle until eleven or 11.30; given your lunch; locked up in your individual cells; let out between two and 2.30 and again allowed access to that quadrangle; and then again by 3.30 your food would come in and by four o'clock you'd have your food and by 4.30 at the latest you'd be locked up again.

Q.   *Is any day — for example Sunday — different?*

A.   On Saturdays and Sundays you are locked up for longer periods. You are opened up later and closed earlier. At lunch breaks on weekends and public holidays you do not have access to your fellow prisoners; you are locked in your individual cells. Otherwise the days are the same. But, I run away from the description of monotony because in a certain sense it is true the days are monotonous but in another sense every day is also a different day for a prisoner because of the fact that you are able to talk with each other and develop friendships, you develop comradeship and find that you have new things to talk about. You also re-live some old things over and over again.

Q.   *What library facilities are available to Mandela, what magazines and what writing facilities?*

A.   Writing facilities: you are only allowed a certain amount of paper according to how many letters you are allowed to write. Other writing facilities may be available if you are a student. In fact recently a life prisoner has permanently lost his privilege to study because the authorities say he abused his study privileges by making notes of his life.

Library facilities: there were reputedly library facilities in the prison in the sense that they had books donated by, amongst others, Foyles, when Foyles closed down its Cape Town branch in 1964. But these books were not available to Mandela and the comrades in the single cells. Eventually as a result of demands they gave us about 250 books. Over the years we fought for the right to change these books periodically so that in the single cells one cell has now been set aside as a storage area for library books. These books are obtained from the main library in the prison maybe once a year. There are a limited number. The Prisons Department claims in its publications that there are over five thousand items in the library but we've not seen anything like that. The maximum we've seen in our section is about 250 books. I think I've read every book in that section.

The quality of the books is a major problem. They are subject to censorship and the result is that you have the peculiar situation where, though they say they would like to censor books which deal with sex and crime, these are in fact the books that are available on a wide scale. But serious books, ones that we are interested in — history, economics, the geography of the world, social questions, social developments — these are very scarce. Good novels are very scarce. I remember, the year I was leaving, the Red Cross donated money for the purchase of books. The authorities didn't tell us this. They claimed that they were buying them for us. They gave our section 30 new books, 25 of which were by Daphne Du Maurier.

Q. *What about magazines?*

A. By about 1974-75 they allowed us to subscribe at our own expense to certain magazines. At present they allow you the Afrikaans weekly *Huisgenoot* (a family weekly), subject to censorship and it's pretty badly cut by the censors. You are allowed the *Farmers' Weekly*, which is also cut, and the *Readers' Digest*, subject to censorship. You are allowed a soccer magazine from South Africa, which is cut very badly because of so-called 'mixed' sport developing. You are allowed a British soccer magazine I think called *Soccer*, also subject to censorship. Even the South African government publications such as *Panorama* and *Bantu* are censored.

Q. *What recreation is available?*

A. As I said, we had a volleyball-cum-tennis court. We eventually got indoor sport too in the form of table tennis, and the rest are sedentary games, cards, draughts, chess. We have demanded soccer but they refuse to allow us to play with other prisoners as it means taking us out of the yard. They did, however, introduce cinema, subject to censorship, once a month for us in our section.

Q. *A recent Prisons Department brochure spoke of South Africa being blessed with a 'temperate climate'. Winters of course can be very cold in South Africa. Is adequate provision made for prisoners to keep warm in winter on the island?*

A. The island has got terrible extremes of climate. It can be blistering hot in summer, and even more punishing in the lime quarry. The reflection from the lime catches the sunlight and throws it back on to you and it can be extremely sharp and scorching. In winter it can become bitterly cold, raining or drizzling most of the time, with gusty winds. Even worse is the fact that our cells, the single cells, are bitterly cold. There is no heating whatsoever. In the communal cells, if 60 are packed into a cell meant for 25, body warmth, communal body warmth, at least changes the temperature of the place, but in a single cell, you are in that space alone and your body warmth can't do anything to change the temperature of the room. On the contrary, all that happens is that the room temperature affects your body temperature and you get very cold. Blankets: we started off by being only allowed two blankets, then we demanded more and were given slim increases, one by one till today blankets are adequate, a minimum of five. All bedding in the form of bedsheets, pillows, bedspreads, pyjamas are not provided for black political prisoners. Clothing: this used to be made out of khaki and sail cloth, with one thin jersey given to you on 25 April and taken away on 25 September irrespective of whether it was going to be hot or cold in the intervening period. You were given short pants, with Indians and Coloureds allowed long pants in winter, but these things have changed, they've given us a warmer type of cloth for our jackets, they've given us long trousers which they now allow us to wear at any time of the year, African, Asian and Coloured. The jersey remains one still given to you on 25 April and taken away again on 25 September, and is inadequate for single cells. Rain capes: they gave us no rain capes for work until recently and in any case it is just a rubberised sleeveless mackintosh to enable black workers to continue working with a pick and shovel in the rain. It provides no warmth at all.

The authorities surprised us somewhere round 1972-73 by calling us one day and issuing each man two pairs of trunks and two vests. Then a few weeks later the Red Cross arrived. Those vests were left with us and were replaced for about one year but from 1974 we couldn't get replacements for the vests.

One point: in your cell you weren't allowed to take a blanket and wrap it around you when you sat and read and studied to have the warmth of a blanket. We had to fight that and got permission in the end. It is now allowed, but it depends on the whims of a commanding officer, who changes at least every two years. When a new commanding officer comes back you start the battle all over again, because he says the rules say all blankets must be folded throughout the day.

Q. *What about gathering seaweed in the cold water?*

A. You gather it on the seashore when the tide is out but you have to go into the water a bit. We of course refused, we said they must properly equip us with the necessary clothing. In the end they provided gumboots for use at work; otherwise you work with your bare hands. We protested in fact in 1976 just before I left because in the winter [June-July] there was a crisis, which we thought was related only to the work conditions but of course this coincided with

243

the start of the Soweto uprising. We came back from work accused by the warders of not working properly. It was a bitterly cold day and we came back filthy from the seaweed, which dirties your body and clothes, so we rushed into the shower and switched the taps on. They were cold; there was no hot water. We were then taken out to work on days when the weather made it impossible to work because it was too cold. It was already drizzling and we refused to go out to work. We tried to negotiate the matter by going to the authorities, they refused to come and we reached a critical point. We did not want to act spontaneously — we wanted the opportunity to try and consult among ourselves — but the prisoners were so incensed that a number advocated that we should spontaneously refuse. But of course to refuse in that fashion lays you open to a charge on which you can be found technically guilty and punished.

We had, you see, to find formulas as prisoners where we only refused to do a thing that was against one's dignity and therefore justified the type of action where one is prepared to take on an open confrontation. But otherwise we say: we are prepared to go to work but they must fulfil these conditions the regulations require them to fulfil; we are not refusing. So we had to look for that type of formula. In this instance, we were compelled to lead a deputation to the prison authorities, long discussions took place and we were forced out to work. We ended up by refusing on particular days: our cold water was put off, the music was cut off, we were locked up in our cells. But within a month we'd won that battle — because we virtually forced access to the Commanding Officer and charged that he was doing this deliberately. At which point the authorities responsible said: no, it's a sheer accident, it's not deliberate that the water is cut off, the warder that took you to work acted wrongly but you should have obeyed him and gone out, then come and seen me afterwards.

Q. *Could you say how the treatment of Mandela and other single cell men has changed over the years, and what has caused the changes?*

A. Mandela's treatment I should emphasise is exactly the same as the other prisoners in single cells. So if I describe the general conditions they also apply to Mandela. And things have changed. In the early years we had not only psychological forms of pressure but also open brutality. Now in this sense we in the single cells were better off than prisoners in the main sections. A number of us were assaulted and beaten up but it was not as common a phenomenon as it was in the main sections, where assaults were communal in character, what the prison staff called a 'carry on', when they used not just batons but even pick handles. In our section we believe in the early years, in so far as open brutality was concerned, there was restraint because in that section we had people of international status and the world was watching what was happening to them. The attention of the world was focused on comrades like Mandela and the Rivonia trialists. So this did, I think, restrain the authorities. None the less, individual assaults were carried on where you'd be beaten up alone so that nobody else would be a witness to that; you'd be taken to a cell or office and beaten up. Nelson himself was never beaten but faced violent situations. The last mass assault in our section took place if I remember correctly on 21 March 1971, when 28 of us were beaten up in our individual cells at about ten at night by a group of something like 30 warders. This was the time when the Namibian comrades were also beaten up. Since then the assaults have died down but psychological pressures have increased.

The reason this treatment fluctuated — and I believe that assaults even on a mass scale are likely to return at any time, and indeed they did return to the section after I came out in 1976 — is because we are actually political hostages. One of the best ways of knowing what was happening outside was through our treatment. When SWAPO took to the armed struggle and the first attacks took place in Namibia, we found our conditions changing and we realised something was happening in the country. A few weeks later we smuggled in the news that SWAPO had begun its armed operations. Similarly when the attack took place by the ANC-ZAPU combined forces in Rhodesia we knew that something had happened through our rougher treatment, although it took us some time to find out exactly what it was. Interestingly, open brutality was not used in 1976 with the uprisings that will go down as Soweto and post-Soweto, but the pressure was intense. And there was a desperate effort by the authorities to cut us off from whatever sources we used for smuggling news. There was a drive to try and work out how we were smuggling and to sever those links. And for a period, there was a month or two of total isolation from the news because the authorities, not I think by knowing exactly how we were smuggling news, in the general tightening up, disrupted our illegal methods of getting news.

As I say, therefore, we are political hostages; our treatment fluctuates. However, we believe that our conditions still embody the basic aims of the prison authorities: whatever techniques are used are designed for one purpose — to demoralise us both as human beings and as freedom fighters. How do we then account for changes? To the extent that improvements take place, the approach of the regime is that, where it is forced to give in and grant an improvement, it will then undo it by tightening up in some other way.

Improvements have taken place firstly because of the struggle of the political prisoners themselves. We've acted individually and collectively, and in our actions men like Nelson have played a leading role in bringing us together and leading us into these battles, acting as our spokesmen. We have waged hunger strikes, we have waged go-slows. We have petitioned, filed written complaints and verbal complaints. We've even gone on deputations to see persons like the Minister of Justice Jimmy Kruger.

Then there has been the campaign outside — outside the country and inside the country, but outside prison. The campaign has centred mainly around the question of releasing political prisoners, but it has an adjunct: the question of the treatment of political prisoners. I've only become fully aware of the magnitude and extent of this campaign since my release, but we were aware of it and we could see evidence of it. There were the visits by the Red Cross and prominent people coming to the island in order to meet Nelson. These have been the main

245

forces, but I also believe that our treatment is also related to the general development of the struggle in southern Africa.

Q. *How did international pressure over prisoners' conditions help improve conditions on the island?*

A. I think to answer this question I have to widen it and show you what I understand by conditions. I have indicated that there have been changes even in our diet and clothing, even in the times that we work, and in the conditions under which we work. These are physical things in which we can see changes. But I think that international opinion and pressure has played another and very important part which is not easy to measure, and that is that it has helped to maintain morale and spirit because man can adapt to the worst of conditions if he feels he is not alone, if he feels he has support in what he is doing and that why he is there is for a just cause and a cause that will triumph. And I feel that international pressure has helped to keep up our morale. It has not been the only factor in keeping up morale but in this sense too it has altered our relationship to our physical conditions to the extent that our spirit is better; even conditions which were the same have now changed. You are no longer as oppressed by those conditions, so in this double sense international pressure has played, I believe, an important part. It has not managed to make any significant or fundamental changes but it has always managed to make us survive our imprisonment to the point where even those who are serving life and are told that they will never walk out alive remain convinced that they are in prison not in a lost cause, and that they will walk out alive.

Q. *Some well-publicised visits by journalists to the island have taken place since the mid-1960s. What is the attitude of Mandela and the other prisoners to these visits?*

A. Only one publicised visit took place, that is, of the 22-25 journalists in April 1977. There have been visits by other journalists, one a Mr Newman, I think, who visited the island in 1964 and an Australian journalist by the name of MacNichol. We met him and I'm interested because I later read his reports (we asked for a copy but never got it), but he certainly saw the prison through different eyes to our eyes. Now the publicised visit was in April 1977. I was already out — you know I filed complaints with the Press Council line by line challenging the reports of the press, because of their inaccuracies and distortions.

Our attitude has changed over the time. Our experiences with Newman, who saw Nelson and Walter [Sisulu], and with MacNichol, who saw several people selected by us including Nelson, and the news that filtered back as to how they had distorted and reported differently from the way they'd discussed matters with us, convinced us that comrades like Mandela who are leading figures cannot allow themselves to be put into a situation where without warning they are simply called by the Prisons Department, and told this is so-and-so and then confronted by an interview and a discussion. This is because statements are made and they are taken as statements by the leadership and the movement in prison.

Our attitude has been that we are not afraid of interviews but we must be given advance warning and the reporters who come must themselves negotiate with the prison authorities so that despite their ban on news what they publish as a result of their visit and interview must be made available for us to check what they have written, because we have no right of reply. The ordinary citizen can write a letter or call a press conference to challenge a statement attributed to him — we can't, and yet our statements are taken as authoritatively reflecting our position on the political developments of the country. So our position now is (at the time I left in November 1976) that we would still welcome the press on the basis that we must be told honestly by the prison authorities with some warning who is coming and from which paper and be properly introduced. We must have the right to determine which of us will speak to them so that we appoint the people to speak in our name. Not the Prisons Department calling Nelson then an hour or two later calling some other prisoner whom the prison authorities have tried to persuade to say something that is favourable.

Q. *Were you able to make contact with other prisoners in the non-single cells section of the prison?*

A. Well, I'll answer you in this way. In trials taking place in South Africa today it is alleged we are in touch with each other despite the fact that we are isolated between one section and another. You can draw your own conclusions from that.

During my time there were three separate sections and we were separated from the other two sections by a 30 ft wall, and the prison authorities do everything so that you don't get a chance to get a glimpse of each other. However, hunger strikes have repeatedly taken place in all sections. A strike will start in one section in the morning and by lunchtime and at the latest the evening all three sections will be on hunger strike. I think the authorities know, and we have not hidden the fact that we do not accept their isolation, that we will make efforts to communicate with our comrades from one section and another. The only problem is how we do it. We have not hidden the fact that we do it but we do not say who does it and how it is done. In fact, as far back as 1967 we put forward from the single cells the demand that we want the isolation to end and that we should all be housed together.

Q. *What studying has Mandela been able to do on the island? What barriers are there to study?*

A. Nelson was fortunate, when he was sentenced in 1962 the flood of prisoners into prisons had not yet commenced. The prosecutor agreed even before he was sentenced that he would be allowed to continue with his studies, and he was registered to do the London LL.B., although he never finished that because it was never possible for him to get his prescribed material. (The British law exams require you to be acquainted with current developments in British law and have gone further by the late 1960s and early 1970s, I think, requiring acquaintance-ship with European Common Market law.) Nelson has never been able to get his books on time. Those exams that he has passed — his intermediate prelims, he passed on the basis of outdated material. In any case, the LL.B. is regarded as a post-grad. course and law was cut out by 1968-69 together with most graduate subjects. Nelson was told after representations that he would be allowed a short specified period within which he should complete the course, but as it happened he didn't complete and then he was told he would not be allowed to. By 1976 if I remember our discussions correctly he was planning to do the Bachelor of Commerce degree — not because of any special interest in the field but because of the need to have some intellectual stimulus. Side by side with this of course he went to prison as a person who couldn't speak, read or write Afrikaans. He took up Afrikaans in prison and did the Taalbond exam, which is the Standard 6, then did the matriculation and went on to university level.

Q. *Is all this studying purely by correspondence, even, for example, learning Afrikaans?*

A. Completely — he never gets tutoring on pronunciation. We help ourselves at work. I only learned Afrikaans to read the smuggled Afrikaans papers and I wanted to understand what the warder was saying.

Q. *What effect do you think the imposed ban on studying for university and higher education courses will have on prisoners?*

A. The ban on post-grad. studies imposed in 1968 was bad enough but it only affected a small number. It affected me, for example, I couldn't go on to post-graduate studies so I had to go on and accummulate something like 40-45 subjects at undergraduate level. But the present ban on all university studies is an extremely vicious ban: a) it affects a large number; b) it tells every prisoner when he takes advantage of the opportunity to study and to educate himself that the limit is matriculation — and even within matriculation they have prohibited certain subjects, such as history. So by this act they have deprived all political prisoners of the main source of intellectual stimulation outside of their conversations with each other. They have closed the doors to all stimulating literature and books and they have left virtually only the library books, the bulk of which are merely the sort of thing that people read to while away the time while travelling on a plane or sitting on a train.

Q. *As there are only a limited number of subjects available at matriculation level, prisoners will presumably soon run out of subjects that they are able to study?*

A. In fact, there are two problems there. If I know the mentality of the prison administration, if someone in my position asks for permission to take a matriculation subject the answer will be: 'No, you have matriculated already.'

But let us suppose we go on fighting as prisoners and that they allow someone to do book-keeping, say, because he hasn't done it. The matriculation subjects available depend first of all on the colleges through which you may study by correspondence, and the Prisons Department has indirectly cast a slur on many correspondence colleges in South Africa. Now these colleges offer about twelve subjects at most, and in languages perhaps Tswana, Xhosa, Zulu, Afrikaans,

English, French, German — but we are not allowed to do all these. We are only allowed English, Afrikaans, Zulu, Xhosa. Other languages, even African languages like Tswana, are not allowed — the argument being they haven't got censors to censor that material. Then there is a prohibition on all law subjects so something like commercial law at matriculation is not allowed. Then you have a subject like shorthand and typing: not allowed; and history: not allowed; so you are confined to maths, biology, geography, physical science: you can't do physics, chemistry or geology because they are practical and need laboratory work. So I would say at most, speaking off the cuff, you have a selection of something like ten subjects and at matriculation level you'd polish them off even if a prisoner took it one a year.

The argument of the Prisons Department in curtailing our studies is that this has been abused by the prisoners. The abuses are not spelt out. But it is clear what they are aiming for — they want to remove studies altogether to stop, as Kruger has indicated, prisoners having access to stationery and writing material. If you are doing matriculation you still have writing material, so the objective of the Prisons Department is the total removal of studies, which they are doing in stages, so as to lessen the shock and to prevent effective opposition being mobilised.

Q. *What is the truth behind the recent announcement that political prisoners are now to be allowed to listen to news broadcasts from the South African Broadcasting Corporation?*

A. Well, these won't be 'live'. In fact they will play canned broadcasts over the prison internal broadcasting system, but they will only relay news items that they want the prisoners to hear. They will cut out all that they don't want prisoners to hear. The whole arrangement is actually a package deal to try to take the steam out of protests over their action to remove study privileges from political prisoners.

MANDELA THE MAN — HIS MORALE AND POLITICAL BELIEFS

Q. *What personal impressions do you have of Mandela?*

A. Well firstly, as a personality, Nelson is a very friendly and warm person to meet, but one also feels that he maintains a distance. To get to know him really well takes time — in my own case it took a lot of time before we became intimate friends. When I did get to know him well I realised that initially I hadn't really known him after all; his initial friendliness makes one think one knows him.

Secondly, he has obviously cultivated a deliberate policy of concealing his anger. In his political line in the early years he gave vent to the anger he felt. In prison he has got his anger almost totally under control. That control has come about through a deliberate effort by Mandela, for political reasons as well as personal.

His warmth comes out in his real sense of concern for his comrades in prison. In an unobtrusive way he finds out if anybody has problems and he tries to spend time with them if they do. Although he is completely committed to the ANC his approach to *all* prisoners is always warm.

When something is worrying him, he does not come out with it easily. Both his eldest son and his mother died while I was in prison with him — both deaths were severe blows to him. He was very close to his son. When he returned from hearing the news, he just stayed in his cell and kept out of the way. However, Walter Sisulu noticed that he was quiet and went to his cell and asked him what was wrong. Nelson then confided in him, and Walter stayed with him a long time, talking to him. By the next morning Nelson was his usual self again.

In relation to his personal problems, Mandela never complains to other prisoners. However, when taking complaints to prison authorities concerning his personal problems and the problems of other prisoners, he shows tremendous persistence and stubbornness.

In his manner he is kind, gentle and warm, but he has steeled and hardened himself. When he acts he wants to act in a cool and analytical way, and then follows through his decision with tremendous perseverance.

Q. *How do you assess the morale of Mandela and the other prisoners in the special section, and on the island generally?*

A. In many ways, like all of us Nelson has been changing over the years. I think that the basic change in Nelson is that as he has been living through prison his anger and hatred of the system has been increasing but the manifestations of that anger have become less visible to a person. They are more subdued, more tempered. They've become more cold and analytical in focusing on the evils of the system. His morale has been such that he has been one of the men that has inspired all who came into contact with him. He isn't the only one, there are many who've played this role, in truth all of us in our own small way have helped each other, but Nelson has been outstanding. He has had the confidence of all prisoners whatever their political persuasion and has been accepted by all as a spokesman of the whole prisoner community. He has often sought and guided us in the campaigns we've waged so that even though we were fighting on losing ground, that is, ground controlled by the enemy, the campaigns we waged would at least bring us some benefit.

His confidence in the future has been growing. I do not recall a time when he showed any despondence or gave us any clue that he may be thinking in the back of his mind that he would never live through prison. He has always shown this belief in private and in public, and I believe I can say this, knowing him intimately, not even when Winnie was in jail, detained, or when news came out of her torture or whatever demoralising actions were taken by the enemy, has Nelson flagged. His spirit has been growing, and I think the reasons for this high morale amongst us are very deeply related to our conditions. First of all, I believe that the enemy's treatment is counter-productive, it's a dead loser. You never fail to be reminded every moment in prison that you are there not just as a prisoner but as a black man, and that alone tells you that the only way to survive, even if you haven't thought it out, is to fight back.

It is a very important element in our morale that we are able to find ways to fight back: we feel we have something to do, we have a programme in prison, we want to put our demands. Our central issues are: a) release, unconditionally; b) interim treatment should be that of *political* prisoners; c) remove all racial discrimination. Now that on its own is a limited programme which we know we cannot win altogether, since it is dependent on the wider struggle, but it has given us something to fight for. The fact that we come to prison as political fighters and are kept together gives us this opportunity to act as a collective.

The next element has been the recognition that our freedom won't come from negotiation with the enemy. The enemy could only afford to release us from a position of strength, and any semblance of strength that it may have had, say between 1965 and 1969 when it could claim, as it kept on claiming, that South Africa was calm and peaceful — although this had been achieved at the cost of a terrible campaign of intimidation and terror — has now been lost. Today every day brings the regime more and more against the wall. So that any such act will be perceived as an act of weakness, and it is clear that our release won't come from them and we see that it is related directly to the struggle outside. There our morale and spirit is helped by the fact that, even with all the repression and intimidation, our operations have continued to survive underground. The struggle has carried on despite the blunders and the casualties. The jail doors have been drawing in more and more people, testifying to the presence of the organisation, to the fact that it continues to live, continues to fight. Then the mood of our people: the evidence from round about the 1970s of a mounting mass of campaigns from our people, a rising tide of anger culminating in the explosions of Soweto and post-Soweto, all these have shown us that the conditions are there for our victory.

Q. *How is Mandela regarded by the other prisoners on the island?*

A. Well, first of all Nelson Mandela is accepted and recognised by the Congress and its allied bodies as one of its leading members. His image in prison is that of the first commander-in-chief of Umkhonto we Sizwe. He therefore is seen as symbolising the new phase in our struggle — a phase where we have turned our backs on the view that non-violent struggle will bring us our victory. He therefore symbolises that spirit, that aspiration, and he symbolises the recognition that to talk of change by violence is not enough, that violence has got to be organised and that campaign of violence has got to be rooted in the masses. This is the image that Nelson has. In prison of course his stature has grown, just as it has grown internationally. As I said, in the campaigns in prison, his guidance and leadership and advice have made him accepted by all political movements in prison as a spokesman of the prisoners. This was true too of the 'younger generation' of prisoners, those who began to come in from the so-called 'black consciousness' groups from 1973 and the young people imprisoned after Soweto.

What was interesting was that, after all these years of imprisonment, with the organisations driven underground and these young men and women growing up under Bantu education, educated by the enemy as he desires, exposed only to the propaganda of the enemy, with no knowledge of the history of our struggle and only surreptitious information given in darkness, none the less their first connection was Nelson Mandela, this was the first thing they'd ask you about. This indicated that his name was even by that generation accepted as a leader in the country. Of course this has interesting implications, because the enemy has tried to show that what happened in Soweto and post-Soweto was exclusively the work of some new crop, 'historically unrelated', with no roots. But their very questions and interest and acceptance of Nelson show that there is an organic connection. Furthermore, no black group which claims to be standing for the rights of the black man and for the ending of national oppression, however much they may differ even on tactics and theory and strategy, fails to mention Nelson Mandela when it talks of a future South Africa. Thus not only does the ANC recognise him as a leader, but he is accepted as a national leader in the country as a whole by all the people whatever their colour, and no future plans can afford to exclude him from their calculations.

Q.   *How much does Mandela know of what is happening in South Africa and in the world as a whole?*

A.   My comrades, myself and others who have come out of prison have indicated we were very aware of things happening outside. But now that I've been out of prison for a year and a half I've become increasingly aware of how uninformed we were. But I think that it is fair and correct to say that comrades like Mandela and others in prison are pretty well in touch with the basic lines of development inside the country. We have been obliged by the forced inactivity of prison life to sit back and look at the whole scene. In prison one is pulled out from the rush of everyday activity where one only sees one corner of one's world, the corner and sphere in which one is active. This opportunity therefore has given us the chance to see the general direction. There are times when we do not know the detailed manoeuvres of the enemy or of the struggling forces, but I think on basic issues we have managed successfully to see the general direction of developments and changes. So I think all in all, despite the news censorship, we have kept abreast. Sometimes in certain respects we have done this better than our colleagues abroad, especially those who are concerned with some specific aspects of work in the underground, but I cannot claim that we know more than our comrades outside. We've recognised this from prison too, they have not only the same general perspective that we have but have more of the flesh on the bones. We prisoners may know it in its bone and marrow form, but I think the comrades outside have it in a fuller form.

Q.   *Has Mandela changed in any of his major political attitudes over the years, for example, does he still think that international sanctions against the apartheid regime are so vital?*

A.   When Nelson spoke of sanctions in the 1962 speech at the Addis Ababa conference he called for total sanctions, but he emphasised that even total sanctions will not bring the regime down, that the real struggle is inside the country. Now the perspective within which he sees the role of international sanctions is very clearly understood by him, and as we have switched over from non-violent forms of struggle to the armed struggle we have been able publicly to articulate our position more clearly and forthrightly. Nelson clearly grasps this point. He does not see sanctions or any other form of struggle even inside the country as being a form of struggle that has to be seen in isolation.

Nelson's view as he put it to me in conversation is that the armed struggle is central to our liberation, but that sanctions will play a very important subsidiary role by helping to alter the tactical balance of forces involved in the struggle, by depriving the regime of the underpinning that international trade and investment give it.

Nelson's views, in so far as conditions have allowed, have been developing and changing: changing in a sense that even his understanding has been deepening and I think that in this process the fact that he has been put together with all those comrades, given the opportunity to exchange ideas, has also led to his benefiting from it.

There have, for example, been questions of the tactics of the struggle. Now we in prison, Nelson included, have felt that it is not our role to determine the tactics, that these are matters to be determined on the basis of actual concrete conditions obtaining at any given time, and that given the dearth of information and the fact that our smuggled information is derived from enemy sources, it is quite inappropriate for us to work out tactics. Nelson has been absolutely clear on this point. Nelson's position, and the position of comrades in the ANC and in the prison, has been unqualified support for the leadership of the ANC, be it inside the country or outside; we see no distinction between the ANC and its allies on that basis. We give them complete support, but this support is not just an act of faith, we try always to recognise and develop the basis of our support. So when you get an item of news you will be concerned whether the right tactics are being employed, and this is particularly so of those who came from the heat of battle: people like Nelson who sat in the innermost councils of the movement in determining strategy and tactics. The most punishing thing about prison life is that you are outside that area; you now have to accept that you are in that sense on the sidelines, you have to trust to your comrades. But the fact that you can trust them is because you know those comrades and, in the case of someone like Nelson, you helped to develop those who are now at the helm.

When it comes to the manoeuvres of the government, there have been a large number of rumours which I've become aware of since I came out of prison — reports in the press, statements by some of the Bantustan puppets like Matanzima that he was going to demand the release of Nelson Mandela and all Xhosas. The strongest of these, one of the most pernicious and persistent rumours, has been that Nelson has been approached by the Transkeian regime;

that they will make representations to have him freed on the basis that he will come out and be given a job in the Transkei cabinet. The facts of the matter are that Nelson was never approached (at least up to November 1976) by the Transkeian regime — no offer was made to him. The most that happened was that in December 1973 for the first time in the history of our imprisonment a cabinet minister visited the island and met us — that was Jimmy Kruger. We had discussions with him; we sent deputations to see him and make representations on our conditions. He saw Nelson, and the deputation from the single cells which I led. When we compared notes and reported back to our comrades one of the things that intrigued us was why Kruger had chosen to come, and as we examined the interviews it became clear. On the face of it he conducted the discussions in his typical fashion which seems to endear him to his white laager electorate — he came at us like a bulldog. But in working out his objectives we thought it possible that he had come there on a kite-flying mission to find out whether there was scope amongst us political prisoners and the leading people — without betraying his hand — that possibly the regime could find a negotiating base on the basis that separate development would be the accepted principle. He went back without gaining anything — our answers quite clearly proved that we cannot compromise on separate development.*

Kruger also tried to put us on the carpet on the armed struggle, and Nelson put him on the carpet instead when Kruger confessed that he was not aware of the history of our struggle and the efforts we had made through the ANC, even when we were driven underground and Nelson led the strike of 1961. We still entertained the possibility of a peaceful transformation through the strikes and the letters written to the Prime Minister. So the interview ended with Nelson saying to Kruger, 'I think you'd better go back to the Prime Minister's files and see the letters written by the ANC': letters written by Nelson himself, letters written by Chief Lutuli, letters written by various presidents of the ANC at different times and during different campaigns. But the purpose of this visit seemed to be a possibility that Kruger came there to say — he said so bluntly at one point — if you are prepared to accept separate development I will be prepared to allow you to function politically within that thing even though you disagree with me.

When he left some of us argued the matter — was he being honest and sincere? Many of us realised and argued that he was being insincere; some were inclined to say: look, grant him the benefit of the doubt. But of course his actions immediately after he left the island betrayed his position. He made a statement in parliament — from the protection of parliament against a prisoner who had no access to the court — with a statement saying Nelson Mandela was a card-carrying communist (which he has never been able to prove and they never even succeeded in having Nelson named as a communist), so we think that it was just a

---

*The term 'separate development' was introduced by the Verwoerd administration in the early 1960s as a euphemistic replacement for 'apartheid'.

kite-flying exercise as we saw it at the time. Our answers and Nelson's were unequivocal: that he will not be prepared to entertain any basis of discussion or negotiation with the regime if it meant that separate development remains: we could only talk on the basis that separate development must go.

Our approach has always been that Nelson does not hold views to be acted upon by himself in a public capacity except if he is in consultation with the leadership of the ANC outside prison, and that means specifically with President General Oliver Tambo and the national executive of the ANC. We have always maintained the position that if the conditions should arise where, because we are hostages and the enemy tries to exploit us, whatever designs it has, our duty would be never to give an answer to the regime no matter how attractive the package offered, except to say: if the package justifies it on the surface then we must be allowed to consult the leadership of the ANC and put what has been put to us to them. In fact, our short answer is: 'Go to the accredited leadership of the movement which is conducting the struggle.'

Helen Suzman put the matter the other way to Nelson in 1969. We wrote a petition signed by 22 of us on behalf of all prisoners, demanding our release — the main signatory and draftsman was Nelson.* Helen Suzman as a Progressive Party MP visited the island and he explained to her very cogently the demands we put to the then minister (Pelser). We had argued very cogently, using South African historical experience, how white political prisoners who had taken to arms had been sentenced to far shorter periods in prison and had been released before they had even served as much as a third of their sentence; and we demanded the same. We had shown how Nazis like Robey Leibbrandt in the service of Nazi Germany had been sentenced to death, had their sentences commuted to life imprisonment then, when the Nats. came to power, were released after serving nothing more than four to five years. Having outlined those cases, showing that our treatment was discriminatory because it was the black man now in revolt, we demanded our release. Helen Suzman in a discussion with Nelson said, 'The difference Nelson is, are you prepared to say that you'll abandon violence and the armed struggle? Because your struggle is ongoing — true, the rebels of 1918 were released, the Robey Leibbrandts had been released, but their struggle had been defeated, now yours is ongoing, it weakens your case and I cannot demand your release.' Nelson's answer to this, made in 1969, and he stands by it to the present, is that we are never prepared to do that. Because this demand for our release is a politically motivated demand and he and all of us are prepared to sit on in prison. We will never put an impediment to the development of the armed struggle.

In short, I would say that whether we look at the cosmetic changes, whether we look at the manoeuvres of the government, whether we look at the build-up of pressures from certain western countries who are trying to create a negotiating position with the regime in order to influence changes, Nelson's position has

*See document 12(a), pp.184-9.

grown stronger and firmer. His position is, centrally: a) that the changes will not come solely through outside work and pressure, outside pressure is merely a subsidiary and adjunct to our main struggle; b) that no pressures which seek to bring about a change of heart in the regime will bring about changes initiated by the regime in the correct direction: those are not possible in our situation; c) that the armed struggle will be central to our struggle.

He is completely opposed to collaboration with the regime and acceptance of bantustans or any of these manoeuvres which aim to divide our black people, whether they be Indian, Coloured or African. I would go further to say that Nelson made many statements in the past showing how he changed in the early 1950s from a position of narrow nationalism — almost appearing to carry racialistic undertones *vis-à-vis* other population groups — and from a sectarian position in the sense of being anti-communist. But what is interesting in his development has been his analysing of the situation in the country. Today he analytically tries to see problems on the regime's side and on the side of the people. His approach to the regime's side is that we must look for the contradictions in there in order to see how we can widen them, so as to narrow the social base of the regime. But amongst the people his approach has been we must look for the unifying points, and therefore also the danger-points that the enemy may use to disunite us, and here he has consistently isolated anti-communism, and he has gone further and tried relating it to its social basis. He has gone on to analyse the question of racialism and tribalism: and again in prison as he has reflected on these issues he has again related them to the social and material basis which allow these divisive ideas to thrive. So he has become more conscious of the need to fight against these divisive positions, not just in theory but to fight them daily.

My own impression, having read his past writings before he went to prison, is that Nelson has deepened his outlook on these matters even though our information as prisoners is not up to date and does not enable us to feel intimately the pulse of what is happening in our country and the international community. But we are very clear and he is clear: that the way we analyse things in prison is in order to keep informed so that our loyalty to the struggle and to the ANC is not blind but is reasoned.

2 'COMRADE MADIBA' BY MICHAEL DINGAKE

Michael Dingake was released from Robben Island in 1981 after serving a 15 year prison sentence, having been convicted in 1966 on charges of sabotage and holding office in an illegal organisation, the ANC. What follows are extracts from a book by him due to be published in 1986.

On Robben Island, the bell, up to the late 1970s, or the music in later years, woke up every prisoner at 5.30 am. The bellringer, that is, the night-duty warder, clanged the bell with such vigour, it could raise the dead. The soundest sleeper, except for one or two comrades, could not outsleep the racket of that bell . . .

With the passage of time many of us did not need the bell or the music, the routine was in our system, and we jumped out of the blankets without effort.

The cell doors were opened at 6.45 am. The next hour and a quarter was devoted to a number of routine duties: rolling up the blankets and the mats,* tidying the cell, greeting fellow inmates in the opposite cells (those who could see you through the window) with a raised clenched fist, doing physical exercises, and washing one's face in the upturned lid of the sanitary bucket, or 'ballie'.

When the doors opened, everybody rushed out to empty and wash his ballie. Those who did not fancy washing in the small upturned ballie lid inside the cell, had their chance to wash in the limited wash basins provided in the bathroom. Everything moved fast after the unlocking of cells. Joggers at varying paces circled the small prison section yard. Those whose turn it was to 'phaka'** got on with the job.

Breakfast done, the shout 'Val in' (fall in) brought us in twos to our first gate. Then it was the next gate and the next. Each had its own attendant warder. Before each, we halted, usually accompanied by orders of 'Stilte in die gang!' (Silence in the passage) and 'caps off'!

The 'caps off' order irritated many prisoners. Cloth caps for African prisoners and black, cheap felt hats for Asian/Coloured prisoners, soon vanished as part of prison uniform, because prisoners stopped wearing them on the way to the quarry.

The walk of one and a half kilometres to the lime quarry was usually interesting. There was a possible glimpse of some communal section span,*** hidden in the wood along the road to give us a clear passage. The lovely morning breeze of the sea contributed to the buoyant morning conversation along the route. 'Mind the landmine!' some one would sing out, on sight of dog shit on the road, and the orderly marching line broke slightly to avoid the danger.

---

*At that time the prisoners did not have beds, only mats on the floor.

**Dish out food.

***Span, ie. team. These teams of prisoners were kept away from the political leaders.

Past Mangaliso Sobukwe's cottage, we strained to catch a glimpse of the PAC President. Robert Sobukwe, after completing his three-year sentence in 1963 for PAC activities, had been detained on Robben Island for another six years under some special law called 'the Sobukwe clause'. He was kept alone and allowed occasional visits from his wife, who stayed with him in the cottage while she visited. 'The Sobukwe clause' was a definite psychological torture to many political prisoners who were doing short-term sentences. Under this law, anybody could be detained indefinitely after completing a sentence imposed by a court.*

Each lime quarry day had a full (unofficial) programme for each prisoner, along with the hard labour. Each prisoner's programme varied from day to day. In the morning one might be busy with something in one group, and the afternoon, with something else, in another group. The main preoccupation was 'study classes'. The more subjects one studied, the busier one would be.

Generally, discussions in class carried on without notes. Where notes were unavoidable, then they were held in such a way that the warder in charge would not notice, otherwise there might be trouble. Picking, shovelling and loading the lime had to go on without obvious interference from the classes.

Another preoccupation was political discussion. When I arrived in the single cells section, ANC members were discussing the history of the ANC. Needless to say we had no written guides, but Comrade Walter Sisulu, who led these discussions, was a walking history of the organisation. Comrade Walter's memory was phenomenal. Not only did he remember events, and the names associated with them, but also the circumstances under which they occurred.

Political discussion was prohibited on Robben Island: it flourished notwithstanding.

After the history of the ANC, which took a vast period because of its richness and the complexity of its evolution, other topics were tackled: nationalism, Marxist theories, and current national and international topics. Consensus was never the object in discussions of a general political nature. The aim was to learn from each other.

Comrade Nelson among all the inmates was the most tireless participant in discussions — in formal discussions restricted to ANC members and in informal, bilateral or group discussions with members of other organisations.

Some of us, whenever we could, preferred to engage in 'Mlevo' (palaver/idle talk). Not Comrade Nelson. Every day, but every day, in addition to his organisation's programmes, he had numerous appointments with individuals, always on his own initiative, to discuss inter-organisational relations, prisoners' complaints, joint strategies against prison authorities and general topics. Nelson Mandela is an indefatigable activist for human rights.

Two book titles, *The Struggle is my Life* and *No Easy Walk to Freedom*, summarise his political perception, commitment and dedication to the struggle

---

*In fact, the law was never used for anybody else — but it was there as a threat to anyone coming up for release.

for liberation of the oppressed masses in South Africa. 'Madiba', as he is respect-fully addressed (using his clan name), is a man who lives for nothing else but the struggle of his people, outside gaol and inside gaol.

Nelson is a forceful debater, some say controversial and dogmatic. The opinion appears slanted when you get to know him better. Perhaps it is his direct, fiercely candid approach, which depicts him in an unfavourable light with some contrary opinion holders! In argument against someone with insubstantial facts, Nelson can be vicious, by adopting a modified socratic method. Very few people like to be cross-examined and exposed in their vagueness or ignorance.

Quite a few times I have come out of an argument with Madiba 'bloodied' and humiliated. None the less, I have found such experience fruitful in the long term.

For it has taught me to look at both sides of the question, to attempt to give an objective and honest answer to it. An objective approach to social questions in particular, sometimes brings one to unpopular conclusions. Frankly, it is better to know the unpleasant truth than delude oneself with popular fallacy. Such con-clusions might form a precarious base for future programmes and plans.

Those who have read the two books referred to above, will have a good image of Mandela, the man. Forthright in his condemnation of government oppression, unequivocal about the society he is striving for, and forceful in his pledge to fight for a better society. He has not changed in gaol. On the contrary, his daily contact with the most extreme forms of repression, in the heart of the ultimate in state machinery, inspires him with tireless militancy and dignified resistance.

Whenever I have watched Madiba present his own or general complaints to the prison authorities, stressing every word and every syllable of every word he uttered, I would be reminded of Chief Lutuli's favourite precept, 'Let your courage rise with danger.'

In the early 1960s, when gaol conditions were atrocious, Nelson played very much the role of a battering ram. He was one prisoner whom officers could not ignore, not only because of his status, but because he would not 'let them do it'. Comrade Mandela's attitude and conduct was that physically he was in prison, but psychologically he was free. That is why he could seriously tell Colonel Aucamp, the head of security in gaol, that he demanded the right to correspond with O R Tambo and exchange views on the liberation struggle!

The Commissioner of Prisons (COP), General Steyn, also came under systematic pressure from Comrade Nelson. To start with, the COP, to give his officers an unimpeded opportunity to institute a rule of terror on Robben Island, made it his policy to stay away as long as possible from the prison. Mandela, as the popular spokesman of prisoners, took up the strategic absenteeism of the COP from Robben Island strongly, by correspondence.

In reply, the COP usually stated, as his excuse not to visit Robben Island, that he was too busy, and pressure of time. To move from the defensive to the offen-sive, as befitted the COP in the apartheid state, General Steyn constantly warned Nelson to stop speaking on other prisoners' behalf. Each prisoner had to raise his own personal complaints and not assume the mantle of spokesman. 'And Nelson, you are a prisoner!'

This theme was taken up by all officers, junior and senior. The COP's attempt to enforce the injunction on Nelson was unacceptable. It was simply ignored. Similarly, the officers on the spot were also ignored.

In his correspondence with the COP, Mandela defiantly continued to describe general conditions. The rest of the prison population resolved to make it a duty of each prisoner to lay personal complaints at every opportunity to demonstrate the unfeasibility of a single warder taking down each prisoner's complaint at the weekend! It soon became apparent that it was just impossible for the limited staff of warders over the weekend to cope with the taking down of complaints from every single one of the more than a thousand inmates.

Officialdom is generally coy to admit retreat from previously held sacred lines. Consequently, the rule that each prisoner had to be his own spokesman, even on common grievances, was repealed by practice. Individuals or groups of individuals from respective sections were simply mandated to present their section's grievances. Since they were not turned back nor reprimanded for acting the role of spokespersons, the practice developed into a tradition and replaced the former misguided official policy.

The victory, therefore, over the 'each-prisoner-for-himself' prison strategy belonged to the combined effort of the whole prison population. The objective of the strategy was to intimidate prisoners, to isolate troublemakers, to identify the pliable ones and employ them in the nefarious efforts of the Prisons Department to divide the prisoners and undermine their morale.

The attempt failed due to the concerted effort of the prison community. Nelson Mandela's role in the success of the campaign deserves a special place, none the less.

As soon as it was evident that deputations were tolerated by the authorities, Comrade Nelson was the first to encourage appointment of inmates other than himself to represent prisoners on some occasions. Where the issue was regarded as urgent and weighty, especially when the officer to hear it was of senior rank or a visitor from outside, Nelson was invariably appointed alone or with a couple of other inmates. Generally, outside visitors requested to interview Nelson.

Nelson Mandela was among the very first modern political prisoners in South Africa to be incarcerated on Robben Island, in late 1962.

In those days, says Nelson, the conditions were mixed. Bad and not so bad. It was before the flood of arrests and convictions triggered by the passing of the Sabotage Act and the report of Justice Snyman's Commission, appointed to investigate the Paarl unrest said to have been initiated by Poqo, the militant group within the PAC. The report, while connecting the immediate unrest with Poqo, warned that the more experienced and resourceful ANC was more dangerous in the long term, and to be watched.

According to Nelson, when they arrived two notorious prison officers, the Kleynhans brothers, were already there. Nelson pays glowing tribute to the unintimidated attitude of his pioneer comrades. It is the standard of his extreme modesty that he will often underplay his own role while he highlights that of his comrades.

However, it appears that during those early days, the harassment imposed by the Kleynhans brothers was mitigated by the covert sympathy expressed by the Coloured warders. These warders would smuggle tobacco, newspapers and any little contraband comfort to the political prisoners. Their contrast with the naked Boer brutishness was a psychological balm.

Unfortunately, these black warders had to be transferred from Robben Island when the avalanche of prisoners inundated the place. Robben Island became a maximum security prison under all-white warders, whose racial prejudice and political indoctrination ensured that they dealt with black prisoners without mercy of any kind.

Back from the Rivonia trial with his six other colleagues, Walter Sisulu, Govan Mbeki, Ahmed Kathrada, Andrew Mlangeni, Raymond Mhlaba and Elias Motsoaledi, Nelson found a 'refurbished' Robben Island, designed to intimidate and demoralise. The seven were segregated on arrival in some old section of the prison, while a new, specially built section was under construction.

Later, some members of the YCC* and a few leading PAC and ANC members from the communal sections were transferred to join them.

The policy of segregation was designed to keep the prisoners considered influential away from others, ostensibly for effective administration. That is why the theme of prison administration was, at this juncture, each prisoner for himself. Organised representation might upset the gaol applecart; the authorities might find it hard to maintain order and discipline. Was it not as organised entities that the prisoners made a nuisance of themselves and landed in the mess they were in? Well, they were not going to be afforded the opportunities that misled them while outside. 'Die plek se naam is tronk.' (The place's name is prison.) 'No PAC or ANC shit here!'

Shortly, it transpired that General Steyn, the Commissioner of Prisons, had been a prisoner of policies which were somewhat alien to his suave personality. A frequent visitor abroad, he showed himself more cultured than he appeared to be while he barricaded himself in his ivory tower at Prison Headquarters in Pretoria. Neat, in his expensive shoes, suits and fashionable shortbrimmed hat, which he doffed gracefully to prisoners, he soon won himself some personal regard from prisoners. His visits to the island still lagged far behind our demands, but they were beginning to be regular, as they coincided with the parliamentary sessions. Occasionally when some foreign visitor called on the island, the COP played the role of escort.

Before the presence of such visitors, General Steyn's etiquette could be dazzling to inmates more acquainted with abuse from junior officers. While the COP was not changing his essential policies, his manners were improving.

---

*Yu Chi Chan Club — an anti-apartheid sabotage group that existed briefly in the early 1960s.

'Gentlemen', he addressed us one day, as he introduced advocate Henning of the American Bar Association, 'will you elect your spokesman to place your complaints before Mr Henning, if you have any'. 'Mandela', responded several voices to the rare offer. 'Mr Mandela, the floor is yours', said the COP, bowing slightly while making a hand gesture towards advocate Henning.

The advocate soon revealed himself as being to the right of the right in the American Bar Association. He seemed totally inexperienced with regard to aggrieved political prisoners, who made it their duty to challenge orthodox prison practices. Moreover, he had apparently been briefed in advance on the sort of complaints to expect. As a result he was a very bad listener. 'No', said Madiba, slight exasperation in his voice, 'you did not listen. I did not say we "dunna wanna chup wod"! What I am saying is that chopping wood is a temporary occupation, our permanent work is the quarry work, the monotonous, back-breaking, picking and shovelling of the lime.' Henning looked stumped and obviously in need of a handy spittoon. He continued to counter every complaint raised by Madiba with comparisons from backward penitentiaries in the USA. He missed the burden of Madiba's representation, namely that as political prisoners we demanded rights and treatment commensurate with our political status. Our demand was for human dignity, right inside the gaol walls. In a nutshell, that was Madiba's message to Henning.

Although the COP looked absorbed in the argument between advocate Henning and attorney-at-law N R Mandela, he kept his peace and declined to be involved.

Representations by prisoners to visiting dignitaries hoped to win sympathy for the point of view of the prisoners. Since the visitors were considered to have the government's ear — otherwise they never would be given permission to visit — they were expected to comment favourably on prisoners' demands to enable the government or the prisons department to reassess their prison policies. The openly unsympathetic visitors, of the kind of advocate Henning, had to be humbled for their support of primitive practices in a civilised world. None could better Comrade Nelson when it came to performance of that task. He was the expert. His handling of the conservative Henning thrilled us.

Comrade Mandela is articulate, confident, factual, assertive and persuasive. His representations did not always yield immediate results but they were never without lasting impact. He was a great inspiration in our campaign for improvements in gaol.

Comrade Mandela was also a shrewd tactician in dealing with prison administration. He made it a point to size up every Commanding Officer who was posted to Robben Island prison. As soon as the new OC arrived, he sought an interview with him. At such an interview he might get a slight insight of the man. More important, he made it his duty to outline prisoners' pending grievances, and acquaint the new OC with some of the unfinished programmes of the previous OC which were to the advantage of the prisoners.

Colonel Badenhorst, alias 'Kid Ruction', alone, as far as I can remember, declined Madiba's request for an interview. It transpired later that Kid Ruction was an appointee on a special mission to 'discipline' our 'undisciplined' section.

Entrusted with that sacred mission, Kid Ruction suspended prison regulations and instituted a rule of terror, particularly in our section. Whenever he came on inspection he walked through our lines with head bent. He had no time to greet or be greeted by a prisoner, let alone to pause for a prisoner's complaint.

The only time Kid Ruction spoke to a prisoner was when he pronounced punishment: isolation, spare diet, straitjacket, downgrading from a higher to a lower grading, loss of study privilege, etc. He dealt ruthlessly with strikes. His warder thugs were mobilised against our section one night, to demonstrate their disapproval of the hunger strike that was going on.

Armed with batons, they raided our single cells in batches of three or four. 'Teen die muur!' (Against the wall). 'Trek uit' (Strip).

A number of prisoners in the segregation section were assaulted. They had their balls twisted, they were punched and kicked. Andimba Toivo ja Toivo, the SWAPO leader, was one of those who were severely beaten. After the assault, like the other victims of that 28th day of May 1971, he was forced to clean his blood-splattered cell. It is typical of habitual criminals to destroy any evidence or exhibit that might be used against them in future investigations. The South African police torturers and prison warders have developed the expunging of evidence to a fine art. Afterwards, in court or administrative enquiry, they can deny the allegations and lie with innocent faces, thankful that their consciences will not betray them.

Colonel 'Kid Ruction's' regime of terror lasted for two years. During the two years, on the average half our number were locked up in punishment cells. This made it very difficult to organise any effective inside counteraction. Although it was not so easy to mobilise the outside, because of harassment of visitors (including the clergy), curtailment of the privilege of legal visits and stricter censorship of letters, slowly the harsh events of our existence filtered to the outside. Relatives of some prisoners, through legal representatives, instituted enquiries about the systematic harassment and arbitrary withdrawing of study privileges.

Then one day, a strong contingent of judges visited us at work, accompanied by senior prison officials, including Kid Ruction. During their interview with Comrade Nelson, Kid Ruction butted in and made threats to Nelson: 'Nelson, did I ever order you to be punished, since I arrived here?' asked the OC, emotion in his voice. 'No', said Nelson 'not me personally, but what you have been doing to some of my colleagues affects all of us. You are persecuting us.' 'Nelson!', interjected Kid Ruction, fuming and shaking his finger at Nelson, right before the eyes of the judges, 'You'll pay for this!'

Nelson in an eloquent dumb expression, turned to the judges. It was an invitation to the judges to corroborate the oral evidence just interrupted.

One of the judges was Justice Steyn, the director of the Urban Foundation — the organisation concerned with black urban conditions, particularly housing. He seemed to take strong exception to the OC's outburst. There was a minor commotion as some of the judges who had been chatting with other prisoners on the side overheard Badenhorst's threats. The judges' expressions appeared to invite Kid Ruction to repeat such utterances inside a court of law. Unhappily for them, Robben Island was not a court of law, but a notorious prison where Kid Ruction and his ilk ruled supreme, in defiance of the judiciary and the rule of the law. In fact, had Badenhorst decided to be nastier, he might have told the judges they authorised his administrative conduct. After all, it was the judges who sentenced the prisoners under the apartheid laws and he was merely implementing the apartheid legislation on victims of apartheid courts in a typical apartheid fashion. Authority was conferred on him by the legislature and the courts.

However, the favourable international opinion of the South African judiciary appears to have some desirable influence on some of them. After the Madiba-Kid Ruction encounter, we believed the OC would not wag his tail much longer on Robben Island. Whether by coincidence or the logic of events, indeed Badenhorst's contract was not renewed for the second term. In spite of his harassment, oppression and persecution he had dismally failed to break us. That was his sacred mission, to break us: to humiliate, undermine our morale and force us to surrender our principles.

Like some of his predecessors he failed and left — that is what some of us long-termers used to say, 'Warders/officers come and go, we stay on!'

In his relations with prison officers, Comrade Nelson's conduct, whether by design or by instinct, differentiated between senior officers and junior officers.

With junior officers who knew their position, Nelson was charming and fatherly. Many young warders were friendly to him, occasionally soliciting advice from him in connection with their jobs or social problems. Some brought him greetings from their parents, who wanted very much to meet him, and envied their sons who were priviledged to know this great man in person. Afrikaners, like all groups, are not homogeneous in character.

The top officers constituted Madiba's target. They not only had to answer his attacks on the rotten administrative practices, they had to field critical questions and allegations against their government. 'Why are you oppressing us?'

'The colour of your skin does not make you superior. We are all humans. We demand political status. We demand to be released from goal. Robey Leibbrandt the traitor and Nazi sympathiser was amnestied. We are not traitors. We are patriots. Allow us to write our memoirs.' They might deny some of the allegations or refuse to accede to Nelson's demands, but he persisted and rubbed it into their thick skins until they squirmed in embarrassment.

Often these top officers and ministers exasperated him with their ignorance. Jimmy Kruger, then Minister of Prisons, was one such ignoramus.

When he visited Robben Island in 1978 he had a long interview during which Madiba raised prisoners' demands as well as discussing topical questions. Madiba came back from his meeting with Kruger very much disappointed and shocked. The Minister, according to Madiba, was completely blank on the history and policies of the ANC. He could not argue on the Freedom Charter of the ANC, he had not read it. This of course did not stop him from condemning it as a Communist document! What justice could one expect from such a Minister of Justice and Prisons?

Obviously only prisons and imprisonment!

Comrade Mandela, though disgusted by ministerial ignorance, urged Jimmy Kruger to study the history of the ANC and the Freedom Charter. He probably tried, for he lost his portfolio thereafter! Who knows, one of his ambitious security officers might have caught him reading the 'banned document' and opened an unflattering dossier under his name!

Comrade Mandela's relations with the middle rung of the officers were uneasy and poor. In their aspirations to climb the hierarchical ladder, they behaved more top than topmost officers. Madiba made short shrift of them whenever they assumed such airs: 'Look here, you are a junior. You cannot take such a decision. I want to see your seniors . . .!'

Lieutenant Prins, the head of prison, who once stopped Andimba Toivo ja Toivo's outgoing letters because they bore the name Namibia,* was typical of the middle-rung prison officers. He was never tactful, always blurting out the first thing that came into his mind, without weighing the implications of such a gaffe.

Nelson went to see Lieutenant Prins in connection with his wife's application to visit him. The application had been turned down on the unheard-of grounds that Nelson did not want to see her. Nelson did not want to see his wife? Preposterous!

Without investigating Nelson's complaint, Lieutenant Prins put his foot in it, by alleging that Winnie was just seeking publicity. Publicity, my foot! The constant persecution of his wife by the apartheid system, and this absurd remark by a prison Jack-in-office, made Madiba lose his head. He told Lieutenant Prins off in untypical intemperate language, shook his hammer fist at him, and stormed out of the office banging the door behind him.

He was still panting when he came back into the section. Someone whispered that he needed tranquillisers in view of his blood pressure.

The prison administration soon indicted Nelson for his misconduct against the head of the prison.

Ironically, Comrade Nelson looked forward to this case. It became his pre-occupation. He prepared a counter-indictment against Lieutenant Prins, against his superiors, against the whole prison administration and against the source of all the black man's woes, the apartheid system.

His defence lawyer was not happy with that line of defence. It was likely to antagonise the court and the administration. Antagonising the court or the administration was not Nelson's bother. In any case, the white administration as

---

*The official term was 'South West Africa'.

well as the white court was antagonistic and hostile to the interests of all blacks. The antagonism was enshrined in the attitudes, policies, constitution and programmes of the white government. The line of defence Madiba opted for was necessary to show that blacks had passed the crawling stage. Blacks were on the 'standing up' stage. Everywhere, outside or inside gaol, it was time to stand up against the tyranny of white supremacy. To stand up and let the white racists see our height. Gaol, the institution, made specially to cow and force blacks to crawl on their bellies and chant 'my baas' every minute of the day in South Africa, was the very place to stand up and show the stature of the black man.

Thus Comrade Mandela's line of defence. There were to be no apologies, but counter-accusation and bold challenge.

Unfortunately, the case did not come off. It was withdrawn, after the authorities had got scent of Nelson's line of defence.

They were not supposed to know, but they did, by bugging the room where Nelson consulted his lawyer. The client and his lawyer had actually discovered that some listening device had been installed to monitor their conversation.

The discovery led to another contest, when Nelson challenged the unlawfulness of the prison administration's effort to meddle in his legal consultations.

The prisons headquarters had to amend prison orders to legitimise their illegal action retroactively.

Shortly after the authorities had discovered Mandela's line of defence, there were attempts to confiscate the documents he was drawing up for his defence. All attempts and intrigues had failed, however, due to Nelson's alertness and long experience with the strategy and tactics of the enemy right in his own base. Nelson's familiarity with legal principles, prison regulations and his tremendous guts in awkward terrains, helped him to win exciting temporary victories.

The prison administration, with its overwhelming advantage and resources, was plotting a dramatic coup. After the bugging incident, Nelson's consultations suffered a setback. Every application of his lawyer to visit Robben Island was deferred by the authorities to some unsuitable future time. An attempt to proceed with the case without Nelson's lawyer was successfully challenged by him.

Then suddenly one day, things seemed to look up. There was a letter from the lawyer stating he would be arriving on a definite date for the case. The prison authorities also confirmed that the case was to take place on the day mentioned in the lawyer's letter, and permission had been granted for him to represent his client. Without informing Comrade Mandela, a few days before the set date for the case, the lawyer was told not to bother to come to the island as the case against his client had been withdrawn.

Meantime Nelson had not been informed. Only on arrival in court did he learn his lawyer was not around.

The court proceeded with its sham formalities of withdrawing charges against the accused.

266

Hardly had Madiba recovered his shocked breath when he was surrounded by officers demanding his defence documents. It was a neat administrative ambush. Since the case was over, the authorities had the right of access to any prisoner's property. Nelson handed the papers over under protest.

If the prison authorities believed their ambush was a 'coup de grace' they had another think coming. In spite of the dispossession of the papers, Nelson argued that the documents were his, and he instituted action to recover them. After a long legal contest the documents were returned to him.

Nelson's objective all the time had been to have the documents reach the outside officially through his lawyer. The prison authorities knew this, that is why they were compelled to withdraw the case.

After the return of the documents Nelson continued to insist that his lawyer had the right to see them and keep them on his behalf. Alternatively, if the authorities disapproved of the suggestion, his wife could keep them while he was in goal.

Needless to say, the authorities were not prepared to let such dynamite fall into 'irresponsible' hands. It was quite safe with Nelson in his cell. There it could do no harm, being defused by the narrow space.

Comrade Nelson has not given up the fight to get this time-bomb outside to explode. It might do damage to propaganda and lies about the duckling-to-a-swan 'reformed' apartheid. Nelson never gives up. He thinks the struggle twenty-four hours per day in his life. His dreams and actions reflect his thoughts.

He has amazing stamina for discussion, too. In our section he never missed an opportunity to draw each of his fellow-inmates into some political discussion.

In discussion he is a wonderful listener. He never misses any point raised in a discussion. His capacity to retain what he hears made him an excellent reporter after interviews with authorities. He could be detailed not only in the substance of the point made, but in reporting expressions and innuendos of the participants.

Comrade Nelson's tendency to examine all aspects of a question sometimes sets him off as a controversial figure on topical events. Moreover, he is not a man to leave any important discussion hanging. He prefers to arrive at a principled conclusion. This tendency does not necessarily emanate from the desire to dominate an argument, but rather from the natural desire to see behind the other man's argument — to learn from a contrary viewpoint.

Comrade Nelson does not consider himself a political genius nor an extraordinary leader within his organisation. He believes that his organisation is a contribution of diverse talents now and in the past. He is very much conscious that he is a creature of South African conditions and, in that regard, a creature of his own organisation, the ANC. He speaks with the greatest admiration of all his former colleagues and the present ones. Moses Kotane, J B Marks, Chief Albert Lutuli, Dr Yusuf Dadoo, Bram Fisher, Lilian Ngoyi, Helen Joseph and others.

He has amazing confidence in all his colleagues now leading the struggle outside. He was very much offended at one time to receive a letter, from one of his non-ANC admirers in exile, which insinuated that, had he been free, the struggle would have been on a different level. Since the letter had come through unofficial channels, it had to be answered through the same channels. It implied indefinite delays, which kept Comrade Nelson tense and unhappy. Only after he had answered the letter did Nelson relax.

To place him above his colleagues, those in the leadership, was blasphemous to the image of the ANC, a misconstruction of its history. ANC and its leaders are a reflection of the concrete conditions in South Africa. As long as the conditions remain what they are, there shall always be the ANC and the right calibre of leadership to steer it through a particular phase. That is Mandela's firm belief.

Again, there was a period when the international press 'appointed' Comrade Mandela as the President of the ANC (recently I have even heard him referred to by the media as the 'life president' of the ANC). Well, such unofficial appointments do not flatter Comrade Nelson. To Nelson, more than any of us in prison, these reports were wild and far-fetched. Were they true, they might betray some internal strife within the organisation or a loss of perspective. This was a source of anxiety to him.

One of Nelson's great virtues is his simplicity. Like all the leaders of the ANC, there is no image of cultism around him. In prison he could easily have used his national and international image to amass personal privileges from the authorities. All Commanding Officers including Kid Ruction would have been happy to be in the good books of Madiba. That is why Kid Ruction was so offended when Nelson exposed his fascist tendencies. That is why, in the beginning, General Steyn the COP did his best in an attempt to coerce Nelson to speak for himself. In the process, Nelson would have destroyed his image in relation to his colleagues. No leader of principle, let alone of the calibre of Nelson, would compromise himself that easily.

A true revolutionary leader must be one with the people. Thus, in gaol Nelson sought no personal privileges and participated fully in all common duties in the section. Each one of us of course cleaned his own cell and washed his own clothes. Besides the cells there were the section yard, the corridor, the recreation hall and the shower room to clean. For these duties we divided into a number of work spans who rotated the cleaning of these areas weekly. Nelson belonged to one of the spans and performed all duties involved just like anybody else.

In the 'phaka' spans Nelson featured like everybody else too.

At work, there was our toilet bucket to clear and wash. We all did it in turns, including Nelson. None was exempted.

Ever since the first sentence of Madiba in 1962, the demand for his release has been growing. As I write this chapter P W Botha has made a conditional offer to release him. The US administration, the British government, along with some members of the white Progressive Federal Party in South Africa are almost falling over each other in their praise of the statesman-like gesture of P W Botha. This happens after Mandela has been in gaol for more than 22 years!

The noises these governments and parties have been making in this connection expose their misconception of the liberation struggle in South Africa, as well as the role and commitment of Nelson Mandela in it. Winnie Mandela, the revolutionary wife of Nelson, hit the nail on the head in answer to P W Botha. Says Winnie, 'Botha talks about the freedom of my husband, but my husband talks about the freedom of the oppressed!' Why isn't there a single spokesman in some of these establishments who can grasp this simple truth?

The answer is that they do not care. They do not know what it is like to be oppressed. Nor can they imagine what it is like to yearn for freedom. The liberation struggle is about unconditional and absolute freedom of the oppressed masses from the tyranny of apartheid. It is about equal opportunities, freedom from exploitation of man by man, and human dignity. Offer of conditional release of Comrade Mandela is an insult to his revolutionary image. It is an attempt to discredit him by implication. It implies that during all his years of struggle and sacrifice, he was misled, and that he must now admit that the concept of freedom he has fought for is an illusion, a political mirage, some Utopian dream of the never-never.

The challenge to progressive mankind today is to apply pressure on P W Botha to stop insulting Comrade Nelson and the oppressed masses of South Africa, to force him to abandon his political gimmicks which threaten to engulf the whole of Southern Africa in a blood bath. Nelson Mandela must be free to lead his people and South Africa to peace and prosperity.

Appendix 1

AUTOBIOGRAPHICAL NOTE, 1964

Notes written by Mandela about himself while on trial for sabotage (see document 12) at the request of James Kantor, one of the accused against whom the charges were later withdrawn. *

I was born in Umtata, Transkei, on 18 July 1918. My father, Chief Henry, was a polygamist with four wives. Neither he nor my mother ever went to school. My father died in 1930, after which David Dalindyebo, then acting Paramount Chief of the tribe, became my guardian.

I am related to both Sabata Dalindyebo, the present Paramount Chief of Tembuland, and to Kaizer Matanzima, Chief Minister for the Transkei. Both are, according to Tembu custom, my nephews.

I hold the degree of Bachelor of Arts from the University of South Africa, and am a qualified solicitor. I married Winnie, daughter of Columbus Madikizela, the present Minister of Agriculture in the Transkei, in 1958, whilst an accused in the Treason Trial. I have five children, three by a former marriage and two with Winnie.

My political interest was first aroused when I listened to elders of our tribe in my village as a youth. They spoke of the good old days before the arrival of the White man. Our people lived peacefully under the democratic rule of their kings and counsellors and moved freely all over their country. Then the country was ours. We occupied the land, the forests and the rivers. We set up and operated our own government; we controlled our own armies, and organised our own trade and commerce.

The elders would tell us about the liberation and how it was fought by our ancestors in defence of our country, as well as the acts of valour performed by generals and soldiers during those epic days. I hoped, and vowed then, that amongst the pleasures that life might offer me, would be the opportunity to serve my people and make my own humble contribution to their struggle for freedom. At 16, as is our custom, I went to a circumcision school on the banks of the Bashee River, the place where many of my ancestors were circumcised. By the standards of my tribe, I was now a man ready to take part in the 'parliament' of the tribe Imbizo. At 23, my guardian felt it was time for me to get married. He loved me very much and looked after me as diligently as my father had, but he

---

*From James Kantor, *A Healthy Grave*, Hamish Hamilton, London 1967, pp. 144-6.

270

was no democrat and did not think it worthwhile to consult me about a wife. He selected a girl, fat and dignified, paid lobola* and arrangements were afoot for the wedding. I escaped to Johannesburg.

I applied for a job at Crown Mines. I had left home with my nephew, who was four years older than I, Chief Justice Mtirara, now a member of the Transkeian Territorial Authority. It was arranged that he would start off as a learner mabalana (clerk) and I as a policeman. After a short time, it was said, when a vacancy occurred, I would become a clerk. I left the mines and worked for a year as an estate agent at £2 per month plus commission. It was the most difficult time in my life. In 1942 I was articled to a Johannesburg firm of attorneys — Witkin, Sidelsky and Eidelman. To Mr Sidelsky, I will always be indebted.

Two of the experiences I had in the firm are worth recording. On my first day at the office the White senior typist said, 'Look, Nelson, we have no colour bar here. When the tea-boy brings the tea, come and get yours from the tray. We have brought two new cups for you and Gaur Radike — another African employee. You must use them. Tell Gaur about your cups. Be careful of him, Nelson, he is a bad influence.' I duly told Gaur, whose response was, 'I will show you. Do exactly as I do.' When the tea arrived Gaur boycotted the new cups and picked one of the old ones. I had no desire to quarrel with him or the senior typist, so for months I did not drink tea.

Some months later a new typist, also White, was in the habit of asking me for work when she had nothing to do. One day I was dictating to her when a White client came in. She was obviously embarrassed and, to demonstrate that I was not her employer, she took 6d. from her purse and said, 'Nelson, please go and get me some hair shampoo from the chemist.'

In 1944 I joined the African National Congress. The movement grew and in 1952 I was elected President of the Transvaal branch. The same year I became Deputy National President. I was ordered to resign in 1953 by the Nationalist Government. In 1953 I was sentenced to a suspended sentence of nine months' imprisonment for my part in organising the campaign for the Defiance of Unjust Laws. Then in 1956 I was arrested on charges of high treason. The case lasted for five years and I was discharged in March 1961. Early in April 1961 I went underground to organise the May strike, and have never been home since.

In January 1962, I toured Africa, visiting Tanganyika, Ethiopia, Sudan, Egypt, Libya, Tunisia, Algeria, Morocco, Mali, Senegal, Guinea, Sierra Leone, Liberia, Ghana and Nigeria. I also visited England. In all these countries I met the Heads of State or other senior government officials. In England I was received by Hugh Gaitskell, then leader of the Labour Party, and by Jo Grimond, leader of the Liberal Party.

---

*Lobola = 'bride-price'.

Appendix 2

DETAILED INDEX OF SPEECHES, WRITINGS AND DOCUMENTS IN PART II

The documents not composed solely by Mandela are distinguished by the symbol '‡'. Material new to the second edition is marked by the symbol '*' and material new to this third edition is marked by the symbol '†' (*see* Publishers' Preface for further information).

1. **ANC Youth League and Programme of Action 1944-49**

    (a)   ANC Youth League Manifesto.‡*Issued by the Provisional Committee of the ANC Youth League in March 1944.*

    (b)   ANC Youth League Basic Policy Documents.‡ *Issued by the National Executive Committee of the ANC Youth League in 1948.*

    (c)   ANC Programme of Action.‡ *Statement of Policy adopted at ANC Annual Conference, 17 December 1949.*

2. **National Day of Protest 1950**

    (a)   National Day of Protest.‡ *Statement by the National Executive Committee of the ANC issued after an emergency meeting on 21 May 1950.*

    (b)   National Day of Protest.‡ *Report issued by the Secretary-General of the ANC, 26 July 1950, initialled by Mandela.*

3. **Defiance Campaign 1952**

    (a)   'No Easy Walk to Freedom.' *Presidential address by Mandela to the ANC (Transvaal) Conference, 21 September 1953.*

    (b)   'The Shifting Sands of Illusion.' *Article written for the monthly journal* Liberation, *June 1953.*

4. **Congress of the People 1955**

    (a)   Call to the Congress of the People.‡ *Leaflet issued by the National Action Council of the Congress of the People, 1955.*

(b)   Freedom Charter.‡ *Drafted by a sub-committee of the National Action Council from contributions submitted by groups, individuals and meetings all over South Africa, approved by the ANC National Executive and adopted at the Congress of the People, Kliptown, Johannesburg, 25-26 June 1955.*

(c)   'Freedom in our Lifetime.' *Article on the Freedom Charter published in* Liberation, *June 1956.*

5.   The conflict hardens 1955-59

(a)   'People are Destroyed.' *Article on the effects of apartheid, and in particular the pass laws, on people's lives. Published in* Liberation, *October 1955.*

(b)   'Land Hunger.' *Article on the coercive methods used to make the bantustans into reserves of labour, and in particular on the situation in the Transkei, published in* Liberation, *February 1956.*

(c)   'Bantu Education Goes to University.' *Article on Bantu Education and the introduction of segregated universities, published in* Liberation, *June 1957.*

(d)   'Our Struggle Needs Many Tactics.' *Article on political tactics, in particular the boycott weapon, published in* Liberation, *February 1958.*

(e)   'A New Menace in Africa.' *Article on American imperialism, published in* Liberation, *March 1958.*

(f)   'Verwoerd's Tribalism.' *Article on the bantustan policy published in* Liberation, *May 1959.*

6.   The Treason Trial 1956-60

Extracts from the testimony by Mandela, responding as spokesman for the accused to questions from the bench, the prosecution and the defence lawyers.

7.   All-in African Conference and Stay-at-Home 1961

(a)★   Consultative Conference of African leaders, Orlando, 16 December 1960: Resolutions.‡

(b)   All-in African Conference, Pietermaritzburg, 25-26 March 1961: Resolutions.‡

(c)   'The Struggle for a National Convention.' *Article written in March 1961.*

(d)   Appeal to Students. *Leaflet issued by the All-in African National Action Council, April 1961, signed by Mandela.*

(e)★   Appeal to the People of Namibia. *Leaflet issued in April 1961 by the All-in African National Council, signed by Mandela.*

(f) Letter to the United Party. *Written in 1961.*

(g) 'Stay-at-Home.'‡ *Leaflet issued by the National Action Council calling for a nationwide stay-at-home on 29, 30, 31 May 1961.*

(h) 'General Strike.' *Statement by Mandela on behalf of the National Action Council following the stay-at-home of May 1961.*

8. 'The struggle is my life' — press statement 1961

Press statement issued by Mandela on 26 June 1961 from inside South Africa, following his decision, in accordance with the advice of the National Action Council, to carry on his political work underground.

9. Armed struggle

(a) Manifesto of Umkhonto we Sizwe.‡ *Issued by Umkhonto we Sizwe, 16 December 1961.*

(b) Address to the Pan-African Freedom Conference. *Address on behalf of the ANC delegation to the Conference of the Pan-African Freedom Movement of East and Central Africa held in Addis Ababa in January 1962.*

10. 'Black man in a white court'

Court statement by mandela during his trial in 1962.

11. The Rivonia trial 1963-64

(a) 'I am Prepared to Die.' *Mandela's statement from the dock in Pretoria Supreme Court, 20 April 1964, at the opening of the defence case.*

(b) Statement by Chief Lutuli. *Press statement by Chief Albert Lutuli issued by the ANC, 12 June 1964 following the Rivonia verdict and released by the ANC office in London.*

12. Robben Island

(a)* 'Release us or treat us as political prisoners.' *Letter addressed to the Minister of Justice, Cape Town, from Nelson Mandela, Robben Island, dated 22 April 1969. Published by the ANC in 1978.*

(b)* 'Unite! Mobilise! Fight on! Between the anvil of united mass action and the hammer of the armed struggle we shall crush apartheid!' *Message from Mandela after the Soweto uprising of 1976, published by the ANC on 10 June 1980, with an introduction by O R Tambo, President of the ANC.*

13. Pollsmoor

(a)★ 'I am not prepared to sell the birthright of the people to be free'. *Mandela's response to an offer of conditional release by the State President of South Africa on 31 January 1985, read on his behalf by his daughter to a mass meeting in Soweto on 10 February 1985.*

(b)★ Message to the second National Consultative Conference of the ANC, Zambia, 1985.‡ *Message from the leaders in Pollsmoor and Robben Island prisons, and signed on their behalf by Nelson Mandela, read to the conference and later presented to a press conference in Lusaka on 25 June 1985 by the President of the ANC.*

14. Victor Verster

(a)† Document prepared by Mandela and given to P W Botha before Mandela met him on 5 July 1989. *First published in* South *newspaper 25 January 1990.*

(b)† 'A document to create a climate of understanding.' *Forwarded by Nelson Mandela to F W De Klerk on 12 December 1989. Not previously published in full.*

15. Release

(a)† Address to rally in Cape Town, 11 February 1990.

(b)† Address to rally in Soweto, 13 February 1990.

(c)† Address to rally in Durban, 25 February 1990.

(d)† Address to rally in Bloemfontein, 25 February 1990.

NOTES ON SOURCES OF DOCUMENTS IN FIRST EDITION

The documents reprinted in the first edition, with minor editorial amendments and explanatory footnotes, are mainly reproduced in the following publications:

1. *From Protest to Challenge: A Documentary History of African Politics in South Africa 1882 – 1964,* edited by Thomas Karis and Gwendolen M. Carter and published by Hoover Institution Press, Stanford University, California.

   Vol. 2: *Hope and Challenge, 1935 – 1952,* edited by Thomas Karis (Stanford, 1973).

   Vol. 3: *Challenge and Violence, 1953 – 1964,* edited by Thomas Karis and Gail M. Gerhart (Stanford, 1977).

   This publication is referred to below as Karis and Carter (eds.).

2. Nelson Mandela, *No Easy Walk to Freedom,* edited and introduced by Ruth First (London, 1965; new edition 1973).

Index

This is a subject index except for the inclusion of names of Mandela's fellow prisoners (indexed under 'prisoners, political') and names of authors of statements or writings about Mandela.

INTERNATIONAL DEFENCE AND AID FUND FOR SOUTHERN AFRICA

Canon Collins House, 64 Essex Road, London N1 8LR

The specific mandate of IDAF is to ensure the legal defence of the victims of apartheid, to aid their families and dependants, and to inform the world about apartheid and the struggle against it.

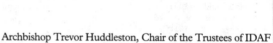

There can be no real peace in Southern Africa until South Africa has been liberated.

There are increasing demands on the work of IDAF. Despite the release of Nelson Mandela and other leaders, there are still many other political prisoners. While organisations have been unbanned, apartheid is still in place. Repression continues: trials and imprisonment, detention and torture, violence, killings and forced removal go on remorselessly.

A very special concern for IDAF is the children, who have been made a particular target of the apartheid regime.

We urgently need your support. Make your contribution to a free, just and peaceful Southern Africa. The current developments have not diminished the urgency of the need for assistance of this kind. Send your donation, large or small, to our Fund at its Head Office at the address above, or to one of the addresses below.

Archbishop Trevor Huddleston, Chair of the Trustees of IDAF

The International Defence and Aid Fund for Southern Africa is a humanitarian organisation founded by Canon L. John Collins, dedicated to the achievement of free, democratic non-racial societies in South Africa and Namibia.

The International Defence and Aid Fund for Southern Africa is associated with a registered English charity, The Sol Plaatje Educational Project Limited, which assists with the education of children who are victims of apartheid.

IDAF has National Committees in various countries. Their accounts are audited and they are part of the Fund. For convenience supporters may wish to send contributions to them at the following addresses: please address your donation to Archbishop Trevor Huddleston.

CANADA
IDAFSA-Canada
294 Albert St # 200
Ottawa K1P 6E6
Tel: (613)-233-5939

IRELAND
IDAFSA-Ireland
PO Box 1974
Dublin 18
Tel: (01) 895035

NETHERLANDS
DAF-Nederland
Kromme Nieuwegracht 10
3512 HG Utrecht
Tel: (30) 313194
Postgiro a/c no. 2989732-Hilversum

NEW ZEALAND
NZDAF
PO Box 17303
Karori
Wellington 5

NORWAY
IDAF-Norway
PO Box 2
Lindeberg Gaard
N-1007 Oslo 10
Tel: (2) 301345
Postgiro a/c no: 2616670

SWEDEN
International Defence and Aid Fund (IDAF)
c/o Lennart Renöfelt,
Månskensgatan 34F,
S-80274 GÄVLE
Postgiro a/c no: 4093290-7

UNITED KINGDOM
BDAFSA
22 The Ivories
6–8 Northampton Street
London N1 2HX
Tel: (01) 354 1462
Postgiro a/c no: 5 11 7151